THE FORGING OF NATIONHOOD

The Forging of Nationhood

Edited by

GYANENDRA PANDEY • PETER GESCHIERE

SEPHIS

MANOHAR
2003

Dedicated to the memory of T.K. Biaya and Ravinder Kumar, two very different but equally insistent voices in the search for new dialogues across continents and nations, one a contributor to this volume, the other central to the organization of the conference out of which it came. They will both be greatly missed.

First published 2003

ISBN 81-7304-425-2

Published by
Ajay Kumar Jain for
Manohar Publishers & Distributors
4753/23 Ansari Road, Daryaganj
New Delhi 110 002

Typeset by
Kohli Print
Delhi 110 051

Printed at
Lordson Publishers Pvt. Ltd.
Delhi 110 007

Contents

The Forging of Nationhood

The Contest over Citizenship, Ethnicity and History

Gyanendra Pandey and Peter Geschiere

Is there anything left to be said about the forging of nationhood after so many learned articles and books have been published and so many political battles fought on this issue? What is the need for yet another collection on the contest over citizenship, and over equality and exclusion within and between nations, especially when the very centrality of the national idea and of nation-states seems to have been called into question? The following pages will, we hope, provide their own justification for this renewed foray.

This book is the product of a somewhat unusual initiative—a 'South-South Exchange Programme for Research on the History of Development' (also known as SEPHIS) which held its first Conference in Delhi in 1996 on the theme of 'The Forging of Nationhood and the Contest over Citizenship, Ethnicity and History'.[1] The exchanges at the conference made it clear how little we still know about different trajectories of 'modernity' and 'development', and diverse struggles over nationhood, citizenship and history, in what used to

[1] SEPHIS was founded in 1994 by a small group of historians from various parts of the South and the Netherlands, in close collaboration with the Dutch Ministry of Development Cooperation which agreed to finance the programme. It provides scholarships and other subventions to historians established in the South and organizes conferences, workshops and guest lectures in different locations in the South. The 1996 Delhi Conference was organized by SEPHIS in collaboration with the Nehru Memorial Museum & Library, New Delhi and the Indian Council for Historical Research. We remember with gratitude the late Professor Ravinder Kumar, the then Director and Chairman of these two institutions, and also thank the staff and members of both institutions, for enabling the holding of this conference and for helping to make the occasion such a success.

be known as the 'Third World' and is now—more innocuously, but also perhaps more disingenuously—called the 'South' and, by extension, how much we have assumed about the universal, theoretical meaning of several of these terms. It indicated, too, how much there is to learn about these facets of the modern world from closer attention to the experience of the directly or indirectly colonized parts of Asia, Africa, the Caribbean and Latin America and, no less importantly, from direct interaction between scholars from these regions. It is our hope that the selection of papers published here will reflect at least something of the intellectual excitement and political energy that was generated at the Delhi meeting.

The question with which we begin arose naturally in the wake of the conference. What is the value of a collection of investigations on the forging of nationhood at a time when the nation-state is so evidently threatened by global flows and transnational networks? One answer to the question is that *that* is precisely its importance. What does the historical moment of the forging of nationhood look like now, at the moment of the nation's apparent decline? In addition, as the deliberations at the conference indicated, and a good deal of other evidence has done as well, we may yet have to ask questions about just which nationalisms, and whose nation-states, are under threat.

The intricate intertwining of capitalism, nationalism and modernity has a complex history. A hundred years ago, capitalism was closely articulated with a nationalist, not to say jingoistic, imperialism. Paradoxically, perhaps, this was the time when nationhood came to be recognized as the hallmark of modernity: to be 'civilized' was to have a nation. A hundred years on, in the age of a new 'globalization', matters appear to be rather different.

In the new configuration, marked by the generalization of new technologies of communication and transport, the mobility of people, goods and especially images on a vastly accelerated and truly global scale, and the demand for ever greater mobility and 'flexibility' of labour,[2] the link between capitalism and nationalism seems far less evident. Yet, the contrast in this respect with the earlier stage of the political and economic expansion of capital should perhaps not be exaggerated.

[2] Cf. A. Appadurai, *Modernity at Large, Cultural Dimensions of Globalization*, Minneapolis: University of Minnesota Press, 1996.

It is notable that authors on globalization and transnationalism continue to pay a great deal of attention to the vicissitudes of the nation-state.[3] The new phase of globalization is marked by a powerful drive from the West to engulf and homogenize—not to say Americanize—the world. Predictably, the process has triggered strong feelings of chauvinism, both in the South and in the North. The complex articulation of globalization and nationalism in the explosion of the atomic bomb by the Bharatiya Janata Party led regime in India, as a climax of national pride but also as an event of worldwide significance, shows how potent the concept of the nation remains despite the changing global constellation.

This is one good reason for returning anew to a number of well rehearsed questions regarding nationalism, modernity and development. The old 'development' debate of the 1960s and 1970s showed up the gross inadequacy, and Eurocentric bias, of the notions of 'development' and 'underdevelopment' as formulated in the 'advanced' social science and political establishments of the world.[4] What it failed to do, to the same extent, was to question the very meaning of the terms 'modernity' and 'development' as articulated in these quarters, and the privilege that was assigned to them. Among other things, the present collection of papers on nationhood and nationalism proposes the necessity of such an interrogation.

As in the case of the 'development' discourse, writings on nationalism have also been dominated by the 'advancement' and the historical experience of the North. Even authors who have paid considerable attention to the vicissitudes of nationalism and nationstatehood in the South have derived their models from the development of these ideas and institutions in the North.[5] In some

[3] In addition to Appadurai, op. cit., see M. Featherstone (ed.), *Global Culture: Nationalism, Globalization and Identity*, London: Sage, 1990; and U. Hannerz, *Cultural Complexity: Studies in the Social Organization of Meaning*, New York: Columbia University Press, 1992.

[4] For a couple of classic statements, see Andre Gunder Frank, *Development and Underdevelopment in Latin America: Historical Studies of Chile and Brazil*, Harmondsworth: Penguin, 1969; and Samir Amin, *Le développement inégal: essai sur les formations sociales du capitalisme periphérique*, Paris: Minuit, 1973. A trenchant, summary statement is found in Amiya K. Bagchi, *The Political Economy of Underdevelopment*, Cambridge: Cambridge University Press, 1982.

[5] For example, see the stimulating studies of nationalism by B. Anderson, *Imagined Communities, Reflections on the Origin and Spread of Nationalism*, London: Verso, 1983; E. Gellner, *Nations and Nationalism*, Oxford: Blackwell,

ways this is understandable. It is a reflection of a historical inequality, and the increasing dominance of one part of the world over the rest. It will be pointed out, too, that the idea of the nation as the selfevident basis for the state emerged in Europe (even though its historical antecedents were to be found in the Americas), and that it spread from there to other parts of the globe. To the extent that these ideas were accepted and actualized in these 'backward' regions, they joined the 'advanced' sections of the modern world, we are told. To the extent that they diverged from the 'norm' or lagged behind, they have remained 'underdeveloped'.

Yet it is now all too clear that the story of nationhood and nationalism, modernity and 'development' has not been quite so straightforward. The struggle to realize nationhood and sovereign status, democracy and development has necessarily encountered different obstacles and charted different paths in different parts of the world. Not the least marked of these differences have been those between the once colonized, now 'postcolonial' countries of Asia, Africa, Central and South America, on the one hand, and the excolonial powers of Europe and North America, on the other. There is a growing recognition today of the need to complicate and enrich our understanding of the modern world by bringing to the fore the experience of those regions that have long been seen as secondary, 'backward' and even unhistorical.

The forging of nationhood, it will generally be acknowledged, is about the transformation of subjects into citizens; the move from being subjects of one's own King or Queen to being citizens of one's own State, but, more commonly perhaps, from being subjects or slaves of another race or 'people' to being independent (or newly integrated) citizens in a new nation-state. Theoretically the right to citizenship is now accepted as a universal right. Yet, this general acceptance may mask not only the very novelty of the citizenship/nation idea—surely one mark of the singularity of our 'modern' age—but also the highly incomplete realization of this 'universal right' in practice. For the story of nationalism is also the story of

---

1983; B. Kapferer, *Legends of People: Myths of State*, Washington: Smitsonian Institute, 1988. For an important new perspective, see Partha Chatterjee, *Nationalist Thought and the Colonial World: A Derivative Discourse*?, London: Zed Books, 1990, and his *The Nation and its Fragments: Colonial and Postcolonial Histories*, Princeton: Princeton University Press, 1994.

the naturalization of a most unusual belief—the idea that human beings are automatically born into nations, that nations (and the people constituting them) ought to be sovereign, and that nation-states are the appropriate, indeed the only (the 'natural'), form of the political existence of peoples.[6]

So successfully have some of these notions been imbibed in the political consciousness of our times that it is easy to forget how long and difficult has been the struggle—first within Europe and the Americas, and later on a global scale—to establish the claims of popular sovereignty and political equality as *universal* rights; and, no less important, how very incomplete has been its victory. For, as is now well recognized, the rhetoric of the *inclusive* claims of liberty and equality that nationalism (and other related movements) promote, is accompanied by the practice of *excluding* numerous classes and communities from precisely those claims. Indeed, as we shall argue, the story of nationalism and of modern 'civilization', could scarcely have been written without such exclusions.

Over the last two centuries, as notions of the equal rights of all (nations as well as individuals) have spread, popular sovereignty has been repeatedly denied—often in the name of 'the people'; and citizenship rights have been withheld—frequently in the name of 'the citizens'. The story of the struggle to realize nationhood and sovereign status has also been a story of how to deprive certain groups and peoples of citizenship. This, in a regime of citizenship across the globe as well as in individual countries. Even today in every part of the world, 'North' or 'South', the struggle to attain the full rights of citizenship continues, in one form or another, for a small or a large section of the population. It is the necessity of this struggle that this volume seeks to highlight.

There has been a certain reluctance on the part of political thinkers and activists in the once colonized territories of Asia, Africa, Latin America and the Caribbean to mount a critique of nationalism and

[6] Our colleague from Kerala, southern India, the late M. Muralidharan was one of those who pointed out the Eurocentrism of a social analysis that finds the criterion of birth for the determination of caste so primitive and irrational, while being blind to its own acceptance of birth as the automatic criterion of the 'national'; M. Muralidharan, 'Nation, State and Community: the Problem of Identity and Institutions', in J. Athya and J. John (eds.), *Religion, State and Communalism: A Post-Ayodhya Reflection*, Madras, 1992, p. 25.

to examine its limits and inconsistencies. Having succeeded only after long and hard intellectual-political battles in establishing the applicability of these ideas to all communities and peoples (and not only to 'Europeans'), and having seen something of their liberating potential, social scientists and other concerned citizens in these regions have been loathe to criticize the grounds upon which their modern polities and societies have been constructed. Such a critique may seem even more risky at a time when globalization, and the global advance of right-wing movements, threaten both to run down the autonomy of the nations of the erstwhile 'Third World', and to marginalize the struggles of progressive forces and disprivileged groups and classes within them.

Precisely for this reason, however, it seems necessary to examine the uses to which some of the central ideas and institutions of modernity (nationalism among them) have been put by dominant groups and classes in different parts of the world, whether on their own or in alliance with ruling groups of other countries. It is necessary too to recognize the variety and complexity of the contests involved in the long drawn out struggles for nationhood and democracy—for the dream of equal opportunity and justice for all—if we are to give our understanding a measure of historical depth and think of ways forward from the present demoralization. It is as a small part of this enterprise that we present the following reflections on nationalism and its own internal discontents. What are the conditions and limits of this once ennobling ideology? What are some of its more common oppressions?

The contributions that follow vary greatly in tone and style. Some are distinctly scholarly and academic, others far more personal; more than one is self-consciously partisan and even polemical. This diversity of presentation reflects something of the diversity of conditions of intellectual production and debate in different parts of the excolonial ('developing' or 'under-developed') world. As such it is itself a significant indicator of the specific, unstandardized and not easily assimilable struggles towards which we wish to draw attention. As editors, we have made no attempt to iron out, or standardize, the varying textures of different contributions.

However, in all their diversity, the papers published here converge in their common attention to the simultaneous act of inclusion and exclusion in the forging of nationhood, and their suggestion that the criteria for inclusion/exclusion are never easily determined, nor arrived at without a prolonged contest. It is the complex history of these prolonged struggles, spanning a period of two centuries and more, that the contributions seek to highlight.

The novelty of the 'nation' idea needs no reiteration. It is dramatically reflected in this volume in Zhang Haiyang's contribution on China's struggle with the nation concept over the last century and a half. When China was drawn into the 'family of nations' towards the end of the last century, its scholars searched for and then launched the term *minzu* as their equivalent for the modern 'nation'. They spoke of the *han minzu*, the Han Chinese as a nation which could claim a history going back 5,000 years or more. Yet the very concept *minzu* turns out to be a recent borrowing, probably from the Japanese; and it is so elastic that it can apply to any group claiming a common origin. Zhang draws attention to what might be called the 'mendacity' of the state, which has sought to manipulate the very elasticity of *minzu* to assign it very different meanings in different contexts. In this century the concept has been used not only in the sense of 'nation', but also for 'minority nationality' and even for 'ethnic group'; it has also allowed for occasional references to a unity with all Chinese in the diaspora.

Nevertheless state manipulation is only a part of the story, in China as elsewhere. The ambiguity of the 'nation' is clearly evident in the 'original' European experience too. What needs to be stressed, perhaps, is the essential *untranslatability* of the nation idea, not only as between cultures, but also as between ideal and reality. In short its *unrealizability* in some perfect form. Taking the novelty and the unrealizability—and, with that, the vitality—of the modern 'nation' for granted, the contributions in this volume focus directly on the question of how these new, 'natural' political communities, of the eighteenth to twentieth centuries have been constructed. These constructions are crucially dependent, they suggest, on a search for 'authenticity' in the new community called the 'nation'. This search in its turn necessitates the adoption of different modes or criteria for inclusion or exclusion from these modern political communities, the claim of 'authenticity' being one such manoeuvre. In dealing with the question of how the nation is to be constituted, our Latin American colleague, Andres Guerrero, poses a central problem faced by the 'national' regime. How does nationalism solve the problem of domination in a regime of equality, or, turning the terms around, propose the equality of citizenship in a situation of actually existing inequality[7] which is, of course, the precise condition of all actually existing nationalisms, past and present. How have nationalisms of different kinds—colonial, anticolonial and postcolonial—coped with the competing demands of equality and domination, or to shift ground a little again, with the competing requirements of homogeneity (seen as the prerequisite to equality) and difference?

The history of nationalism and imperialism suggests that political leaders have found two kinds of answers, not always exclusive of one another, but perhaps worth separating for analytical purposes. One is to declare sections of the population politically (civilizationally) 'unfit' for the benefits of citizenship; the other is to declare them culturally 'alien'. Let us first outline the terms of the former solution, which was found particularly handy in the heyday of imperialism and imperialist-nationalism.

Along with, perhaps more than, Enlightenment ideas and notions of the 'rights of man', conquest and capitalism were the harbingers of the new world. What would come later to be described as 'ethnic cleansing' characterized European expansion into the Americas, north and south, as into South Africa, Australia and New Zealand. It has continued to be a feature of 'modern' politics down to our own day—in the Germany of the 1930s and 1940s and similarly in Bosnia in the 1980s and 1990s, as also in the Indian subcontinent in 1947 and, more recently, in Sri Lanka or Rwanda. The earlier 'conquests' and massacres were accompanied by the rise of a massive slave trade and the transport of large number of people to far-off places, often as indentured or bonded labour of various kinds, in conditions only slightly less severe than slavery.

The ideas of Freedom and Rationality followed 'conquest'; or, rather, they came initially to these parts of the globe only as an excuse for confiscation of land and conquistador capitalism. Their extension to human beings everywhere as their 'natural' right and property occurred much later; and then, as we have noted, it was far from universal. For a long time in the history of the 'modern' world, the notion of citizenship served in practice to distinguish the 'civilized' from those who were not. Citizenship was the preserve of the 'civilized', that is to say of those (men in the main) who were supposedly mature adults, capable of negotiating one with

[7] See Guerrero's contribution.

another and determining their rights and duties through rational argument.

To be 'civilized' was, as we have said, to have a Nation, to have History and the (modern) State; outside these lay 'violence', chaos, raw human emotion unrestrained by Reason. These propositions were very much in place in the nineteenth century. History, as Hegel put it, was the progress of Freedom and this was possible only in the State. The life of peoples, as individuals and even communities, before the State belonged to '*pre*-history'. Hence Hegel's well-known comments on India:

> India not only has old books of religion and brilliant works of poetry but also old codes of law—which above were mentioned as a condition of the formation of history—and *yet it has no history*. In that country the impulse to organization, which begins to differentiate society, was immediately petrified into the natural distinctions of caste. . . . Because of that bondage of the caste system, in all historical relation there is *wild arbitrariness, ephemeral bustling*, indeed, *raging* without a final purpose of progress or development.[8]

Hegel was, of course, even more drastic in excluding Africa—that is *das eigentliche Afrika* 'south of the desert'—altogether from the realm of reason and therefore from the progress to Freedom. Yet Kant, one of the main *Begründer* of the Enlightenment, was perhaps the most categorical in this mania of exclusion: 'Humanity reaches its greatest perfection in the white race. The yellow Indians have already more limited talents. The negroes are lower and the lowest are some of the American peoples.'[9]

[8] G.W.F. Hegel, *Reason in History: A General Introduction to the Philosophy of History*, tr. Robert S. Hartman, Indianapolis: Bobbs-Merrill Co., 1953, pp. 74–5 (emphasis added).

[9] E. Kant, *Physische Geographie*, vol. II, Königsberg, 1802, p. 15. Cf. also C.M. Neugebauer, 'The Racism of Hegel and Kant', in H. Odera Oruka (ed.), *Sage Philosophy*, Nairobi: African Centre for Technology Studies, 1991, pp. 247–57, for a philosophical refutation of Hegel's and Kant's racism. This author emphasizes that especially Kant's racism has received far too little attention. The quotation above is preceded by the following remarkable statement: 'Die Mohren, . . . haben eine dicke Haut, wie man sie denn auch nicht mit Ruthen, sondern gespaltenen Röhren peitscht, wenn man sie züchtigt, damit das Blut einen Ausgang finde, und nicht unter der dicken Haut eitere' ('The black Moors, . . . have a thick skin; it is therefore that they are beaten with a split cane instead of with a rod in order to create an opening for the blood to get out so as not to let it fester under the thick skin'), E. Kant, 1802, p. 11.

Colonialism and closer contact with the diversity of 'irrational' peoples of the world occasionally led to a certain nuancing. But the domain of the excluded did not contract markedly; it simply became a banal fact of life. As James Mill had it in his classic *The History of British India*, commenting on an early nineteenth century example of Hindu-Muslim conflict in the city of Banaras in north India, '... the disturbance was characteristically illustrative ... of the discordant elements of Indian society, which are alone restrained from frequent and destructive conflict by the vigilance, vigour, and impartiality of the ruling [British] power'.[10] Or Lugard a century later, in justifying segregated 'colonial' and 'native' dwelling areas in tropical Africa:

> The Indian or the African gentleman who adopts the higher standard of civilisation and desires to partake in such immunity from infection as segregation may convey, should be as free and welcome to live in the civilised reservation as the European, provided, of course, that he does not bring with him a concourse of followers. The native peasant often shares his hut with his goat, his sheep, or fowls. He loves to drum and dance at night, which deprives the European of sleep. . . . For these people, sanitary rules are necessary but hateful. . . .[11]

'Equal rights for all civilized men', Cecil Rhodes once famously declared.[12] The extraordinary African or Indian 'gentleman' might indeed (one day) qualify, but as a rule the proposition distinguished the European nations from the rest of the world. Around the time when the Second World War ended, as Sartre noted, the earth still consisted of 2000 million inhabitants—500 million 'men', and 1500 million 'natives'.[13]

In his contribution to this volume, Biaya describes the disappoint-

[10] James Mill and H.H. Wilson, *The History of British India: From 1805 to 1835*. In three volumes, vol. I, London: James Madden, 1838, p. 336. For a fuller discussion of colonial constructions of this and other instances of Hindu-Muslim conflict in India, see G. Pandey, *The Construction of Communalism in Colonial North India*, Delhi: Oxford University Press, 1990, Chap. 2.

[11] F.D. Lugard, *The Dual Mandate in British Tropical Africa*, London: Cass, 1965, pp. 149–50 cited in Mahmood Mamdani, *Citizen and Subject: Contemporary Africa and the Legacy of Late Colonialism*, Princeton, New Jersey: Princeton University Press, 1996, p. 16.

[12] Ibid., p. 17.

[13] See Frantz Fanon, *The Wretched of the Earth*, English paperback edition, London: Penguin, 1967, Preface by Jean Paul Sartre (1961).

ment of the Luba elites of Congo/Zaire who—as trusted auxiliaries of the Belgian 'colonial trinity' (State, Church and Business)—believed that they had become 'civilized' enough to claim the status of *évolués*. Biaya sees the bland rejection of their 'Luluabourg Manifesto' by the colonial authorities in 1944 as marking the beginning of Luba radicalism against the colonial state.

However, it was not only between countries and continents, an external imperialism and a colonized 'native', that the distinction between the 'civilized' and the 'uncivilized' was made. *Within* individual countries too, both in the North and in the South, there were many groups who were excluded from the ranks of citizens because they were deemed 'unfit' (or 'not yet fit') for the exercise of full rights in the modern political community. These were rights that the majority of women, labouring classes and other subordinated groups could not exercise until the second half of the twentieth century.

Guerrero and Barragán pose the problem squarely for the newly independent Latin American countries of Ecuador and Bolivia respectively. The signing of a modern constitution was to introduce these countries, with one stroke of the pen, as it were, into the modern age, and the constitutional proclamation was celebrated with something like religious fervour. Yet, the application of the new constitutional principles immediately posed a problem: how to deal with the Indians and other 'dependents' who constituted the majority of the population? Maintaining a formal, separate status for them as dependents, as in earler colonial legislation, was out of the question, since it went against the very principle of a 'modern' constitution. Yet, including them among the citizens was equally unthinkable.

One 'solution' that was found is what Guerrero calls 'archival amnesia'. The indigenous population becomes 'invisible', disappears from the archive, and their domination is made into a private affair of hacienda owners. By legal fiat they were 'attached' to 'master citizens' who became their representatives in all political matters: the Indians themselves disappeared from the records. It required two major 'indigenous uprisings', in 1990 and 1994, before they finally became visible again.

For Bolivia, Barragán focuses along similar lines on the subtle ways in which *patria potestad*—patriarchical authority, not only over Indians, but also within the house, over women, children and domestics—was combined with a nationalist discourse which claimed to be modern and liberal, to perpetuate existing forms of domination. As the author shows, it was no accident that it was at first only literate, male 'householders' who were granted the status of 'citizens'.

One scarcely needs to add that similar forms of exclusion have marked the history, even the very recent history, of the so-called 'advanced' countries of the modern world. In the USA, where modern 'nations' and 'representative governments' were conceptualized fairly early, a variety of disqualifications kept the majority of Afro-Americans, and other groups too, from the vote till as late as the 1960s. In France, where the Revolution announced the arrival of the modern world, women got the vote only after a referendum in October 1945; in Switzerland even later.

By the mid-twentieth century, however, the openly imperialist and masculinist notions of civilization and citizenship that underwrote the conditions discussed earlier were becoming a little more untenable. Many of the procedures of exclusion described in the preceding paragraphs survived in practice. Think of the near impossibility, until a few elections ago, not only for Blacks in the USA, but for the Ainu and for Korean-born Japanese in Japan, and for *dalit* ('untouchable') peasants and labourers in much of rural India to exercise their right to vote. For the last-named the votes were regularly cast by their landlords and landlords' goons. The position of many women, and of other subordinated groups, was not always very different. Yet, as this kind of exclusion became less legitimate and less passively accepted, and as an increasing number of countries joined the ranks of the 'civilized' as nation-states, a culturalist argument took the place of the argument about political 'unfitness' to ensure the dominance of particular groups in these societies.

The criterion for citizenship now increasingly took the form of a new kind of cultural test, having to do not so much with 'civilization' (literacy, 'rationality', settled existence, cleanliness, what have you), though some of that survived too, as with 'homogeneity'. Which were the groups and individuals who properly fitted into the *cultural community* called the nation, who belonged to the 'real', uniform, national culture, or at least, conformed to the 'mainstream'? What this produced was something perhaps even more insidious than the citizens/children distinction that marked the civilized/uncivilized discourse. It produced a politics of those who belonged—'naturally', as it were, which is to say, in general, by birth—as against those who could never quite belong.

Earlier, equality had been limited to those who were already 'equal'. Now it was to be restricted to those who were culturally the same. Equality was now tied to homogeneity and the wiping out, or minimizing, of difference 'within', so as to maximize the difference with the 'real' outsiders. It is a proposition that the women's movement, and along with feminists, the spokespersons of other marginalized groups, have had to do battle with for a long time now.

One might, then, posit the existence of two different moments in the history of nationalism—a 'democratic'/'political' moment (the people-nation as a *political community*), and a 'culturalist' moment (the *volk*-nation as a 'natural', *cultural community*). This contrast is often equated with a contrast between France and the Americas (the Revolutions as political moments), on the one hand, and Germany (notably Herder's romantic version of nationalism), on the other. There is of course no denying the existence of powerful, if more implicit, culturalist trends in French and American history, and of the political dimension of German nationalism. Without the politics, indeed, there would be no nationalism. Yet, the separation of these two moments may be helpful in understanding different trajectories of the inclusive and exclusive tendencies of 'national' political arrangements.

From 'the nation of the French' and the nations of German-speakers and Italian-speakers in the nineteenth century, to the propaganda about autochthonous as against allochthonous inhabitants in our own day—claims of true, original Englishness, and even more astonishingly, of being 'real' Americans and 'original' (White Settler) Australians—the notion of a 'natural', unquestionably belonging, national inhabitant claiming historical respectability, has had a long innings. It is perhaps unnecessary to point out the sleight of hand, or sometimes sheer brazenness, that is required to advance claims of this kind. Much has been written about the transformation of 'peasants into Frenchmen' (i.e. into speakers of a shared language that would from this time on be called 'French'), a process that was not anywhere near complete at least until the period of the First World War, and about the invention of national traditions in England, Italy, Spain and elsewhere, to say nothing about the very long history of Australasia and the Americas which the latecomers of recent centuries tried to suppress.[14]

Essential to the culturalist project of nationhood is the claim to 'purity' and a distinguished, preferably 'ancient', lineage. The idea of the 'natural','original' inhabitant is grafted on to the notion of the real, true, trustworthy citizen—fully French, Nigerian, Thai, or whatever, a figure that is arrived at only by the suppression of several other (non-'national') attributes of the same person, or by the unstated assimilation of these to the notion of the French, Nigerian, Thai, etc. The search for this figure, and the contradictory practices that allow it to emerge, are by no means new. This is well illustrated in the Chinese, Indian, Sri Lankan (Ceylonese) and Thai cases discussed by Haiyang, Chandra, Wickramasinghe and Tejapira in this volume. It is worth emphasizing once more that this pure national figure and these contradictory practices are by no means confined to the colonized and semi-colonized countries of Asia, or other parts of the 'South'.

A powerful example of the quest for national homogeneity and of its consequences is found in Kasian Tejapira's paper on the exclusion of the Chinese from the emerging Thai nation after 1900. King Rama VI, one of the main protagonists of this nationalism, specialized in shockingly racist vituperations against the Chinese as the arch-enemies of the Thais, characterizing them as 'different' in every respect and using them as an integral part of his efforts to consolidate the Thai nation. There was no attempt to base this exclusion of the Chinese from the nation on some opposition of 'civilized' *versus* 'non-civilized'. Indeed, this would have been difficult in view of the king's close collaboration with the Chinese as indispensable business partners. Rather, the Chinese had to be excluded because they were culturally 'different', not *quite* the Thai citizen, and as such a menace to Thai national unity. It is a conception of nationalism with which, as Tejapira so eloquently shows, the Chinese and other non-Thai citizens of Thailand can scarcely be comfortable.

[14] See, for example, Eugen Weber, *Peasants into Frenchmen: the Modernization of Rural France, 1870–1914*, Palo Alto, California: Stanford University Press, 1976; Eric Hobsbawm and Terence Ranger (eds.), *The Invention of Tradition*, Cambridge: Cambridge University Press, 1982; and Henry Reynolds, *The Other Side of the Frontier: Aboriginal Resistance to the European Invasion of Australia*, Ringwood, Victoria, Australia: Penguin Books, 1983.

Nira Wickramasinghe and T.K. Biaya offer further examples of other ways in which the state (colonial as well as postcolonial) becomes the self-proclaimed guardian of the nation's authenticity in such totalizing projects. Wickramasinghe's theme—the return of a cranium from a British museum to Sri Lanka in 1948—may appear to be somewhat eccentric, but it was the outcome of a long and concerted project to construct a Ceylonese nation around an 'authentic' Sinhalese heritage. The cranium was Keppetipola's, the famous leader of the Kandyan rebellion against the British in 1817; Wickramasinghe examines how Kandy, in the interior of the island, was constructed as the cradle of Ceylonese (itself equated with Sinhalese) authenticity. Along similar lines Biaya analyses the heavy pressure of Mobutu's notorious *authenticité* project on the efforts of the Luba of Mbujimayi to create space for a more or less autonomous regional development. In both cases the colonial-postcolonial continuity is striking.

The British, once they had achieved the 'pacification' of Kandy, followed their own strategies in erecting this relatively isolated area as some sort of a symbol of the 'real' Ceylon, using it as a counterweight against the incipient nationalist movement in the coastal regions. However, after some hesitation, the nationalist leaders saw the advantages of such 'authenticity'. Wickramasinghe characterizes Keppetipola's cranium as 'a national treasure . . . built up by both the colonial rulers and the nationalist leadership'. Mobutu's *authenticité* was similarly built on colonial conceptions of 'traditional' Congo; in fact, in constructing his new ideology, Mobutu seems to have been closely advised by Belgian Freemasons.[15] Biaya shows also how stifling such statist constructs of the nation can be. In his view, the Luba of Eastern Kasai only succeeded in realizing regional growth, both economically and politically, in a striking contrast to the stagnation of the country as a whole, by relating to the dynamics of local political culture instead of to artificial, static constructions like Mobutu's *authenticité*.[16]

[15] René Devisch, 'Frenzy, Violence and Ethical Renewal in Kinshasa', *Public Culture*, 7 (3), pp. 593–629.

[16] See for a somewhat different interpretation of this trajectory Filip de Boeck, 'Domesticating Diamonds and Dollars: Identity, Expenditures and Sharing in Southwestern Zaire', in Birgit Meyer and Peter Geschiere (eds.), *Globalization and Identity: Dialectics of Flow and Closure*, Oxford: Blackwell (also special issue of *Development and Change*), 1999, pp. 177–211.

Sudhir Chandra, writing about an important debate on the position of Indian women at the end of the last century, also emphasizes the convergence between the worlds of the colonizer and the colonized, Victorian England and nineteenth century India, but suggests implicitly that the initiatives of the state were not always the sole force in the making of 'modern' identities. His careful analysis of a long polemic between a leading writer and a social publicist about the emotional attachments and marital arrangements that were permissible for an 'ideal' Indian woman point both to the great difficulty of establishing the 'authentic' in any situation of 'becoming' (here, forging nationhood), and to the centrality of the 'excluded' (in this instance, women) in the construction of the national authentic.

In these detailed analyses of the contest over citizenship, ethnicity and history at the moment of the forging of nationhood, we suggest there is much food for thought about our current political condition. One disturbing trend in regard to political arrangements at the end of the twentieth century, and the beginning of the twenty-first, is that far from declining, the culturalist conception of the nation has on the contrary appeared to grow in strength at the cost of its political conception. This culturalist view has now acquired such a hold in common sense political understanding that the earlier conception of the nation as a new and newly imagined political community, constituted in common struggle, is in danger of disappearing altogether.

The much increased mobility of indentured and other workers, and the general dislocation of large bodies of people under colonialism, which has been carried further by subsequent capitalist aggression, had already contributed not only to the flattening and homogenizing of labour, but also to the objectification of 'culture', and renewed drives to preserve what was 'authentic' or 'traditional' in the culture of the displaced people, as well as in that of the societies they 'contaminated'. Culturalist nationalism, if that is the term we want, which had already begun to insist on the erasure of 'difference' and the homogenization of national cultures and histories, has only tended to become more militant in this context.

A striking illustration of the changes involved here is the evolution of the notion of the 'autochthonous' in African politics. In many parts of the continent autochthones used to be distinguished as some sort of subject stratum from the rulers who explicitly claimed to be later immigrants. In the traditions of the Mossi (Burkina Faso), for instance, *les authochthones* are described as some sort of pre-cultural people who only became fully human after they were subjected by the rulers, the 'real' Mossi, who, as in so many other African societies, prided themselves on coming from elsewhere.[17] However, especially since the onset of the recent wave of democratization, it has become vital to prove that one is 'really' autochthonous not only to the nation, but also to the region or the province where one claims to belong. Democratization, and the contest over who is allowed to vote where, has triggered a complex politics of belonging, often with violent implications, in which the qualification of 'autochthon' has lost its subservient connotations to become instead a vital asset.

It will be conceded that everywhere the concept of nation/people has come into being historically through struggles to define and advance the national interest. Everywhere, however, there is a simultaneous, and it seems almost necessary, desire to present the nation as a given, an already formed totality, even a spirit or essence. Everywhere, it seems, once the 'nation' comes to have a state of its own or to be realized in the nation-state, to use nationalist parlance, this essence, this totality, comes to be concretized in the state and its territory, and the national interest comes to be equated with the integrity of the state and its boundaries.

Even in the 'advanced' countries of the West, where nationalism is said to be in retreat, such reductionist (and, simultaneously, totalizing) claims in the name of the 'nation' seem to have acquired a new vigour in recent decades. In France, Le Pen has excercised heavy pressure on the political establishment with his claim that the state should protect the purity of the nation. Enoch Powell's warnings against the Asian flood are well known and Thatcherite Britain appeared to have accepted them very substantially. In Belgium, people seem to be less and less sure whether they are one nation. Yet de Winter—the leader of the new right, who is invariably described as someone who seems to be a 'model son-in-law'—has great success with his slogan '*Eigen Volk Eerst*' (our own people

[17] Cf. Izard M., *L'Odyssée du pouvoir. Un royaume africain*, Paris: EHESS/MSH, 1992; S. Luning, *Het Binnenhalen van de Oogst. Ritueel en Samenleving in Maane*, Burkina Faso, Leiden: CNWS, 1977.

first). The United States even coined a new term for this nationalist subterfuge: 'unAmerican', a term which speaks volumes for what was taken to be axiomatically 'American' and which applied to all things that the American political leadership and military-industrial establishment did not like—not least, the suggestion of opposition to American military adventures abroad.[18]

Mahmood Mamdani's contribution on the ethnocide in Rwanda in the 1990s shows how dreadful the consequences of building the nation on such reductionist, and at bottom colonial, notions can be. The key question during his interviews in that country was: 'How did you know whom to kill? How did you know whether someone was a Tutsi or a Hutu?' After the obvious replies about racial traits were discarded—mixed marriages have become as common in Rwanda as in many parts of the former Yugoslavia—the staggering answer was that the identity card, as imposed by the Belgian colonial state, served as the ultimate identification. Authenticity, when based on colonial classifications (and are not all such classifications in today's globalized world in some sense 'colonial'?), can have particularly damaging and divisive effects. As Mamdani emphasizes, the real cause of the crisis is the nature of the state, the postcolonial version as much as its colonial predecessor. His argument is that the nation-state needs to be acknowledged forthrightly as a historically-constituted, political community, and not one based on cultural essence.[19] We could not agree more.

The proponents of an emancipatory politics must necessarily

[18] We are grateful to Professor U.R. Ananthamurthy for drawing our attention to this point.

[19] Cf. also Lisa Malkki's study of Hutu refugees from Burundi in Tanzania—L.H. Malkki, *Purity and Exile-Violence, Memory and National Cosmology among Hutu Refugees in Tanzania*, Chicago: Chicago University Press, 1995. She observes a sharp contrast between the historical perspectives of refugees who have now for more than twenty years lived in camps, and others who stay more or less illegally in border-towns. The first seem to imprison themselves ever more in a vision of the Hutu-Tutsi divide as the crux of Burundi history, reversing the colonial view—since the Hutu are the real autochthones, Burundi belongs to them; the Tutsi have no rights there since they came later—but retaining its basic categories. In contrast, the refugees outside the camps prove to be rather reluctant to discuss these categories at all. In general, the debate on ethnicity in Africa has been lately dominated by the question to what extent it is a colonial creation, a view that is often, but maybe somewhat erroneously, attributed to the influential collection by J.-L. Amselle and E. M'Bokolo (eds.), *Au coeur de l'ethnie: Ethnies, Tribalisme et Etat en Afrique*, Paris: Editions la Découverte,

challenge the assumption that the nation is a *natural*, eternally existing *cultural community*, to which *some* automatically belong, and *others* never quite. The 'we', that is, the idea of the nation that much of the world has inherited from colonial capitalism and imperialist nationalism, cannot be a pre-constituted, unchanging cultural community. It has to be a common *political* community, forged in struggle, out of shared difficulties and shared dreams. That struggle to build the new political communities of the future is clearly ongoing.

Marx wrote in his reflections 'On the Jewish Question' of the distinction between the 'living individual' and the abstract citizen: 'The difference between the religious man and the citizen is the [same as the] difference between the merchant and the citizen, between the day-labourer and the citizen, between the landowner and the citizen, between the *living individual* and the *citizen*.'[20] The observation is of importance. It is precisely the emancipation of living individuals and communities that we must seek.

Nationalism and modernity have insistently staked their claims on notions of the 'pure'. 'Modern civilization', modern states and nations, have demanded clear, unambiguous, uniform identities—purely this or purely that,[21] where the 'this' and 'that' have usually been 'national' terms. 'Impurity', 'difference', 'resistance', 'complexity', shall we say, 'richness' have, however, never been wiped out. If ever they were, we would be in serious danger of being reduced to the lowest common factor of human life: a race, or races, of uniformly dressed and uniformly driven, unthinking, men and women occupied only with earning, eating and surviving.

1985. Whatever the answer is—and it is clear that it will differ for the various parts of the continent—there is, in this respect as well, a striking colonial-postcolonial continuity. Especially since the recent wave of democratization, many postcolonial regimes in Africa seem to deem it in their interest to actively encourage ever more vicious forms of ethnicity, often also on an ever smaller scale. Cf. P. Geschiere and Francois Nyamnjoh, 'Capitalism and Autochthony, The Seesaw of Mobility and Belonging', *Public Culture* (*Millennium Issue*), 2000, 21, pp. 423–53 and D.W. Cohen and E.S. Odhiambo, *Burying SM, The Politics of Knowledge and the Sociology of Power in Africa*, London: Currey, 1992.

[20] Karl Marx, 'On the Jewish Question', *Early Writings*, London: Penguin Books, 1975, pp. 220–1

[21] For an elaboration of this point, see G. Pandey, 'Can a Muslim be an Indian?', *Comparative Studies in Society and History*, 41, 4 (1999).

One further point. The forging of nationhood—the promotion or imposition of uniformity and homogeneity in economy, culture, history, and the promotion or hindrance of the struggle for rights, equality, difference, justice—has long been dominated by, or appeared in association with, the need to build a modern state. A critique of the state is, therefore, a necessary part of the current exercise of critiquing the nation. We are caught in something of a bind here. The self-questioning and political reflection which has occupied many of us show that we cannot do without the modern state; nor can we do very well with it as it exists. Even if we are able to overcome the demands of a homogenizing, flattening and to some extent impoverishing 'nationalism' and 'natural' nationhood, we are not so easily going to be able to dispense with the need for a centralizing state to organize complex economic and political activities.[22]

Tejapira, contributing one of the more passionate and politically committed pieces in this volume with a trenchant personal testimony of how a member of an excluded group can suffer from nationalism's impatience with difference, concludes with the hope of reforming the nation-state. We have argued that the concept of the essential, cultural nation—and perhaps therefore the idea of the nation itself, as this has been handed down to us—needs serious questioning. Along with that questioning, the struggle to democratize the state, and with it the state's management of difference (of gender, caste, class, race, region)—must, however, remain among the more urgent of the political-intellectual tasks facing men and women in different parts of the world today.

[22] The dilemma—of not being able to do without the state while not doing very well with it either—is graphically illustrated by the striking reversals in the World Bank's dealings with the state in Africa. Its 1989 report on Africa brought a first abrupt reversal. After sticking, ever since independence, to the postcolonial state despite increasing criticisms, the Bank decided abruptly that the state had become an obstacle to development instead of an instigator. The slogan of 'bypassing the state' then led to a rapid proliferation of NGOs which often were only 'non-governmental' in name, but which also actively participated in the politics of belonging and autochthony in quite problematic ways. Its reports on Africa over the last few years indicate that the Bank is now again seriously reconsidering its position.

Citizenship and the Administration of Dominated Populations

The Case of Postcolonial Ecuador

Andres Guerrero

This essay explores neglected aspects of the construction of a republican regime of citizenship. It focuses notably on the paradox that this regime of citizenship was formally based on political representation, but incorporated simultaneously and organically, forms of domination which were antagonistic to the very idea of citizenship as based on equal rights. I am most concerned with those aspects which I call the 'administration of populations': the management, under republican regimes, of demographic groups, particularly in the nineteenth century, which were not considered apt for the everyday forms of exchange inherent to the relationship of equality among citizens; that is, for the most part, populations classified as uncivilized.

This problematic is part of a wider discussion about the various forms of citizenship which may arise in different historical contexts. Where the various perspectives of class, ethnicity, race, gender intersect, some authors have raised the problem of citizenship conceived not merely as a modality of inclusion and egalitarianism (which seem to be inherent in its own universalizing discourse), but as a historical construction tinted by the semantics of domination and contingent upon social conflicts and relations of power.[1] This problem, in my view, is particularly pertinent for those postcolonial states (like the Republic of Ecuador) which harbour significant indigenous populations under conditions of social, political, and economic subordination.

*I thank M. Thurner for the translation and his suggestions.

[1] M. Mann, 'Ruling Class Strategies and Citizenship', *Sociology*, 21 (1987), pp. 339–54; C. Pateman, 'The Fraternal Social Contract', in J. Keane (ed.), *Civil Society and the State: New Perspectives*, London: Verso, 1988; B. Turner, 'Outline of a Theory of Citizenship', *Sociology*, 24 (1990), pp. 189–217; M. Thurner, *From Two Republics to One Divided: Contradictions of Postcolonial Nationmaking in Andean Peru*, Durham-London/Duke University Press, 1997.

Today, in the Andes and in Mesoamerica, the so-called Indians have assumed frontline roles in social movements. They have now come out upon the public stage and on the national political scene, provoking specific political crises, albeit under a doubly paradoxical sign. First, these movements emerged precisely at a moment when the architecture of citizenship and of republican representation—which will in the next decade commemorate 200 years of construction—seemed to be totally consolidated.

Second, they occurred at a moment when the public opinion of 'citizens in the practical sense' (a notion I will define below, but by which here I mean the Creole or White-Mestizo population) was convinced, as a sort of consensus among the dominant, that Indians were essentially obliterated populations or at best 'witnesses' to a past long gone. In other words, they were 'fossil' cultures or perhaps remnant peasant communities cornered in remote 'refuge regions'.[2] In effect, under the shadow of citizenship, indigenous peoples were rendered invisible populations stripped of social and political rights, their economic and cultural contribution to the nation was strongly reduced; thus, they seemed to lack all political relevance. Indians constituted a kind of historical residue, peoples and cultures which silently faded away before the open gates of national integration, globalization, migratory movements and, above all, the process of *mestizaje* or miscegenation which implied the bodily incorporation of natives in the ideal image of the White-Mestizo national citizen.

As a means for bringing this problematic into focus, I have adopted a modality of narration which does not intend to unravel a historical intrigue, but which does seek to draw taut associations between three levels of analysis.[3] I begin by sketching two key-events of a historical conjuncture which left an enduring mark on the formation of citizenship in Ecuador. Cutting the thread of this historical narration, I then intercalate four 'detours' on connected methodological and theoretical considerations. I will thus spin a web of linkages which associate both the events with two kinds of problems. The first problem, which is theoretical, derives from the

[2] Alfonso Caso, *La comunidad indígena*, Sep-setetas, México, 1971; D. Ribeiro, *Las Américas y la Civilización*, vol. I, 'Los pueblos testimonio', Centro Editor, Bs. As., 1969; Aquirre Beltrán, *Regiones de refugio*, FCE, Mexico, 1989.

[3] On the notion of intrigue as organizing thread of historical account, see P. Ricoeur, *Temps et récit*, vol. II, Paris: Seuil, 1983 and J. Rancière, *Les noms l'histoire. Essai de poétique du savoir*, Paris: Seuil, 1992.

necessity to think through the paradox of a form of citizenship which is constructed as a system for the administration of populations. The second is the methodological problem of how to write, on the basis of the available archives, the history of citizenship as an everyday relation of domination in a postcolonial republican context. These problems, imposed upon the historian by both past and present social realities, arise when she/he attempts to decode and analyse the documents at hand.

The two events are located in 1843 and 1857. They both concern the constitution of citizenship by initiative of the state. The first removed the dust from a failure buried among the many amnesias of the national cause. In effect, the recently founded nation-state attempted in 1843 to amplify the juridical equality of citizenship and extend it to all the populations of the Republic, including the indigenous. However, the state had to backtrack in the face of a social rebellion ignited by the White-Mestizo population, and particularly by the popular classes that formed part of this group of de facto citizens.

In contrast, the second event in 1857 achieved an enduring success: without dissent the Parliament voted for the legal equality of the indigenous population with the rest of the country's citizens. Nevertheless, this juridical levelling did not solve the problem of the administration of the dominated populations; on the contrary, it made it all the more urgent. A shift occurred in the system of domination, from an explicit form of management—concentrated in the state and the legacy of the colony—to a republican form which decentered domination towards the diffuse and variegated periphery of 'fields of power'—in Bourdieu's term—located in the private sphere. A system of domination over the indigenous population was implanted which was compatible with republican principles and laws, and even inscribed in citizenship. In summary, in 1857, the management of the indigenous population (the de facto not-citizens) was delegated to the private sphere—that is to the patriarchal and patrimonial institutions of the de facto citizens.

I have selected these two events since, in my view, they accentuate crucial aspects, both theoretical and historical, of the architecture of citizenship. They can help us to understand that the effective content of this relationship, in everyday life, is the contingent result of a specific historical process—of the conjuncture and relations of power under which it was imposed. In other words, under certain circumstances citizenship may integrate modalities of domination over those populations classified and discriminated against as not citizens, by internalizing the habitus of the politically, culturally, and racially 'legitimate' population. This leads me to formulate theoretical considerations which, in my 'detours' into the usages of the notion of citizenship, I attempt to link back to the historical narrative.

Over the course of my ongoing research on the relation between the formation of the republican state and indigenous populations in the nineteenth century, it has become increasingly clear to me that—in the Ecuadorian context and also for other countries of the region with large indigenous populations—to adhere to the conventional, merely juridical definition of citizenship, or to define it exclusively in terms of relations between populations and the state, is to render the notion reductionist. The issue of a form of domination decentred away from the state and delegated to the periphery of private power remains unelucidated within the context of a political system which implanted, relatively early on, juridical equality among all adult male inhabitants of the country. This is what occurred in Ecuador after 1857 and continues to the present. Everyday problems of discrimination and marginalization can then, at most, be interpreted as the result of intersubjective relations between individuals and of intolerance as a consequence of ethnic sensibilities. In any case, they do not seem to constitute a pertinent subject for the history of the political construction of the Republic.

The question for us is, therefore, what conceptual tools can be employed to achieve a deeper theoretical understanding of the problematic, but apparently basic, relation between citizenship and inequality? The possibility which I explore in this essay consists of orienting the analysis toward a notion of citizenship conceived of as a field of power for social agents in the political public sphere (to borrow Habermas' concept). This perspective requires removing citizenship from its formal relation to the state, and resituating it in the context of immediate and everyday strategies of power between populations. Thus, I heed Foucault's warnings about the insufficiency of any juridical explanation of power (which fits so well with the notion of citizenship conceived only in terms of rights), and about the need to reveal aspects of domination hidden under the notion of the 'administration of populations'. I also make use of two theoretical propositions drawn from the feminist critique of the political. In order to analyse the constitution of the dominated subject and of those who dominate, I draw upon, on the one hand, Pateman's proposal to interrogate the forms of domination nested in the myth of the social contract, the notion of citizenship, and the separation of public from private; and, on the other, on Butler's suggestion that forms of domination demarcate a domain of politics by setting up a 'determining exterior' that is 'pre-' or 'non-' political where the 'Other' is situated.

A final theme in my detours has to do with the political representation of the indigenous population under a regime of citizenship. In Ecuador, the construction of citizenship was accompanied by a process of making certain populations invisible in the public-statal sphere, as the logical consequence of the 'legitimate' discourse of the dominant social agents in this sphere. Given that indigenous peoples as a group of populations were pushed into the distant recesses of the public sphere of citizens, subordinated to the sphere of private powers, and situated in a 'constitutive outside', two questions arise. First, under such conditions, how is the political representation of this type of population (which is, ultimately, one of subjects) executed under a regime of citizenship? Second, what significance may the historian assign to those archival documents called 'representations' which are addressed to state functionaries, and in which invisible populations emerge? How should we interpret documents written by citizen intermediaries, the social agents who put words into the mouths of Indians and then down on paper? Who speaks and what is being said? My conclusion will be that this is a form of representation which is best characterized as ventriloquy.

CITIZENS AGAINST UNIVERSAL EQUALITY

In 1843—thirteen years after the foundation of the Republic of Ecuador—the country's first president drew a grim picture of the nation's fiscal situation before the Parliament.[4] The newly founded nation-state was bankrupt. The bureaucracy had not been paid for

[4] Territories and populations belonging to the Royal Audiencia of Quito (a colonial district) were organized into an independent nation-state in 1830, when the Republic of Colombia was divided up (1822) into the nation-states of Colombia, Bolivia, Ecuador and Venezuela.

months; the authorities were without funds for public works and other planned projects. Funds had to be collected somehow. The President asked senators and deputies—the country's first generation of 'representatives'—to vote for a new law designed to resolve the financial crisis. He made two alternative proposals aimed, he explained, at solving not only the fiscal crisis, but also a 'painful and flagrant' political contradiction, an injustice nested in the very principles of the Republic. In effect, his two proposals for revenue collection eliminated a longstanding political distinction—rooted in the colonial period, and not suppressed by the foundation of the Republic—which had existed between two types of populations.[5] On the one hand, Spanish-speaking Creoles or 'Whites' and Mestizos, those who the state recognized as active or passive citizens, composed what one might call the 'natural' members of the Republic, endowed with obvious contextual and implicit historical rights, and thus embodying the *sens pratique* which informed the founding fathers of the nation-state.[6] However, and despite being citizens, they paid no personal or poll tax and, as the President announced, they 'contributed almost nothing toward the maintenance of the state'. On the other hand, 'indigenous taxpayers', i.e. adult males of dominated populations, paid a 'tribute or contribution' (in the form of a head tax) in cash, for no other reason than the tautology of having been classified by the Republic as indigenous persons.

The President gave the Parliament two options. The first was a straightforward abolition of the tribute now paid by indigenous persons, to be replaced, in accordance with sound republican principles, 'by other taxes imposed on every citizen in proportion to his assets'. The second option was to generalize tribute to all citizens: 'to extend the contribution (*the tributo de indios*) to that part of the people (*la parte del pueblo*) otherwise exempt from its payment—that is the White-Mestizo population (AG)—so that, extended or generalized in this manner, two great goals may be

[5] The Status of Indian tributary was suppressed in 1821 during the War of Independence, and citizenship was extended to all populations; however, in 1828, S. Bolivar reestablished the tribute.

[6] P. Bourdieu, *Le Sens Pratique*, Les Eds. de Minuit, Paris, 1980, Chap. 3. This notion has been translated into English as 'practical mastery' as well as 'the logic of practice'. See Calhoum Craig (ed.), *Bourdieu: Critical Perspectives*, Chicago: University of Chicago Press, 1993, p. 225.

reconciled: that of justice, by abolishing a bad principle, and that of [the state's fiscal] necessity, which forces us to close the deficit. . . .'[7]

Both proposals would produce the necessary revenues to continue the project of republican statemaking, while at the same time establishing the principle of civil equality (both fraternal and patriarchal) among the various populations of the Republic.[8] The proposals were certainly innovative. By suppressing Indian tribute they broke the back of colonial domination inherited from Spain. The bond of tribute between the Spanish Crown and the colonized peoples had been forged since the beginnings of colonial rule (1570); it lent coherence to a complex architecture of material and symbolic ties of domination which were in place long before the foundation of the Republic.

In contrast, the President's proposals sprang from ideals which had guided the independence struggle with Spain: the utopia born with the Enlightenment and the Anglo-American and French revolutions. It was about constructing a new and rational political order, making a clean sweep of history, and erecting the sovereign people's state. In short, building a republic of free and equal individuals, based upon universal principles of citizenship.

Once the collection of the universal levy was decreed in 1847, an event took place which, if regarded from today's perspective—that is, from categories constituted under current national systems—presents a historical paradox. A violent rebellion swept the most densely populated area of the country from north to south, the region inhabited by Whites-Mestizos and Indians.[9] Except for Quito, the capital of the Republic, site of the domestic life and political activities of the ruling White-Mestizo urban classes and landowners, where there were no confrontations, revolutionary fervour spread through the villages and towns of the Sierra. The President ordered

[7] 'Report from Gral. J.J. Flores, President of the Republic to the Senate', *Gaceta del Ecuador*, 24 January 1841.

[8] C. Pateman, 'The Fraternal Social Contract', in J. Keane, op. cit.

[9] By 'Mestizo' or 'White' I mean that social group which under the Colony was classified into different juridically defined 'castes'. Under the Republic, this group identified itself as 'White'. I am using 'White' as a qualifier and as a classification parallel to 'indigenous' which was used by the state and citizens, and today is still in use in everyday life. In addition nowadays former populations qualify themselves as 'Ecuadorian indigenes'.

the army to stamp out the insurrection; pitched battles, death, and destruction ensued for nearly three months. Spirits were calmed by a further decree. Finally the rebellion ceased as the government backed off. The President revoked the act which had extended the levy imposed on Indians to the adult male 'White' population—that is, to that part of the population defined as citizens both de facto and by law, by the state *and* in the 'logic of practice'.

Meanwhile, the levy was maintained for the indigenous population, who had always, over the last three centuries, paid tribute to the state in their capacity as colonial subjects. In effect up to the mid-nineteenth century the republican state partly financed itself—to a level fluctuating around 30 per cent of its total income—by means of this levy.[10] In the words of the Minister of the Interior and Finance, the state kept itself afloat thanks to a levy based on 'an outrageous inequality, so very contrary to the republican form of government we have adopted'.[11] It is worth pointing out that this Minister of the Interior, Ecuador's first to advocate universal republican equality, was himself a member of the landlord class, the owner of an *obraje* (textile mill) and several haciendas. As such, he administered several generations of indigenous families on his properties and in his house.

Detour 1

When talking about citizenship in the early nineteenth century one must keep in mind that it was still a notion in formation, not only in Ecuador but around the world. It was part of a growing debate in everyday life, signifying adherance to a political system which was both vast and still scarcely codified.[12] In the early years of the

[10] M. Van Akken, 'La Lenta expiración del tributo indígena en el Ecuador', *Cultura*, no. 16, 1983, Quito.

[11] *Informe* from Gral. J.J. Flores, op. cit.

[12] 'The inevitable consequence (of the extended use) was that the term "citoyen" was packed with multiple, ambiguous and contradictory meanings, and that, between 1789 and 1800, it became a focus of passionate political struggles', W.H. Sewell Jr., 'Le Citoyen/la citoyenne: Activity, passitivity, and the Revolutionary Concept of Citizenship', in Colin Lucas (ed.), *The Political Culture of the French Revolution*, Oxford: Pergamon Press, 1988, p. 106. See also Ferdinand Brunot, *Histoire de la Langue Français des origines à nos jours*, T. IX: *La Révolution et l'Empire*, 2 partie, 'Les événements, les institutions et la langue', Paris: A. Colin, 1967, pp. 678–98.

Republic one can distinguish a spectrum of meanings which range, first, from tacit and quotidian rights, derived from the logic of practice of that part of the population that was sensitive to Independence; and, secondly, to those rights which were progressively defined in a restrictive way by Republican laws, particularly political rights. The general usage granted, as many documents demonstrate, a de facto right of citizenship to every White-Mestizo 'civilized' adult. Such usage did also include White-Mestizo females, albeit in a situation of paternal and conjugal subordination. Simultaneously, it excluded categorically indigenous persons. Indeed, in law, the extension of citizenship to include the exercise of representation rights, as elector and elected, was limited by propriety and by other restrictions.[13] Obviously, those laws which granted full rights to active citizens referred only to adult males. Thus, they ratified the double legal exclusion—applied unequally—of women and Indians (men and women). Furthermore, the term 'citizen' was in many official papers interchangeable with the word 'Ecuadorian'—a usage which was widespread in administrative and political discourse, and determined by the logic of practice rather than by any juristic codification. As the nineteenth century unfolded, the state's definition annulled and prevailed over usages anchored in this *sens pratique*. Citizenship was converted into an almost purely juridical notion defined in terms of a state which 'recognized' a certain population and excluded the rest.

THE PARADOXES OF EQUALITY

To understand this rebellion of the citizens, one must pause to look at the manner in which the popular sectors of the White-Mestizo population perceived the government's attempt to generalize the contribution paid by the indigenous population and thereby implement the principle of equality. Official accounts and the sporadic writings of the rebels (handwritten by themselves, being Spanish speakers) coincide as to the reasons for the rebellion. Both indicate that these people rebelled because they understood that the government intended, in an underhand way and via the pretext of a 'universal tax' (contribucion general), to impose upon them a levy which—by analogy with the colonial *tributo de indios*—they qualified in their pamphlets as *a tributo de blancos*, or White tribute.

[13] *Leyes de Colombia: 1821–7*, Caracas. Imp. V. Espinal, 1840.

This fiscal equalization under the Republic was not entirely new; it had colonial antecedents. In the 1780s the Bourbon State attempted to expand the tax base of the colonial system by similarly extending the Indian tribute to include 'Cholos' and 'Mestizos'. Moreover, in the 1810s, the liberal Cortes of Cadiz momentarily suppressed the fiscal and civil distinctions between Indian and non-Indian populations in the Americas. In 1788 in the region of Riobamba (south of Quito), for example, a significant uprising took place which was led by the so-called Mestizos of the towns and cities, bilinguals who strove to situate themselves in a non-Indian condition. The rebellion was a response to the Bourbon reforms which attempted to extend the caste categories. The fiscal equalization enacted by the state may have been experienced as a symbolic degradation by these people, returning them to the condition of Indian tributary. It is conceivable that the rebellion of 1788 against downward equality still reverberated sixty years later in the acts and words of the poor White-Mestizos rebelling against the new Republic in 1847.[14]

It is highly probable that the use of the word 'tribute' contained meanings which resonated in the mental perceptions and emotional sensibilities of the citizen rebels. It signalled the government's transgression of what E.P. Thompson called a 'moral threshold of political legitimacy'. In effect, 'poor whites' in the Andes constituted a social group which in the postcolonial context both fits and clashes with the gramscian notion of 'subalterns'. White-Mestizo peasants with scarce lands, wage workers, artisans, itinerant merchants, shopkeepers, muledrivers, day labourers or domestic servants were all dominated, even though they belonged to the dominant colonial group. They shared a common colonial class consciousness: they saw themselves as White-Mestizos, and on their farms and in their homes, and in those of their masters as well, they dealt with and dominated indigenous persons (both men and women) who worked for them in a permanent or sporadic capacity.

The equalization of rights decreed by the state had great repercussions especially for this poor White-Mestizo group. According to a report written by a colonial magistrate (*corregidor*) to the Royal tribunal in 1778, there were three categories of 'Mestizos'

[14] On colonial fiscal reforms in Peru, see M. Thurner, *From Two Republics*, pp. 20–5. On the 1788 rebellion, S. Moreno Yanez, *Sublevaciones indigenas en la audiencia de Quito*, Puce, Quito, 1985, pp. 208, 224.

which tried to escape the Indian tribute. These were the 'cholos' who were Indians but had ceased being so culturally; the children of white and indigenous unions; and the illegitimate children of 'gentlemen' born of Mestiza women.[15] These were social strata which, due precisely to their cultural and generational proximity to Indians (being bilinguals with Indian forebears), accentuated symbolic and material strategies of distinction especially in urban society. The payment of a 'universal contribution' would necessarily resituate them on the same plane as the indigenous population from which they strove so hard to differentiate themselves. As such, it must have been resented for bringing an abhorrent equality. So much so that one rebel denounced, using the same phrase that for this 'part of the people' as the President had employed in his discourse. The levy implied that sooner or later they would succumb to the necessity of having to 'sell oneself into bondage on the haciendas'. To pay the tax, the 'poor whites' would have to work as *peons*; they would be enslaved, or in any case be 'attached' (*adscritos*) to the landlords for generations to come, with their spouse and children. In short, they would, in the end, be reconverted into Indians.

In effect, the tributary circuit which linked the state to the haciendas and its indigenous populations was an integral part of an ancestral colonial habitus. This circuit benefitted from the difficulties peasants faced in obtaining cash in an agrarian economy with restricted money circulation and a broad subsistence sector where barter prevailed. Obviously, landlords—whether big, medium or small—had access to cash since they sold their harvests in urban centres. Ever since colonial times, the state knew about, and took advantage of, this circuit. Thus, when a peon was contracted to a hacienda the state required the landlord to assume payment of the peon's tribute on a semester basis.[16]

The 'Attached Condition' of the Indian

Nevertheless, the financial obligation imposed on landowners was not unilateral. They were politically compensated with an acknowledgement of rights. In return for paying the tribute of their indigenous workers, the republican state adjudicated to landowners

[15] Cited in Segundo Moreno Yanez, *Sublevaciones indigenas*, o.c.
[16] *Gaceta del Ecuador*, 3 November 1842, v. 1841–2, ABFL, Quito.

a modality of rule over a space and its inhabitants. A circular issued by the Minister of the Interior in 1831 defined the so-called 'attached condition' of indigenous labourers on the haciendas.[17] In essence, it consisted of a sort of delegation of republican sovereignty to a 'master citizen' (*patrón ciudadano*) for the administration of indigenous persons who, grouped in communities, inhabited his private property.[18]

In this 'attachment' the republican state acknowledged a set of power relations of colonial origin. It constituted a realm of domination inscribed in everyday modalities of assymetrical reciprocity, material and symbolic, between landlord and indigenous families. For instance, peons could hardly abandon their masters, and their children were dependent on the proprietor's tutelary power. In turn, the master citizen 'took charge' of 'his' indigenous workers, securing the reproduction of generations, and providing protection; he administered some sort of justice at the hacienda courtyard (*patio de hacienda*); and his powers stretched over individual and domestic life cycles, as well as the generation cycle of the population. Finally, the master citizen presided over the ritual calendar, and his acts of power were endowed with sacral meanings.[19]

With rare exceptions, the circuit I have just described was aimed at conquered populations. It concerned the King of Spain's colonial 'subjects,' not the 'Creoles' and 'castas' (or Mestizos), who were excluded from this domain as the privileged colonial group. Thus, in the early Republic the rebellion of the poor 'Whites' against 'tribute' meant that citizens from lower strata ('notables', mainly land-owners, were not involved in the revolt) violently rejected a generalization or extension of the colonial situation intrinsic to 'Indian' populations.[20]

[17] Circular issued by the Minister of the Interior on 18 November 1831, ABFL, Quito.

[18] Compare this postcolonial situation with the features highlighted by E. Hobsbwam in the constitution of the nation state, which eliminates intermediary bodies of power and establishes a direct link between individuals and the state: 'In short, the state ruled over a territory, its agents increasingly reaching down to the humblest inhabitant of the least villages', E. Hobsbawm, *Nations and Nationalism since 1780, Programme, Myths, Reality*, Cambridge: CUP, 1990. p. 80.

[19] A. Guerrero, 'La semántica de la dominación: el concertaje de indios', Libris Mundi, Quito, 1991, pp. 119–213.

[20] Report from a civil servant, 'Correspondance from the Governor of Imbabura to the Minister of Interior', 16 August 1843; ANH, Quito.

In summary, universalizing the principle of equality elicited a paradox. The Republic appeared to demote 'common' citizens from their colonial status. It annulled the social hierarchies that impregnated the concrete signifiers of citizenship and equated them with a colonial preeminence. It converted 'poor white' citizens into state subjects, since they became obliged, like the indigenous population, to enter the sphere of power of the landowners.

THE REPUBLIC'S INVISIBLE POPULATIONS

The Weight of Demographics

Which groups qualified as citizens in the practical sense during the first decades of the Republic? The importance of this question for the construction of postcolonial citizenship is accentuated when we consider its demographic proportions, which are so clearly marked by the power relations between dominant and dominated colonial populations which with Independence had become citizens and administered subjects.[21]

In 1846 some 7,00,000 inhabitants were living in the Royal Audiencia of Quito, the administrative unit of the Spanish state over which was mapped out the Republic of Ecuador with its own territory, inhabitants, and state. The national census of that year classified the population (male and female) by ethnic and juridical categories: 'Whites', 41 per cent; 'Indians', 52 per cent; 'Free Mulattoes', 4 per cent; 'Mulattoe slaves', 1 per cent; 'Free Blacks', 1 per cent; 'Black slaves', 1 per cent. Plagued by errors and absences, these figures were more an ideal construction than a reflection of quantitative realities. They were the products of an imaginary demographics, which may therefore serve all the better as a qualitative index of the problems besetting the construction of a republican citizenship from the existing modalities of administering the populations.[22]

[21] The literature on republican citizenship in Latin America is immense. Still, the problem of the administration of populations subject to the state is at best mentioned as a problem of 'exclusion', or following T.H. Marshall (*Citizenship and Social Class and Other Essays*, Cambridge: CUP, 1950), of 'unfinished processes', or perhaps as impediments which 'distort' the historical formation of the citizenry and the 'political culture'. See for instance J. Murilo de Carvalho, 'Dimensôes da Cidadania no Brasil do seculo XIX', presented to the Bogota seminar on citizenchip in 1994.

[22] 'Report from the Minister of Interior to the Senate in 1846', BAEP, Quito.

Only one part of the population could, according to its own colonial classificatory system, be included without hesitation in the republican ideal of equal treatment of de facto citizens in public and quotidian exchanges. This was the broad category of the 41 per cent 'whites', which included 'Creoles' (or 'Mestizos', the old colonial 'castas'). In the early nineteenth century, this was a motley minority group of Spanish speakers, although many were bilingual Quichua speakers. They enjoyed a privileged colonial status, even though abysmal economic, cultural, and political inequalities prevailed within this group. Especially this part of the population had shown itself disposed to a revolutionary sensibility, actively pushing for Independence. In contrast, there were examples of 'Indian' communities in the Andes who, even if they did not actually oppose Independence, pursued their own strategies, supporting indiscriminately and alternately, the 'Creole Pioneers', but also the Spanish colonial troops.[23]

On the other hand, the 52 per cent of 'Indians', although included as Ecuadorians by the state, unquestionably fell—according to the mental maps and social strategies of 'white' citizens—on the other side of the frontier of what constituted a 'rational being' (an expression from common speech)—that is citizenship. Thus, the majority of Ecuadorians (the 'Indians') became republican subjects, to be administered by the de facto citizens.

In 1830 the delegates of the 'Whites', that is the 'notables' (big landlords, miners, merchants, and intellectuals) met in 'constitutive assemblies of the Republic' and founded the Parliament of Ecuador. They saw themselves as the unquestionable 'representatives of the people' and of the 'Republic'.[24] They wrote the Political Constitution of the State. In their vision, it was only logical that the sovereign power of citizens would reside in the juridical body of those persons who had invented the identity concerned: the nation of Ecuadorians within the borders of the Republic.

It was as logical that this same act of instituting a republican reality excluded 'Indians'. The foundational myth classified,

[23] J. Lynch, *The Spanish American Revolutions, 1808–26*, New York, 1986. C. Mendez, 'Rebellion without Resistance: Huanta's Monarchist Peasants in the Making of the Peruvian State, Ayacucho 1825–1850', Ph.D. dissertation, SUNY-Stony Brook, 1996.

[24] Both terms appear interchangeably in the constitutions of the Republic of Ecuador from 1830 to the present.

implicitly and by consensus, the rest of the population as being 'outside' of the rational and civilized. Thus, it succeeded in excluding, hiding, and shutting out the demographi- majority throughout the nineteenth century and even up to the end of the twentieth. It created the internal 'alien', the Indian subject of the Republic, as a hidden limit to the 'citizen', constituting a tacit and indefinable category. Conceptually, it created a 'blank space' which was constitutive of the sovereignty of republican law. As a domain external to the principles of 'the people', this space granted legitimacy to a political system based on deliberation and common accord. It was an undefined space which, nonetheless, traced a border in social, political, historical, and ethnic respects, structured by a matrix of colonial classifications which distinguished the 'white' population from the rest. Thus, in turn, it permitted the definition by contrast with the legitimate citizen and established an historical goal: civilizing the rest of the population.[25]

This constitutional blank indicated to which extent the formation of the Republic and the construction of citizenship depended on the play of power. The Republic had to emboss the indigenous populations as 'rational' Ecuadorians whose faces carried the effigy of the White-Mestizo individual. An obvious continuity unfolded between the colonial process and the postcolonial construction of the civilizing nation-state with the administration of the population as its crucial task.

EXTENDING CITIZENSHIP

However, the above-mentioned demographic proportions of republican state formation raise an urgent, although apparently less obvious, question: Does the form of domination change when rights of citizenship are extended to all adult males? Or, to put it more precisely, exactly how were Indian subjects administered under a generalized system of citizenship?

In 1857, the Ecuadorian Parliament approved a law which suppressed the status of 'indigenous tributary', establishing that

[25] N. Elias emphasizes the unambigous relation between the 'civilizing process', colonial expansion, and the formation of national states. *El proceso civilizatorio. Investigacions sociogenéticas y psicogenéticas*, Mexico: FCE, MEXICO, 1987, pp. 95–6.

> in the Republic the tax known by the name of *contribución personal de indigenas* is abolished, and individuals of this class are now equal to the rest of the Ecuadorians in terms of the obligations and rights imposed and granted by the fundamental charter [the Constitution] of the Republic.[26]

This problem is well illustrated by the position of the heads of peasant households (*huasipungueros*) on the haciendas. In the Andes, the hacienda was firmly institutionalized as a formation of power: it was recognized both by the state as a domain of private property and reinforced by a nearly autonomous structure of social relations of domination, characterized by reciprocity among unequals. During three centuries of colonialism, the Ecuadorian haciendas had achieved an unrivalled dominance over land and people. For this reason they—and notably the dominated groups included within them—offer a strategic setting to explore the shift in domination induced by the mid-century extension of citizenship into the periphery of the republican order.

In order to understand the practical consequences of the suppression of indigenous status and the amplification of equality, it is necessary to keep in mind two dimensions which together define the changing strategies of domination: in the first place, the organizational logic of the republican state; and secondly, the economic interests of *hacendados* (landlords) as a class.

According to the logic of the nation-state, to maintain a tax, in the form of tribute, designed exclusively for certain populations (the natives) while exempting others (the white citizens) was a 'barbaric' violation of principles. All adult male Ecuadorians should enjoy the same rights and obligations; all should 'contribute to the state each according to his fortune'.[27] No reason could possibly justify that one 'part of the people' be made to pay a form of tribute derived from a classificatory scheme elaborated under a colonial political rationality—that is, by an exogenous logic contrary to the principles of citizenship and popular sovereignty. This irrationality was accentuated above all in the judicial system. Under the postcolonial tribute system, natives were assigned a threefold status: they were seen as Ecuadorians, as tributary populations and as 'miserable persons'. Contradictory and ambiguous, this last

[26] Congressional Law of 21 October 1857, ABFL, Quito.
[27] Proceedings of floor debate and commissions, 1856–7, ABFL, Quito.

category served to integrate Indian subjects in the code of citizenship, but in a situation of state tutelage: the state's judicial system classified the dominated populations as Ecuadorians who were unfit to exercise the rights of citizenship. Thus, a series of judicial procedures were prescribed and a corps of 'Indian protectors' was organized to 'represent' the Indians in the courts and before the state.[28] The relationship between the state and indigenous peoples was thus mediated by a strata of intermediary functionaries—a bureaucracy for the administration of populations. This situation contradicted the logic of the Republic, including one of its cornerstones, the republican regime of direct representation.[29]

Moreover, the extension of citizen's rights to natives coincided with our second dimension, the economic interests of *hacendados*. Indeed, in the vote for the abolition of tribute there was no opposition but instead wide consensus in a parliamentary body where landlords were preponderant.[30] How is this to be understood? In my view we must revisit the economic circuit linking state, tribute and haciendas. In effect, the state treasury collected from the *hacendados* the tribute which, in principle, they assumed on behalf of those indigenous workers (*huasipungueros*) who inhabited their estates. With the abolition of the state-tribute-haciendas circuit the landlords were freed of the obligation to pay the tax. The other side of the coin was that, by mid-century, if not before, the hacienda had consolidated its own forms of recruitment, maintenance, and reproduction of the indigenous labour force. The tributary circuit was no longer indispensable; the haciendas had achieved autonomy from the state.

For its part, the Republic continued to recognize the 'attachment' of workers to the haciendas until the late nineteenth century. This meant that, part de facto and part de jure, the practice of ad-

[28] Laws relevant to tribute: 15/10/1828 in *Indice del Registro Oficial de la República de Colombia* (1828–9), *Registro Oficial*, nos. 20, 21, pp. 156–63; Law of 3 June 1851 in *El Nacional*, no. 370, 29 July 1851; Law of 23 November 1854 in *El Seis de Marzo*, no. 132, vol. on 1851 and 1854, ABFL, Quito.

[29] A history of republican political representation in Latin America may be found in F.X. Guerra: 'The Spanish American Tradition of Representation and its European Roots', *Journal of Latin American Studies*, 26 February 1994, pp. 1–35. This study deals with the premodern impediments that 'distort' republican representation, but it barely mentions the exclusion of indigenous populations.

[30] Proceedings of floor debate and commissions, 1856–7, ABFL, Quito.

ministering populations as consolidated by the power relations on the landed estates was legalized. Even the legislative activity of the formulation and approbation of a few flaccid guidelines for 'labour contracts' between landlords and peons was delegated to the lower level of the Municipal Councils of the rural countries. Obviously, in these local bodies the interests of landlords prevailed with few in-hibitions. Thus, the central state delegated the codification of labour relations between citizens and natives to the private sphere, or at least to the confines of the public-statal sphere.[31]

Detour 2

This brings me to the question of the historical forms, both processes and structures, that the administration of populations adopted under a regime of citizenship of the postcolonial type—that is, to the problem of domination when equality under the law is generalized. As an historical variant, this is a 'state of domination', to use Foucault's term, that is almost the opposite of an 'apartheid' type system, and in which no attempts are made to impede access, either by juridical or political means, to the equality of citizenship.

In an 'apartheid' type system the administration of subjects (the de facto not-citizens) falls within the public-statal sphere. As in the colonial tributary situation before the mid-nineteenth century, it requires a legal corpus and an administrative apparatus; it even assigns territorial circumscriptions for populations. Its government embodies the citizenly concern for the 'common good' and the administration of dominated populations is, therefore, a public affair. Indeed, when a republican system erects an impenetrable juridical 'wall' between citizens and subjects, the domination of the latter requires the state to directly assume at least six inescapable functions: the identification, registration, locating, tracking, protection, and repression of the segregated part of the people. Such a 'state of domination' must locate the management of these 'technologies of rule' over populations in the nucleus of the public-statal sphere. In this form, government itself becomes a weapon in the political struggles of the citizens.[32]

[31] 'Leyes de Regimen Municipal', in *El Nacional*, no. 54, 20 June 1861, ABFL, Quito.

[32] The reference to Foucault is mandatory here, because of the ways in which he develops key notions like 'administration', 'technologies of rule', 'population',

However, as we have seen, the Republic of Ecuador followed very different strategems.

DOMINATION AND THE PRIVATE SPHERE

The derogation of republican tribute and the legal extension to all populations of the equality of citizenship unleashed a curious 'strategy of power'. Displaced with respect to the public-statal axis, a specific field is configured for the citizens to exercise power over the indigenous peoples. In Ecuador, in the second half of the nineteenth century, the administration of populations was no longer a public affair, and so it remained until the indigenous uprisings of 1990 and 1994, which paralysed the country. What is more, at first glance this 'strategy of power' seems to depict the dismantling of the functions realized by the state's 'administrative technologies': domination appeared to disappear. Nevertheless, seen from up close what happened was that the extension of citizenship, particularly in the case of the haciendas, consisted in the state abandoning the administration of indigenous tributaries. With the abolition of tribute the specific statutes and juridical codes, and the whole bureaucratic apparatus of intermediaries which permitted the state to recognize its 'indigenous contributors' were suppressed. Natives thus became invisible in the public-statal sphere. The new strategy displaced the administration of populations toward the private sphere, and particularly toward the haciendas and the territorial power of propertied citizens.

Detour 3

After 1857 the astonished and frustrated historian is confronted by an archival amnesia: oversight seems to attack the official memory of the state. In the national archives—of the executive, the Parliament, and the courts, housed in the Capital of the Republic—the word 'indigenous' or 'Indian' vanishes. A gap is left on the archive's shelves and a blank space in the documents. In the 'instruments' of

---

'state of domination', 'strategies of power'. See: 'Cours du 14 janvier 1976', in *Dits et Ecrits*, vol. 3, Paris: Gallimard, 1994, pp. 178–98; and 'L'ethiqué du souci de soi comme pratique de la liberté', in *Dits et Ecrits*, vol. 4, Paris: Gallimard, 1994, p. 728.

rule—official reports and correspondence, laws, decrees, and regulations—the equality of citizenship erases the words that had once made it clear that certain measures pertained only to a 'part of the people,' that is, to the 'Indians' or 'indigenous'. For the historian, it becomes indiscernible whether the information refers to dominant or dominated populations. Thus, in the censuses, the columns which hierarchically ordered the body of 'Ecuadorians' under three rubrics—'Whites', 'Indians', and 'Blacks'—disappear. The activity of recounting, in both senses of enumeration and narration, grants an instant identity to the social group being recounted and which recounts the 'Others'; it is a practice that ratifies the 'natural' citizens, as defined by the dominant habitus. The state and the citizens verify their reality, and the 'demographic people' becomes real in the objectification of the columns of figures unfolded within the national borders: they become places, towns, cities. The censuses, particularly in the nineteenth century, are ritual acts which etch a symbolic representation in the social imagination. The White-Mestizo citizens verify their reality in the numerical tables published in the *Diario Oficial*—the place of the state's legitimate public word—where the collectivity of literate citizens reads itself and at the same time comments upon the nation. With the abolition of the tribute and the erasure of the classification of Indian the statistics bear witness to a fact deemed natural because it is biological: they delineate a body-contour organized in three parts which seem to be outside history: 'men', 'women', and 'minors'. The image of the nation as a human biological group crystallizes as unitary and ultimately, without differences.

The universalization of the rights of citizens rendered Indian peoples invisible in the official registers. But when the historian leaves the Capital of the Republic and abandons its national archives, she/he, both surprised and intrigued, discovers that this forgetfulness does not affect texts produced in the periphery. The specifications 'Indians' and 'indigenous' reappear in papers piled up in places which do not quite qualify as archives, and even less as depositories of official memory. The omitted appellations appear in the correspondence of petty functionaries, in the proceedings of the Municipal Councils, in the case files of the lower courts, in the account books of the haciendas. These are texts which, in the written word, scrape the barrel of the oral tradition and the living marks of practice. The fiction of the naturalized, unitary and homogenous body-nation is rendered dim.

Indeed, the researcher cannot fail to notice that these provincial functionaries reinsert the omitted words, even when applying the measures dictated by the central government. This is an obvious necessity: after all, the law is executed in the context of everyday strategies of power between Whites and indigenous in the confines of the public sphere, and also in the private one, of motley local bosses at the periphery. The postcolonial logic of practice reveals that, rather than being forgotten, those words are actually avoided by the republican state. Nevertheless, in the process of writing the 'instruments of rule' they are very much present in the thought of those who apply the new laws.[33]

From a heuristic point of view, the hacienda presents greater advantage for the historian. It offers a dense mass of documentation different from other formations which, because they are inserted in a misty and evanescent quotidian orality, devise more furtive plays of power. Such is the case, for example, of the strategies of symbolic domination obtaining among a certain kind of White-Mestizo village intermediaries who assume a ritual role: the so-called 'founders' of christian cults, or the *compradazgo*, the fictive godparents of an unequal kinship between White and indigenous families. For such formations of power the historian may only intuit—by means of a retrospective gaze activated by an ethnographic present—the many intrigues and machinations of the field of intimate and immediate domination.

The delegation of power to the haciendas offers examples of a more evident and institutionalized modality of the private administration of populations. Besides constituting a geographical space, the hacienda is, in effect, a consolidated power formation endowed with symbolic codes, rituals, and mechanisms of repression and consensus-making. Moreover, it unambiguously belongs to the private and patriarchal sphere where landlords conserve a jealous autonomy in the management of their properties, which are a 'private affair'. Although the hacienda is the most obvious case, it was not the only peripheral power formation that assumed administrative functions. In reality, everything having to do with Indian people was pushed out toward the limits of the state, ending up in the realm of a nebula of powers located either in the hacienda as the

[33] A. Guerrero, 'La coutume et l'Etat: curagas et lieutenants politiques à Otavalo au XIX siècle', *Annales E.S.C.*, Paris, March-April 1992, pp. 331–54.

plexus of the private sphere, or on the blurred threshold of the public, in the hands of petty functionaries who confused the public with the personal and the domestic.

Let me summarize the shift in domination that occurred in 1857 as a result of the abolition of tribute and the extension of citizen's rights to include the indigenous populations.

(a) The generalization of republican rights carried with it the familiar trick of concealment and exclusion.[34] It displaced the administration of populations from the dense nucleus of the public-statal sphere toward the dispersed plexus of the private. Among citizens it opened a polygon of forces in relation to indigenous populations: it became an issue in the private sphere.[35]

Thus, it delegated domination to a periphery of quotidian and heterogeneous patriarchal powers. It was a 'state of domination' ruled by the furtive and velvet strategies of practice and symbolic violence. With one trick the Republic achieved several objectives. First, it preserved the purity of the principle of citizenship as established in the Constitution. Second, it delivered to citizens direct, personal and private access to indigenous populations. This access was a prerequisite for the material and symbolic reproduction of the dominant social group, who became citizens in the nineteenth century.

(b) Of special interest here is the suggestive work of Pateman, who includes civil society and the state in the public sphere, while the private is seen as a domain of conjugal and patriarchal power. The division derives from the imaginary, liberal institution of political society as a social contract among '*fratres*'. However, in Andean Ecuador the private sphere was not constructed nor defined merely by a process of differentiation from the public-statal sphere. It was not a sphere of familial sensibility, centred on the 'intimacy' of the home. Rather, it outlined a terrain of strategies between citizens and subjects, between the private (as domestic and patriarchal) and indigenous (as domestic and communal) domains.[36] The state con-

[34] C. Pateman, 'Feminist Critique of the Public/Private Dichotomy', in Benn and Gauss (eds.), *Public and Private in Social Life*, London: Helm, 1973, pp. 281–2.

[35] C. Pateman, op. cit., pp. 102–3.

[36] For J. Habermas the 'petty patriarchal family' is, in Europe, the formative nucleus of the private ('Prefacio a la nueva edición alemana', in Gili (ed.), *Historia y Crítica de la Opinón Pública*, Barcelona, 1994, pp. 8–9). About

citizenry and the government directly. With these two mass actions—which were articulated in political forms with powerful ritual significance—they instituted themselves as social agents in the public sphere. Thus, the emerging movement of Ecuadorian Indians dramatically recast the political field. It elaborated its own discourse, with its own interpretation of the political forces (parties, pressure groups, intellectuals, labour unions, the Church). The Indian people now delegate their representation to their own leader-intellectuals (men and women) who claim to speak on behalf of 'the indigenous people of Ecuador', rejecting pre-existing forms of domination in the name of the 'common interest of the people'. They denounce oppression in general—of Indians and peasants, but also of the White-Mestizo urban poor; outline political economic measures; elaborate legislative proposals for official recognition of their languages and cultures in the Constitution of the Republic; demand cultivable lands; protest against the decline in living standards; and solicit social services. Most importantly, they declare themselves to be an autonomous 'people' which includes various 'nationalities' whose representatives should be recognized by the Republic.

During the two uprisings the President and his ministers had to reiceve the indigenous leaders, now collaborating in one 'national' organization, in the old colonial palace of Carondelet, which is the present seat of government.[41] They initiated a long series of negotiations which were broadcast on radio and television, day by day. This act—the mass diffusion of the scene of negotiation—disrupted the national concept. For the first time in republican history, natives were seen taking their own positions in the political field and negotiating directly and publicly with the big powers, whether government, landlords, industrialists, the church, or the military. In public opinion—for the state, the political parties, and the military—natives thus became an essential and modern social agent located in the plexus of the public sphere. Their organizations are now among the primary forces of the country, represented by intellectuals who have emerged from their own ranks, and with

[41] The 'Confederation of Indigenous Nationalities of Ecuador' (CONAIE), founded a decade and a half ago, coordinates at least seventeen provincial organizations in the Ecuadorian Sierra.

their own discourse. The subjects, having broken the barriers of the private, passing from everyday forms of resistance to public action, became political agents.[42]

I return now to the nineteenth century to clarify the significance of the eruption of indigenous peoples in today's public sphere. As said earlier, how to arrange for the representation of the invisible populations of subjects under a regime of citizenship became a central issue during this century. In effect, with the two 'indigenous uprisings' of 1990 and 1994, a breaking point had been reached with the colonial and republican past. A nodal aspect of the republican 'state of domination' was that, with the construction of citizenship in the mid-nineteenth century, the indigenous populations came to form a 'constitutive beyond' for the public and private spheres. The process of exclusion situated indigenous peoples in a third sphere, a space of domination of colonial origin in the Republic. To raise the question of self-representation, or of the legitimacy of their discourse, was irrelevant. Moreover, the words of the traditional leaders were simply un-intelligible to the state and the political forces; in the public sphere, they were populations not yet civilized.[43]

What these populations and their discourses 'said' through the mouths of their spokesmen only acquired sense within the limits of the private sphere. In everyday practice it was a translucent discourse; it arose in the personalized gambits that were hatched by peripheral power formations (haciendas, domestic units, municipalities, local functionaries). It was the constitutive discourse, with its ritualized utterances and gestures, of the fields of everyday power.

How then, could the Indian populations as subjects be represented in the political sphere of citizens? The historian sifts through the local documents, he dusts off the mid-nineteenth century correspond-

[42] A similar process has happened in Mexico. The indigenous organizations in Chiapas erupted in the political public sphere, forcing the state to negotiate, and thereby constituting themselves as social agents. On the uprisings of 1990 and 1994 in Ecuador, see J. Leon, *El levanamiento indígena: de campesinos a ciudadanos diferentes*, Quito: Cedime, 1994; A. Guerrero ,'Le soulevement indigène national de 1994: discours et représentation politique', in *Problèmes d'Amérique Latine,* Paris, 19 Oct.–Déc. 1995, pp. 51–75.

[43] A. Guerrero, 'A Ventriloquist Image: Liberal Discourse and the "Miserable Indian Race" in the Late 19th Century Ecuador', *Journal of Latin American Studies*, vol. 29, pt. III, October 1997, pp. 1–36.

ence between provincial functionaries of the Republic and the Minister of the Interior; he reads some proceedings preserved in a file labelled 'representations'. In bureaucratic jargon these are solicitations, complaints, and problems expressed by Indians before a state authority. One such document begins 'I, Jose M. de la Cruz, governor of natives, before your excellency, for his part and in the name of the rest [of the natives], respectfully say . . .' (*Jose M. de la Cruz gobernador de indígenasante Usted respetuosamente por si y por los demás digo . . .*).

The phrase exhibits an obvious grammatical error that I wish to emphasize. In correct Spanish it should say 'I . . . for my part . . . say' (*por mi . . . digo*) to indicate that the same person carries out two actions: he speaks and writes. But here one reads for his part (*por si*), in the third person, followed by say (*digo*), the first person conjugation. The (grammatical) 'person' of the pronoun does not agree with the verb form.[44]

The error, the discordance in the grammatical person, opens an ambiguity about the historical person who realizes the act of speaking and writing. Who speaks in this document? He who speaks or he who writes? It is obvious that the governor of Indians did not write the representation in his own hand. To address the functionary and state his problem he resorted to an intermediary who did the writing for him. Embedded in the text is a social agent, a scribe, who, although indispensable to the act of speaking via writing, nevertheless remains incognito and, yet is present in the words. In effect, and as it must be, the indigenous authority, not the writer, signed the petition. What functions did this intermediary fulfil who, in the end, made it possible that the governor of the natives was rendered comprehensible to the state functionary, and who, in the public sphere, represented for his own part and in the name of the rest?

There are several levels involved here. The function of the scribe who produced the document was not entirely derived from his control over the writing. It was also not reduced to the problem of translating from oral Quichua—the tongue of the populations the governor of natives represented—to written Spanish, the language of the Republic and its citizens. The unknown intermediary carried

[44] Correspondence of the Governor of Imbabura Province to the Ministry of Interior (Solicitudes), 1856; ANH, Quito.

out at least two additional functions. On the one hand, he became a ventriloquist since he made a voiceless indigenous authority speak in the public-statal sphere. He stated the problem in the state's code, assembling a legitimate and legal discourse. On the other hand, as he wrote the 'representation' he was the author of a strategy. He carried out both functions insofar as he was an individual who possessed a recognized presence in the public sphere, knew the 'rules of the game' in the political field and, above all, knew the functionaries personally. In short, he was a White-Mestizo, a citizen.

As the historian reads the text he notes that the document does not reproduce the words spoken aloud to the scribe by the indigenous authority. This is what the syntactic slippage in the phrase explains: 'for his part' (*por si*) is the scribe who speaks, practiced in law; 'I . . . say' (*digo*) is the ventriloquist who makes the indigenous governor speak to the state functionary. Thus, the intermediary agent neither transcribed nor translated: he elaborated a complex practice which may be defined as trans-writing (*trans-escritura*). His writing seeks a performative effect that prolongs the text beyond the words.[45] In the 'representation', the historian does not discover the words spoken by the native governor. Still, the document offers something more: a kind of geometric semblance. In drawing up the document the scribe delineated on a reduced scale the local political polygon, and he centred its axis on the conflict related by the indigenous authority. On the margins of his outline, but in the outer confines of the political, he arranged, first, the shadow of the governor who he tried to represent 'for his part and . . . the rest' of the natives (*por si y los demás*); he then tried to provoke state intervention in that no-man's land between the private citizen sphere and the dominated, or among the latter. But to do this he must possess a guide's knowledge of the topography of the political terrain. Thus, secondly, the scribe made a calculation of the local vectors, interests and forces, which impinged upon the subject. Finally, he oriented the text toward a key social agent, addressing it to a state authority. In order to play the part of strategist, the ventriloquist must have been a seasoned player who occupied a position in the local play

[45] On this notion see my: 'De protectores a tinterillos: la privatización de la administración de poblaciones indígenas (dominadas)'; in H. Bonilla (ed.), *Las sociedades indígenas en Mesoamérica y los Andes*, INAH-México, Universidad de Santander, Colombia, 1996.

of material and symbolic interests. He must have had first-hand knowledge of how to plot gambits of attack and defence, and he must have been capable of analysing the positions of social agents and thus propose alliances. In a word, he possessed a political skill embodied in the dominant habitus.

The above leaves open an analysis of the complex plays of power, the webs of clientage, assymetrical reciprocity and symbolic domination implied by this system of representation by ventriloquy. But it is clear that it will be worthwhile to further explore the consequences that this political ventriloquy carries with it: the undeniable transformations that a conflict, raised in the indigenous domain, undergoes when it is made to emerge in the public sphere. The prismatic divergence which mediates between the play of the indigenous governor and the play of the scribe contains the strategies of representation in the domain of the voiceless and dominated, and circumscribes their audibility in the public-statal sphere.

The Spirit of Bolivian Laws: Citizenship, Infamy and Patriarchal Hierarchy

Rossana Barragán

On 2 April 1831, the capitals of departments and provinces woke to the sound of cannons, announcing the reading of a presidential decree and the celebration of *te deum* masses in all the churches of the land.[1] The newspaper published a poem to honour the sun-father and source of light, who had ripped away the veil of infernal darkness and brought wisdom inscribed in sacred books.[2] That same day, 'the most classical document of civilization in the youngest

*I am grateful to SEPHIS, The Indian Council of Historical Research and the Nehru Memorial Museum & Library, for their invitation to the 1996 Conference at Delhi on 'The Forging of Nationhood and the Contest over Citizenship, Ethnicity and History'. My thanks are also due to Gyanendra Pandey, Peter Geschiere, Silvia Rivera and Sudhir Chandra, and my colleagues Seemin Qayum, Tristan Platt and Sinclair Thomson for their valuable comments on previous versions of this paper, as well as for their corrections of the English translation done by Rose Marie Vargas.

[1] 'Decree of 26 March 1831', in *El Iris de La Paz*, Thursday, 31 March 1831, p. 2.

[2]

Cual suele el padre de la luz del día	As the father of the light of day
Veloz marchando en carro luminoso	Flying swiftly in a luminous carriage
Rasgar el velo de la noche sombria	Sweeping aside the veil of the night's shadow
Imagen del avérno tenebroso;	Image of infernal gloom;
Asi se ve brillar sabiduría	So wisdom shines forth
En las líneas sagradas, libro hermoso	In the sacred lines, beautiful book
Honor eterno al Héroe, cuya mano	Eternal honor to the Hero, whose hand
Borró las leyes del poder Español!!!	Banished the laws of Spanish power!!!

'On the occasion of the publication of the Codes', in *El Iris de La Paz*, Thursday, 31 March 1831, p. 4.

of Republics' was dedicated to a woman who was both wife and mother.[3]

These celebrations hailed the promulgation and publication of the Civil and Criminal Codes and the Code of Procedure in 1831 and 1832.[4] The father, hero and philosopher who ruled with the son and dedicated his works to the love and care of a woman's heart was none other than President Andrés de Santa Cruz. His wife, Francisca Cernadas, celebrated her birthday that same day and received the codes in her safe-keeping, recalling the manner in which Napoleon had paid homage to his wife the Empress Josephine. The preamble and dedication to Cernadas declared: 'The Penal Code classifies crimes whose perpetration will cause you to invoke justice, and punishments whose application will incite in you neither injustice nor cruelty but rather compassion for miserable human beings. In the Civil Code, the duties of spouse, mother, and tutor will complement your own sentiments, reflecting maternal feelings toward the sons of Bolivia.'[5]

Three features stand out in this ceremonial presentation of the codes. First, the codes are regarded as sacred books, like the Bible, which commemorate the foundation of the new Republic. Second, the image of the philosopher-hero—embodiment of rationality and civic religion, incarnated as the sun-father who illuminates the

[3] 'Dedicated to her Excellency Francisco Cernadas de Santa Cruz' from Jose Manuel Loze in the first edition of the code (see, Santa Cruz Shuhkrafft, 1976–92, p. 40; see also note 4 below).

[4] According to the decree of 28 October 1830, the codes were to take effect beginning on 1 January 1830, but due to delays, they were finally instituted three months later (Santa Cruz Shuhkrafft, 1976–92, p. 37 and V. Abecia, 1976–92, p. 86). The Constitutional Assembly declared on 15 July 1831 that they be called the Santa Cruz Codes (Santa Cruz Shuhkrafft, 1976–92, pp. 33, 39).

[5] One of the authors of the Code, José Manuel Loza, wrote to Francisca Cernadas: 'A literary genius offered the Napoleonic Code fashioned in elegant verse to the Empress Josephine; I, a guest in the house of belles lettres, and with utmost respect for the literal text of these laws, present to you, Madam, the Santa Cruz Codes. Who else but the wife of a philosopher could possess the sublime work imposed by him with his virtues which he attained with his talents? You, Madam . . . you cannot but appreciate the most classical document of civilization of the youngest among the Republics. The Codes of Bolivia, the Codes of your beloved Country, deserve to be placed over your heart. . . .

'The Codes, then, have inspired me to award your property to you, as a tribute . . .' (in Santa Cruz Shuhkrafft, 1976–92, p. 40).

darkness of barbarism and inaugurates civilization, and offering as tribute the product of masculine reason to the mythical hero's wife, who cradles justice in her lap and offers compassion—reflects state conceptions about gender relations and social hierarchy. Last, the imitation of contemporary French political iconography highlights the themes of Enlightenment and so-called 'modernity.'

These features naturally raise the issue of the ruptures and continuities between the colonial and 'modern' historical periods. In recent decades, historiography has conceived of the Republic, founded in 1825 after sixteen years of independence wars, in terms of colonial continuities in economic and social structure. This contrasts with the representation of the elites of the time, who conceived of the Republic as a total rupture with the past. The discrepancy forces us to reconsider the forging of the Bolivian nation.

A much-quoted study of this general process is that of Anderson (1991), who proposes that the nation is an 'imagined political community' that emerged in the late eighteenth century in close relation to capitalism. According to Anderson, the possibility of imagining the nation arose with changes in cultural conceptions about language, society and time. As part of the process of thinking this new political community, he emphasizes the importance of print-capitalism, crucial for the emergence of secular egalitarian communities (1991, pp. 36–7). Anderson also draws attention to the pioneer role of American Creoles, who expressed their conception of the nation well before most of Europe (1991, Chap. 4, p. 50). This, he argues, was due to the importance acquired by colonial administrative units which came to appear as 'fatherlands' because they framed the professional ascent of Creole officials. Newspapers and official tours ('pilgrimages') were the vehicle which allowed them to think of themselves as a community.[6] Thus, ideas of nation-states, citizenship, and popular sovereignty came to supercede those of dynastic empires, inherited nobilities, serfdoms, and so forth. Anderson also emphasizes the homogenizing quality of this national

[6] 'What I am proposing is that neither economic interest, Liberalism, nor Enlightenment could, or did, create in themselves the kind, or shape, of imagined community to be defended from these regimes depredations; to put it another way, none provided the framework of a new-consciousness—the scarcely-seen periphery of its vision—as opposed to centre-field. . . . In accomplishing this specific task, pilgrim creole functionaries and provincial creole printmen played the decisive historic role' (Anderson, 1991, p. 65).

imaginary. Referring to a famous decree of the Creole liberator José de San Martín—'the aboriginal people shall not to be called Indians or natives; they are children and citizens of Peru, and they shall be known as Peruvians'—Anderson asserts that the 'logic of San Martin's Peruvianization was at work' (op. cit., p. 49). Other analysts of nationalism have made some of the same points, if somewhat differently. Gellner, for example, points out that nationalism reflected an objective need for homogeneity because the modern industrial state requires a mobile, literate and standardized population (1988, pp. 67, 177).

In Latin America and Bolivia these themes have aroused the interest of two French scholars, Guerra and Demélas, who propose a paradox in the form of Latin American modernity in the nineteenth century: the juxtaposition of modern legal, political, and constitutional forms with a traditional society. Demélas argues that the modern democratic system, based on the equality of individuals within a representative system of government, was imported rather than created. It coexisted with a stratified social order quite unlike that of modern social classes (Demélas, 1992, pp. 13, 35, 46). Guerra, on the other hand, argues that the revolutions of independence were in fact cultural revolutions of Enlightenment and modernity (1992. pp. 14, 31 and 85), and the new societies were formed by equal individuals freed from the ties of the old corporate society. The new social pact deposited legitimacy and sovereignty with the people, thus forming a nation (ibid., pp. 13, 85, 86, 89 and 91). However, this modernity was the exclusive province of the elites, because only they were acquainted with modern democratic culture.[7] Thus a 'cultural chasm' divided modernizing elites and the corporate society of the ancien *régime* (ibid., pp. 52–3 and 359).

This set of studies, whether adopting a global (Anderson and Gellner) or regional (Guerra and Demélas) perspective, is marked by a series of unresolved problems. First of all, San Martín's 'Peruvianizing' declaration should be considered a desire and a project, not an actual achievement. The emergence of the new Republics, which arose under the impulse of the Creole 'pioneers', mark the beginning of a long process, rather than the crystallization of an

[7] 'The only citizens in the modern sense of the word are the members of the elite who have internalized their condition as citizens, that is, the democratic modern culture' (Guerra, 1993, p. 361).

'imagined political community'. Second, in societies with an Indian majority and in which local Creole elites were responsible for imagining the new 'national community', the process of forging the nation must be understood as part of a social struggle. The elite imaginary, for example, was nourished by conflicts between the 'Spanish' colonial state and the Indian population which had demonstrated its power and autonomy during the great insurrections of the eighteenth century. Recognized as 'Spanish Americans'[8] by the colonial bureaucracy itself, these local Creole elites began to assert themselves by omitting the epithet 'Spanish' and by affirming their sovereign rights and ability to govern the Indian population better than 'foreigners' (Barragán, 1996a). Third, there was no correspondence between the emergence of these nations and an industrial system of production, a link that is strongly emphasized by leading authors on nationalism like Gellner. Nor do we find the conception of a civil society based on the principle of equal citizens, a conclusion we will demonstrate through our analysis of the new legislation of the Republic. But should we therefore conclude that the absence of full industrial and capitalist development, virtually until the first decades of this century, meant that there was no process of nation formation, or that the historical changes were strictly political?

Démelas and Guerra posed the problem in terms of a dichotomy and contradiction between traditional society and modern political structures. After this initial point of agreement, their arguments differ. For Démelas, modernity was a foreign product and alien to Bolivian society, while Guerra considers that modernity was an attribute only of the elites. The superstructure consisting of modern legal texts, such as the Latin American constitutions, is imagined by Demélas as completely divorced from society, and the modernizing elite is conceived of by Guerra as struggling against the archaic nature of society and the people. In both cases, the nineteenth century seems to constitute a long transition to an incomplete modernity. To a certain extent, then, we are presented with an old argument, also found for example in the work of the

[8] In the disputes and conflicts between the 'Spaniards' and the 'Creoles' at the end of the eighteenth century and the beginning of the nineteenth, in fact, there were Spaniards and Creoles on *both* sides. This means that the decisive factor was the insertion of the latter in local society (Barragán, 1996b).

Bolivian historian Alipio Valencia Vega, in which the French and European models are the hidden measuring sticks for analysing the new Bolivian Republic. Thus the Eurocentric perspective appears to lead, as Chatterjee has shown (1993, p. 12), to the discovery of historical paradoxes and anomalies, incomplete and copied projects destined to failure (either because they did not correspond to reality, or because the 'masses' did not partake of the appropriate culture, an attribute only of the elites), and conflicts between so-called 'tradition' and modernity.[9]

The study of these elites becomes even more urgent because the historiographic renewal which took place in Bolivia from the 1960s on, and particularly after 1976, has turned all its interest, in the face of the official historiography, towards the rural space of the Indian communities. This emphasis leads us, however, to a vast gap, because the new proposals and problems analysed for the 'subaltern groups' are not paralleled for the dominant groups. In the Andes, small hillocks have been created on the basis of new studies of Andean societies, but the great mountains erected by the traditional, elitist historiography remain intact. This gap has emerged because the bridges and paths connecting hillocks and mountains have been forgotten.[10]

In this article, I wish to examine the relation of foundational laws and constitutions to society as a whole. This article emphasizes the dominant institutional and discursive sphere because it is fundamental for understanding the complex overall interaction between modernizing elites and the subaltern groups considered 'traditional' social sectors. The historical formation of the 'Nation' must be seen as the outcome of changing power relations between

[9] Anderson speaks of the 'failure' of the Spanish American experience to 'generate a permanent Spanish America-wide nationalism that reflects . . . the level of development of capitalism and technology' (Anderson, 1991, p. 63). Chatterjee wrote: 'It is the perversity of Eurocentric historical theories that has led to the search for similar developments everywhere in the world. Whenever that search has proved fruitless, the society has been declared incapable of producing a true historical dynamic. . . . The practice has been to see the history of "backward" countries as a history of "lack", a history that always falls short of true history' (1993, p. 30).

[10] One of the results of the historical approach to the two domains, the elite's and the subaltern's, had 'been precisely the demonstration that each domain has not only acted in opposition to and as limit upon the other, but, through this process of struggle, has also shaped the emergent form of the other' (Chatterjee, 1993, p. 12).

these groups: the result of the partial successes and failures of elitist projects, the strategies and tactics elaborated by 'subaltern groups', the daily intersection of contending social forces.

My concern is to consider whether the ideology of 'modernity' was in fact the spirit of the body of laws adopted and what its impact was on social and political life. My first hypothesis is that the body of laws directly affected social conditions and cannot be considered merely as discourses or ideological phenomena that were strictly superstructural or divorced from 'reality'. My second hypothesis is that the law is crucial to the making of the nation because it created a contested field which shaped the strategies used by the indigenous and Mestizo population in their relationship with the state and which fueled the dynamics of identity.

This paper will mainly focus on the analysis of one of the clearest expressions of the new Republican state: its legislation—particularly the collection of Constitutions, Civil and Criminal Codes, the Code of Procedure and the Military Code. This body of nineteenth-century legislation is conceived of as an expression of the interplay of social, cultural and political forces, rather than a superficial or arbitrary ideological representation of society at the moment of Independence. Since it established rules and marked the limits of what was permitted and what was forbidden, it ranked and classified social groups and legitimized the way power was exerted. Rather than being a set of dead texts, it provided the basis and norms for nineteenth-century social relations and this played an active role in reorganizing and structuring society. The presentation of the legal codes by Santa Cruz, which we recalled at the start of the article, may therefore be described as 'a rite of institution' and a rite of legitimation that established, assigned, and imposed social rights and categories. At the same time, it was a 'solemn act of categorization', which served to grant privileges to some while subordinating and excluding others (Bourdieu, 1982, pp. 121 and 125–6),[11] as well as constituting the new nation.

[11] Following Bourdieu, such rituals mark 'a line which establishes a fundamental division in the social order. . . . In truth, what is most important, and what goes unnoticed, is the division which it effects. . . . Hence there is a hidden ensemble in relation to which the instituted group is defined. . . . The *ritual* consecrates the difference. . . .' It is 'the effect of socially instituting a difference by an act of *constitution* . . .'. *Instituere* or *institutio* also suggests the idea of an 'inaugural act of constitution, of foundation, leading . . . to lasting dispositions, habits, usages . . .' (Bourdieu, 1982, pp. 122–3, 128–9).

The first part of this paper, focussing on the constitutions and codes as touchstones of the nation, will analyse the specific content of the Criminal Code. In the second part, I will examine the structural axes of the legislation as a whole, that is to say the spirit of the laws. In the third part, I will show how this ideological framework was applied in court, where it became one of the most important links between state and society; I will consider as well the specific implications of this body of legislation for social and ethnic dynamics.

I. FOUNDATIONS OF THE NATION AND ENLIGHTENED STANDARDS OF CRIME AND PUNISHMENT

The number of constitutions that Bolivia has had—a total of 11 in the course of the nineteenth century[12]—shows how different presidents sought to legitimize themselves through a symbolic refoundation of the Republic. This was even more apparent in the codes, approved between 1830 and 1832, only five years after proclamation of the Republic, since political autonomy, as represented in the constitutions, had to be matched by judicial and legal autonomy.[13]

Old laws in force until then had to be abolished, as they were seen to be anachronisms in the new era;[14] they belonged to 'feudal

[12] New constitutions were introduced in 1826, 1831, 1834, 1839, 1843, 1851, 1861, 1868, 1871, 1878, and 1880. Our reference to the constitutions is based on the compilation by Salinas Mariaca, 1989.

[13] 'A colony of Spain before its fortunate emancipation, it can be said that it remains so in the judicial realm.' ('Letter from the Ministry of State from the Office of the Interior to the President of the Supreme Court of Justice, Chuquisaca, 17 September 1829', in *El Iris de La Paz*, Saturday, 29 November 1829, p. 2.)

[14] 'If the prevailing Roman legislation in Spain was later intermixed with that of the Goths, Vandals, the Alani-Swabians and the Arabs; if the *Partidas*, the most complete and regular body of laws which has existed since the thirteenth century in the Peninsula, is only a trace of those already mentioned; if these and even the royal authority had to be observed in absence of the collection compiled in Castile in the sixteenth century, without mentioning the newest one which for lack of sufficient publication is not commonly used in the Courts . . . , would it be just and convenient that men of the nineteenth century be ruled by laws whose origin is lost perhaps in the uncertainties of time and in the successive multitudes of its authors?' (in *El Iris de La Paz*, Thursday, 31 March 1831, p. 3).

times',[15] the 'horrors of serfdom',[16] the spirit of 'conquest . . . and oppression', and the perpetuation of colonialism.[17] They were declared an obstacle to entry into the new century, the age of Enlightenment, philosophy, freedom and morality.[18]

The first of the founding laws of the Nation and the Republic was the Criminal Code of 1831 which regulated behaviour, defined crimes and imposed punishments. The Criminal Code distinguished crimes against society from those against individuals. Punishments were classified as pecuniary, corporal and non-corporal. The last basically involved the judicial condition, legal rights, honour and employment of individuals, for example, the declaration of infamy, suspension of certain civil rights, loss of employment and public office, imprisonment as corrective punishment, surveillance by the authorities and public apology. Corporal punishments were those affecting the convict's literal or figurative 'body', such as death and different forms of deprivation of liberty.[19]

[15] 'Decree of the Marshall Andrés de Santa Cruz', in *El Iris de La Paz*, Thursday, 31 March 1831, p. 1.

[16] 'Legislation', in *El Iris de La Paz*, Saturday, 12 June 1830, p. 3.

[17] 'The Iris', in *El Iris de La Paz*, Thursday, 31 March 1831, p. 3.

[18] 'We dare to declare that as long as this and other American states which used to be colonies of Spain find themselves under the influence of the laws of the old metropolis, they will never reach that level of morality and illustration of which they are capable' ('Legislation', in *El Iris de La Paz*, Saturday, 12 June 1830, p. 3). It was also pointed out that they did not take into account the 'habits and tendencies, and even the vices of the majority of our population'. It was argued also that there were more than 15,000 confused laws, including those of the *Novísima Recopilación* and the *partidas* which were still prevalent dating back to 1805, written in an obsolete and even incomprehensible language, tending to preserve injustice, the arbitrariness of the trials and the judicial despotism ('The Iris', in *El Iris de La Paz*, Thursday, 31 March 1831, p. 3). Another article read: 'A monstrous and complicated legislation, most of the time in contradiction with our habits and tendencies. . . , it has the capacity to mislead the jurist and the magistrate. In this labyrinth of things, it seems that the integrity of the judge was the only recourse for the innocent, while the accused feared the rigour of the punishments as much as the most notorious criminal. What a vast space for arbitrariness and corruption! How many pretexts for an undeserved compassion, for impunity and clemency disguised with the veil of equity, with the silence of the law, with the atrocity of the penalty' ('Administration of Justice', in *El Iris de La Paz*, Sunday, 24 April 1831, p. 4).

[19] These forms were labour for fourteen years, public work, confinement in a work house, imprisonment in a fortress, confinement, prison, exile, and deporta-

The visual and exemplary role of the death penalty, and of the chains used to prohibit the movement and liberty of prisoners (as well as a variety of other punishments) were related to a complete classification of crimes. The severity of the punishment corresponded to the seriousness of the crime. This marked a break from the dark and barbarous past, as President Andrés de Santa Cruz emphasized and newspapers proclaimed,[20] just as it had in Europe.

As in Europe, reforms of the Criminal Code sought—as Foucault would put it—'not to punish less, but to punish better; to punish

---

tion. In 1831, the physical punishments were: (1) death; (2) fourteen years' labour, (3) deportation; (4) exile or permanent banishment from Bolivia; (5) prison; (6) public work; (7) confinement in a work house; (8) to witness an execution; (9) imprisonment in a fortress; (10) confinement in a town or district; (11) life or temporary exile in a town or district. Non-physical punishments were: (1) declaration of infamy; (2) inability to exercise an employment or profession or hold government office in general or of a certain sort; (3) deprivation of employment, honours, profession or public office; (4) suspension of the aforementioned; (5) arrest as a merely corrective punishment; (6) subjection to authorities; (7) obligation to post bail for good conduct; (8) retraction; (9) satisfaction; (10) judicial warning; (11) judicial reprimand; (12) to hear the sentence publicly; (13) correction in a house for women and minors (Art. 28, Chap. 3, *Código Penal Boliviano*, 1831). By 1843 corporal punishment had been modified, although modestly; penalties were reduced to nine, disappearing or being joined to others (fourteen years' labour joined with the public work, and deportation joined with excile, *Código Penal Boliviano*, 1845).

[20] On the occasion of presenting the Penal Code to the North Peruvian State, the Marshall Santa Cruz commented: 'The Penal Code presents to you a logical and well classified nomenclature of crimes and penalties; a summary of the most accredited laws with which since the renaissance of enlightenment in Europe, the Philosophical Legislators have tried to purify this most important part of social institutions. Humanity shuddered to see the refinement of afflictive and cruel measures; the iniquitous inequality of punishment; the painful and useless barbaric system of prevention which dishonored the criminal Legislation of our forefathers. You will be emancipated from this barbaric yoke. The Laws . . . will protect your security against the attacks of violence and passion. . . . They will intimidate only the wicked; they will not squander the blood of men in the expiation of their crimes, which satisfaction does not demand such sacrifice. . . . They offer secure guarantees to the citizen, against perversion of the course of justice, malice and the arbitrariness of public officials. They save the life of men, and but in a small number of cases they do not shut for them the doors of society, to which they can go back to after having satisfied it' (in Santa Cruz Shuhkrafft, 1976–92, p. 72). See also the article 'Codes', in *El Iris de La Paz*, Sunday, 31 January 1831, p. 4.

less severely . . . , to punish on more universal terms'. Following the 'Linnaen' scheme for crimes and punishments, the punishment should be proportional to the crime (Filangieri), and should 'punish just enough to prevent it' (Foucault, 1975/93, pp. 85, 86, 97–8, 102–4).

One might argue, then, that European 'legal and criminal modernity' was rapidly and fully enforced by the new Republic. The paradox is that this criminal code, which was to 'break the chains with Spain', was precisely the result of a revision of the Spanish Code of 1822, using the work of the Spaniard Calatrava, the Frenchman M.B. Constant, and the Englishman J. Bentham. It is important to underline two elements that emerge when analysing the Bolivian Criminal Code: extensive application of 'infamy' and an implicit conception of the society as heterogeneous, hierarchical and non-egalitarian.

The Bolivian Criminal Code of 1831 included as punishments: (1) the loss of public office and political rights in the public sphere (*inhabilitación*); (2) the loss of family rights (*interdicción*), also known as private or civil rights, such as paternal and marital authority and the ability to administer and dispose of property; and (3) infamy. Infamy, the main non-corporal punishment, involved three elements: (1) deprivation of political rights or the loss of citizenship; (2) deprivation of the legal right to act as accuser, witness, executor, or guardian; and (3) prohibition against holding public office and joining the army. Infamy was applied during a vast period, longer than in Europe, where it eventually disappeared from French and Spanish criminal codes in the course of the nineteenth century. In Bolivia, infamy was the punishment in cases of common crime of robbery, irrespective of the circumstances or the amount stolen.[21] Also, if an individual repeated the offense within a period of 7 years, he was sentenced to the maximum punishment of 14 years of hard labour.

II. THE CONSTITUTIVE AXES OF THE LAW

Another noteworthy aspect of this body of legislation was that society was not considered to be composed of equal individuals. Although social distinctions were not obvious in the Criminal Code, certain

[21] Art. 699, 'All crimes included in this chapter [Theft] carry infamy with them', in *Código Penal Boliviano*, 1831.

details reveal their presence. The need to distinguish between social groups is revealed only under careful scrutiny, but it constitutes one of the axes of the interaction of law and society.

Four main axes clearly reveal the logic of hierarchy and difference present in the legislation: citizenship and infamy; paternal or marital authority and legalized violence; honest women *versus* prostitutes; and legitimate *versus* illegitimate children.

1. CITIZENSHIP AND INFAMY

Citizenship and infamy involved not only inclusion or exclusion with regard to the exercise of political rights, but also distinctions between citizens and Bolivians, as well as inclusion and exclusion with regard to civil rights.

a. *Exclusion from Political Rights*

To begin with, the constitution established a distinction between the general category of Bolivians and the subset of Bolivians who were citizens. Bolivians were simply all people born within the Republic, while citizens were those Bolivians who were male, over 21 years of age or married, literate, and not domestic servants. This distinction between Bolivians and citizens thus evokes the distinction between active and passive citizens in France, and even more so the distinction between Spaniards and citizens found on the Iberian peninsula.[22] In the case of Bolivia, the requirements for

[22] It is worth underlining the similarity between the requirements for citizenship in Spain and Bolivia. The Political Constitution of Cádiz from 1812 (CPC-E-1812) and that of Bolivia from 1825 (CPB-18-25) stipulate, with regard to the definition of citizenship and its suspension or loss:

—(Suspension or loss)

'For criminal prosecution' (CPC-E-1812)

'For criminal prosecution' (CPB-18-25)

—'After 1830 . . . they should know how to read and write' (CPC-E-1812)

'Know how to read and write; though this ability will only be required starting in 1836' (CPB-18-25)

—(Suspension or loss)

'For a sentence in which defamatory or grievous penalities is imposed, if no rehabilitation is obtained' (CPC-E-1812)

'For having suffered defamatory or grievous penalty due to judicial conviction, if no rehabilitation is obtained from the Legislative Body' (CPB-18-25)

citizenship implied the exclusion of the great majority of the population. Since the Indian and Mestizo majority was mostly unlettered (the native languages were not written down) and had a subordinate, dependent status, it could not exercise the political right to vote or be elected to office. The analysis of requirements for citizenship in the various nineteenth-century constitutions shows no changes until 1939.[23]

b. *Citizens, Bolivians and 'all classes of people'*

But the legislation also distinguished between people with 'good reputation' and those who lacked it. The former were granted the privilege of not being imprisoned together with delinquents, or being sentenced to major corporal punishments.[24] Distinctions among people also affected rights to bail; if a crime was not serious enough for corporal punishment, people of 'publicly known honesty and wealth' were not required to pay for bail.[25]

—(Suspension or loss) 'For being a bankrupt debtor or in debt to the public treasury' (CPC-E-1812)

'For the disqualification of being a fraudulent debtor' (CPB-18-25)

—(Suspension or loss)

'For having no employment, profession, or recognized way of life' 'For being a domestic servant' (CPC-E-1812)

'[Must] have employment or work, or a scientific or artistic profession, without being subject to another person as a domestic servant' (CPB-18-25)

We may recall that the first Bolivian constitution was proposed and approved with some modifications by Simón Bolívar.

[23] In the 1939 constitution, the condition of property and of not being subject to another person as dependent disappeared, while the condition of reading and writing as well as of being registered in the civic registry remained.

[24] 'Generally, men of good reputation, against whom prison is decreed, will be placed in separated quarters from criminals, caring only for their safety' (Art. 822, *Código de Procederes Santa Cruz*, 1852). Furthermore, honour associated with and intrinsic to certain occupations and 'estates', such as the ecclesiastical estate, established that no priest, deacon or subdeacon could be condemned to the major physical penalties such as fourteen years labour or public work. These penalties were replaced with prison or exile (Art. 68, *Código Penal Boliviano*, 1831).

[25] Bail for defendants in cases in which the crime did not merit any physical penalty were not necessary for those of 'notorious honesty and known property'; these defendants were subject only to the simple 'juratory caution' (Arts. 841, 843 and 844, *Código de Procederes Santa Cruz*, 1852).

Distinctions were also made inside the army. Soldiers and officers were differentiated according to literacy, civic knowledge, and the power to give orders and to punish. Soldiers, for example, were obliged to learn the 'catechism of the Political Constitution' and had to pass a literacy test in order to be promoted to corporals.[26] Once they did so, they were given a stick with which they could punish soldiers, especially drunkards, 'not exceeding two or three strokes'.[27] In the case of the army, it is interesting to note the parallels that existed between educational level, the power to inflict punishment, and knowledge about the Republic and its laws. Soldiers were required to read and write and to know the 'catechism of the Political Constitution of the State'. Sergeants—besides having to pass a literacy exam in order to rise to corporal and, as said, thereupon receiving a staff with which to punish 'drunken soldiers'—had to know the four rules of arithmetic, keep up registries, and know the penal code; they also had the jurisdiction to arrest and jail their subordinates. Finally the high officials were allowed to have their own servants.[28] The parallelism thus evokes in attenuated form the differentiation between citizens and Bolivians which in this case corresponded to the high command and soldiers.

Distinctions were also made between different kinds of crimes and their corresponding punishments. Drunkenness, for instance, was associated with specific classes; and corporal punishments like arrest and imprisonment, for example, were mostly reserved for soldiers. Corporals, sergeants, officers and generals suffered, instead, a loss of employment or reduction of salaries.[29]

[26] Arts. 96 and 101, *Código Militar*, 1843.

[27] Art. 119, *Código Militar*, 1843.

[28] For the Articles pertaining to common soldiers, see especially 13, 87 and 96; for corporals, see 101, 117, 119, and 130; for sergeants, see 183, 185, 247; and on servants, see 501.

[29] Punishment for a first offense consisted of fifteen days arrest; for the second offense, two months and, during the first eight days, 'one hour of campaign stocks in front of his body'; and for the third offense, three months in prison (Art. 228 of the *Código Militar*, 1843). For corporals and sergeants, even though the arrest for a first offense was the same, for a second offense they were removed from their jobs (Art. 230). In the case of officers and chiefs, for the first offense they were sent to a fortress or to another region with one-fourth their pay, and were removed from their jobs for three months; on a second offense they were discharged ignominiously from the service (Art. 231, *Código Militar*, 1843).

Consequently, while the legal codes did not establish specific juridical categories for the different social and ethnic groups, distinctions were made when administering and distributing punishments. Although laws and resolutions did not explicitly differentiate between Indians and non-Indians, Mestizos and Creoles, distinctions were made in their application and (re)surfaced as a result of their application. There was no need for discriminatory laws, since behind legal equality was a practice of inequality. For example, the consequence of the application of corporal punishment to one type of crime and non-corporal ones to others meant that public officials were generally exempted from corporal punishments, except in the case of serious crimes.[30] And, of course, few public officials were Indians. Moreover, in the case of the army, soldiers and officers could commit the same offence, but were penalized with different punishments.

c. *Infamy and Citizenship as Exclusion from Civil and Private Rights*

Citizenship not only involved political rights, but also civil and personal rights. In this regard, there were two key and complementary concepts: loss of citizenship and infamy. Citizenship could be permanently or temporarily lost. Suspension, according to the constitutions, could be applied to the insane, fraudulent debtors, drunkards, gamblers, beggars (Constitution of 1826) and those involved in a criminal case, or suffering either defematory or 'degrading' corporal punishment (Constitutions of 1831, 1861, 1871). Infamy, on the other hand, was associated with 'the power of the word',[31] reputation and honour. In nineteenth-century Bolivian legislation, infamy was a variant of what in older Spanish Legislation was called 'civil death', since loss of citizenship rights meant that the person in question could not act as plaintiff in any trial, except

[30] Corporal punishments were applied preferably for crimes against persons, such as homicide and theft, while non-corporal punishment was applied for crimes against society, such as those involving public servants and family affairs. This implies that those guilty of crimes against society, except in the case of serious offenses, suffered only the loss of their employment and 'honours'. (See, for example, Art. 407, *Código Penal Boliviano*, 1831.)

[31] Infamy stems from the Latin negative *in* and *fama*, as in reputation, related to the Greek *pheme* from the root word *bha* which means 'to talk' (*Grand*

his own, nor act as witness, executor,[32] guardian (except to his children), enter into public office or serve in the army, militia or navy.[33] And suspension, loss of citizenship, interdiction, disablement and infamy were widely applied.

Another criterion for differentiation within society was based on sex and age. Because of their sex, women were not only excluded from citizenship, they were not allowed to file accusations, except in cases in which they were directly and personally involved. Similarly excluded were minors and those whose occupation or profession did not yield a minimum annual income of 300 pesos. This brings us to the second axis of the law.

2. PATERNAL AUTHORITY AND LEGALIZED VIOLENCE

Patria Potestad in colonial legislation was 'the power of parents over children and grandchildren, and over all those of their lineage

---

Dictionnaire Universel du XIXème siècle, 1873). In the laws of Alfonso The Wise, fame was defined as 'the good state of man', that is, he who 'lived decently according to the law and good customs' (Tomo 4, Séptima Partida, Tit. VI, Ley I, folio 468, in *Las Siete Partidas del Rey D. Alfonso el Nono*, c. 1250/1851). Infamy was applied automatically to procurers, mountebanks, usurers, adulteresses; or was obtained by law due to sentence for treason, falsehood, adultery, theft, robbery with fraud, bribery and injuries (Tomo 4. Séptima Partida, Tit. VI, Leyes I to V, folios 468–73, in *Las Siete Partidas del Rey D. Alfonso el Nono*, c. 1250/1851). *Hombre infame* was applied in the nineteenth century to 'men hated because of their public behavior, but that act so as a result of their self-interested desire; regardless of the harm done to others, and against rules of morality and justice, as established by society. Infamous means without reputation, and reputation is only applied to those who act correctly with fellow men and civilize them. To do the opposite then is to be infamous' (*Primer Diccionario Etimológico de la Lengua Española* by Roque Bárcia, Tit. III, f. 188) (hereafter folio and folios have been abbreviated as f. and ff. respectively).

[32] It should be remembered that the penalties of forced labour and exile also entailed infamy (see footnote 24).

[33] Art. 73, Código Penal Boliviano, 1831. Regarding civil death, a Spanish jurist commented at the end of the nineteenth century that it was a penalty in which 'all the legal consequences of natural death were imposed to a living man. . . . He is no longer a son, he is no longer a father, he is no longer a husband; he can no longer acquire property. . . . He lives, if that can be called living; but he lives outside not only of society, but of human nature. Everything, absolutely everything in the order of rights has ended for him' (J. Pacheco, 1848/1870, p. 343).

born of honourable marriage'.[34] In the Republic, it was restricted to unmarried, under-age children. Paternal authority meant that children were not allowed to leave home without authorization, nor behave disrespectfully.[35] However, that same authority exerted by mothers and fathers over their children was exerted by husbands over their wives. If a spouse were disobedient and refused to change her behaviour despite 'warnings and moderate domestic punishments', she could be taken before a judge to be reprimanded.[36]

If a woman committed adultery, she not only could be sent to a reformatory for a period not exceeding six years, but could also lose all her marriage rights, including her dowry and her part of the joint property.[37] In cases in which the husband had found his wife committing a carnal act and had killed the man, his punishment was less than that usually applied for 'murder'.[38] Brothers and fathers-in-law were also assigned less than the full punishment for such an act.[39]

[34] Tit. XVII, Ley I, in Ots Capdequí, 1945, p. 94. 'Tómase esta palabra, que es llamada en latín potestas, que quiere decir . . . poderío, en muchas maneras . . . se toma . . . por señorío, así como . . . el poderío que ha el señor sobre su siervo . . . ; se toma por jurisdicción . . . como el poder que han los reyes. . .; se toma por el poder que han los obispos sobre sus clérigos . . . ; se toma . . . por . . . sujeción y castigamiento que debe haber el padre sobre su fijo . . .' (Tomo 3, Cuarta Partida, Tit. XVII, Ley III, file f. 149, in *Las Siete Partidas del Rey D. Alfonso el Nono*, c. 1250/1851).

[35] If they committed several offenses, they could be taken to a correctional house for anywhere from six months to two years (Art. 519, *Código Penal Boliviano*, 1831).

[36] Arts. 516, 521 and 525, *Código Penal Boliviano*, 1831. In the opposite case, if a woman were able to prove that her husband were morally reprobate, he could be sentenced to a maximum period of one year (Art. 526, *Código Penal Boliviano*, 1831).

[37] Art. 629, *Código Penal Boliviano*, 1831.

[38] Imprisonment was anywhere from six months to two years (Art. 575, *Código Penal Boliviano*, 1831).

[39] Art. 576, *Código Penal Boliviano*, 1831. Another law referred to the death caused by parents and grandparents when they exceeded themselves in their 'right to reprehend their children and grandchildren. . .'. This case was considered as 'involuntary homicide committed because of levity' and extended also to the masters' authority regarding 'their servants, disciples or other persons in their charge' (Art. 581, *Código Penal Boliviano*, 1831). 'Involuntary homicide' led to arrest for anywhere from three months to two years of exile (Art. 583, *Código Penal Boliviano*, 1831). Intentional murders merited the death penalty.

The authority of parents over children, of husbands over wives, and that of masters over their servants also included legalized violence. As already mentioned, 'moderate domestic punishments' of children and women were allowed as part of this authority. 'Physical injury, offense and physical ill-treatment' were not punished if they were inflicted 'unintentionally', and inflicted by parents on their children and grandchildren without permanent injury.[40] Punishment thus reflected hierarchical gender, generational and class relations, a conception that was also present in colonial Spanish law.[41]

The Military Code of 1843 also revealed a pattern of authority, subordination and legalized violence. The essence of the army was, of course, obedience, since disobedience was considered the 'most severe charge' that could ever be brought against an officer, especially one in the top ranks.[42] Violence was also inherent in the relationship of authority and obedience. The death penalty was applied to any soldier who did not arrive at his post on time in case of 'alarm, at the battlefield, or in any other function', but also for soldiers, corporals and sergeants who refused to obey the higher ranks in service matters, or who had physically abused an officer, even if it was in retaliation for punishments they had received.[43] In addition, punishment was also inflicted if orders were not carried out either in service or out of service. In such cases, soldiers and corporals would receive one hundred strokes of the rod and four

[40] 'The parents and direct ascendants . . . will not be responsible in these cases, except when exceeding themselves in their faculties they would injure one of their children or grandchildren in the terms expressed in Article 598. If they commit this offense, they will suffer arrest for anywhere from six days to a month' (Art. 614, *Código Penal Boliviano*, 1831). Article 598 refers to cases in which another person is voluntarily injured or hit, with premeditation and intent of ill-treatment to cause injury or sickness.

[41] 'The father can punish his son moderately, as the master his slave or servant and the master craftsman his disciple' (Séptima Partida, Tit. VIII, Ley IX, f. 497, in *Las Siete Partidas del Rey D. Alfonso el Nono*, c. 1250/1851).

[42] Art. 503. Article 5 of the *Código Militar* (1843, Sucre) stated that the armed forces were 'essentially obedient'. In this spirit, it was forbidden to express objections by 'murmuring' nonconformity with salary, work, food, dress, discomfort, etc., instead of following adequate channels (Art. 504). Furthermore, everyone of lower rank 'who spoke ill of his superior' should be 'punished severely' (Art. 506), and should be 'mortified in proportion to the irregularity of the case' (Art. 507, *Código Militar*, 1843, Sucre).

[43] Arts. 238, 247, 255, *Código Militar*, 1843, Sucre.

months' imprisonment.[44] Such acts of disobedience, which were considered the most serious crimes and could even be punished with death, took into account hierarchical and class differences. For instance, an article which applied to 'all' the army community ended by stating that punishment should be imposed according to the 'quality of the persons affected'.[45] This same difference can be observed in punishments inflicted for identical crimes. Thus, a soldier who stole between 6 and 25 pesos was sentenced to eight years in prison and to death if the theft exceeded that amount; but in the case of an officer, robbery was called misappropriation, and he was merely suspended from employment, while still receiving a third of his salary.[46]

3. WOMEN OF GOOD REPUTATION *VERSUS* PROSTITUTES

The 1831 Criminal Code clearly distinguished between 'uncorrupted women, those with good reputation', and those of blemished reputation or prostitutes. Punishment for sexual offenses committed against a prostitute was half that for a crime against women of good reputation.[47] Abuse of a married woman was punished with two to four years of public labour; that is, this crime was punished in a similar way to minor theft of hats or capes, since the latter was punished with two to six years of public labour.[48] Molesting women 'against their will' (sexual abuse), on the other hand, was punished with eight years of public labour and banishment.[49] Such

[44] Art. 249, *Código Militar*, 1843, Sucre.

[45] Art. 261, *Código Militar*, 1843, Sucre.

[46] Art. 283 and 291, *Código Militar*, 1843, Sucre.

[47] Dishonest abuse and deception of women who were not prostitutes implied for the aggressor the penalty of three to six years in public work, plus exile for the same period of time; while if the victims were prostitutes, the penalty was reduced to half, from one to three years (Art. 644, *Código Penal Boliviano*, 1831).

[48] Art. 643, 644, and 687, *Código Penal Boliviano*, 1831.

[49] Article 620 stipulated that whoever took someone by force and against that person's wishes, in order to harm or abuse, would receive the penalty of two to four years of public work. Article 622 stipulated that whoever abused a person would also suffer the penalty for abduction, four years of public work and life exile from the city. Thus if we add the maximum penalty from Article 620, four years, to the maximum of Article 622, we have eight years (*Código Penal Boliviano*, 1831).

a sentence was reduced to half that period if it was committed against a prostitute.[50]

4. ADULTERY, CONCUBINAGE AND FILIAL LEGITIMACY

The differentiation among men and between men and women also corresponds with a differentiation among women and, consequently, among their children. This distinction is evidently related to old Spanish customs of concubinage (the women involved were known as '*barraganas*') as well as Spanish notions of lineage. The differentiation established among women assumed the existence of a small female elite of good reputation, expected to be sexually chaste, as well as a group of 'dishonourable' women. In ancient Spanish law, *Patria Potestad* permitted men to have concubines ('*barraganas*') who were women over twelve years of age and not virgins. Etymologically, the term evokes a 'gain' (or profit) which, whether materially or symbolically, in this case refers to male access to and acquisition of the female body and sexuality.[51] We are thus confronted with a socially and legally specified class of women who were suppliers of extramarital sexual relations for men and, at the same time, the mothers of illegitimate children.

It is within this context that we can begin to understand the colonial social dynamics of premarital unions despite the existing cult of female chastity, and of extramarital unions despite the general censure of such unions. In both cases, sexual 'virtue' was expected only of certain women. This pattern involved not only the institution of marriage which separated women as wives and mothers from the figure of the mistress, but shaped also male access to other women, and wives' acceptance of such extramarital relations. The dishonour of many plebeian women was thus the underside of the honour of gentlemen and ladies. A lady's honour was also linked to

[50] Arts. 625 and 626, *Código Penal Boliviano*, 1831.

[51] 'This term was taken from two words, from "*barra*" which is Arabic, meaning "outside" [*fuera*] and "*gana*" which is Latin for "gain" [*ganancia*]. These two words joined into one mean "gain which is obtained outside the law of the Church". As a result, the children are known as "gained children" [*hijos de ganancia*].' 'Any man may have a concubine [*barragana*] if she is not a virgin and not younger than twelve years, nor an honest widow' (Tomo 3, Cuarta Partida, Tit. XIV, Leyes I, II, ff. 127–8, in *Las Siete Partidas del Rey D. Alfonso el Nono*, c. 1250/1851).

patrilineal norms of kinship descent—a married woman would be conferred the 'honours and dignity' associated with her husband, and above all the 'highest honour' of having her children inherit her husband's patrimony.[52] Illegitimate children, on the other hand, were considered to have been 'conceived against law and natural reason', and had no right to property from their father's side.[53] In other words, the 'quality' of the children also depended upon the condition and 'virtue' of the mother.

Republican legislation established a similar distinction between women of good reputation and those of low reputation or prostitutes. This reflected a general social practice of premarital or extramarital unions which frequently occurred across socio-ethnic lines, the men being of a higher social stratum than the women involved. In terms of the offspring of such extramarital unions, republican law distinguished between two types. *Illegitimate* children were those not acknowledged by the father and conceived in circumstances socially or morally forbidden (e.g. outside of marriage), or those 'stained' for some other reason (e.g. non-Catholic religious background). Such children could not inherit, but had the right to be maintained until they came of age at twenty-five years.[54] *Natural* children were those acknowledged by the father, and conceived and born in circumstances in which the parents would have been able to marry. These offspring were allowed to demand a fifth of their parents' property.[55]

[52] Tomo 3, Cuarta Partida, Tit. II, Ley VII, f. 24, in *Las Siete Partidas del Rey D. Alfonso el Nono*, c. 1250/1851.

[53] Tomo 3, Cuarta Partida, Tit. XV, Leyes I and III, ff. 130 and 132, in *Las Siete Partidas del Rey D. Alfonso el Nono*, c. 1250/1851.

[54] Article 493 of the Civil Code. The food allowance varied in accordance with the means of the parents. In 1845, the two illegitimate children who survived the impoverished presbyter José María Ybarburu were assigned 400 pesos annually from his property, that is so say, less than 1 peso a day for each. See ALP CSD 1845 C. 82. Dossier compiled on the behalf of D. Ysabel Quisberto regarding the filiation of her sons, the minors Rafael and Florencio. ff. 12–12v. and 17.

[55] 'Toro's Law No. 11 in Book 10 of the *Novísima Recopilación* defined the natural son as one who is born outside of marriage, of parents who could marry without dispensation at the time of conception or birth, it being necessary that the father acknowledges him or that he has had in his house the woman who bore him' (ALP CSD x 1850, Blue covered dossier. Doña Ignacia Medina with D. Jacinta Medina . . . , f. 24v.).

Although the distinction was important for inheritance purposes, both illegitimate and natural children were characterized as 'infamous' because of the conditions in which they were conceived and born, and thus both were despised by dominant groups because they expressed dishonour, 'sin' and shame, and frequently 'illicit' interclass and interethnic unions. It seems clear, then, that such vertical gender relations were key elements in the articulation of different social groups. Each maintained its own contours, yet was linked by the logic of *Patria Potestad* within a chain of hierarchical relations.

III. SOCIAL DYNAMICS IN THE COURTS

It is important to turn to the courts of justice in order to analyse the relation between the legislative corpus and society, to identify particular strategies deployed by popular sectors, and to help specify identity dynamics in republican Bolivia. While hegemonic class and gender ideologies certainly prevailed in the courts, regulating what should or should not be stated and how one should address oneself, they also constituted arenas of intersection, tension, and struggle between elites and subaltern groups.

Lower-class men and women faced a constant questioning as to the validity of their legal testimony. To begin with, they needed to justify their presence in the court by declaring a socially legitimate trade or occupation. Some forms of employment were not recognized as granting credibility, or were considered of low grade. The case of day-workers and seasonal workers (*colonos*) on agricultural estates—the great majority of whom were indigenous people—provides a good example. These types of workers were grouped under the category of 'vagrants' (*vagos*), defined by police regulations in 1845 as anyone whose 'trade, occupation, destination, property, rents, or honest livelihood is unknown'.[56] In a related category were those 'dubiously engaged' ('*mal entretenidos*'), including artisans and similar manual labourers who 'do not apply themselves due to their vices and laziness'. Furthermore, petty

[56] Others within this category were all sorts of healers or ritual specialists ('*romeros y santeros, adivinos, agoreros, hechiceros y sorteros*') and 'vagabonds' without fixed domicile. Cap. 6, Art. 68, Reglamento de Policía, 10 de Junio de 1845. *Colección Oficial de Leyes, Decretos, Ordenes. 1ero de Marzo de 1845 al 28 de Febrero de 1846. Tomo Décimo*, Sucre, 1863.

officials or apprentices were seen as equivalent to dependents, estate workers, or domestic employees.[57] Ultimately, to fall under the category of 'vagrant' or someone 'dubiously engaged' meant not to be considered a citizen. In this context, lower-class testimony could easily be rejected, as is shown by the reply of a master accused of beatings and mistreatment:

> Article 786 . . . and 787 of the Procedural Code prohibit people from making accusations if it is not on their own behalf, if they do not have employment which brings in at least three hundred pesos annually, and in general if they do not exercise citizenship: you know very well that a few miserable estate workers [*colonos*] lack this franchise. The following article prohibits dependents [*criados*] from challenging their master; estate workers are nothing but domestic servants and dependents subject to the lord and owner of the estate.[58]

But let us take, as another example, the case of an indigenous hatter who sued a merchant over debts arising from a work contract.[59] The merchant based his defence and his opposition to the hatter's witnesses around four arguments:

1. Some witnesses were related to the plaintiff or were coerced, while others were living in his house or were 'servants'.
2. One of the witnesses was a concubine (*amasia*) of another, and furthermore she was 'dim-witted and lacking in judgment'.
3. They belonged to a special substratum of society, a 'class which is barely visible', and were 'obscure . . ., unknown people',[60] 'miserable people . . . without any role in society'.[61] These slurs were made against two men and a woman who declared themselves employed as a trader and tailor, a tribute-paying hatter from the parish of San Sebastián, and a seamstress.[62]

[57] Art. 26, Tit. 2°, Cap. 1 del Reglamento de Policía. Reglamento de Policía. 10 de Junio de 1845. *Colección Oficial de Leyes, Decretos, Ordenes. 1ero de Marzo de 1845 al 28 de Febrero de 1846. Tomo Décimo*, Sucre, 1863.

[58] ANB Corte Superior de Chuquisaca, 1851, No. 2. Criminal seguido contra el ciudadano Pedro Gironda por suponérsele haber seducido para revolución a los indígenas de su hacienda de Lajrachira y construcción de un cuartel en ella. f. 18v.

[59] ALP CSD 1849 C. 101 E. 2.

[60] ALP CSD 1849 C. 101 E. 2, ff. 44, 42v.

[61] ALP CSD 1849 C. 101 E. 2, f. 74.

[62] ALP CSD 1849 C. 101 E. 2, ff. 21, 27–8, 30, 29, respectively.

4. For these reasons, their attestations were suspect—the witnesses 'do not merit credibility . . . in their declarations due to their lack of or bad reputation'.[63]

This attempt to insinuate intimacy between the witnesses and the hatter, and even bribery, aimed to suggest a condition of dependency and to disqualify the witnesses. Thus, as the contending party sought to deny them any status as citizens, the witnesses for the prosecution were converted into accused who fought to assert such status. It is noteworthy that the attack against them insisted on their 'obscure' and 'unknown' condition. In the end, given the lack of any specific juridical criterion concerning Indians and Mestizos within the new liberal legal framework, elites tried to redeploy preexisting hierarchical differentiations while using a different language.

This language centered around the issues of credit and credibility, competence and 'invalidity', rationality and 'lack of judgement'. The emphasis on and frequent recourse to references to a person's 'unknown' condition served to impugn their trustworthiness and credibility. The word of an unknown person was suspect and likely to be untrue. To be an 'invalid' person (the condition of *desvalidez*) contrasted with the definition of a credible person, implying a lack of subordination to the dominant social logic and a lack of ties to society's 'worthy' representatives. For they were the source of recognition and validation for any individual and social existence. Yet this gave rise to a trap: without relations to those who were credible or credit-worthy, one was simply unknown; but with such relations, one could be taken for a dependent, a non-citizen, and someone subject to corruption.[64] The use of language such as 'concubine' and someone 'lacking reason' was also significant as a way to recuse or disqualify a female witness. Such language sought to define an inferior and dependent identity: as a woman and as a woman without honour.

In this fashion, dominant groups exercised authority and the power to attribute negative social essences to subaltern groups

[63] ALP CSD 1849 C. 101 E. 2, ff. 42v, 44.

[64] In one trial, a witness declared that she had been told that 'Doña Atanasia Cordero pleaded for her to declare in her favor and that, in compensation, she would buy all her food for her and would protect her husband should he be enlisted as a soldier or engaged in any other labor' (ALP CSD 1847 C. 88. Sin Título. Josefa Mérida por insultos, f. 4).

(Bourdieu, 1982, pp. 126–8). This served ultimately to deny recognition of their place in society, converting them into murky beings whose humanity was virtually erased:

> [Should the] attestations of such miserable, obscure, and unknown entities . . . , who play no role whatsoever in society and whose figure, for all we know, may not even be human . . . , merit more faith than those of . . . witnesses so notable for their character and other social circumstances?[65]

Backed into this corner, how could one escape? What resources could an Indian hatter deploy to avoid such an assault? In fact, he would risk to lose everything not only the final payment and the financial credit advanced to him to fulfil the contract, but also his reputation and moral credit. This hatter, like others in similar straits, saw himself forced to undermine his opponent's case by working within the same logic: he farred the opposing witnesses by demonstrating their condition of servitude and dependence; he had to prove that his own witnesses were credible and not dependents, drawing on other testimony to demonstrate that they were experienced and reputable workers. Courts of justice thus became arenas of social contestation. Those subject to discrimination knew how to counter the accusations levelled at them in order to demonstrate their credibility and honour. They did so by employing, often simultaneously, a variety of strategies, both appealing to patriarchal logic and defying discrimination in the name of equality.

One of these tactics consisted of rejecting essentialist and negative stereotypes attributed to them because they did not follow the norms of dominant groups in their individual, family, and social conduct. In 1846, for example, a young man accused of assassination assured the court he was 'raised and fed' by his mother, and asked for an inquiry to prove that in fact he had 'lived as an obedient son under the *Patria Potestad*' of his mother.[66] Another accused thief presented witnesses to address a set of questions: (1) Whether they had known him to be of 'unstained honour?' (2) Whether his parents had educated him 'with delicacy and under the auspices of proper morality?'

[65] ALP CSD 1847 C. 88. Sin Título. Josefa Mérida por insultos, f. 74. The syntaxis of the quote has been slightly modified in the interests of comprehension.

[66] ALP CSD 1846 C. 84. Criminal seguido contra los autores de la muerte de D. Manuel Casablanca, f. 13.

(3) Whether he had remained under their protection and in the paternal home up until the present? (4) Whether he had all his necessities met since his parents provided him with everything, being a 'child of the family?'[67] The true situation of these legal suspects could in fact be quite different from what they alleged: many could be of distant provenance and hence without near kin; many may not have been maintained by others and may have lacked the resources necessary for their education. The assertion that one was a 'child of the family' thus constitutes a typical response to common questioning. Such questioning also provoked the need to demonstrate personal ties to members of higher social strata, since to bring suit or to obtain liberty from detention required the role of guarantor. Without such backing, legal suspects could remain in jail for months even if they had been absolved of wrongdoing.[68] Legal practice in the courts of justice thus required not only social recognition of the individuals involved, but also a socially shared set of values and, ultimately, the institution of vertical social relations. We find here a terrain propitious for introducing asymmetrical relations of *compadrazgo* (ritual kinship)—a useful strategy for developing vertical alliances—as well a sign of the importance that clientelistic networks acquired in the nineteenth century.

As for the Indian hatter, he sought to accredit his own character by asking the authorities of his community to provide assurances as to his 'conduct as a tributary . . . and his behaviour'. He also requested the principal master of his guild to testify to the 'honesty' with which he had 'behaved as an artisan without the slightest mar to his character and honour'. Moreover, this information was channelled through the police authorities, who issued the certificate of his 'morally immaculate' behaviour.[69]

Yet the artisan's adversary again counterattacked, declaring that 'Everyone knows, and the court over which your honour presides

[67] ALP CSD 1848 C. 95. Testimonio de oficio seguido contra el reo ausente Manuel Cesareo Cordero por robo de varias especias al Presbítero Matías Cordero.

[68] In 1845, for example, two Indians stated through their legal defender that they had been in detention for over three months without being able to find garantors (ALP CSD 1845 C. 80. Criminal contra Mariano Ortiz . . . , f. 10). In another case, an ironsmith had been held in prison for over a year, despite having been declared innocent, because he had no guarantor (ALP CSD 1847 C. 88 Manuel Mamani contra Norverto Aguilar, f. 84).

[69] ALP CSD 1849 C. 101 E. 2., ff. 104–5v.

knows better than anyone, that such documents [the certifications of conduct] are worth nothing, and that this recourse is excessively manipulated and hence has no credibility even among the most ingenuous of people'.[70] This 'excessively manipulated recourse' was precisely one of the legal channels opened up by subjects like the Indian hatter in order to confront their opponents, and one of the discursive strategies they deployed *vis-a-vis* the state.

Another tactic they drew upon was to assume the role of poor and ignorant victims who required the patriarchal protection of the authorities. In 1850, a group of Indians in La Paz, who had been subject to retaliation for having denounced their *corregidor* (canton official), continued to challenge the local authorities while calling on the President of the Republic, whom they described as a 'fighter' for the 'Indian caste', to defend them.[71]

Such testimony clearly falls within a hegemonic state discourse, since popular sectors were seeking a favorable solution by taking on the role of 'invalids' or, alternatively, by demonstrating honourable conduct as a response to imputations of discredit. It was part of an uphill battle, for daily life was made up of actions considered by dominant groups to be morally unacceptable. The ostensible discrepancy between what subaltern subjects said and did can be seen as part of a repertoire of strategies *vis-a-vis* their social superiors, and would help to explain the deep Creole disgust at the reputedly 'two-faced' behaviour of Mestizos and Cholos (best expressed by Alcides Arguedas). This double attitude developed because the authorities and dominant sectors promoted a form of communication that required discursive alignment with their norms, hierarchy, and patriarchal role. Thus, they encouraged humility, submission, and recognition of their superior power.

It is also clear, however, that subalterns employed a different strategy which obliged the state to follow through on its own liberal and egalitarian discourse. The same Indians who pleaded for presidential protection argued, for example, that they were as Bolivian and as free as anyone else![72] Another Indian couple appealed to the patriarchal logic of the government, but also simultaneously to juridical equality:

[70] ALP CSD 1849 C. 101 E. 2, ff. 110v–11.

[71] ALP P.E. 1850. The Indian Quispehuana complaints about abuses.

[72] See footnote 71 above.

We wish to say that we unhappy Indians continue to suffer ignorance both in fact and in law, and therefore we have not improved in condition or fortune although the Supreme Government tries daily to relieve this unfortunate caste . . . My Lord, you are authorized by the Nation and by the Law, acting in rigourous Justice, to protect Indians such as ourselves by showing us to be equal before the Law. (ALP CSD 1846. C. 85. Exped. seguido por María Pabón, ff. 11–11v)

In conclusion, the introduction of a new collection of laws can be seen as contributing to the weaving of a 'fabric' of social identities in the nineteenth century. The laws set up conditions for the interaction between different social groups and between these groups and the state. Yet the image of a woven fabric may be rather too innocuous. For these interactions can also be taken as a sort of daily social battle. On one hand, the dominant classes consistently disqualified and negated popular subjects because of their subordinate social and ethnic position, reanimating old colonial divisions in new discursive terms. On the other hand, however, those who were discriminated against often rejected these stereotypes and labels. Faced with the stigmatization and condemnation of their social existence, they often sought out creative new responses and forms of self-representation *vis-a-vis* hegemonic forces.

IV. MODES OF CONTINUITY AND CHANGE

The next question that needs to be addressed is whether the new juridical corpus in the nascent republic did in fact represent a rupture with Spain, as the discourse and rhetoric of the elites proclaimed, did Independence indeed break the chains of national subordination? While it is not our objective to analyse either the intellectual genealogy or the juridical models for the Bolivian Penal Code of 1831, a brief comparison of the structure and content of this legislation reveals that the model was not the Napoleonic Code but the Spanish Penal Code of 1822! The elites and their legislative authors simply copied in large part the legal code of 'Mother Spain'.[73] This is a striking

[73] See for example the literal translation in the following articles: Art. 561 of the Santa Cruz Penal Code of 1831 (SCPC) and Art. 605 of the Spanish Code of 1822 (SC); Art. 569 of the SCPC and Art. 612 of the SC; Art. 569 of the SCPC and Art. 613 of the SC. . . . The list could be extended at length. The articles from the Spanish Code are given in Pacheco (1848–70).

finding since one might have expected republican legislation to be clearly differentiated from that of the Spanish metropolitan power, for example by adopting the post-revolutionary French code. So, to return to our question for this section: to what extent had a rupture really taken place *vis-a-vis* Spain, and for which social sectors?

For the elites, the answer must be ambivalent. There was indeed a rupture in the sense that Independence from Spain brought about their rise to political power. In another sense, however, the rupture and innovation of Independence had less to do with Spain or Europe than it did with a past which these modernizing elites sought to leave behind. In effect, both the Napoleonic and the Spanish Codes, each with their own particularities, were framed within Enlightenment and Liberal thought. If Creole elites subscribed to this ideological framework it was not only because they identified closely with Europe (as American-born Spaniards), but because this framework was conceived as representing universal civilization. In a letter addressed to President Andrés de Santa Cruz, one of the authors of the Criminal Code stated:

> The Criminal Code . . . ? is the product of wisdom and any criticism of it is groundless. . . . It was drawn up by eminent men of the Spanish Courts. Not satisfied with Calatrava's six years' work . . . it was revised by Benjamin Constant and the most profound of legislators, Bentant [Bentham]. According to the former's opinion, this is the most perfect Code ever issued in Europe. The latter's opinions were in the same vein. . . . Thus who in America would ever dare to condemn it? One would have to be superior to these notable men, or very arrogant, which would not be advisable. After all, Sir, the code is wise, perfect, almost divine, and anyone who dares to find fault with it does not know what he is doing, and his lack of intelligence gives rise to his arrogant criticism. (Santa Cruz Shunkrafft, 1976-92: 37)

But we can also respond to our question by noting that there was no rupture insofar as adopting a foreign Spanish model implied an ongoing form of dependency, now primarily cultural and ideological, though no longer based on direct colonial domination. But why was the Spanish Code adopted, rather than the Napoleonic Code? It would seem fundamentally because the Spanish Code retained what we have termed the 'constitutive axes' of social hierarchy, permitting the maintenance of culturally engrained discrimination on the basis of educational level, morals, and social affiliation. The Spanish Code offered a functional model that reserved citizenship for honourable and reputable men, as opposed to infamous, tainted and illiterate men, and to privileged women of good credit *versus* those of low or 'unknown' reputation. There is indeed a recognizable relationship between the colonial Spanish concept of civil death and the republican use of infamy, exclusion from citizenship, interdiction, and disablement. In other words, in the new framework Bolivian society was still conceived of as being formed by unequal and hierarchical groups, and this framework could disguise and refunctionalize old colonial divisions.

But as for the majority of the population, the indigenous sector whose 'Indian' identity was a colonial creation, what was the particular significance of the new republican laws? It is a historiographic commonplace that the division between conquerors and the conquered, colonizers and the colonized, was expressed in the dualistic conception of colonial society as composed of a 'Spanish Republic' and an 'Indian Republic'. This division was found in the legislated segregation of colonial space and of the colonial population, and in the two separate spheres of political jurisdiction.[74]

The situation was much more complex, however. The foremost legal reference in the colonial period—the *Recopilación de las Leyes de Indias*—made no explicit juridical distinction between the two Republics. The political autonomy of indigenous society was limited and indigenous authorities were ultimately subject to the superior authority of Spanish officials.[75] For Solórzano, the preeminent jurist for the colonial Indies whose organic notion of society derived from Plato and Aristotle, Indians could be conceived of as the 'feet of the [social] body'.[76] In sum, social segregation was not clear and

[74] Spaniards, Mestizos, Mulattos, and Blacks were not allowed to reside within indigenous towns and territory. Furthermore, as part of the framework for indirect colonial rule, Indian communities were governed by their own ethnic authorities: whether traditional Andean authorities, the *caciques, kurakas*, and '*principales*' who exercised political jurisdiction in Indian towns; or new Indian authorities, such as the *alcaldes* and *regidores*, whose posts were created by colonial officials in imitation of Spanish municipal goverment (*cabildo*) (Libro Sexto, Tit. I, l. l, xv–xvi, *Recopilación*, T. II, 1774, ff. 200–200v). The caciques were nonetheless subject to Spanish provinicial governors known as *corregidores*, who were later replaced by *subdelegados* within the Intendency system. On the indigenous authority system in the colonial period, see Thomson, 1996.

[75] Libro Sexto, Tit. VII, l. v, *Recopilación*, T. II, 1774, f. 220.

[76] Solórzano, Libro II, Cap. VI, 77, Cap. XXVIII, f. 206.

consistent, and there did indeed exist integral conceptions of the colonial order.

What was the specific juridical situation of Indians in the colonial period?[77] Following upon the controversies provoked by the conquest, Indians were declared free vassals not subject to servitude.[78] However, they paid tribute in recognition of the dominion of the Spanish kings and their role as Protectors and Administrators of the Indies.[79] Also, though unremunerated personal service for private benefit was prohibited, they were obliged by the state to carry out a series of tasks in the mines, on haciendas, and in public works. This corvée labour obligation was justified because of their 'limited capacities',[80] the 'benefit' which Spanish intervention entailed for them,[81] their similarity to 'rustics' in Spain, and their 'more apt nature' for labour.[82]

There was hence an apparent contradiction, since they were 'free vassals' obliged to perform given services only incumbent upon them.[83] They also had a particular legal-juridical status as 'miserable' individuals (*miserables*) 'for whom we naturally feel pity due to their state, quality, and labours'. This status was determined by their 'imbecile nature' and poverty, their recent conversion to the Faith, their lesser capacity for rationality, and their 'inability to govern themselves'.[84]

[77] We lack studies of the legal and juridical situation of Indians in diachronic perspective. Commonly, as in the treatment here which is designed to compare their situation in the colonial and republican periods, the issue is dealt with generally and without regard for the changes which occurred over the three centuries of colonial domination. Yet such changes took place throughout this period. In the early seventeenth century, Solórzano commented on the subject of caciques: 'Already in our own time the role of these caciques is new, and they are very limited in their powers' (Libro II, Cap. XXVII, Solórzano, 1947, T. 1, f. 194.)

[78] Libro Sexto, Tit. II, l. i, *Recopilación*, T. II, 1774, f. 194.

[79] Libro V, Cap. XIX, Solórzano, 1739, T. 1, f. 152.

[80] Libro II, Cap. IV, Solórzano, 1739, T. 1, ff. 71, 77.

[81] 'That which is compensated by a greater good is not wrong' (Libro II, Cap. VI, Solórzano, 1739, T. 1, f. 80).

[82] Libro II, Cap. VI, Solórzano, 1739, T. 1, f. 78.

[83] Solórzano, however, justified the contradiction: 'It is not in opposition to say that in Spain free vassals are not obliged to perform similar services . . . because every province requires its own laws and customs'. (See Libro II, Cap. V, Solórzano, 1739, T. 1, f. 79 and ss. See also ff. 72–4).

[84] Libro II, Cap. XXVIII, Solórzano, 1739, T. 1, ff. 203–5, 207–8.

The status of 'miserable' individuals carried with it certain 'privileges'.[85] Their legal cases were to be expeditious without having to follow all of the regular juridical procedures,[86] and they were not required to take oaths because as rustics it was thought they were prone to lying. For this reason, the testimony of six Indians was equivalent to that of one 'proper' individual.[87] Finally, they were represented in the courts by the Protector of Indians.[88] In other words, they resembled 'poor children' who received given 'privileges' due to their inferior condition.

What then were the changes and continuities in the legal situation of Indians in the first decades after Independence? In keeping with the ostensibly egalitarian principles of Liberalism, Indians had no juridically specific status either in the constitutions or legal codes (penal, civil, or procedural). They were not even named in these texts, which evidently suggests that they were cast along with all others in the categories of Bolivians and citizens. And yet another body of laws which were more conjunctural in nature—the Laws, Decrees, Orders, and Resolutions—display an abundance of specific dispositions which do refer to 'Indians' and reveal that in fact their juridical situation was not altogether transformed. Among these dispositions, for example, was the legislation regulating the 'indigenous contribution', a neo-colonial form of tribute to the state. Despite initial attempts to abolish this differential tax, as a colonial vestige incompatible with enlightened liberal principles, the Bolivian state was fiscally unable to do without it (Lofstrom, 1983). The specific and practical situation of Indians as tributaries thus remained unchanged.

Indians were no longer considered 'miserable' persons, but they

[85] Libro II, Cap. XXIX, Solórzano, 1739, T. 1, f. 211.

[86] The law allowed this 'exemption' since it was assumed that they would not be able to deceive others (ibid., ff. 206–7). In the *Leyes de las Partidas*, rapid or 'verbal' trials were reserved for 'poor and vile men' (Tomo 2, Tercera Partida Tit. XXII, Ley VI, f. 778, in *Las Siete Partidas del Rey D. Alfonso el Nono*, c. 1250/1851).

[87] Libro II, Cap. XXVIII, Solórzano, 1739, ff. 207, 208. This evokes the old laws of Alfonso the Wise: 'A man of another law, such as a Jew, Moor, or heretic, cannot testify against a Christian' (Tomo 2, Tercera Partida, Tit. V, Ley VIII, ff. 588–9, in *Las Siete Partidas del Rey D. Alfonso el Nono*, c. 1250/1851).

[88] See Libro VI, Tit. VI, *Recopilación*, T. II, 1774.

made up the bulk of those acknowledged to be 'notoriously destitute' (*pobres de solemnidad*). This was a category inherited from the colonial period which had no specific 'ethnic' attribution, and which was applied instead to anyone lacking a minimum annual income. It carried with it reduced charges for any legal transaction.[89] Given the general absence of a specific legal status for Indians, the colonial position of the Protector of Indians disappeared.

The novelty of the republican situation was this absence of a specific legal statute and jurisdiction for Indians. The consequence was a redefinition of the bases for social differentiation. A new system was thus inaugurated, in which (1) social and ethnic stratification was not recognized but continued to exist; (2) the rights and so-called 'privileges' of indigenous people disappeared; and (3) the stigma of belonging to certain groups and categories, and the ambiguity involved in defining social identities, became a social battleground.

CONCLUSIONS

This study permits us to rectify two frequent historiographic assumptions. One is that in the new nation-states emerging after Independence in the nineteenth century, hegemonic discourse was divorced from or alien to social reality. Another is that the dominant superstructure and discourse was thoroughly 'modern' and liberal. First, then, the analysis of the social dynamics in the courts allows us to appreciate the importance and consequences of the new legislation in the interrelations among different social groups. The supposedly 'dead letter' of the law in fact had precise and concrete effects. The dominant discourses which acted to constitute social subjects, essentializing and stigmatizing subaltern identities, gave rise to important cultural tensions and confrontations. This dynamic demonstrates the articulation between discursive and practical social relations.

[89] The 'notoriously destititute' were defined as individuals who had no rents or income above 200 pesos a year (Arts. 751 and 763, *Código de Procederes Santa Cruz*, 1852). In 1835, Indians were explicitly included in the category of pobres de solemnidad (Orden de 14 de Noviembre de 1835, in Bonifaz, 1953, f. 51). This status was linked to the 1826 decree that 'those Bolivians formerly called Indians' should employ special paper, bought at reduced rates, for legal business (Ley de 14 de Diciembre de 1826, in Bonifaz, 1953, f. 16).

Second, and even more importantly, the detailed examination of the juridical corpus upsets the common image that Creole elites introduced a consistently modern and liberal legal framework in the nineteenth century. The adoption of a single criminal, civil and procedural code and a constitution for all Bolivians could lead us to believe that the new legislation reflected an ideology of juridical equality for all individuals. However, the above shows that the content of the legislation does not fit with this familiar historiographic vision. The 'constitutive axes' of the juridical corpus clearly reveal that society was thought of, in subtle and implicit ways, as composed of different and differently ranked groups and castes. Juridical equality, the foundational ideology that ostensibly marked the breakup of a 'feudal society' in Europe and the modernizing projects in independent Latin American countries, was actually not consistently applied. In fact, Creole elites were bearers of a 'modernity' which was far from being perceived as a regime 'founded on individuals who freely associate by contractual, corporative, or communitarian links', as argued by Guerra (1992: 359). The essential structure was still one of difference and hierarchy. The 'modernity' of the elites—a term which must be taken advisedly—was bound up with a patriarchal hierarchy formulated as *Patria Potestad*. Enlightenment ideology and the imitation of Europe allowed them to think of themselves as the patriarchal leaders who would bring light, civilization, and progress to barbarous and backward people. A door was left open to equality, at least at a juridical level, but in order to attain equality and citizenship, it was necessary to undergo a process of 'civilization', as Rivera (1993) and Platt (1991) have observed.

The analysis of early Bolivian legislation also suggests that the construction of 'citizenship' involved not only a 'civilizing' process but a procedure for reconstituting the 'rule of colonial difference' (Chatterjee, 1993). While the Indian population was not excluded from the nation, while it was an integral part of the new state, it remained in its subordinate position. The mission to transform 'children' and 'savages' was an effective discourse which legitimized the power of Creoles, the offspring and heirs of the former Spanish masters, to lead and govern.

But the fact that the criminal, civil, and procedural codes and the constitution did not recognize differentiated juridical statutes or jurisdictions for different sectors of the population did entail a certain change in the dynamics of identity formation. It meant that social differentiation was defined in terms of less obvious and more 'hidden' oppositions (Rivera, 1993). Since the new legislation did permit subtle discrimination, the assignment of differentiated social identity did become contentious. In the conflicts generated, dominant groups constantly categorized and subordinated popular groups by the power of their word, while subalterns just as often rejected elite attempts at exclusion. Their responses included both the evasion of discriminating stereotypes and the pursuit of citizenship as the exercise of civil rights. Since the arenas of conflict and confrontation were part of everyday relations with the state, there were few grounds for organized popular struggles or outspoken demands for citizenship. In these dynamics, the enforcement of the laws and regulations adopted in the nineteenth century involved the weaving and interweaving of social identities, redefining the relations among different groups and *vis-a-vis* the state.

REFERENCES

PRIMARY SOURCES

Aldeano, *Bosquejo del estado en que se halla la riqueza nacional de Bolivia con sus resultados, presentado al examen de la Nación por un Aldeano hijo de ella. Año de 1830*, Plural Editores y Facultad de Humanidades y Ciencias de la Educaciòn, Universidad Mayor de San Andrés, 1994 (1830).

Codigo de Procederes, *Código de Procederes Santa Cruz. Nueva edición con notas que indican las disposiciones legales que han derogado o alterado algunos de sus artículos, y con un suplemento que contiene las leyes, decretos, órdenes y resoluciones referentes a los Códigos de la República*, Imrenta Paceña, La Paz, 1852.

Código De Procederes, Santa Cruz. Edición con notas I. Suplemento. Tipografía de Gutiérrez, Cochabamba, 1862.

Codigo Militar, *Código Militar para el réjimen, disciplina, subordinación y servicios de los Ejércitos de la República Boliviana de orden de S.E. el Presidente*, Imprenta de Beeche y Cia, Sucre, 1843.

Codigo Penal Boliviano, *Código Penal Boliviano*. Imprenta del Colegio de Educandas, Paz de Ayacucho, 1831.

——— *Código Penal Boliviano*, Imprenta de Beeche y Cia, Sucre, 1845.

Coleccion De Leyes, Reglamento de Policía, 10 de Junio de 1845. *Colección*

Oficial de Leyes, Decretos, Ordenes. 1ero de Marzo de 1845 al 28 de Febrero de 1846, Tomo Décimo, Sucre, 1863 (1845).

Compilacion, *Compilación de las Leyes del Procedimiento Civil Boliviano.* Edición particular. Imprenta Bolívar, Sucre, 1890.

Constitucion, *Constitución Política de la Monarquía Española*, promulgada en Cádiz a 19.3.1812. Cádiz, 1812.

Dictionnaire, *Grand Dictionnaire Universel du XIXéme. siecle, par Pierre Larousse*, Tome Neuvieme, Paris, 1873.

Las Siete Partidas, *Las Siete Partidas del Sabio Rey D. Alfonso el Nono, copiadas de la edición de Salamanca del año de 1555.* Cotejadas con varios còdices antiguos por la Real Academia de la Historia y glosadas por el Licenciado Gregorio López del Consejo Real de Indias de S.M., Paris, 4 Tomos, 1758–1851.

Recompilacion, *Recopilación de Leyes de los Reynos de las Indias*, 4 Tomos, Madrid, 3era. edición, 1774.

Pacheco, Joaquín Francisco, *El Código Penal concordado y comentado.* 4ta. edición, Madrid, 1870 (1848).

Solórzano Pereira, Juan de, *Política Indiana*, 2 Tomos, Madrid, 1739 (1646).

——— *Política Indiana*, *Antología*, 2 Tomos, Selección y Prólogo de Luis García Arias, Madrid, 1947 (1646).

SECONDARY SOURCES

Abecia, Valentín, 'La obra legislativa del Mariscal Santa Cruz', in *Vida y Obra del Mariscal Andrés de Santa Cruz y Calahumana.* Edición de la Honorable Municipalidad de La Paz, La Paz, 1976–92.

Albo, Xavier, Greaves, Tomás y Sandoval, Godofredo, *Chuquiyawu. La Cara Aymara de La Paz III. Cabalgando entre dos mundos.* CIPCA, La Paz, 1983.

Anderson, Benedict, *Imagined Communities: Reflections on the Origin and Spread of Nationalism.* Ed. Verso, London, New York, 1991 (1983).

Barragán, Rossana, 'Entre polleras, lliqllas y ñañacas. Los mestizos y la emergencia de la tercera república', in Arze, Barragán, Escobari y Medinaceli (Comp). *Etnicidad, Economía y Simbolismo en los Andes.* II.do. Congreso Internacional de Etnohistoria, La Paz, 1992 a.

——— 'Identidades indias y mestizas: una intervención al debate', in *Autodeterminación No. 10, Análisis histórico-político y teoría social,* La Paz, 1992 b.

——— 'Un Aldeano Ilustrado', in *Bosquejo del estado en que se halla la riqueza nacional de Bolivia con sus resultados, presentado al examen de la Nación por un Aldeano hijo de ella. Año de 1830.* Ed. of A.M. Lema. Plural Editores y Facultad de Humanidades y Ciencias de la Educación, Universidad Mayor de San Andrés, 1994.

——— 'Españoles patricios y españoles europeos: conflictos intra-élites e identidades en la ciudad de La Paz en vísperas de la independencia 1770–1809', in Walker Charles, Comp., Compê in *Entre la retórica y la insur-gencia: las ideas y los movimientos sociales en los Andes, Siglo XVIII*. Centro Bartolomé de las Casas, Perú, 1996a.

——— 'Los múltiples rostros y disputas por el ser mestizo', in *Mestizaje: Ilusiones y Realidades*, Museo Nacional de Etnografía y Folklore, La Paz, 1996b.

Bernand Carmen y Gruzinski Serge, 'La Redécouverte de l'Amérique', in *L'Homme*, Nos. 122–4, Paris, 1992.

Bonifaz, Miguel, *Legislación Agrario Indigenal*, Imprenta Universitaria, Cochabamba, 1953.

Bourdieu, Pierre, *Ce que parler veut dire*, Paris, 1982.

——— *Le sens de la Distinction*, Paris, 1993.

Buisson et al., *Problemas de la formación del Estado y de la Nación en Hispanoamérica*, CIP, Colonia, 1984.

Chatterjee, Partha, *The Nation and its Fragments: Colonial and Post-colonial Histories*, New-Jersey: Princeton University Press, 1993.

Damen, Frans, La fiesta de la Exhaltación en Obrajes. Conferencia Episcopal de Bolivia. Departamento de Diálogo y Cultura, La Paz, Inédito, 1994.

Demelas, Marie Danièlle, *L'invention politique. Bolivie, Equateur, Pérou au XIXe. siècle*. Ed. Recherche sur les Civilisations, Paris, 1992.

Foucault, Michel, *Vigilar y Castigar. Nacimiento de la prisión*, Siglo Veintiuno Editores, México, 1975/93.

Gellner, Ernest, *Naciones y Nacionalismo*. Ed. Alianza Universidad, Madrid, 1988.

Guerra, Francois-Xavier, *Modernidad e Independencias*. Editorial Mapfre, España, 1992.

Hobsbawm, Eric, 'Introduction: Inventing Traditions', in Hobsbawm and Terence Ranger. *The Invention of Tradition*, Cambridge University Press, 1983.

Lofstrom Lee, William, *El Mariscal Sucre en Bolivia*, Edición e Imprenta Alenkar, La Paz, 1983.

Mertz, Elizabeth, 'Legal Language: Pragmaticas, Poetics and Social Power', *Annual Review of Anthropology*, 23, 1994.

Morner, Magnus, *Estratificación de la sociedad hispanoamericana durante la Colonia*, Estocolmo, 1980.

Ots Capdequi, José María, *Manual de Historia del Derecho Español en la Indias y el Derecho propiamente Indiano*, Ed. Losada, Buenos Aires, 1945.

Platt, Tristán, 'Liberalismo y Etnocidio', in *Autodeterminación No. 9, Análisis histórico-político y teoría social*, La Paz, 1991.

Rivera, Silvia, 'La Raíz: colonizadores y colonizados', in Albó Xavier y

Barrios Raúl, Coordinadores. Violencias encubiertas en Bolivia. Cultura y Política, CIPCA ARUWIYIRI, La Paz, 1993.

Salinas Mariaca, Ramón (Comp.), *Las Constituciones de Bolivia.* Especialmente compiladas por el Dr. Ramón Salinas Mariaca, 1989.

Santa Cruz Schuhkrafft, Andrés de, 'Notas y apuntes para la historia de Don Andrés Santa Cruz. Génesis de la primera codificación republicana', in *Vida y Obra del Mariscal Andrés de Santa Cruz y Calahumana*, Edición de la Honorable Municipalidad de La Paz, La Paz, 1976–92.

Thomson, Sinclair, *Colonial Crisis, Community, and Andean Self Rule: Aymara Politics in the Age of Insurgency* (*Eighteenth-Century La Paz*), Ph.D., University of Wisconsin, Madison, 1996.

Wrestling with the Connotations of Chinese Minzu

Zhang Haiyang

While it is possible to talk about the forging of Chinese nationhood and contests over citizenship, ethnicity and history in China, it is necessary to ask first which China are we talking about. Given the fact that the map of China exists in more than one version (those put out by mainland China, by Taiwan and by other countries, such as the US and the UK, especially in relation to the status of Mongolia and Taiwan), we have reason to doubt that China as a physical entity conjures up the same picture in every mind, let alone what the abstraction 'China' stands for. Inevitably, this paper represents only the narrator's personal perception of the theme and his own view of the 'elephant'. This entitles the readers to ask why the elephant is perceived in this particular way.

I am from mainland China, born in 1955 in a village between Beijing, the capital city, and Tianjin, a port city 100 km to its south-east. In an era when 100 km can be covered in two hours or so, it is difficult for us to imagine how different it was only 25 years ago, specially in China.[1] I remember clearly that in 1971, if one wanted to go to Beijing by train, one had to produce a certificate

*The writer thanks Tony Saich for his recommendation, Gyanendra Pandey and Peter Geschiere for detailed advice on how to improve the first draft. He thanks all the participants of the SEPHIS Delhi Conference 1996 for their criticism, especially his discussants Sabyasachi Bhattacharya and Issa Shivji for their insightful comments.

[1] It has to be said that 100 km is a relative distance. At a time when the automobile was not available and public transport was controlled by the government or when people could not afford a ticket, it could mean a distance beyond reach. Anyway, I did not go to Beijing until 1972, when I was 17 years old. I went on a borrowed bicycle, and I had to pedal back the same day.

issued by the Revolutionary Committee of one's county to the station master, which could not be obtained unless one had a certificate from the Revolutionary Committee of one's commune, which in turn required one from the Revolutionary Committee of the production brigade (usually coinciding with a village on the north China plain). Otherwise, a ticket would be denied. A good reminder of proletarian dictatorship in China of the time. My family had been classified as that of a 'landlord' in the early 1950s, the time land reforms took place. Before 1961, my father was a teacher in a Muslim primary school, but after 1961, my father and the family were sent down to our village. Thus, though not a member of any minority ethnic group in China, I, as an offspring of an outcast class, grew up on the margins of the mainstream society. For this reason, I was deprived of middle school education that was nominally popularized during the Great Cultural Revolution (1966–76). I didn't enter university until 1978 when China began to 'reform and open doors'. My graduate education (1982–5) was completed in the Central Institute of Nationalities (the Central University of Nationalities since 1994), a higher learning institution for ethnic minorities in China. I experienced some cultural shock there at first but eventually become comfortable with its cultural relativism and have taught there since 1985. The theme of the SEPHIS Conference is interpreted in this paper based on my specific experiences and observations during this career.

THE CONCEPTION OF NATIONHOOD AND LINGUISTIC RELATIVITY

Though there are hundreds of books (and reference books) which deal with the subject, the definition of nation, states, nationalism and nationhood, and their relation to each other, the task remains difficult. This paper will skirt the task for two reasons: First, I have no new definition to add to the existing ones. Secondly, this paper aims to depict a process rather than delineate the product, although the diachronic change in connotation is a focus of my interest. With this in mind, we can save on time and start by quoting the definition of nation and state given in the *Webster Dictionary*.

Nation is 'a community of people composed of one or more nationalities and possessing a more or less defined territory and government' (Webster, 1961).

State is defined as 'a territorial division containing a body of people of one or more nationalities (ethnic groups) and usually characterized by relatively large size and independent status' (ibid.).

It is imperative to approach the concept of nation and state in the light of nationalism, which, according to the same *Webster*, is 'an attitude, feeling, or belief characterized by a sense of national consciousness, and exaltation of one nation above all others, and an emphasis on loyalty to and the promotion of the culture and interests of one nation as opposed to subordinate areas or other nations and super-national groups'.

Nationhood, as defined in the 1989 edition of *Webster* is 'the state or quality of having status as a separate and independent nation'.

Definitions in this field are subject to modifications, such as those explored by James Goodman's *Nationalism and Transnationalism*' (1996, pp. 9–32). However, so long as the basic ideas propounded by Jean-Jacques Rousseau (1712–78), John Gottfried von Herder (1744–1803), James Mill (1773–1836), Giuseppe Mazzini (1805–72), and their elucidation by authors like Carlton J.H. Hayes, Hans Kohn and so on, remain pertinent to us, we can assume that their basic definitions are workable, at least in the linguistic world that gives birth to them. A diachronic and cross-cultural comparison will show that this terminology which sounds so international and universal is neither international nor universal in origin. It has become so as a result of modern history in which the Western powers enforced their own interpretation and agenda throughout the world.

With basic concepts described in this way, we will apply them to the facts and see what further questions are raised. This is necessary because the world today is trapped in clashes of nation-states and nationalism or nationhood just as crucial, if not more crucial than the clash of civilizations perceived by Professor Hungtington. While both of these are 'imagined communities', nation-states have a much more direct influence on us. This is because in the modern world, a civilization cannot claim sovereignty, while the sovereignty of a nation 'is fully, flatly and evenly operative over each square centimetre of a legally demarcated territory' (Anderson, 1983, p. 26). Thus the concept of nation-state deserves continued scrutiny.

It is commonly known that the nation-state as an omnipotent actor in inter-national politics is a fairly modern one. It attained the current connotation (sovereignty, equality, independence, etc.)

in the late eighteenth century or even later (Gellner, 1982; Anderson, 1983; Hobsbawm, 1990; Parker, 1993, p. 210). Nonetheless, it has restructured the world since then and continues to do so. Since the First World War, the number of nations has more than tripled (Evans and Newnham, 1990, p. 261). Today, there are more than 180 nations in the world (Running Press, 1995, pp. 7–8). There are more candidates waiting, fighting, or ready to fight for it. Macroscopically, the UN is a club that denies entry to those who are not nations. Microscopically, we are born equal and free, until we apply for a passport, or a visa, or stand in front of a frontier post. Then we realize that we are neither, at least until we have obtained our nationality or nationhood.

This then is the nation; it is easier to know the 'what' and 'how' of its history than its 'why'. Some scholars have concluded that as a concept, it does not have coherent, explicit and empirical logic (Birch, 1989, pp. 1–7). For others it is an imagined community which arouses wonder and amazement (Anderson, 1983, pp. 14–16). But everywhere it provokes zeal and enjoys the esteem of even its opponents. It is politically correct to belittle a party, community, tribe or sectional group, but never a nation.

Impressed by the potential and overwhelmed by the recurrent discourse, many have become convinced that ever since the genesis of the world, nation is a being *per se* and dividing people along the line of nationhood is an expression of the law of nature. Thus, we find numerous efforts to trace a nation's history back to the prehistory of humankind. In China, some scholars have zealously traced the origin of *han minzu* (the Han Chinese as a 'nation') to as far back as 5,000 years ago and fiercely assailed all the speculations about 'Western origins' (Xu Jieshun, 1992, pp. 1–5). The same spirit works to produce arguments about Indians or Egyptians as nations from the most ancient times (cf. Choudhury, 1990).

One cannot deny that people probably did have group identities even in the Neolithic Age. The question is whether these identities can be described as 'nation'. What is of concern is the fact that, using 'nation' in this context, the authors cited above presuppose that China, Egypt and India each have people who are the physical descendants of their forebears who shared a national identity thousands of years ago, as they do now. This is an anachronism. But this anachronistic use of 'nation' is not unusual (see Wang Mingfu, 1983, pp. 2–3).

The Sapir-Whorf hypothesis on linguistic relativity suggests that people

> dissect nature along lines laid down by our native languages. The categories and types that we isolate from the world of phenomena we do not find there because they stare every observer in the face; on the contrary, the world is presented in a kaleidoscopic flux of impressions which has to be organized by our minds—and this means largely by the linguistic systems in our minds. We cut nature up, organize it into concepts, and ascribe significance as we do, largely because we are parties to an agreement to organize it in this way—an agreement that holds throughout our speech community and is codified in the patterns of our language. (Whorf, 1988, p. 270)

I agree with this proposition that 'language does have some effects on what we think about most readily and on how we think much of the time' (Crape, 1986, p. 123).

The discourse of 'thousands-of-years-old nations' provides a good case. It testifies that human thought is susceptible to the influence of the extant word as the carrier of concepts. Furthermore, one observes that besides the anachronism, there is dislocation of concepts in another way, pointing again to how thought succumbs to language. If one compares the connotation of the word 'nation' in different languages, one will see that the same concept in different languages attains a discrepancy from its original connotation. If one goes further by arranging similar connotations of a word and its usage into categories, and try to understand it in terms of its own historical experience, one may get some sense of the 'inner' contour of world civilizations as well as the obvious global power structure of nation-states. One ought to examine the case of '*minzu*' in China.

A SQUARE PEG IN A ROUND HOLE

All languages do not share equivalent terms for social cultural realities, including the concept of nation. Pamela Crossley has observed that, in contrast to the ethnology of the (former) Soviet Union, neither English nor Chinese scholarship has recourse to a definitive vocabulary distinguishing various types of cohesive identities from one another.

> Where English flounders attempting to distinguish 'nation-state' from 'nation', 'nation' from 'people', 'people' from 'nationality' or 'ethnic group', Russian offers the compact *natsiya* (where we might write 'nation-state'),

narod (where we might write 'people', 'nation', 'nationality'), *etnos*, (where we might write 'people', 'nationality', 'subnationality' 'ethnic group') and *etnicheskaya gruppa* (where we might write 'people', 'nationality', 'ethnic group'), among other precisions. In nearly all of these instances, Chinese is obliged to make do with *minzu*, and it is not surprising that both Chinese and Western academic writing on ethnicity attempts to orient itself with frequent allusions to the precisions of Russian terminology. (Crossley, 1990, p. 12)

To confirm the observation that Chinese as a language is particularly weak in defining nationhood, even the omnipotent *minzu* is not of Chinese origin. Crossley notes that it was borrowed from the Japanese neologism *minzoku*, strongly associated with a populist, nativist discourse in early modern Japan: and its usage in China has not been traced earlier than 1895 (ibid., pp. 19–20).

Before Crossley, at least three Chinese scholars had traced the earliest appearance of the word in Chinese writings to 1883 and 1874 (see Han and Li, 1985, p. 4; Peng, 1985, p. 9). In fact, Peng asserted it was introduced directly from English rather than via Japan (Peng, 1985, p. 9). If this is the case, it falls neatly in line with the fact that by 1880, 'China had been drawn into the "family of nations" much to her dismay and certainly not without reluctance' (Yu, 1994, p. 155). Or, in a macroscopic observation: 'Well before the end of the nineteenth century, it was obvious to Asian rulers and elites from India to Japan that the Western powers were in control. It was time to react against that dominance' with the weapon of nation and nationalism (Wang Gungwu, 1973, p. 85).

The English translation of the Chinese *minzu* is split as 'folk or common people' for *min* and 'consanguinity, or lineage' for *zu*. Literally, it means a community of ethnic folks with a common origin. Traditionally, a similar connotation was conveyed in such terms as *zu, bu, zhong, lei, luo min*, denoting lineage, tribe, genre, category, neighbourhood and folk respectively, or the derogatory *man, yi, rong, di*, i.e. the uncivilized in the four cardinal directions respectively (Han and Li, 1985, pp. 1–14). Before *min* and *zu* were joined together, these terms were preserved for those not civilized enough to be addressed as *hua'ren* (people of glory), *guoren* (people of the capital or state), or *hanren* (people of Han dynasty and later, those who followed the ways of that dynasty). In modern Chinese *minzu* means people of the same origin. That is the reason why it is frequently attached to 'family'. It is a Chinese cliché to refer to

China as a *minzu da jiating* (the big family of ethnic groups). The term has no connotation whatsoever of popular sovereignty.

However, the meaning of *minzu* has not been rendered always in one way. It has varied with time, circumstance, and the agents of its coinage and circulation. In the case of China, the later nineteenth century was an important time. The agents were the Chinese elite interacting with the Western powers. The circumstance was that the Sinocentric elite were ruled by the culturally peripheral Manchu, who in turn were bullied by the far more peripheral Western powers. This brought an unbearable sense of humiliation to the elite who considered their country (*guojia*, state and family, or country and hometown) as the centre of civilization. Therefore, ever since the Taiping Heavenly Kingdom Revolution (1851–64), an overwhelming sentiment among the dissident elite was that the Manchu were illegitimate rulers, for they had failed to ward off the Western powers preying upon the civilized Central Country. Against this background, the newly borrowed word *minzu* immediately attained a double connotation. Internally, it refers to the Han Chinese—all those who were once conquered by the Manchu from the north-east, including all ethnic groups except the Manchu and its allies—as a *minzu*, aiming at toppling the corrupt Manchu regime and establishing self-government. Externally, it denotes China and Chinese (including the Manchu) as a *minzu*, aiming at reinstating the proper world order, and thus its own central position 'under-heaven'.

It is this inherited ambiguity—both containing positive or sacred values—that leads to an academic conundrum later in China. It has become the focus of a chronic, even hopeless debate over the definition of *minzu*. (Wu Wenzao, 1990, pp. 19–36; Pan Guangdan, 1995 and *Minzu Yanjiu* as a bimonthly official journal of ethnic studies since 1983, especially in 1986.) Professor Li Yifu has observed it involves five concepts, and he prescribed six alternatives to modify its use (Li, 1986, pp. 13–17). But relating them to the Chinese linguistic context, none sound feasible. Thus Crossley observes: 'Chinese as yet has no technical term for ethnos, or for nation, and thus *minzu* plays many contradictory roles in academic and popular writing, a fact frequently lamented by spokesmen in the field' (Crossley, 1990, p. 20).

The fact that the Chinese did not have the word *minzu* in their vocabulary until their encounter with the Western powers in the last century, and the fact that the single word *minzu* lumps together conflicting concepts, are salutary reminders of a different history. Before being engaged with the Western powers we should remember that China was something different from a nation-state and also that it never endorsed the concept. It is imperative for a nation to recognize its equals. China did not reach this perception until the late nineteenth century. Before that, it lumped together non-Chinese of all sorts as barbarians or 'foreign devils'. Westerners to the Chinese were 'big noses', and Dutchmen, 'red bearded devils', reflecting as one author has put it 'a great ignorance and unreality about the world' (Taylor, 1991, p. 23). While the modern 'nation' is new everywhere, certain particularities of the Chinese past need to be remembered.

First the different relevance of the traditional *chao* (dynasty) and the state (*guo*). In traditional Chinese, *chao* is something relevant to time while *guo* is relevant to space. In fact, the Sinitic ideograph of *guo* is a territory defended by a weapon and circled by a wall. It denotes a feuding power, and especially its capital. The feudal state is relative to its peers but subject to the same sovereignty of the overlord, the emperor as son of heaven. It is recorded in ancient Chinese classics that in the time of the Xia Dynasty (twenty-first to sixteenth century BC), there were 10,000 states; in the Shang Dynasty (sixteenth to eleventh century BC), there were 3,000; while in the Zhou Dynasty (eleventh to eight century BC), less than 1,000. The relationship between 1 and 1,000 or more explains why in ancient China, those who had the sovereignty over other states always referred to themselves as the *chao* and never a *guo* (Xu Xinjian, 1992, p. 23). Time, with its cycles of date, month, season, year, etc., was linked with heaven, giving the emperor, as son of heaven, his ultimate mandate or legitimacy.

Second, the particular novelty of national history to Chinese historians. Ying-Shih Yu once observed that 'the conception of "national history" in its current Western usage was wholly unfamiliar to Chinese historians before the 20th century. This was primarily because there was no notion of "nation" in traditional Chinese political parlance' (Yu, 1994, p. 154). 'Even after the Treaty of Nanking in 1842, many high-ranking Chinese officials at the Imperial court still insisted that there could be no more that two or three "nations" in the Western World.' In 1872, James Legge, a great translator of Chinese classics, criticized China's officials and people for their failure to 'realize that China is only one of many independent nations in the world'. It was not until 1864, when W.A.P. Martin completed his Chinese translation of Henry Wheaton's *Elements of International Law*, that the Chinese Foreign Office (*Tsungli Yamen*) formally acknowledged the fact that 'nowadays there are many nations outside China' (ibid.).

Third the chronic blending of foreign affairs with ethnic affairs. Before the contact with Western powers, China perceived itself as the world. 'Under-the-heaven' (*tianxia*) was the Sinocentric symbolic universe at the time. As a conceptual world order, it regarded China as the centre of civilization surrounded by countries and peoples who were not only culturally inferior but also actively sought to be 'transformed' into civilization. This was encouraged at the time, like a layman's interest in the church is welcomed by the church today. As the sole sovereignty under the heaven, dynastic China made no distinction between foreign affairs and ethnic affairs. Dealing with people other than those of China proper was always considered a part of internal affairs, just as an imperial court dealing with its vassal states (ibid., p. 156). Therefore, the basic bureaucratic framework of six ministries (Official, Household, Protocol, Defence, Punishment and Industry) since the Qin Dynasty (221–207 BC) represented nothing as foreign. Usually the Ministry of Protocol, in charge of the ceremonial and educational affairs, was responsible for receiving tributary envoys from afar, and they needed instruction and training before being ushered into the court. The branch in the Ministry of Protocol dedicated to this function was entitled the Department of Guest-Hosting (*zhu ke si*, in the Qin Dynasty), the Department of Grandeur Display (*hong lu si*, from Han to Song: 206 BC–1279 AD), the Office of Administration Decree (*xuan zheng yuan*, in Yuan, 1271–1368), and the Office of Vassal State Administration (*li fan yuan*, in Qing, 1644–1911) (Bai, 1989, pp. 31–141).[2]

In brief, ethnic and foreign affairs were lumped together before 1861 and co-managed by the Ministry of Protocol and the Office of Vassal States. The division of responsibility was as follows: with Beijing the capital as the centre, the Ministry of Protocol was responsible for those from the south and east by the water route, and the Office of Vassal States for those from the west and north by land (ibid., p. 134). After 1861, the imperial court readjusted its

[2] The Ming Dynasty (1368–1644) between the two ethnic dynasties, the Yuan and the Qing, assumed the official system of the Song (960–1279).

edifice according to the situation (its second failure in the Second Opium War 1859–60). Foreign affairs were separated from ethnic affairs and transferred to a new institution. But the title of the new institution reflected the old conception. It was addressed as 'Overall Administration of Affairs of All the States' (*zongli geguo shiwu yamen*), much like the UN Security Council. It was not until 1901, under the 'threat and pressure of imperialist countries', that the title of *Zongli Yamen* was changed to Ministry of Foreign Affairs. It was from then on that China had its seventh administrative ministry, and this was positioned as heading the other six ministries (Zhang, 1984, p. 7).[3] The new establishment signified the end of the traditional system. If, as Gertjan Dijkink has it, foreign policy is 'a "boundary-producing" phenomenon', and 'is sometimes the only, or the most, explicit indicator of the prevailing visions of a country, then the establishment of the Ministry of Foreign Affairs is really the hallmark of a nation-state which China did not achieve until the beginning of this century' (Dijkink, 1996, pp. 5, 142).

All these facts remind us that nation as a concept is subject to the reign of cultural and linguistic relativity, and that it does not have a universal presence. This presence was shaped by forces of international political economy sustained by a universally effective technology first developed in the northern Atlantic region. China, before it was affected through the expansion of Western powers, was in a different symbolic universe that might be describe as culture-sensitive but *minzu*blind. 'In Confucian historiography, a non-Chinese dynasty would be regarded as being in possession of the Mandate of Heaven if it successfully ruled a unified China according to the standards of Chinese culture' (Yu, 1994, p. 156). This notion is well reflected in a widely quoted saying by Mencius: 'Shun (a legendary founder of the Xia Dynasty in 2100 BC HY) was an Eastern Barbarian and King Wen (founder of the Zhou Dynasty, 1100 BC–710 BC HY) was a Western Barbarian. Yet when they had their way in the central kingdoms, their actions matched like the two halves of a tally-stick. The standards of the two sages, one earlier and one later, were identical' (cited in Yu, 1994). In short,

[3] It is interesting to note the fact that, with seven ministers (instead of six or eight) in the Court, the arrangement of a balanced pattern with the emperor as the central figure became impossible.

the traditional Chinese *tianxia* was defined in cultural rather than in ethnic or national terms (see Yu, 1994, p. 156). Whoever practices the Chinese way can rule China.[4]

As a result, people speaking virtually different languages compete for the authenticity of their Chineseness. As for the unity of the physical Chinese nation, especially the Han Chinese, one could borrow a succinct comment from David E. Apter and Tony Saich in their analysis of the revolutionary discourse of the Communist Party of China: 'everything before the Opium Wars (1839–1942) is prehistory' (Apter and Saich, 1994, pp. 92–5).

THE CHINESE NATION AND FOREIGN POWERS 1911–1949

The separation of foreign and ethnic affairs is an indicator that China reluctantly put on the straitjacket of a nation-state at the beginning of this century. This was deeply interwoven with the following factors: (a) the presence of powerful foreign nations, including Japan; (b) their breach of the sovereignty and expropriation of territories of the Central Country, including the forced concession of Hong Kong and Taiwan.

It is ironic that the Manchu regime could not take advantage of the nationalism ignited in China by the foreign powers. In 1911, at the high tide of the Chinese nationalist movement, it was overthrown. The leading body of the movement that toppled the Qing Dynasty was *Tong Meng Hui* (Chinese Revolutionary League), the corporate founder of the Republic of China in 1912 and the predecessor of the Nationalist Party (KMT). Headed by Dr Sun Yat-sen, an overseas Chinese from Guangdong, the incubating province of the Taiping Revolution, *Tong Meng Hui* was composed of Chinese nationalists who proclaimed themselves as the Han Chinese. Its programme consisted of four points: 'To expel the Northern barbarians (*quzhu dalu*); to restore the Chinese reign (*huifu zhonghua*); to establish a nation-state (*jianli min'guo*) and to equalize

[4] Because the history of China is so long, it is often assumed that there has always been a unified group of Chinese people. My own view is that while the ideal of a higher civilization has always been there, the carriers of the ideal have always been a mixture and have changed over time.

the land ownership (*pingjun diquan*)' (Hu, 1981, p. 127). It is remarkable that the different connotations of *minzu* (for Chinese as a nation, and for the Han as an ethnos) were reflected in the programme. In fact, the ultimate aim of the programme was to restore the past glory of China against the encroachment of foreign powers. The Manchu had to be driven out of power, not because they were Manchu, but because they had lost the mandate of heaven as indicated by their failure in warding off the foreign powers. The programme that led to the 1911 Revolution also laid the foundation for the Republic of China in the next four decades, except for the replacement of barbarians (*-dalu)* with foreign powers (*lieqiang*). The whole period of KMT rule in mainland China was charged with the struggle for restoring the 'national' pride of the country against the foreign powers, especially against the aggressive Japanese.

As soon as the Manchu regime was overthrown, the new Republic of China proclaimed itself a multi-*minzu*, instead of a Han one, thus confirming the observation that 'minority' is the by-product of nationalism in a new nation (Wang Gungwu, 1973, pp. 85–6). The new discourse was *wuzu gonghe* (the republic of five ethnicities, i.e. the Han, Manchu, Mongol, Muslim Hui and Tibetan). All were components of the Chinese nation (*zhonghua minzu*). The common adversary of the Chinese nation were the foreign powers trying to partition China. It was against this background that a new version of Chinese national identity evolved.

Various discourses, ranging from social Darwinism, fascism and anarchism to communism, were advocated for national salvation and integration. The most conspicuous among them was the racial nationalism put forward by Chiang Kai-shek, which emphasized the common ancestry of all the Chinese, and it categorized the minority ethnic groups as sub-lineages of the Han (see Huang Guangxue, 1993, vol. 1, pp. 273–4) The 'racial' connotations of the discourses were so obvious that, in retrospect, Franc Dikotter confers various titles to the years between 1915–49, including that of 'race as nation', 'racial nationalism', 'race as species' and 'race as seed' (Dikotter, 1992, pp. 97, 123, 164, etc.). What he fails to mention is the fact that this racial rhetoric was either an immediate borrowing from the West or a backlash to it. In comparison, Jay Taylor's observation sounds more relevant: 'China, in the first decades of the twentieth century, had endured civil war, economic collapse, and piecemeal imperialist exploitation, culminating in the Japanese effort to dominate all of China. The banner of Chinese nationalism went to the strongest military movement and the leader who seemed most patriotic' (Taylor, 1991, p. 44).

The contribution of foreign powers to the formulation of Chinese nationalism was substantial. Between 1903 and 1937, *minzu* became the buzzword of Chinese intellectual and political discourse. The frequency of *minzu* in public use was very high. In a number of articles, Pan Guangdan, a renowned sociologist, vehemently attacked the abuse of the term, and he wrote a series of articles to clarify the difference between ethnos, nation, state, and race, all being called *minzu* (see Pan, 1995, pp. 1–130). So did Wu Wenzao, writing in 1926 (Wu, 1990, pp. 1–36). In the end, the Japanese invasion rendered more power to the political parlance that regarded *minzu* as a common blood lineage; and it was the anti-Japanese war between 1937 and 1945 that gave shape to the integration of the Chinese nation.

The anti-Japanese war was the first that China had ever won against foreign encroachers over the hundred years since 1840. It is here that one should rein in the proposition of linguistic relativity and emphasize the effect of international political economy on the universal popularity of nationalism. In a world that denies all but the sovereignty of a nation-state, it is natural that nationalism finds itself welcome everywhere. It can even override the gaps between social systems. As Jay Taylor commented in his macroscopic comparison between China and India in the decades after the Second World War:

> A communist regime and a democratic government each gave higher priority to nationalistic and ideological objectives than to raising consumption and living standards. . . . Both sought to restore their pride and sense of greatness by creating an economic base for national power that would not only predominate in its region, but would also be a major, independent actor on the world stage. (Taylor, 1991, p. 97)

This is insightful but has an obvious lacuna. It neglects the international context of the cold war, the two ideological blocs as an overall framework after the Second World War. It also overlooks the heavy Soviet influence over the early People's Republic of China (PRC), especially in the fields of education, academics and ideology.

SOVIET THEORY AND CHINESE PRACTICE: 1949–78

The triumph of the CPC (Communist Party of China) in China and the founding of the People's Republic of China in 1949 ushered in a new period of Chinese nationhood. However, as Taylor notes, 'the new social, economic and political structures created by the Communist Party were even more foreign and revolutionary in China than they had been in European Russia' (Taylor, 1991, p. 47). A vigorous campaign for socialist transformation followed immediately.

> The physical liquidation of hundreds of thousands, if not over a million landlords, and assignment of the remainder to a new, inverted, hereditary class order was as sweeping in its effect as Qin Shi Huang's elimination of the feudal system in the third century BC. The abolition of private land ownership, which had existed for over 2,000 years, and the collectivization of agriculture and division of harvest and income within a village on the basis of hours worked were reforms unprecedented in scope and nature. The mass purging of intellectuals, and the creation of a whole new value system had also not been attempted for over 2,000 years'. (ibid.)

Consequently, the PRC was transformed into a socialist nation-state, as well as a pawn of the communist bloc. This partially obliged it to enter into the Korean War in the 1950s and the Vietnam War in the mid-1960s to early 1970s, in addition to giving lavish support to other anti-imperial movements around the world.

What is of interests is the impact of this drastic social change on the hundreds of millions of Chinese as individuals, many of them in minority ethnic groups. In this context, one can take *minzu* as ethnicity (such as minority ethnic groups) and *minzu* as citizenship (such as *zhonghua minzu*, the Chinese nation) as two foci of attention. For *minzu* as internal minority ethnic groups (*shaoshu minzu*), the PRC took a circuitous route. In the 1950s, Mao and the CPC, 'in keeping with Marx, believed that ethnic distinctions would disappear when class distinctions were eliminated. Thus nationality characteristics, including religion, could be tolerated until the true communist stage emerged.' During the 1960s and 1970s, 'the CPC radicals who emphasized a class-struggle approach to integration of the minorities actively pushed abolition of minority customs and special privileges, attacked the special autonomous area system, and insisted on immediate adoption of the Han Chinese communist model of economic and social organization'. Since 1978, there has been 'a backlash in China to some of the concessions given to the minorities, not only on special educational and job opportunities, but also in their exclusion from the country's rigorous birth-control restrictions' (Taylor, 1991, pp. 197–8).

It is important to note the context of these changing positions, including the ideational effects behind the turn around and the change of power structures reflected in it. The starting point is the fact that in the early 1950s, the CPC not only tolerated the ethnic diversities but also encouraged their visibility through a series of major political manoeuvres. They were:

— Sending Governmental Delegations to Visit the Minority Nationalities (1950–2), repenting for all the wrong doings on behalf of the Han (read government);
— Carrying-out Official Ethnic Identification (mainly between 1950–3); and sanctioning their eligibility for all the affirmative actions;
— Carrying-out a General Survey on the Social History of Minority Nationalities (1956–64), intended as a benchmark to demonstrate the social progress made since the founding of the PRC;
— Designing (creating) ethnic writings (1951–80s), intending to first use them to enhance the development and their automatic disuse once communism comes true.
— Founding Colleges of Nationalities (1950–4), aimed at training ethnic officials and converting the ethnic nobility to work in the ethnic area with the government (see Huang Guangxue, 1993, vol. 1, pp. 48–123; vol. 2, pp. 302–8; Jiang Ping, 1994, pp. 51–2).

It is not convincing to condemn all these manoeuvres as measures of cultural assimilation. It is an indisputable fact that most of them obviously construct divergent ethnic identities rather than otherwise. In fact, it is highly doubtful whether the communist leaders had as clear a concept of the Han in their mind as many Western scholars seem to, though the concept of China is never absent. Communism has its own logic that requires understanding. In relation to the international context, we conclude that the manoeuvres were the result of a combination of conceptual mislocation (or anachronism), communist idealism and the traditional condescension of the Chinese rulers.

By conceptual mislocation, I refer to the CPC's misreading of Leninist revolutionary strategy contrived in reference to the situation in Europe of the early twentieth century. The strategy regards nationalism as a positive force for fighting imperialism, thus it should be encouraged rather than curbed. Founded in Shanghai (1921), with most founders from central and south China and overwhelmed by the discourse of saving China with the help of Leninist theory, the young CPC accepted the theory without much awareness of the multi-ethnic situation in China. This was quite in accordance with the spirit of communism, which at least ideally should be *minzu*-blind. Until 1931, the CPC Soviet Republic in Jiangxi Province still carried the stipulation in its Constitution: 'Recognize that the minority nations (*shaoshu minzu*) have their right of self-resolution, to the extent that each of them has the right to separate from China and establish its own independent nation-state (*guojia*)' (Huang, 1993, vol. 1, p. 28). This conviction did not shatter until the 10,000 km Long March between 1934–6.

The Long March must have been a very good instructor of China's cultural geography to its participants. Most of its route was mountainous along the demarcation line between the core area (China proper) and the peripheral (ethnic) areas. How much the CPC owed to this ethnic mosaic it is difficult to tell. But it is un-questionable that the cultural barriers, as well as the physical barrier, frustrated the KMT's endeavour to eliminate the communists. After the Long March, the CPC found its new base in Yanan, a place much closer than its previous Jiangxi-Hunan base to the Mongols to the north, Tibetans to the south-west and compact Muslims communities to the west. This location resulted in *The Issue of Hui Nationality* (*Hui Hui Minzu Wenti*), a CPC monograph on ethnic issues.[5] It was in Yanan that the CPC attained its identity in its policy toward minority ethnic groups, namely the ethnic autonomous system, which resembles neither its former proclamation nor the Soviet Republics. But to keep in line with the Communist Bloc, the anachronistic Leninist strategy and Stalinist conception of *minzu* remained intact, as reflected in the CPC's later discourse. This discrepancy between theory and practice contributed to the confusion in China's political debates.

By communist optimism, I mean the fact that in the early 1950s, the Communist Bloc was full of optimism that in less than 30 years, it would triumph in the world, and nations would become

[5] The book was published in the early 1940s and has been reprinted at least four times. The latest printing was in 1980.

international. Therefore, it seemed they could afford to sanction the existence of diverse ethnic groups (nationalities at the time), for they would self-destruct later. Communist philosophy (dialectical materialism and historical materialism) believes in no primordial identities. This is shown in the Marxist perception of human nature as a complex whole of social relations, meaning that a good social system will make human nature better. It was also reflected in the CPC's practice, especially in the General Survey on the Social History of Minority Nationalities, 1956–64 (*zhongguo shaoshu minzu shehui lishi diaocha*). In fact, the dictum by Mao Zedong for this survey was 'to rescue the backward' (*qiangjiu luohou*), meaning to record and classify the backward social forms so as to preserve them in the museum or library before they were transformed by social progress (see Liu Geping, 1994, p. 51). Sure enough, in less than two years, the Great Leap Forward came with the slogan of 'surpassing the UK and catching up with the US', with a speed of 'a day equals to twenty years'.

By traditional condescension, I mean that it was routine for powerful and ambitious rulers in China to take pride in manifesting the cultural diversities in their domain. As already noted, from the Han to the Ming Dynasties, the imperial department for ethnic and foreign affairs were called *hong lu si*, the department of grandeur display. The CPC in the 1950s was also powerful and ambitious. Thus it could accommodate the cultural diversity. In fact, when the nationwide ethnic identification started in the early 1950s, the yardstick was Stalin's 'four commons' (common territory, common language, common economy and common psychological make-up demonstrated in common culture). This is essentially a definition of 'nation'. Given the historical facts and the CPC's regional autonomy (rather than *minzu* republics) as a political resolution of its *minzu* question, China needed to have a definition of its own for *minzu*. This must be have done in practice, otherwise China would not be China today. But no verbal modification of Stalin's definition of *minzu* was ever voiced. Officially, China does not have its own definition for *minzu* until today. In fact, Mao Zedong personally took a cynical attitude in this matter. He said in 1953: 'Scientific analysis is another matter. Politically, we needn't distinguish nationality (*minzu*), narod (*buzu*) or tribe (*buluo*)' (ibid., p. 39).

As a result, the 5 *minzu* in the Republic of China before 1949 were eventually recognized as 56 in the People's Republic of China, with numerous groups still trying to gain recognition. Along with this progress, *minzu* attained a special connotation as minority ethnic groups (*shaoshu minzu*) in mandarin Chinese, such as *minzu* policy, *minzu* work, *minzu* population, etc. As for the turnaround in the CPC's policy towards the ethnic minorities, my observation is that it became radical in the 1960s and 1970s, because communism suffered frustrations at home and abroad, resulting in impatience and the attempted assimilation. Since 1978, the policy softened again, because the Party became pragmatic in its sense of mission.

In addition to the ethnic issue, the impact of *minzu* as citizenship in the Chinese nation was also impressive, especially its impact on the peasantry. According to Taylor, during Mao's life (till 1976), all of China's rural population (about 85 per cent of the total population) were denied the right to decide how to organize themselves economically and were denied the last resort of the poor—to pick up and move. The former landlords, rich peasants, and their descendants formed an 'outcast' group at the bottom rung of this economic and social order. In the severe famine of 1960–2, caused by the 1958 Great Leap Forward's disruption of agriculture, the mortality was an astonishing figure of 12 to 24 million.

Peasants had only three ways to leave the village or the locality in which they were born. First, through marriage, in which case the woman usually moved to the village of her husband. Second, by passing the university entrance exam, at which only 3 per cent of the college-age group nationwide and probably about 1 per cent in rural areas succeeded. Or, third, by joining the army (Taylor, 1991, pp. 2, 56–7, 118, 177). It is to this macroscopic nationwide picture that I wish to add some of my personal experiences of the pre-1978 village life that impressed me most.

Among ordinary peasant households, being organized into people's communes and having communized their household stock and even kitchen utensils since 1958, most of them were trapped in the three-year famine between 1960–2. In the most grievous year, 1960, the daily quota of grain in my area was 125 gm per head, not to mention the infringement by the hungry local cadres. As a result, 30 out of the 500 villagers in my village died in that first winter. At the time there were barely enough strong hands to carry the dead out of the village. An indicator of the severity of that time was that few babies were born in those three years in the whole village, except for one or two to the village cadres, which constituted solid evidence of corruption. 'Man had no sperms and woman had no menstrual flow' was the folk knowledge of the time. After the ordeal, household consumption was allowed to resume and most of the households managed to subsist, though expansion was out of the question. Peasants were still bound to production teams attached to a production brigade. The brigade based in the natural village was in charge of every aspect of the villagers' social life. In the poorest area, it was even responsible for equipping its villagers with certificate letters for begging. It was this humiliating situation that was the justification for the spontaneous restructuring of the rural economy pioneered by the peasants in Anhui and Sichuan around the time of the death of Mao Zedong in 1976.

The households of the outcast class (the class-enemies), became targets of all sorts of accusations under the trammels of class struggle since the mid-1950s. In the years of famine, they were denied food and medical relief. Their children were largely denied middle school education, army conscription and the occasional urban job recruitment. During the notorious Great Proletarian Cultural Revolution, household sacking, concentration camps and physicalabuse were commonplace to them. No national law except the ever changeable CPC's policy was sacrosanct. Even Liu Shaoqi, President of the PRC, did not survive. Under the circumstances, no one dared to marry a young male from the enemy class. Marriages of many young males were virtually suspended for more than ten years until 1978 (see also Friedman, 1994, p. 78). The number of these people and their trauma in being enforced into involuntary celibacy in their youth deserves study.

The revolution did not change the patriarchal nature of Chinese society. Class status was inherited through the father, almost through the blood—simply in terms of how the paternal household was classified.[6] In addition to the regular 'enemies' (around 5 per cent of the total households), each political movement marginalized some others to the untouchable class under various labels (see Friedman, 1994, pp. 75–6).

All such discrimination, including the previous class identification and land-reform in the early 1950s, was enforced by the state in

[6] No concepts are more subjective than the rich and the poor, especially in such an unknown country as China in the early 1950s, when transportation and communication in most areas was still minimal. Therefore, the class identification in China was extremely arbitrary.

the name of nationhood and communist discourse. It is difficult to understand why people should have accepted these irrationalities, and how. Nationalism it seems, can easily arouse the imagination of many. The rhetoric which formulated people's perception of the world during the 1960s and early 1970s may help when one seeks an explanation:

— China, the only sizable socialist country in the world was surrounded by US imperialism, Soviet revisionism and the Indian reactionaries;
— Two-thirds of the world's population were struggling in deep water and hot fire for an early emancipation from socialism to communism;
— China was internally threatened by class enemies (less than 10 per cent of the population) composed of the overthrown landlords, former rich peasants, reactionaries, bad elements and the rightists.

Therefore, to safeguard the socialist national security, it was necessary to carry out a consistent class struggle under the leadership of the CPC.

ETHNIC DIVERSITY AND CHINESE IDENTITY: 1980–PRESENT

'Nation-ness is the most universally legitimate value in the political life of our time' (Anderson, 1983, p. 12). In such a time no country can afford to neglect nation-building. PRC's official contact with USA in 1972 confirmed this. It signalled a new era of 'nationalism', overriding other ideologies and systems. However, the ultra-leftist policy in China was to survive for another six years. In late 1978, two years after Mao's death, the reform and open-door policy was inaugurated. In less than three months, the socialist Chinese army briefly manoeuvred against socialist Vietnam which in turn was at war with socialist Khmer Rouge. 'These wars are of world-historical importance because they are the first to occur between regimes whose independence and revolutionary credentials are undeniable, and because none of the belligerents has made more than the most perfunctory attempts to justify the bloodshed in terms of a recognizable Marxist theoretical perspective' (Anderson, 1983, p. 11).

It was after 1978 that nationalism found wider, and greater, entry into the public media. Traditional values embedded in ancient books, folklore, literature and other forms were rehabilitated and promoted. The new rhetoric was to bring out all the positive elements to build the 'four modernizations' (agriculture, industry, science and technology, and national defence) of China. 'Gone are the hoary ideas of class struggle, the continuing revolution, and the goal of an egalitarian society. Improving one's ideological outlook today means essentially to work hard, be honest and unselfish' (Taylor, 1991, p. 241). In any sense, this was a drastic shift of episteme.

As it happened, this reorientation was easy for the CPC. It meant in effect a recovery of the symbolic resources of China. Compared with many other third world countries, CPC was comfortably placed in this respect. 'China embodies the fundamental element of nationalism in its original, tribal, and nation-state form—ethnic homogeneity and historical continuity' (Taylor, 1991, p. 212). This is a matter of interpretation. But Chinese literature has a higher degree of cultural continuation which contains rich resources for the discourse of nation-building. Moreover, the Chinese are not resistant to change with time and circumstance because they have lived in a conceptual world of universality. 'The Chinese do not have to work at being Chinese,' Pye has suggested, and, thus, 'no specific traditions are seen as essential to maintain their identity.' Consequently, they have been able to accept the 'wholesale abandonment of old customs without any sense of being less Chinese because of it' (ibid., p. 48).

Indeed, before knowing the industrialized West, the Chinese did not have to work at being Chinese because China was conceived as the world. Today the US identifies itself with trade balance, global safety, intellectural property and human rights, mostly not in the name of Americanism. It does not even identify itself in e-mail addresses. The same was true for China until the nineteenth century. After that, it became too difficult to resist transformation.

Official attempts to demonstrate the long and continuous 'national' unity has been able to make use of several factors—some of which of course emerged long before the founding of the PRC, or the ROC. Among these are the interlocking maps of different regions of China, which work in favour of centralism. The map of Gains Province is in the shape of a dumb-bell stretching from the central Shaanxi province all the way to the gates of Xinjiang Uygure and Tibet. Only half of China's 3.4 million Tibetans live in the Tibet Autonomous Region. The map of Anhui Province, again, straddles three major rivers (the old Yellow River route, the Huai and the Yangtze down south) and bridges the humid south and arid north. (See Hsieh and Hsieh, 1995, for further examples.)

Other factors that the State can draw upon are the strong Civil Service tradition; the unified writing system; the co-structure of family and state, built on the Confucian assumption that a good ruler should be a good patriarch who can hold his family (household) together in harmony; and the continuous lineages of particular families, such as that of Confucius in Qufu which can trace its roots back for more than 2,200 years.

The endowments are rich indeed. But they are not necessarily endowed for Chinese nation-building. They become so by interpretation, and the interpretation is subject to circumstances. Without reference to the current international political framework, the same factors can be explained as conducive to a hierarchy established 'under heaven'. On the other hand, even interpreted as such, PRC has its own problems for accommodating the cultural diversity in a single national identity against the background of social modernity and the bizzare conglomeration of its own components. Some of these are:

— The challenge of social modernity. Tempered by its bitter experiences in modern history, China's pursuit of modernization has been frenzied since the late eighteenth century. It is only over the last two decades that its endeavour has become more successful. But the success comes not without its problems. While modernization and market economy promote uniformity at the expense of the inherent cultural diversity, the resultant social modernity also erodes authority and generates an awareness of cultural identity (see Gellner, 1983).

— Divergent ethnicity. PRC has officially identified 55 minority ethnic groups since the 1950s. The total ethnic population in China is about 100 million and amounts to nearly 10 per cent of the national population (Chen, 1992, pp. 1662–3).[7] Amid the

[7] According to the official statistics, the ethnic population in China in 1990 was 91,200,000 amounting to 8.04 per cent of the national population. Taking into consideration the effects of affirmative action, we are confident that ethnic population is increasing faster and could have well surpassed 10 per cent of the national population. A careful comparison between the 1982 and 1990 nationwide census would corroborate this estimate.

one billion strong Han Chinese, the Hakka, Tanka, Fulo, Minnan, Canton each has a distinct dialect (or language) and strong sense of community overlapping with regional identity. As the percentage of ethnic population is ever increasing, it is time to speculate on the impact of the ethnic population on China in the near future.

— Parochialism. Owing to their very long history, many provinces and autonomous regions in China have their record of housing parochial kingdoms or local governments (see Taylor, 1991, p. 199; Moser, 1985, Honig, 1992). This is conducive to regional identity. Moreover, traditional Chinese culture gives positive value to one's identity with his or her birth place (*ji guan*). The linguistic groups are another alignment of regional identity.

— The reversion of Hong Kong. A policy of 'one country, two systems' was formulated for Hong Kong's reversion to China in 1997. When the policy took effect, China became the only nation-state that harbours both capitalism and socialism within one regime. While ideology and the social system are no longer burning issues of confrontation, the political and economic discordance will no doubt be a sensitive point for identity issues.

Chinese television news highlights the visit to Peking of illustrious foreign leaders and big events like the hosting of Asian Games and the World Women's Summit. The message to the audience is that China has attained a globally respectable and strong position. The strategy lumps the Party, the State and the Nation together. The challenge to this endeavour is the ordinary person's ever dwindling interest in politics, especially after 1989. More and more Chinese have increasingly become deeply cynical about politics.

The CPC is also quietly shifting from the Leninist view that endorses the minority nationalities' right of self-determination to the current Western understanding of ethnic relations as an expression of domestic cultural variation. One month before the Fourth Women's Summit in September 1995, the English translation of the 'State Commission of Nationality Affairs' was changed into the 'State Commission of Ethnic Affairs', while the Chinese form remained the same as before. The English translation of *minzu teenage*, title of an authoritative journal for the CPC's ethnic work aiming at promoting national solidarity, has also been changed in the same way from the original *Unity of Nationalities* into the current *Ethnic Unity*. This global replacement offers another example demonstrating the naiveté of the Chinese language to the concept of *minzu*.

The diachronic manipulation of history is even more explicit. China has a long tradition of compiling local gazetteers (*xiu fangzhi*). Each administrative unit ranging from county to province, compiles its diachronic, authentic encyclopaedic and authoritative record of the things in the locality. Traditionally, this was a symbol of dynastic prosperity. Since the early 1980s the dozens of provinces and autonomous regions of China, the hundreds of regular and autonomous prefectures, and thousands of regular and autonomous counties, have been 'updating' their local gazetteers. The object is to establish that each of these territories was part of one China from time immemorial.

Common ancestorship is also exploited as a cohesive factor. In Chinese culture, ancestors constitute the common denominator or fountainhead of both *guojia* (state or government) and *minzu* (nation or ethnic group, or both). Currently, this exploitation is reflected in the official discourse of *yan huang zi sun* (offspring of Emperors Yan and Huang), which refers all the Chinese, the nationals and on the mainland all those overseas, to the common ancestorship of two legendary emperors who conceivably lived 4,000 years ago, at least hundreds of years earlier than Yu the Great, founder of the legendary first dynasty. Since the 1911 revolution, it has been common for Chinese leaders (of both KMT and CPC) to pay tributes to the mausoleum of these two imagined progenitors (see Zhang Qizhi et al., 1993, pp. 6–8) A recent inside cover announcement in *New China Digest* (*xinhua wenzhai*), No. 9, 1995, over Jiang Zemin and Li Peng's names informs us that the donation to the Foundation of Yellow Emperor has amounted to 250 million RMB (about US $ 30 million). Currently, the foremost advocate of this discourse in academic circles seems to be Xu Jieshun. His *Development History of the Han Nationality* (1992), attaches the highest value to a common blood tie (*tongbao, or tongzu tongzong*) for the unification and longevity of China (Xu, 1992, pp. 437–40, 584–5). Yet this discourse has the destructive effect of alienating the ethnic minorities in China, especially those of the Altaic and Indo-European linguistic groups.

A new discourse was formulated by the work of a more famous and sophisticated figure, Fei Xiaotong, in the late 1980s. Fei's key 'Plurality and Unity in the Configuration of Chinese Nation' (1989) admits the heterogeneity of Chinese culture and attributes this to the plural ethnogenesis of the Chinese nation in the history of early Homo sapiens (ibid., pp. 3–6). Since the Qin Dynasty (221–207 BC), the regional unification, economic symbiosis and interaction of historical events eventually gave rise to an overarching Chineseness which was a thing-in-itself (*zizai de shiti*, entity by nature). This thing-in-itself evolved into a thing-in-consciousness (*zijue the shiti*, entity with consciousness) through its interactions with the Western powers in the past hundred years, hence the Chinese nation includes all the ethnic groups in China (ibid., pp. 1, 8–35; see also Gladney, 1994, p. 100).

This discourse finds a number of advocates. A strong example comes from octogenarian Su Bingqi, a renowned archaeologist of Beijing University. His 1994 collection, *Hua People, Dragon's Descendants, the Chinese—the Search of Chinese Roots through Archaeology*, though not a book devoted to nation-building, includes a part entitled 'The Origin of Chinese Civilization and the Reconstruction of Chinese Prehistory' (1994, pp. 73–134). This part provides the text for the inscription he presented to the Museum of Chinese History on its eightieth anniversary in 1992: 'Over a million years root system. Ten-thousand years initiation of civilization. Five-thousand years' ancient state. Two-thousand years' unified Chinese entity. These are the basic national conditions of China' (ibid., p. 141).

The direct targeted audience of these discourses is always of two categories: the overseas Chinese, including peoples in Hong Kong, Macao and Taiwan, and the minority ethnic groups in China. But owing to the Herculean territory and population (1.2 billion in 1995), plus the extreme long history that contains as many memories of negative interactions as the positive, each discourse faces serious difficulties. The most difficult is the dilemma of advancing an argument that sounds equally convincing and appealing to peoples from Inner Mongolia, Xinjiang and Tibet, as well as to those from Hong Kong, Macao and Taiwan.

Since I know a little about minority ethnic groups, let me say something about them. It is known that minority ethnic groups in China are officially identified; and that constitutes an objectivized identity. The official recognition of an ethnic group can make 'a considerable difference in obtaining certain entitlements accorded to minorities, including permission to have more than one child, obtaining entrance to a university, access to local political office, special economic assistance, and tax-relief programs' (Taylor, 1991, pp. 96, 198). And minorities have shown the ability historically to exploit the tribute system to obtain trading benefits or self-government. Today, 'by allowing the objectivizing gaze of the state-sponsored media, they establish their identity and right to a voice in their own affairs, appropriating and turning, whenever possible, these objectivizing moves to their own benefit' (Gladney, 1994, pp. 117–18).

That the minorities are no longer passive in their interaction with the state is well illustrated by the discrepancy between the founder's intention and the actual functioning of the Central Universities of Nationalities (originally the Central Institute of Nationalities). It was founded in 1951 with the intention of training ethnic minority cadres for carrying out the CPC's policy in the minority areas. But in four decades it has evolved into a place in Beijing where ethnic groups congregate from all over China. Through frequent celebrations of ethnic festivals marked with ethnic clothing, food, singing, dancing and communication in the ethnic language or local dialects, through annual get-togethers with the visiting NPC (National People's Congress) delegates or officials from the ethnic autonomous areas visiting Beijing for meetings, through information about and comparison between the different areas and their development, most graduates attain a stronger ethnic identity than when they first came.

In the past decades, more and more ethnic intellectuals have become established. They are not only well equipped with a group consciousness, but also learn to use the official revolutionary (or evolutionary) discourses to their advantage. Liu Yaohan, a famous Yi scholar, is a good example in this respect. As a successful historian and ethnologist, he is well known for having invested his experience and resources into training a Yi taskforce for Yi study in the Yi area. Moreover, he masterfully manipulated the once dominant unilinear evolutionary discourse in the discipline, and Chinese ancestry worship in the society, to the point of claiming that Yi people are in fact the cultural ancestors of the Chinese nation. The evidence he has cited includes the fossil remains of *Homo Erectus* in Yunnan (1.73 million years old), the legend of the calabash origin of humankind, the ten-month-cycle calendar used in the Xia Dynasty 40 centuries ago, and the tiger-worshipping content in the name of Lao Tze, founder of Taoism (see Liu Yaohan,

1985). Other ethnic scholars have also questioned the authority of 'ethnic' histories written by scholars from other groups. In short, the progress of China's social modernity has made the formulating of an inclusive discourse of nationhood in some ways more difficult than before.

CONCLUSION

So much for a narration of the saga of the concept of *minzu* and of nationhood in China. Looking at the 1950s world with 1990s eyes, many aspects may seem unrecognizable. Modern technology and the omnipresent market system have taken over many functions from the previously omnipotent nation-states. Individuals and non-government institutions become ever more confident of their ability in advancing such issues as human welfare, human rights, women's rights, social democracy, environment protection and so on. Consequently, in Western countries there is an increasing questioning of the nation-state idea in scholarly and other circles.

But this does not mean that *minzu* discourse (including nationalism, national identity, the sense of nationhood, the sovereignty of nation-states and exertions of ethnicity within a nation-state, etc.) will die down as the world becomes an ever more compact system. Apart from the uses that the Third World countries have made of it to protect their weaker economies and enterprises, the *minzu* concept is in any case too hazy, meaning many different things, and thus has too many lives to completely fade out. Besides, the global happenings in recent years, including the collapse of the former Soviet Union, the painful splitting of former Yugoslavia, the eastward expansion of NATO, are all enhancing rather than detracting the momentum of *minzu* discourse in areas outside north America and Western Europe. This constitutes the context for our discussion of *minzu* discourse in China today.

As important as the international context, the on-going changes in China modify the connotations of *minzu* continuously. In an 'authentic' communist reign (such as Mao's China till 1976), *minzu* was regarded as something obsolete. It was tolerated but not really appreciated. In a pragmatic communist reign (such as Deng's China since 1978), it became complementary: it was appreciated but not without caution. The current developments, including the re-structuring of the economy, the approaching social modernity, the awakening ethnic (or parochial) identity, the faster growth of ethnic populations, the reversion of Hong Kong and Macao with their capitalist systems intact, the burgeoning Taiwanese desire for independent nationhood, the international concern over Tibet, the looming Muslim discontent, the forming of a dissident group in exile, and China's ever deepening international involvement, will contribute to changing China's *minzu* discourse. It remains to be seen what new course the contradictions that underlie the debates on *minzu* and Chinese nationhood will now take.

REFERENCES

Anderson, Benedict, *Imagined Communities: Reflections on the Origin and Spread of Nationalism*, London: Verso Editons and NLB, 1983.

Apter, David E. and Tony Saich, *Revolutionary Discourse in Mao's Republic*, Massachusetts: Harvard University Press, 1994.

Bai Zheng (ed.), *Official Systems in Ancient China*, Beijing: Beijing University Press, 1989.

Birch, Anthony H., *Nationalism and National Integration*, London: Urwin Hyman Ltd., 1989.

Camilleri, Joseph A. and Jim Falk, *The End of Sovereignty?*, Hants and Vermont: Edward Elgar Publishing Limited, 1992.

Chang, Mau-Kuei, 'Toward an Understanding of the Sheng-chi Wen-ti in Taiwan: Focusing on Changes After Political Liberalization', Chen Chung-min et al. (eds.), in *Ethnicity in Taiwan Social, Historical and Cultural Perspectives*, Taipei, Taiwan: Institute of Ethnology, Academia Sinica, 1994.

Chen, Daisun, *The Encyclopaedia of China's Economy*, Beijing: Publishing House of China's Economy, 1992.

Chen, Lian Kai, *A Probing Into the Study of Chinese Nation*, Beijing: Publishing House of Knowledge, 1994.

Choudhury, Paramesh, *Indian Origin of the Chinese Nation: An Unconventional Challenging Theory About the Origin of the Chinese*, Calcutta: Dasgupta & Co. Private Ltd., 1990.

Crapo, Richard H., *Cultural Anthropology: Understanding Ourselves and Others*, Connecticut: The Dushkin Publishing Group Inc., 1987.

Crossley, Pamela Kyle,'Thinking About Ethnicity in Early Modern China', *Late Imperial China*, 11, No. 1 (June 1990), pp. 1–34. By the Society for Qing Studies.

Dijkink, Gertjan, *National Identity and Geopolitical Visions*, London: Routledge, 1996.

Dikotter, France, *The Discourse of Race in Modern China*, Hong Kong: Hong Kong University Press, 1992.

Dittmer, Lowell and Samuel S. Kim, *China's Quest for National Identity*, Ethaca and London: Cornell University Press, 1993.

Evans, Graham and Jeffrey Newnham (eds.),'Nationalism', in *The Dictionary of World Politics—A Reference to Concepts, Ideas & Institutions*, London: Simon & Schuster, 1990, pp. 259–61.

Fairbank, John King, 'The Reunification of China', in Rodrick Mackfarquhar and J.K. Fairbank (eds.), *The Cambridge History of China*, vol. 14, Cambridge: Cambrige University Press, 1987, pp. 1–47.

Fei Xiaotong, *Plurality and Unity in the Configuration of the Chinese Nation* (zhonghua *minzu* duoyuan yiti geju), Press of Central Institute of Nationalities, 1989.

Friedman, Edward, 'Reconstructing China's National Identity: A Southern Alternative to Mao-Era Anti-Imperialist Nationalism', *The Journal of Asian Studies*, 53, No. 1 (February 1994), pp. 67–91.

Gellner, Ernest, 'Nations and Nationalism,' Oxford: Basil Blackwell, 1983.

Gladney, Dru C., 'Representing Nationality in China: Refiguring Majority/Minority Identities', *The Journal of Asian Studies*, 53, No. 1 (February 1994), pp. 92–123.

Goodman, James, *Nationalism and Transnationalism—The National conflict in Ireland and European Union Integration*, Avebury: Ashgate Publishing Limited, 1996.

Han, Jinchun and Li, Yifu, *Data of the Etymological Inquiry of the Word 'Minzu' in Chinese Literature* (hanwen '*minzu*' yici kaoyuan ziliao), Bejing: The CASS Institute of Nationality Studies, 1985.

Hobsbawm, E.J., *Nations and Nationalism Since 1780: Programme, Myth, Reality*, Cambridge: Cambridge University Press, 1990.

Honig Emily, *Creating Chinese Ethnicity: Subei People in Shanghai*, New Haven: Yale University Press, 1992.

Hsieh, Chiao-min and Jean Kan Hsieh, *China, A Provincial Atlas*, New York: Macmillan, 1995.

Huang Guangxue (ed.), *Nationality Work in Current China*, Beijing: Publishing House of Current China, 1993.

Huang Guangxue and Shi Lianzhu (ed.), *Ethnic Identification in China*, (zhongguo de *minzu* shibie), Beijing: Publishing House of Nationalities, 1995.

Huntington, Samuel P. 'The Clash of Civilizations', *Foreign Affairs*, 1993, Summer Issue, pp. 22–49.

Khan, Ali, 'The Extinction of Nation-States: A World without Borders', The Hague: Kluwer Law International, 1996.

Li Yifu, 'On the Establishment of System of *minzu* Concepts in China', (tantan jianli zhongguo *minzu* gainian de tixi wenti), *Minzu Yanjiu* (Nationality Studies), 1986, No. 4, pp. 12–17.

Liu Geping (ed.), *Theory and Practice of Nationality Issues in China*, Beijing: Press of Central Party School of CPC, 1994.

Liu Yaohan, *New Quest on the Origin of Chinese Civilization* (zhongguo wenming yuantuo xin tan), Yunnan People's Publishing House, 1985.

Mcneill, William, H., *Poly-ethnicity and National Unity in World History—The Donald G. Creighton Lectures, 1985*, Toronto: University of Toronto Press, 1986.

Mintz, Sidney W., *Sweetness and Power*, US: Penguin Books Ltd., 1985.

Moser, Leo J., *The Chinese Mosaic: The Peoples & Provinces of China*, Boulder, Col.: Westview Press Inc., 1985.

Pan Guangdan, *Collections of Ethnic Studies by Pan Guangdan* (Pan Guangdan *minzu* yanjiu wenji), Beijing: Publishing House of Nationalities, 1995.

Parker, Geoffrey (ed.), *The Times Atlas of World History*, 14th edn., London: Times Books, 1993.

Peng Yingming, 'A Tentative Inquiry on the History of Concept of "*minzu*" in China' (guanyu woguo *minzu* gainian lishi de chubu kaocha), *Minzu Yanjiu* (Nationality Studies), 1985, No. 2, pp. 5–11.

Pinker, Steven, *The Language Instinct—How the Mind Creates Language.* Originally published, New York: W. Morrow and Company, Inc. *c.* 1994. First Harper Perennial edition, 1995.

Pye, Lucian, *The Spirit of Chinese Politics*, Cambridge, Mass, Harvard University Press, 1968, cited in Taylor, 1991.

Running Press, 'Introduction', *The Running Press World Atlas*, Running Press, 1995, pp. 7–8.

Su Bingqi, *Hua People, Dragon's Descendants, the Chinese: Looking for the Origin of the Chinese Through Archaeology*, Shenyang: Press of Liaoning University, 1994.

Taylor, Jay, *The Dragon and the Wild Goose: China and India*, New York: Praeger Publishers, 1991.

Wang Gungwu, *The Chineseness of China: Selected Essays*, Hong Kong: Oxford University Press, 1991.

——— 'Nationalism in Asia', in Eugene Kamenka (ed.), *Nationalism: the Nature and Evolution of an Idea*, Canberra: Australia National University, 1973, pp. 82–99.

Wang Mingfu, 'Analyzing *Minzu*' (*minzu* bian), *Minzu Yanjiu* (Nationality Studies), 1983, No. 6, pp. 1–23.

Wang Sung-Hsin, 'The Dynamics of Chinese Social System: Network Building Without Group Solidarity', in Suenari Michio et al. (eds.), *Perspectives on Chinese Society, Views from Japan*, printed by Institute for the Study of Languages & Cultures of Asia and Africa, Tokyo University of Foreign Studies, 1994, pp. 16–27.

Webster, Noah, *Webster's Third New International Dictionary*, Massachusetts: G. & C. Merriam Company Publishers, 1961.

Webster, Noah, *Webster's Encyclopedic Unabridged Dictionary of the English Language*, New York: Dilithium Press Ltd., 1989.

Whorf, Benjamin Lee, 'Linguistic Relativity'. Extracted from J.B. Carroll (ed.), *Science and Linguistics in Language, Thought and Reality: Selected Writings of Benjamin Lee Whorf*, MIT Press, 1956. Quoted from Liu Runqing et al. (eds.), *Readings in Linguistics: Seventy-five Years. Since Saussure*, Beijing: Press of Cartography, 1988, pp. 263–74.

Wolf, Arthur P., 'Social Hierarchy and Cultural Diversity: A Critique of G. William Skinner's View of Chinese Peasant Culture', *Proceedings of the Second International Conference on Sinology, Academia Sinica*, Taipei, Taiwan, 1989.

Wu Wenzao, 'Nation & State' (*minzu* yu guojia), *Collections of Anthropological & Sociological Studies by Wu Wenzao*, Beijing: Publishing House of Nationalities, 1990, pp. 19–36.

Xu Jiexun, *History of the Development of the Han Nationality* (han *minzu* fazhan shi), Chengdu: Nationality Publishing House of Sichuan, 1992.

Xu Xinjian, *On Southwest China Studies* (*xinan yanjiu lun*), Kunming: Yunnan Education Press, 1992.

Yu, Ying-Shih, 'Changing Conceptions of National History in Twentieth-Century China', in E. Lonnroth et al. (eds.), *Conceptions of National History: Proceedings of Nobel symposium 78*, Berlin: Walter De Gruyter, 1994, pp. 155–74.

Zhang Haipeng, *Atlas Attached to the Modern History of China*, Beijing: China Cartographic Publishing House, 1984.

Zhang Haiyang, 'China's Cultural Diversity, Ethnic Identity and Cross Cultural Communication', in Ma Qicheng and Bai Zhensheng (eds.), *Ethnology and Ethnic Cultural Devevolopment Studies: Celebrating the 62th Anniversary of Professor Lin Yaohua's Teaching Career*, Beijing: Publishing House of Social Sciences in China, 1995.

Zhang Qizhi et al., 'Several Questions About the Yellow Emperor and Its Mausoleum' (*guanyu huangdi he huandiling de ruogan wenti*), in *Wen Bo* (Cultural Relics and Museums), No. 52 (1), 1993, pp. 3–8.

Zhang Zhengming, 'The Sea in the Land & the Land in the Sea'—On the Centers of Early Civilizations' (*dizhonghai yu 'haizhongdi'*), in *Jianghan Luntan* (Tribune of the Yangtze & the Han Rivers), No. 3, 1988, pp. 42–6.

The Return of Keppetipola's Cranium: The Construction of Authenticity in Sri Lankan Nationalism

Nira Wickramasinghe

I. INTRODUCTION

For a long time now, the Sinhalese community has been differentiated in popular and scholarly perceptions into Low Country and Kandyan Sinhalese, and Kandyan culture has been equated with the authentically Sinhala. As a general rule according to the *The Census of Ceylon 1921*, Sinhalese who trace their descent to a Low-Country district—any of those in the Western and Southern Provinces, the Chilaw district or the western part of the Puttalam district—are considered as Low Country while the Kandyan Sinhalese trace their origin to the Central and North-Central Provinces, the Provinces of Uva and Sabaragamuva, the Kurunegala district and part of the Puttalam district, the Sinhalese divisions of the districts of Batticaloa, Trincomalee and Mullaitivu.[1] It is commonly believed that, as a result of four centuries of Western influence the Low-Country Sinhalese of the southern and western coastal areas who constitute more than two-thirds of all the Sinhalese, tended to diverge in social practices and attitudes from the more 'traditional' Kandyans of the interior, who remained independent until 1815 and were subjected much later, and less intensely, to Western influences.

While interpretations differ about the autonomy of the Kandyan culture,[2] Sinhala in mainstream scholarship is unquestionably equated with Kandyan. Thus, Dewaraja stresses that Kandy had, by the end of the eighteenth century, become a definite cultural

[1] *The Census of Ceylon 1921*, vol. I, pt. II, Colombo, 1922, p. 195.

[2] For example Gananath Obeysekere, in *The Cult of the Goddess Pattini*, Chicago: Chicago University Press, 1984, p. 9, writes: 'The Kandyan civilisation

zone with its own art and architecture, arts and crafts, dance and music. The importance of the Kandyan culture is that it has retained original Sinhala features, she argues, and writes, 'Any form of artistic expression that has survived in Sinhala society today owes its origin to or has derived inspiration from Kandy.'[3] While acknowledging the influence of south India in dance and music (*vannam*) in the Kandyan kingdom, Dewaraja equates authenticity with Kandyan. Interestingly for Dewaraja, who exemplifies the common perception, Kandyanness diluted in Nayakkar culture is considered authentically Sinhalese, while the symbiosis of Low-Country with Portuguese and Dutch cultures is considered hybrid. Clearly the determining factor is the Kandyans' unfailing attachment to Buddhism and the resilience of what is considered 'tradition' due to the very insignificant missionary involvement in the Kandyan districts during the colonial period.

In urban areas today, quite frequently Sinhalese/Buddhist young men and women of the middle classes get married in hotels. The 'traditional' *poruwa* ceremony is performed with great pomp in a hall rented for the occasion. After the ceremony is over, the couple is often seen leaving the hall to the beat of Kandyan drummers dressed in their sumptuous attire. What is curious, apart from the transformation of a village custom into an urban chic one, is the omnipresence of the Kandyan drummers who contribute their joyful beat even if the couple is of Low-Country descent. The Kandyan drummer plays to the authentic rhythm of the nation.

Another example of the importance attached to Kandyan authenticity was related to me by an anthropologist studying the Kaffir community, or Kabiri, in Puttalam. The villagers of Kaffir descent were preparing for the national day celebrations in Colombo to which they were asked to send their representatives. An official who visited them while they were rehearsing apparently suggested adding a few Kandyan drummers to the Kaffir's item, perhaps to dampen the African beat of the Kaffir music. Even a little bit of Kandyanness meant Sinhala authenticity.

Similarly Sinhalese women in the diplomatic service when posted abroad most often wear the Kandyan saree on formal occasions,

---

was not an old continuing tradition but a relatively new phenomenon with a heavy overlay of later South Indian influence.'

[3] Lorna S. Dewaraja, *The Kandyan Kingdom of Sri Lanka 1702–82*, Colombo: Lake House, 1988.

even without themselves necessarily having any link with the Kandyan region. In the same way, the stewardesses on our national airline wear a modernized version of the Kandyan saree or *osariya*, while the stewards for reasons that anthropologists are still trying to fathom, are dressed in the wine coloured jackets which Parisian waiters commonly wear. These examples illustrate how some Kandyan symbols have been selected to become part of the national heritage of the new nation.

I wish to suggest in this paper that the national identity of the new nation-state of Sri Lanka owes much to the colonial articulation of Kandyan things as authentic. I do this by looking at one particular development of the late colonial period, which is the return of artefacts from museums and private collections in Britain in the last decades of British rule. I shall focus especially on the return of the cranium of the Kandyan hero, Keppetipola. This event appears to me to be an important example of the grammar in which colonial ideologies were deployed, and suggests, contrary to nationalist academic thinking, a direct lineage between the colonial and the postcolonial state.

In many ways, the new nation-states inherited much from colonialism: bureaucracy, education system, army, financial system are the most obvious illustrations. In other ways, there was a conscious effort on the part of the builders of the new nation to cut away from the colonial state and its ideology. Nationalist thought redefined the authentic nation, and selected the symbols deemed to be worthy of the new nation-state. What I wish to explore are the politics of selection, of what is remembered and what forgotten, which took place in Sri Lanka in the late nineteenth and early twentieth centuries, and the significance of the colonial ideology in this selection. My hypothesis is that the definition of Kandyanness as 'authentic' in the nationalist era, and the widespread acceptance of this idea today, is inextricably linked to an earlier discourse propounded by colonialism which privileged Kandyan symbols in a particular way.

II. PARADOX OF COLONIALISM: KANDYANS AS ALLIES

It is a paradox that in many parts of the British Empire, the very men who conquered lands in the name of modern civilization valued the 'native aristocracy' far more than the upwardly mobile Western educated sections of the local population. Ranger has shown how Europeans in colonial Africa thought of customary practices with respect and valued the age-old prescriptive rights. They did not fail to compare the sort of title which an African chief held with the gentlemanliness which they laid claim to themselves.[4] In Palestine a basic element in the British perception of the Arab majority was that Palestinians were degenerate Levantines of mixed race and questionable character as opposed to the 'authentic' Arab who was the desert Bedouin, gentleman by birth.[5] The Brahmin in India was considered the 'natural' leader of the Hindus as in Richard Westmacott's 1830 statue of Warren Hastings shown accompanied by two Indians—one a tall, classically proportioned Brahmin with a shaven head and topknot, and the other a seated scribe, bearded and turbaned, the latter representing the Muslims and the former the Hindus.[6] Thus, the authentic Hindu was the Brahmin just as the authentic Sinhalese was the high caste Kandyan, guardian of the admirable qualities of tradition. British respect went to what was regarded as the 'real native not the hybride, university trained mule'.[7]

But just as in India, where the English educated declared themselves committed to the common good and to progress insisting that they and not the 'traditional' aristocratic notables represented the larger public, in Sri Lanka, the Westernized elite mainly from the Low Country tried to show they were more worthy of trust than the feudal Kandyan chieftain. This trust was to be gained painstakingly by the Ceylon National Congress which spearheaded the struggle for Independence from the second decade of the twentieth century onwards. When Ceylon gained Independence in 1948, it was clear that the British had been forced to trust the men whom they had despised a few decades earlier.

The evolution of the attitude of the colonial rulers towards the Kandyans offers a *pendant* to their attitude toward the nationalist

[4] Terence Ranger, 'The Invention of Tradition in Colonial Africa', in Eric Hobsbawn and Terence Ranger (eds.), *The Invention of Tradition*, Cambridge: CUP, 1983, p. 247.

[5] Bernard Wasserstein, *The British in Palestine: The Mandatory Government and the Arab-Jewish Conflict 1917–1929*, Royal Historical Society Studies in History Series 10, London: Royal Historical Society, 1978, p. 12.

[6] Thomas R. Metcalf, *Ideologies of the Raj*, Cambridge: CUP, 1994, p. 82.

[7] R. Kipling cited in Bernard Wasserstein, *The British in Palestine: The Mandatory Gorernment and the Arab-Jewish Conflict, 1917–1929*, London, 1978.

movement dominated by Low-Country Sinhalese. As one lost ground the other gained. As independence became a possibility, colonial rule shifted its support to the modernizing forces in society. The turning point was the sittings of the Donoughmore Commission in 1927 where the federal scheme of the Kandyans was rejected.

In the 1920s Governor Manning had reactivated the ideology of racial differences and through purely political manoeuvres led two groups, the Kandyans and the Ceylon Tamils, to claim minority status. His policy was directed at creating enduring divisions within the elite while organizing the estrangement of minorities from the Ceylon National Congress (CNC). Why he felt that crippling the Congress was worth so much effort remains obscure. Manning perhaps felt that the CNC would represent a danger if it acquired national status and if it succeeded in convincing the Colonial Office that it spoke for all communities even though the political game was restricted to a chosen few. But there was no real risk of the CNC obtaining a Gandhian type of following owing to the dominance of the conservatives in its fold. In the case of the Kandyans, Manning was in fact motivated, not only by a desire to use Kandyan dissent as a counterpoise to the reform movement dominated by Low-Country Sinhalese men, but also by real sympathy with the Kandyan high caste aristocracy (Radalas) who claimed to represent the collective grievances and political deprivation experienced by the Kandyan peasants.

The Kandyan region was regarded by provincial agents and the British in general as the epitome of tradition and they often displayed a patriarchal and protective attitude towards the Kandyans. The Kandyan Sinhalese had been registered separately from the Low-Country Sinhalese for the first time in the 1901 census, forming from then on the second largest community. Inhabitants of the interior of the island, namely, the Central, Uva, Sabaragamuwa and North-Central Provinces, were included. In 1921, the Kandyans numbered 10,89,097 thus accounting for 24.2 per cent of the total population.[8] They were less literate than the Low-Country Sinhalese, and led lives based mainly in the village and ownership of land, largely untouched by the commercial developments which had followed the British exploitation of tea and rubber estates. The inroads made by British capital had, however, created the need for a subordinate entrepreneurship. Low-Country Sinhalese had filled

[8] *The Census of Ceylon 1921, Vol. IV, General Tables*, Colombo, 1922, p. 40.

the void. In the nineteenth century, the antagonism between government agents and these low-Country Sinhalese traders, labourers and arrack renters who settled in the Kandyan province following the plantation boom was widespread.[9] There were many who interpreted the history of the plantation era as a conflict between high caste Kandyans and Low-Country interlopers, and sustained the impression that Kandyans differed fundamentally from Low-Country Sinhalese. Manning's vision of Ceylonese society was in continuity with these ideas.

Thus, when Kandyan leaders began to echo the voice of the provincial agents and appropriate their arguments to press for more political power, Manning lent them unconditional support. The crux of the discord between Kandyans and Low-Country Sinhalese was the discrepancy, real or perceived, in the distribution both of *de jure* power resources—that is, the power resources which accrued to each individual by virtue of his or her citizenship in the state, in particular the right and ability to petition the government and organize political action—and *de facto* power resources such as education and wealth. The more articulate members of the Kandyan community translated this sense of deprivation into an appeal for remedial political action. Manning's task was easy. It consisted in canalizing Kandyan fears and discontent, and presenting their case in a supportive manner to the Colonial Office.

Kandyan leaders clearly did feel threatened by the Colombo reform leaders. The 'Ceylonese' nationalism that the latter articulated was perceived as the announcement of political domination by the Low-Country Sinhalese and the extinction of Kandyan culture and tradition. J.N.O. Attygalle used harsh words against the 'Ceylonese Britishers' whom he denounced *en bloc* as 'nouveaux riches', professional politicians or adventurers, upstarts who were 'averse to be called by their racial names Sinhalese and Tamils which provoked inquiries from outsiders as to the places assigned to them socially by long usage and custom'.[10] What Attygalle suggested was that the Sinhalese who preferred to assume a Ceylonese identity rather than a Low-Country Sinhalese identity belonged to lower castes and did so in order to dilute 'traditional' Sinhala caste hierarchies.

[9] L.A. Wickremaratne, 'Kandyans and Nationalism in Sri Lanka: Some Reflections', *Ceylon Journal of Historical and Social Studies*, vol. V, 1975, p. 51.

[10] *The Ceylon Observer*, 27 June 1918.

In the Kandyan view it was inconceivable that the CNC should arrogate to itself the right to speak for the whole country.

In 1920 there was considerable agitation for a substantial increase in the number of unofficial members in the Ceylon Legislative Council. Congress pressed for the abolition of communal representation and for territorial election and sent a reform deputation to meet Viscount Milner, the Secretary of State for the Colonies.[11] The Kandyan ranks were divided. Dr T.B. Kobbekaduwa, a prominent Kandyan, addressed a message to his community just before his departure for England, in which he stressed the need for a relationship based on trust if there were to be ethnic harmony in Ceylon: 'Scorn the idea that a general electorate does threaten us with extermination or the domination of us by others.'[12] Immediately prompted by Manning, a segment of the Kandyan elite sent a rival deputation composed of three lawyers of Radala status—J.A. Halangoda, G.E. Madawala and T.B. Moonemalle—to London in June 1920. They pressed for the ratio of seats which the Kandyan Association—formed in 1917—had deemed necessary to ensure their distinctiveness in a reformed Legislative Council, that is five seats out of thirteen.[13] Manning, on his side, urged the Colonial Office to recognize the Kandyans as a minority community which needed to be represented in the reformed Council by members elected on a franchise confined to Kandyans.[14]

However, convincing the Colonial Office and the House of Commons, that the Kandyans formed an oppressed minority which could only be protected by extending the communal principle to them, presented some difficulty. In the Commons the Under-Secretary of State was a solitary voice in favour of communal representation. He was strongly attacked by Col. J.C. Wedgewood of the Labour Party who believed that 'consolidation of communal

[11] The Ceylon Reform Deputation led by Sir Ponnambalam Arunachalam was composed of eminent politicians and included a number of Kandyans including A.E. Molamure and T.B. Kobbekaduwa.

[12] *The Ceylon Daily News*, 21 April 1920.

[13] The Kandyan Association Monthly Letter No. 2, November 1920, cited in Calvin H. Woodward, *The Growth of a Party System in Ceylon*, Providence, 1967, p. 33.

[14] The Colonial Office was aware that the Kandyans were protected by Sir William Manning. See for instance CO 54/842, H. Cowell's minute of 30 April 1920.

representation under representative government was a method used to divide and rule'.[15] Finally, unable to withstand Manning's unremitting pressure Milner yielded to Kandyan demands. The Kandyans were allowed to elect their representatives through communal electorates and Manning gloated over the paucity of concessions made to the Congress delegation.

The 1920 reforms were based on the 'balance of power' theory advocated and practised by Manning. Arunachalam who had led the Congress delegation had nursed hopes for something comparable to the Montagu-Chelmsford reforms in India: he had strong reason to be disappointed. Representation had been so arranged that, in the words of the Secretary of State, 'every community shall be represented and while there is a substantial non official majority, no single community can impose its will on other communities if the latter are supported by official members'.[16] For the Kandyan community the reforms meant the addition of only one more representative. The victory, if largely symbolic, was of importance. From this point onwards the Kandyan political leadership had two options: siding with the Low-Country Sinhalese or assuming a minority identity as Manning had succeeded in making their stand as a minority acceptable to those in control.

The Kandyan elite began to detach itself from the CNC after 1924. At the elections of the Legislative Council held that year, with Kandyan electorates having been changed into territorial electorates, only three Kandyans were elected for seven Kandyan seats. The CNC had assured Kandyan leaders that Kandyan electorates would not be contested by the Low-Country nominees of the Congress. The CNC was not, however, a party capable of imposing discipline upon its members and preventing Low-Country Congressmen from contesting and winning in Kandyan areas. The election of non-Kandyans to Kandyan seats was resented and acted as a catalyst to new Kandyan political organizations. An editorial interpreted the Kandyan defeat of 1924 as the result of political ignorance: 'The Kandyans have underrated the difficulties and trusted too much to their influence and prestige. They have never taken the trouble

[15] *Debates of the House of Commons*, 11 August 1920, cited, in D.K. Greenstreet, *Ethnic and Elective Problems of Sri Lanka (Ceylon) 1796–1931*, London: Sasor, 1982, p. 190.

[16] *Cmd. 1809, Ceylon. Correspondence Relating to the Further Revision of the Constitution*, Duke of Devonshire to Governor Manning, 11 January 1923.

to grasp the intricacies of Western politics'.[17] The art of wooing the electorate through organized political campaigns was a novelty for the Kandyan elite. The point was well taken. In November 1924, a meeting was convened in the Kandy Town Hall to discuss the formation of an association of Kandyans based in Kandy. Speakers, one after the other, referred to the Kandyan Convention, to the necessity of safeguarding the rights accruing to them under the Convention and to the intrigues of Colombo Congressmen against the Kandyans.[18] Most Kandyan members of the Ceylon National Congress, T.B. Kobbekaduwa, P.B. Ratnayake and others moved away from Congress and founded a new political association of Kandyan Sinhalese dominated by the chieftain class: the Kandyan National Assembly (KNA). At the first session of the KNA a ceremony destined to reenact the past and herald the future took place. The spirit of reconciliation with colonial rule was propagated, the national identity of the Kandyans was stressed and their privileged relationship with the Crown and its agents was also symbolically emphasized. Indeed the Union Jack was hoisted on the esplanade opposite the Dalada Maligawa; Kandyan chiefs in their national uniform stood at the flagstaff and after the long drum (*Magul Bera*) had been sounded, Kandyan drummers played on, ancient Sinhalese guns fired in salutation and the Kandyan national song was sung. In his presidential address P.B. Nugawela declared: 'We are at the beginning of a great and high adventure namely the rebuilding of our nationality.'[19]

Appearing before the Donoughmore Commission for constitutional reform, the representatives of the KNA reiterated their self-perception now not just as a community but as a nation and proposed a federal scheme for the country:[20] 'Ours is not a communal claim or a claim for the aggrandisement of a few: it is a claim of a nation to have the right to live its own life and realise its own destiny.' Much of the Kandyan case was built on an interpretation of the Kandyan Convention of 1815, which they claimed was an argument between 'two sovereign and equal nations'. They did not accept the view that the Proclamation of 1818, which had followed the Kandyan

[17] *The Ceylon Independent*, 13 November 1924.

[18] *The Ceylon Independent*, 18 November 1924.

[19] *The Ceylon Independent*, 7 December 1925.

[20] Nathan MSS 608, Evidence of the Kandyan National Assembly 19 December 1927. The Rights and Claims of the Kandyan People, Kandy, n.d.

rebellion of 1817–18 against the British presence, had made the Convention invalid. Interestingly the Kandyan National Association tried to build a national identity without ever referring to the role of the British in the fall of their kingdom. The anniversary of the rebellion was conveniently forgotten, as it was not deemed politic in the 1920s to antagonize the British after so many years of peace and friendship.

The scheme the KNA put forward before the Donoughmore Commission entailed the division of the country into three different states, one consisting of the five Kandyan provinces, one of the two Tamil provinces and one of the two Low-Country provinces. In each of these states there would be a legislative council and an executive council to deal with certain matters: for example education, agriculture, provincial administration, land, medical services and the minor judiciary and substantial control over local resources to meet the expenditure under these heads. The central or federal government would have in its charge matters that concerned the whole island—military, public works and railways for instance.[21] It is interesting to note that in the 1920s, plans for federal forms of government were very much in the air. In 1926, S.W.R.D. Bandaranaike had supported such a scheme and declared: 'A thousand and one objections could be raised against the systems but when the object-ions are dissipated I am convinced that some form of federal government would be the only solution.'[22]

However, the Donoughmore Commission was aware that the KNA was expressing the views of feudal chiefs and headmen who were trying to protect their vested interests against the threat of a Ceylon dominated by the more progressive Low-Country Sinhalese. Opposed to the KNA and supported by the Congress were organizations such as the Maha Jana Sabhas and the Sangamayas. The Maha Jana Sabhas were not exclusively Kandyan associations. Most of them were led by Low-Country Sinhalese Congressmen of the area. The Sangamayas were more specifically composed of Kandyans, catered for the lower caste Kandyans and stood for the abolition of communal representation.[23] The commissioners had been notified of the existence of such organizations opposed to the Kandyans of

[21] Nathan MSS 608, op. cit., *The Ceylon Independent*, 17 November 1927.

[22] SLNA 25/25/13, Excerpt from 'Some Memories and Reflections', in *The Tribune*, 12 June 1976.

[23] *The Ceylon Independent*, 11 November 1927; L.A. Wickremaratne, op. cit., p. 56.

high birth. The Madhyama Lanka Maha Jana Sabha, for instance, had asked the Governor in a telegram dated 7 November 1927, to intervene against the 'coercion employed by the KNA through village headmen' to obtain signatures from villagers for a memorial demanding self-government in the Kandyan provinces.[24] Moreover, it soon became clear that the feasibility of the KNA scheme was doubtful, and the motives behind it self-serving.

The Donoughmore Report rejected the Kandyan federal scheme. One of the main reasons put forward by the Commissioners was that a federal scheme would once again isolate the Kandyan community. From the 1930s, colonial rule discouraged the Kandyans from developing a separate political identity. The British had decided to throw in their lot with the moderates of the Ceylon National Congress who represented the forces of unity and Westminster style progress. Yet they continued to harbour the feeling that the Kandyans were more 'authentic' and therefore worthy of special respect. On occasions when etiquette was breached, such as in a 1938 Buckingham Palace reception when Peiris, a Sinhalese of the Low-Country, wore a uniform similar to one of a Kandyan chief, the British expressed their outrage. The Officer Administering the Government (OAG) referred to Peiris disparagingly as 'a member of the *karava* community of inferior social status in no way related to the Kandyans'.[25]

III. THE ABSORPTION OF KANDYANNESS BY COLONIALISM AND NATIONALISM

In the early twentieth century, the proponents of Sinhalese-Buddhist nationalism emerged as the most prominent group within the religio-cultural mainstream of political activity. The brunt of the attacks by Christianity and its evangelical elements had been borne by the Buddhists who formed the largest single religious community in Ceylon. The Buddhist revival of the late nineteenth century gave rise to two movements of protest. The social and religious reformers, Anagarika Dharmapala and Walinsinha Harischandra, led a campaign to protect places of Buddhist worship. They were also leaders of the Temperance movement.[26]

[24] *The Ceylon Independent*, 10 November 1927.

[25] CO 54/960/12, Letter from first and second Adigars and Diyawardane Nilame of Ceylon to Governor Caldecott, 12 September 1938.

[26] *The Ceylon National Review*, vol. 1, no. 1, pp. 113–15.

Temperance had a dual purpose. First it served to reiterate Buddhist strictures against alcohol which amounted to the assertion anew of the validity and relevance of Buddhist values after years of acquiescence to the values of the foreign rulers. Secondly, it represented on the political plane a move to attack the excise policy as an important source of British revenue.[27] With the Temperance movement there was an attempt to unite the masses using religion, Buddhism and anti-Christianity, as binding forces. At the beginning of 1915 this religio-cultural stream of nationalism and the politics of the constitutional reformists were showing signs of convergence: this was apparent at the celebration of the centenary of the Kandyan Convention in March and at the National Day celebration in April.[28]

Interestingly this early nationalism propounded by men from the Low Country such as Dharmapala chose many Kandyan symbols for the new nation they were imagining. But other influences too partook in the process of formation of national tradition. Myths of an Aryan origin of the Sinhalese were reactivated by Sinhalese nationalists.

The Vijayan myth was at the core of the Sinhalese nationalist ideology and the definition of the authentic Sinhalese as children of Vijaya. Dharmapala relates the origin of the Sinhalese in the following manner:

> Two thousand four hundred and forty six years ago a colony of Aryans from the city of Sinhapura, in Bengal, leaving their India home, sailed in a vessel in search of fresh pastures, and they discovered the island which they named Tambapanni, on acocunt of its copper coloured soil. The leader of the band was an Aryan prince by the name of Wijaya, and he fought with the aboriginal tribes and got possession of the land. The descendants of the Aryan colonists were called Sinhala after their city, Sinhapura, which was founded by Sinhabahu, the lion armed king. The lion armed descendants are the present Sinhalese, whose ancestors had never been conquered and in whose veins no savage blood is found.[29]

This short extract capures the essence of the Sinhala identity arti-

[27] Urmila Phadnis, *Religion and Politics in Sri Lanka*, Columbia: South Asia Books, 1976, pp. 67–72.

[28] K.M. de Silva, *A History of Sri Lanka*, New Delhi: Oxford University Press, 1981, p. 381.

[29] Ananda Guruge (ed.), *Return to Righteousness*, Colombo: Anagarika Dharmapala Birth Centenary Committee, Ministry of Education and Cultural Affairs, Ceylon, 1965, p. 479.

culated by nationalists: the Sinhalese as the people of the lion, a pure race of Aryan origin. Dharmapala conveniently omitted the less glorious part of the same Vijayan myth, which the Mahavamsa reveals: Vijaya was the grandson of an Indian princess from Vanga in northern India who had an incestuous and half leonine offspring. He was banished from his land for having led a life of turpitude. It seems the construction of the national heritage was also an exercise in forgetting.

Another leading figure in Dharmapala's nationalism was king Duttagamani who became the sovereign ruler of Sri Lanka in 161 BC after a 15-year war against Elara, a Tamil king from Cola who had conquered the northern part of the island known as the Rajarata, the traditional seat of Sinhalese monarchy. Duttagamani brought the whole island under his sway as a Sinhala Buddhist nation. Interestingly he was a ruler from the Ruhuna, the south of the island. In that sense early Sinhalese nationalism incorporated and integrated symbols and heroes from 'Aryan' India, the Low-Country as well as the Kandyan kingdom. But while the Vijayan myth remained at a purely inner level of perception, Kandyan symbols were exploited and subject to a '*mise en scene*' in an overt fashion by politicians. It was a nationalist need for the ceremonial which was answered in the selection of Kandyan symbols.

The most telling illustration is the dress reform movement Dharmapala spearheaded to restore Sinhalese pride in their culture. The *osariya*, today known as the Kandyan saree , which was considered the true national dress for the Sinhalese woman was promoted by lay preachers throughout the country. One can speculate on the reasons for the choice of the *osariya* as opposed to the cloth and jacket. One possible explanation is that the national dress had to be decorative and flattering as well as regal, since it represented the newly regained pride of the Sinhalese. But at the same time clothes had to be modest and 'decent': women were not encouraged to expose their navel or their ankles. The saree was the morally acceptable dress as it covered the entire body. Dharmapala's recommendations on 'how females should conduct themselves' were quite clear in that respect: 'A proper blouse should cover the breast, stomach and back completely, a cloth ten riyans long should be worn as the osariya or saree.'[30]

[30] Ananda Guruge (ed.), *Dharmapala Lipi*, Colombo: Government Press, 1963, p. 37.

Another possible reason for the choice of the *osariya* as the national dress was its Kandyan origin. While the Low-Country was subjected to an array of cultural influences, the Kandyan kingdom had protected its purity. Portuguese, Dutch and British presence in the island had led to many imitations and syntheses in the dress of the Sinhalese. With the arrival of the Portuguese in the sixteenth century the great majority of women in the coastal belt took to the Portuguese long sleeved jacket rounded at the back and in the front with a V neckline. In the mid-seventeenth century, under the influence of the puritanical Dutch, lace collars, frills and hemlines began to be freely used. In the early nineteenth century, urban women took to wearing European dresses, skirts and blouses. The *osariya* was seen not only as the 'moral' dress, but also as the authentic, unspoiled and 'pure' dress of the Sinhalese.[31]

However, the creation or invention of a national heritage for the Sinhalese did not happen without contest. When the white cloth, banian and shawl was adopted by Sinhalese nationalists as the national dress for men, there were letters to the papers pointing out that this outfit was very similar to the dress worn by the Tamils of Jaffna on grand occasions but in no way reminiscent of the Kandyan traditional costume or that of any other ethnic group.[32] The irony was that the 'authentic' Sinhala costume for men was borrowed from the community that the Sinhalese literati had set apart as 'aliens'.

Conditions in the urban milieu of Colombo had led the Sinhalese Buddhist literati to look for a definition of their identity which could effectively set them apart from the swelling ranks of 'aliens'. Sinhala authenticity developed and matured by creating an other; certain groups were excluded because they were identified as exploiting the Sinhalese, others for descending from south Indian invaders who allegedly destroyed the Sinhala Buddhist civilization. While the Moors were identified as 'the alien traders', the Tamils were perceived as enemies, foreigners, destroyers and vandals.[33]

[31] Nira Wickramasinghe, 'Some Comments on Dress in Sri Lanka', *The Thatched Patio*, vol. 5, no. 1, Jan./Feb. 1992, pp. 1–21.

[32] *The Ceylon Daily News*, 13 July 1931.

[33] The articulation of the 'other' in Sinhala nationalism is studied in detail in Nira Wickramasinghe, 'Migration, Migrant Communities and Otherness in Twentieth Century Sinhala Nationalism', in Crispin Bates and Jonathan Spencer (eds.), *Migration and Communalism in South Asia*, Leicestire University Press, forthcoming.

In the years that followed, the religio-cultural stream of nationalism was overrun by the more modernist and secular reform movement led by the CNC. With the inauguration of the Donoughmore Constitution, the newly elected State Council was established in 1931 under Don Stephen Senanayake's leadership. The new leader played an important role in rekindling Low-Country myths and heroes, and this helped in the evolving of a nationalist spirit where Kandyan Sinhalese and Low Country Sinhalese alike recognized themselves. Senanayake planned colonization schemes in the dry zone—the northern and eastern plains once the seat of the ancient Sinhala kingdoms—in which landless Sinhalese peasants were to become independent peasant proprietors. There were constant references in the speeches of the Sinhalese politicians to the ancient hydraulic civilization which existed in the dry zone. D.S. Senanayake's zeal was legendary and he even tried to claim a hypothetical affiliation of his own family to the ancient families of the dry zone.

The important fact here is that the people identifed as suffering most from landlessness were the Kandyan Sinhalese whose lands had been taken over by the British for tea plantations. In a certain sense the colonization of the dry zone permitted the Low Country nationalists to evoke with pride the feats of king Duttugamunu who reconquered from the Ruhuna in the South the dry zone while at the same time displaying concern for the plight of the Kandyan peasant.[34] In the late 1930s the predominantly Low Country Sinhalese nationalist movement began with even more conviction to look upon the 'conservative traditionally minded' Kandyans as allies.

The Sinhala Maha Jana Sabha (SMS) is said to have been founded by S.W.R.D. Bandaranaike in 1934.[35] Its purpose was clearly stated at the outset: to safeguard the legitimate interests of the Sinhalese race. The aim of the Sabha was to bridge the schism between the Sinhalese communities divided into a Low-Country and a Kandyan group and into competing castes. Only after this first step had been taken was it possible to work towards a higher unity, a unity of all communities. Although the SMS was a unit within the CNC, it

[34] Patrick Peebles, 'Colonization and Ethnic Conflict in the Dry Zone of Sri Lanka', *The Journal of Asian Studies*, 49, no. 1 (February 1990), pp. 30–55.

[35] Michael Roberts, 'Ethnic Conflict in Sri Lanka and Sinhalese Perspectives: Barriers to Accommodation', in *Modern Asian Studies*, vol. XII, no. 3 (1978), p. 360; C.H. Woodward, op. cit., p. 32.

acted as a rival rather than a partner to the Congress, undermining its national or at least pan-Sinhalese pretensions.

The Kandyan political leadership had, from the inception of the nationalist movement, stood aloof from it, owing to its predominantly Low-Country Sinhalese composition. In 1937, the grievances of the Kandyan community were expressed in a memorandum by G.G. Rambukpota, State Councillor for the Bibile area. Only 5 Kandyans had been returned in the 20 seats alloted to the Kandyan provinces, he pointed out. Kandyan candidates lacked funds compared to the Low-Country Sinhalese men, who in his words, 'had money behind them'. Another new danger came from those agitators who preached communist ideas to the plantation workers. It was for all these reasons, Rambukpota argued, necessary to limit the franchise by an education and property qualification.[36]

Another memorial from the Kandyans denounced both the Low-Country Sinhalese and the Indian labour force that worked on tea plantations managed by Europeans: 'the Indian labourers', it was stated, 'servants of the European planter [who] are our masters and rulers', should be excluded from territorial electorates and given representation as agricultural labour on a communal or interest basis.[37] A few years later, Kandyan fears of political extinction were articulated more forcefully by the rejuvenated Kandyan Youth League which had been inaugurated in 1934.[38] All these demands were the work of men belonging to the higher rungs of Kandyan society, mainly of Radala caste. It was not surprising, therefore, that among the demands of the Kandyan Youth League had been the preservation of the headman system; this was turned down.

The Sinhala Maha Sabha's position towards Indians was aimed very much at assuaging Kandyan apprehensions. It denounced the manner in which the restrictions on the Indian franchise embodied in the Donoughmore Constitution had been ignored. The evidence of five years' residence, which was one of the requirements, was not insisted upon, and the second requirement, which was to sign a declaration of permanent settlement, had been a mere formality.[39]

[36] CO 54/979/2, Memorandum from G.C. Rambukpota, 26 June 1937.

[37] Ibid. Memorandum from the Kandyan Community to the Secretary of State, signed by Adigar Ratwatte, T.B. Panabokke and B.H. Aluwihare, 22 June 1937.

[38] CO 54/979/9, Memorial submitted by the President of the Kandyan Youth League to Caldecott, 1942.

[39] CO 54/954/2, Memorandum of the Sinhala Maha Sabha.

The Donoughmore Constitution by granting universal suffrage to those it defined as Ceylonese had effectively established a fixed boundary between them and migrants of Indian origin. Quasicitizenship in the Crown colony Ceylon had been construed as an identity which subordinated all other identities of religion, estate, family, gender, ethnicity, region to its framework of a uniform body of law. Through the vote the boundaries of the Ceylonese nation were affirmed. For the Donoughmore Commissioners the nation was not a group of people who had a common lineage and history but included all those who happened to live within the state boundaries for a period of five years. This perception of an inclusive Ceylonese nation was not shared by all. At meetings of the SMS, Bandaranaike projected a deliberate assimilation of Indian labourers with the imperialist power and preached a bleak future: '. . . before many years pass, we will cease to exist as a people and a few miserable survivors will be left as the slaves of Indian slaves of the British.'[40] In the official perception he grew to become the 'protagonist of the Sinhalese crusade against Indians'.[41] At the end of the 1930s, the Kandyan leadership began to think of Bandaranaike as a possible ally. Similarly, the Kandyan Youth League was seen by the SMS as a useful organization, which could be absorbed in due course and brought under the control of the Sabha.

In 1939, at the celebration of Convention Day organized by the League, Bandaranaike was the principal speaker. The day was also celebrated in Colombo thus symbolizing the growing links between the two Sinhalese communities. The following year, on the same occasion other Low-Country Sinhalese members of the SMS, such as C.W.W. Kannangara, and A.E. Goonesinha of the Labour Party, were present. The 1941 celebration was attended by 1,500 to 2,000 people. D.S. Senanayake, Bandaranaike, and Kannangara were participants. Panabokke Adigar, who was presiding, appealed to his 'Low-Country brethren' to consider the Kandyans as their younger brothers, to cooperate with them and to lead them as 'an elder brother on the path of progress, to obtain Independence'.[42] The language was that of a subordinate ally.

From this time onwards, Bandaranaike and his Sabha were to a

[40] *The Hindu Organ*, 3 April 1941.

[41] CO 54/982/2, Gent to Secretary of State.

[42] CO 54/979/9, Police Report by Sgt B. Langram, Deputy IGP on the Kandyan League, 19 June 1942.

large measure instrumental in forging a stronger sense of cohesion between the Sinhalese communities. His marriage to Miss Ratwatte, daughter of Disava Barnes Ratwatte, was of great political importance. As Governor Caldecott remarked in 1940, the union between a first rank family of the Kandyan highlands with a first ranking family of the Lowlands represented an accretion of considerable political influence to the SMS.[43] Although the new links between the SMS and the Kandyan leadership were grounded more in personal trust than on a reflected common platform, a common opposition to the granting of the vote to the Indian Tamils had brought them together. Kandyan support for the nationalist cause was also reinforced by the incorporation of its traditional leaders in the governance of the country. In 1944, the Board of Ministers recommended that a Kandyan, Sir T.B. Panabokke, the first Adigar who had represented Kandyan interests in the old Legislative Council, be appointed Ceylonese Representative to India as successor to the late Sir Baron Jayatilaka. This choice was clearly motivated by political considerations at a time when it was crucial to present before the British an image of unity. The Low-Country Sinhalese were no longer considered as 'foreigners', invaders or interlopers. The relationship had evolved into one of acceptance by the Kandyans of the benevolent dominance of the Low-Country Sinhalese. The nationalist movement led by the latter had succeeded in coopting the Kandyan political leadership.

IV. THE RETURN OF KEPPETIPOLA'S CRANIUM

Parallel to the nationalist movement's overtures to the Kandyans and the eventual absorption of Kandyan symbols into the new nation, the colonial rulers and nationalist leaders set about defining what in their view were the emblems of the future state of Ceylon. The return of artefacts that had been taken away was one aspect of a wider process of defining the nation: and Keppetipola's cranium was one of the most celebrated of the 'national' objects returned.

The cranium of Keppetipola, one of the leaders of the Great Rebellion of the Kandyan people in 1818, was returned to the Ceylon Government on 9 February 1948, a few days after the country celebrated its independence from British rule. The Duke of Gloucester

[43] CO 54/977/7, 'Things Ceylonese', no. 12, 18 October 1940.

was instrumental in the return to the Colombo Museum of what the *Ceylon Observer* in 1948 referred to as a 'national relic'.[44] Thus the cranium moved from one museum to another; in no uncertain terms, independent Ceylon had inherited the practice and form of political museumizing that began in the nineteenth century with the growth of colonial archaeology.

The origins of the Kandyan Kingdom, situated in the central highlands of Sri Lanka, date back according to 'tradition' to the fifteenth century when Senasammatha Vikramabahu declared his independence from the king of Kotte around the year 1474. The full name of the kingdom was 'Kanda udapas rata' or the five districts. The Portuguese shortened it to Candea using the name for both the kingdom and its capital Senkadagalanuwara.[45] In 1592 the kingdoms of Kotte and Sitawaka were absorbed by the Portuguese. The Kandyan kingdom was the last independent territory, which maintained itself in the interior until March 1815. At that juncture it was ceded to the British by the Kandyan chiefs and the last king of Kandy Sri Vickrama Rajasingha, was deposed. For over three hundred years the Kandyan kingdom had withstood the full brunt of the military power of the Portuguese, the Dutch and the British, in turn. With its demise, the entire island was for the first time subject to Western political control.

The Kandyan kingdom was formally ceded to the British by its leaders, secular and religious. The terms of the Convention, signed on that date by Brownrigg on behalf of the British and by the chiefs on behalf of the Kandyans, had been drafted largely by John D'Oyly. The document was read to the assembled chiefs and to the headmen of the districts gathered outside. People took no part in the ceremony, and, indeed, the townspeople showed not the slightest interest in the proceedings. The Kandyan Convention preserved intact the powers and privileges of the chiefs, the laws, customs and institutions of the country and the Buddhist religion, which in the eyes of the Kandyans was more important than all else.

However, the Kandyan chiefs had called in British help in 1815 for the sole purpose of eliminating an unpopular ruler. They had not contemplated the prospect of the establishment and continuation of British rule and when they woke up to the reality of foreign

[44] *The Ceylon Observer*, 9 February 1948.

[45] Lorna S. Dewaraja, op. cit., p. 22.

control they found it extremely irksome and unpalatable. The Convention was thus a disappointment to the Kandyan elite who yearned for the restoration of the monarchy. They alleged that the British had violated the conditions stipulated in the Convention.

From 1815 to 1817 a plan was hatched to overthrow British power in the Kandyan provinces. In August 1817 the Rebellion broke out in Vellassa. Keppetipola, also known as Monarawila, was Disawa of Uva, a signatory to the Kandyan Convention of 2 March 1815, and brother-in-law of Ehelepola, the last prime minister of the Kandyan kingdom. As Disawa of Uva, Keppetipola assumed command and conducted the insurrection, which spread through the entire Kandyan country.

The British, who did not have adequate troops to quell the disturbance, found themselves in a precarious condition. Martial law was proclaimed throughout the Kandyan provinces and reinforcements were brought in from Madras. By August 1818 the Rebellion was fizzling out, a good many of the leaders having surrendered.

In October, Keppetipola and Madugalle, the second in command, were captured in the seven Korales, brought to Kandy, tried for levying war against the king, and executed. On the morning of their execution Keppetipola and Madugalle were taken to the Dalada Maligawa, since they expressed the wish that they be allowed to pay their last respects to the sacred Tooth Relic. Keppetipola was taken before the relic and after making obeisance, he offered one of the *tuppatis* which he was wearing since he had nothing else to offer. Turning to Mr Simon Sawes, the British agent in Kandy who had escorted him, he said: 'I give you a share of the merit of my last meritorious act.'

He then expressed his *pranthanaya*, the last wish, namely, that he be born in the Himalayas and attain *Nibbana* under Buddha Mettheya. The officiating high priest gave his benediction and said that the *pranthanaya* would be fulfilled. After this Keppetipola and Madugalle were taken near the Bogambara Tank and executed. Just before the execution Keppetipola took out the *Dhammapada*, a book of Buddhist scriptures which he always carried and, as the story goes, he was reciting some stanzas from the text when the executioner severed his head from the body with two strokes of the sword.

Following the Kandyan custom the executioner placed the severed head on the breast of the fallen chieftain.

What happened to Keppetipola's cranium after that makes for a somewhat curious tale. It was taken away from Ceylon and presented to the Phrenological Society of the Edinburgh Museum by Henry Marshall, chief surgeon of the Kandyan Provinces between 1816 and 1821. Phrenology, first known as cranioscopy had been founded by the German anatomist Franz Joseph Gall (1758–1828). There was at the time great interest in methods of determining character and temperament from external bodily configurations, especially the facial, and Gall evolved a new method called cranioscopy, combining the concepts of cerebral localization with the analysis of bodily configurations. He argued that faculties or talents are inborn and dependent upon cerebral structures: therefore the brain is made up of as many 'organs' or areas as there are moral and intellectual qualities. Character and intellect are represented by 27 organs, or psychic qualities, sharply delineated on the cranial surface. Skulls of 'heroes' or any men displaying exceptional qualities were particularly sought after as case studies.

This interest in skulls was not new. In the seventeenth century scientists were making observations on the morphology of the chimpanzee and the orang-outan. The early eighteenth century saw the beginning of anthropology with the works of Buffon, Linne, Camper, Daubenton and others. In the nineteenth century, anthropology officially took a place at the university as the natural history of mankind. Craniology was among the most important subjects taught within anthropology. Parallel to this, the first anthropological museums and the first collections of skulls were created. Appropriately Gall's cranium is still preserved in the Paris museum, Musee de l'Homme.

Gall himself was much more a man of the eighteenth century Enlightenment; he was a social reformer who deduced moral rules from his phrenology.[46] In the nineteenth century, scientists believed that science would be able to explain how a man belonging to an inferior race could act with such bravery as that shown by Keppetipola. Scientific mastery was an important part of the colonial endeavour to control the physical world and was central to the works of social Darwinists such as Spencer. In India, H.H. Risley, census commissioner and ethnologist sought to demonstrate in his

[46] *Encyclopedie Internationale des Sciences et Techniques*, vol. IV, Paris: Les Presses de la Cite, 1970, pp. 604–6.

book, *The People of India*, that the social status of the members of the various castes varied 'in inverse ratio to the mean relative width of their noses'.[47] Most ethnographers of the late nineteenth century accepted the notion that anthropomorphic research had some value: measuring skulls was a part of the preoccupation with social mapping.

Knowledge of the native made for more effective government. Colonial subjects were objectified, scrutinized and classified. For this purpose, museums were established. Anderson has defined the museum, together with the map and the census, as an institution of power that 'shaped the way in which the colonial state imagined its dominion—the nature of the human beings it ruled, the geography of its domain and the legitimacy of its ancestry'.[48] British colonialism was not alone in the collection and collating of such material. As late as in the 1950s, the museum of Bremen contained no less than 2,000 skulls from the colonial territories, out of which 84 from German East Africa were arranged in rows according to their cephalic index.[49]

Thus crania were not only studied by the 'rational' minds of the time, they were also exhibited in museums for the consumption of the metropolitan crowds. Britain had by 1900, 250 natural history museums, and by 1910 more than 2,000 science and natural history museums had been established throughout the world.[50]

The Colombo Museum was established by Sir William Gregory, Governor of the island. In his speech to the Legislative Council he explicitly conveyed what were in his view the aims of a museum:

> The want of a museum, in which may be represented the natural history, antiquities, and industrial products of the island, has been forcibly urged on me. . . . For a comparatively small sum, considering the object in view, a museum may be constructed which shall not be a mere random collection

[47] Cited in Thomas R. Metcalf, *Ideologies of the Raj*, New Delhi: Cambridge University Press, 1994, p. 82.

[48] Benedict Anderson, *Imagined Communities: Reflections on the Origin and Spread of Nationalism*, London: Verso (revd. edn.), 1991, p. 163.

[49] Edgar V. Winans, 'The Head of the King: Museums and the Path to Resistance', *Comparative Studies in Society and History*, vol. 36, no. 2, April 1994, p. 236.

[50] David Jenkins, 'Object Lessons and Ethnographic Displays: Museum Exhibitions and the Making of American Anthropology', *Comparative Studies in Society and History*, vol. 36, no. 2, April 1994, pp. 244–5.

of miscellaneous objects, but a scientific, teaching exhibition, which while ministering to the amusement of many, may convey instruction to all who seek it'.[51]

The purpose of the Colombo museum was articulated as twofold, amusement at the sight of objects of wonder, and education. In 1877 it opened its doors to the public. By 1915 the museum had improved tremendously. Visitors were able to wander through new exhibits from the mineral gallery, the mammalian gallery to the medieval gallery. Exhibits were labelled so as to inform and educate the visitors. A recent addition in 1915 was a wooden four-poster bed of massive proportions which bore the following inscription:

> This bed belonged to the last king of Kandy Sri Wickrama Rajasinghe. In January 1815, the king fled to Madamahanuwara. During his absence the palace was ransacked by different people. Molligoda Adigar took the Royal bed and it was in his possession until his death on 26th October. [1823].[52]

The history or rather the story of the bed was thus encapsulated in an explanatory vignette by colonial archaeologists.

Postcolonial museumizing would follow the same model of displaying selected items behind glass frames thus elevating them to the status of reified exhibits. Just as in the colonial museum each object is then vested with one explanation, one label. The story of the bed, for instance, is almost certainly more complex than that contained in the museum label. But in the colonial as well as in the postcolonial museum, its story is limited, circled to the part it played in the Kandyan Rebellion. Modern museums used the same framework and joyfully classified and labelled all the items in a 'reasonable' way thus carrying on the spirit of the Enlightenment.

The museum that grew out of a typical nineteenth century colonial concern to collect knowledge about the Other and offer a selective representation of this knowledge to the natives, thus standing as an objective demonstration of the colonial appropriation of the world, later became the location for the self-definition of the new nation-state. The reversal of this powerful symbolic process central to colonialism took place with the return of objects such as Keppetipola's

[51] Cited in Bethia N. Bell and Heather M. Bell, *H.C.P. Bell: Archaeologist of Ceylon and the Maldives*, Denbigh: Archetype Publications, 1993, pp. 29–30.
[52] *The Ceylon Independent*, Deubigh, 2 March 1915, vol. 28, no. 206.

cranium. The meaning of artefacts was never more contextual. Keppetipola's cranium, while in Edinburgh, was part of the knowledge system of colonialism. With its return to the Colombo museum in 1948 it became the symbol of the new and independent nation-state.

Into the 1930s and 1940s, the colonial rulers participated actively in defining what they thought was the uniqueness of Sinhalese civilization. The study and preservation of Sinhalese texts was encouraged. The famous German orientalist, Wilhelm Geiger, had completed the translation of the Sinhalese chronicle, the *Mahavamsa*, in 1908. A few years later, the government of Ceylon considered inviting him to the island to catalogue the manuscripts owned by the Buddhist monasteries, but the outbreak of the First World War aborted this project. In 1925, however, under the patronage of the British government in Colombo, Geiger undertook to edit and translate from the Pali the second part of the Sinhalese chronicle, the *Culavamsa*.[53]

There was also a renewed interest in the Sinhalese language. At the end of the nineteenth century, the Ceylon Branch of the Royal Asiatic Society had conceived the idea of a critical philological dictionary of Sinhalese. The original plan was revived in 1925. The aims set out were a better understanding of the language and the building up of a 'really fine modern Sinhalese literature' possibly incorporating modern genres such as the novel.[54] In 1926, work began with the Ceylon government guaranteeing full support. In 1935, the Colonial Secretary constituted a commission headed by Professor Pakeman which aimed at preserving public records, collecting unpublished manuscripts, and translating and publishing Sinhalese documents. There was also a new benevolent attitude in regard to indigenous arts and medicine. The traditional British position, that the local population should be shielded from 'quack' medicine, was abandoned in 1927 and state sponsorship was given to indigenous systems of medicine in the form of a Rs 75,000 grant. A board was appointed to submit to the government definite proposals for the expenditure of the grant.[55]

[53] Heinz Bechert, *Wilhelm Geiger, His Life and Works*, Colombo: German Cultural Institute, 1995, p. 105.

[54] Ibid., pp. 119–21.

[55] C.G. Uragoda, *A History of Medecine in Sri Lanka: From the earliest times to 1948*, Colombo: SLMA, 1987, p. 88; CO 54/891/5, Governor to Secretary of State, 28 September 1928.

It was in this context that, during the last decades of British rule, demands for the restoration of Buddhist relics held in museums in Great Britain began to be received with some amount of sympathy by British authorities in Ceylon. In 1939, the Ananda Bikkhu Sangamaya forwarded a resolution to the Secretary of State requesting that the relics of the Venerable Sariputta and Moggalana in the Victoria and Albert Museum be returned.[56] Governor Caldecott acted as the intercessor on this occasion, as well as a few years later when the demand was made for the return of an ivory tooth representing the Sacred Tooth of Buddha in the Dalada Maligawa in Kandy.[57] Most of the objects returned had been taken away from temples and their return to their original place could be read as a symbolic redemption for past sacrileges. It can also be seen as an acknowledgement that the objects deemed significant enough to be taken away and displayed in western museums were the very objects deemed important by the nationalists. Thus Buddhist relics were placed very high in the list of objects to be returned.

A fairly significant number of objects was returned to Ceylon during this period. And, in instance after instance, the mode of presentation of the 'gift' being returned exemplified the British perception of a nation which was essentially Sinhalese and Buddhist, and which privileged the Kandyan heritage.

In 1934, the *Hindu Organ* reported that 'before a large assembly gathered in the audience Hall the Duke of Gloucester returned to the people of Ceylon the throne and crown of the Kings of Kandy'.[58] The fact that these symbols of Kandyan royalty were initially to be handed over to a social entity called 'the Ceylonese' and were to be placed in the State Council Chamber instead of the ancient Kandyan Audience Hall (this in spite of protests on part of the Kandyan chiefs) reveals the British view of Ceylon as a unified nation as well as the willingness of the leadership in the State Council to construct a Sinhalese identity privileging the prestigious Kandyan heritage. It was only later that the throne was brought back to Kandy.

Interestingly, Sri Wickrama's ceremonial throne and footstool had been fashioned by the Dutch in 1692 as a present for the then king.

[56] CO 54/971/6, Governor Caldecott to McDonald, 21 June 1939.

[57] CO 54/979/2, Governor Caldecott to Viscount Cranborne, 10 September 1942.

[58] *The Hindu Organ*, 27 September 1934.

It was probably made either by south Indian or Sinhalese crafstmen. The throne was covered in gold sheeting and encrusted with jewels, its arms were a pair of lions of Sinhala, and a large sun, symbolizing the origin of the Kandyan monarchs, surmounted its back. Although it had been customary for them to rule from the cushioned *gaddi*, the Kandyan kings had used this Dutch-made throne ever since 1692. After the 1818 Rebellion, it was shipped to England, together with the lion-standard of the king, in the custody of Brownrigg's son who was asked to present it to the Prince Regent. There is further irony in the fact that this throne was used throughout the nineteenth century at Windsor Castle for the ceremony of invest-ing Knights of the Garter.[59]

The renewal of interest in the Kandyan heritage was also evident in the request for the return of a Kandyan gun from Dublin to the national museum in Colombo in 1939, additional articles of the Regalia of the last king of Kandy from Windsor Castle in 1936, and a painting of the Dutch Governor receiving ambassadors from the king of Kandy from the Royal Asiatic Society in 1937.

As independence neared, intellectual circles in Ceylon grew more concerned that a variety of Ceylon's antiquities, including Keppetipola's cranium were still held in museums and private collections abroad. An editorial in 1947 recalled the 'large haul of ancient coins discovered in Gampola which found its way to America' and urged the Ceylon government to follow India's request that Indian antiquities including the celebrated diamond which adorns the Imperial Crown be restored to the Indian people. The return of objects which were part of the 'national heritage' was considered especially important.[60]

On 23 September 1947 the Governor invited D.S. Senanayake, the leader of the UNP to form a Cabinet as his was the party that had won the largest number of seats at the elections. The next day, after a formal ceremony held in Kandy and a religious offering of flowers at the Maligawa shrine, D.S. Senanayake addressed the nation in English, Sinhalese and Tamil. These acts summarized the tensions underlying a seemingly peaceful transfer of power. Kandy symbolized tradition and purity from foreign influences, the

[59] Geoffrey Powell, *The Kandyan Wars: The British Army in Ceylon, 1803–18*, New Delhi: Navrang, 1984, p. 228.

[60] *The Ceylon Observer*, 5 August 1947, 'Antiquities Abroad'.

Maligawa symbolized allegiance to Buddhism and the trilingual address symbolized the acceptance of plurality. The new nation was an interesting conglomerate. A year later three pieces of legislation would disenfranchise the Indian Tamil migrants thus pushing them outside the circle of Ceylonese identity. Keppetipola's cranium and other such symbolic objects, built up by both the colonial rulers and the nationalist leadership as an authentic treasure of the new nation, spoke of the contradictions of nation-building in this land, its richness, and its tensions.

Women's Place in the Nation: An Early Twentieth Century Indian Debate about the Right to Maidenhood

Sudhir Chandra

Among the more contentious issues that comprised the forging of nationhood(s) in colonial India, one related to the place and role of women.[1] In the fast emerging context of national formation, women began slowly to break out of their traditional sequestration within the familial nexus[2] into a slowly expanding socio-political space. They remained anchored, nonetheless, within the family as subordinate to men. Partly because of efforts of those women who felt unhappy with their lot, women's new space became a subject that divided the society deeply. Changes were advocated, acquiesced in, or opposed in such matters as women's education, age at the time of marriage, and acceptance of consensual as against the prevailing mode of parentally arranged marriage. However modest, these changes presaged significant shifts in women's role even within the

[1] The term 'women' for the purpose of this paper will mean Hindu women of the English-educated middle classes, and mostly superior castes, who were getting drawn into what may broadly be described as nationalist consciousness.

[2] Avoiding, in the context of traditional/precolonial India, the binary categorization of the 'private' and the 'public', the term 'familial nexus' locates women within a social universe that, with the family as its epicentre, was primarily governed by the community. Depending upon the given context, community could mean a *jati*—an endogamous caste—or a local/village community. The role of the State in these matters, I believe for reasons that are not germane to the present discussion, was near inconsequential. For a different view, see Uma Chakravarti, 'Wifehood, widowhood and adultery: Female sexuality, surveillance and the state in 18th century Maharashtra', *Contributions to Indian Sociology* (new series), 29, 1 and 2 (1995), pp. 3–21.

family. As wives they were presented with a different, more direct and less constricted, kind of companionship with their husbands that tended to transgress the threshold. As mothers they were expected to be more active in the training and education of their children.[3]

While the need of a 'new' role for women seemed to be felt across the board, acute differences about that role's content, extent and rationale marked the semiotic war over the question of women. These differences acquired an extra edge in that the question of women touched to the quick impulses that ranged from the intensely personal to the politico-cultural. In a colonial context, moreover, the semiotic war tended to be also a civilizational confrontation between the vanquished and the victors.

This paper seeks to indicate the contours of this conflict by focusing on an important epistolary exchange which took place in the first decade of the twentieth century between two Indians—a social reformer and a novelist. The exchange was triggered by the denouement of *Sarasvatichandra*, the first major work of fiction in the Gujarati language. There is a special advantage in focusing on a debate about a work of literary imagination. It reveals the limits of the conception of certain ideas at a given temporal point. However hard to actualize, ideas once conceived release new possibilities, generating impulses that question received assumptions and hegemonic forces.

I

The reformer, Dayaram Gidumal (1857–1927), was unhappy that *Sarasvatichandra* ended with the marriage of an extraordinarily cultivated girl who, contravening the contemporary social ideal of compulsory matrimony for women, had resolved to remain single. To express his unhappiness to the novelist, he wrote to Govardhanram Madhavaram Tripathi (1855–1907), who came up with a wide-ranging defence of the conclusion of his novel.

That conclusion may be baldly recapitulated. Sarasvatichandra,

[3] Aside from larger agendas of social reform and national regeneration, simple considerations of conjugal fulfilment necessitated a reordering of women's upbringing and man-woman relations. The growth of English-educated salaried and professional classes meant the creation of a male population of cultural commuters. Returning home from their place of work and public activities, they would be constrained to speak a different language, both literally and figuratively, to their spouses. That many of these men were exposed to a Western ideal of conjugality only aggravated the risk of alienation and incompatibility.

the male protagonist whose name gives the novel its title, and Kumud are affianced lovers. Sarasvatichandra, forced by circumstances, soon renounces the world and wanders about incognito. Kumud is married to a profligate who dies young. The widowed heroine and the long last hero find themselves together again in an *ashrama*. The situation is tailor-made for a grand rehearsal of the divisive contemporary debate about widow remarriage. Elaborate discussions follow on what the protagonists ought to do. The consensus, both spiritual and lay, favours their marriage. Indeed, taking a *sukshma* as opposed to *sthula*, subtle rather than gross, view of marriage, they are said to be already husband and wife.[4]

But their marriage is not what the stirring defence of widow remarriage and the ardour between Sarasvatichandra and Kumud yield. Sarasvatichandra decides to dedicate himself to national service. Kumud would become a *sadhvi*[5] and help him from a distance. Sarasvatichandra, however, is pronounced to need a wife for his mission to be successful. The only one fit for the role is Kumud's sister Kusum; but this vivacious girl has resolved to remain unmarried. Finally, without much difficulty, Sarasvatichandra and she become man and wife.

This Dayaram found unacceptable. The issue was important enough for him to take it up with the novelist.

What followed was a prolonged discussion on the question of women's emancipation and the profound implications of their right to remain free from marriage. The acceptance or rejection of that right would affect their status as participants in public affairs. As wives, given the contemporary conception of women's twin obligation of matrimony and maternity, they would be their husbands' helpmates in the mission of national regeneration. As maidens, controlling their own lives and commanding a certain autonomous socio-political space, they would vie to be men's equal.

The question of maidenhood gave rise to issues which, though ostensibly parenthetical, seemed to the two correspondents integral to their debate. Their discussion, moreover, was framed within the context of a cross-cultural comparison between India and the West. Indeed, cultural considerations coloured the very semantics of the

[4] The novel applies the *sukshma-sthula* distinction also to love. The thrust of the argument is that though Kumud had been obliged to go through the ritual of marriage with another man who had since died, it is Sarasvatichandra and Kumud who are really in love and, therefore, truly wedded.

[5] Feminine of *sadhu, sadhvi* is a female religious mendicant.

single woman's social function. While Dayaram used the expression 'sister of mercy', Tripathi preferred the indigenous term *sadhvi* which he had valorized through his idealized depiction of a religious order in *Sarasvatichandra*.

This correspondence also reveals that the reformist impulse could find divergent manifestations. The two disputants shared a concern for social reform and a readiness to appreciate the other's reasoning. Yet, their differences could be irreconcilable about what was possible or desirable by way of change. This irreconcilability was more than a reflection of their mutual differences; their respective positions also tended to be internally incoherent. Tripathi oscillated between radicalism and conservatism while Dayaram, so orthodox as to decline tea from the hands of the English Viceroy,[6] went amazingly far in advocating the cause of women.

II

Dayaram and Tripathi had been students together at the famous Elphinstone College, Bombay, in the mid-1870s. At the time of this correspondence Dayaram was posted at Surat as District Judge, and Tripathi was living some hundred miles away in Nadiad, his home town having relinquished a substantial legal practice at the Bombay High Court to lead a life of reflection and writing. That was his mode of serving the nation.

Tripathi, a reflective person with a philosophical bent of mind, believed that he had a special mission to discharge. Conscious of living in a subject country, with no prospect of freedom in the foreseeable future, he wanted to initiate among his 'people' a transformation required for them to be free one day. To do that, he needed to *study*—that was a key word in his lexicon—the past and the present of his 'nation', and envision for it a desirable future. Study would produce the clarity—another key word—which he believed was a prerequisite for action. He was wary of 'the evil consequences which we may inflict on our country by our well-meaning follies'.[7]

[6] Adhering to the rigid Hindu rules of commensality, Dayaram, then a District Judge, found himself at a public function being offered tea by Curzon. Politely he told the Proconsul that his religion did not permit him to accept the tea.

[7] Kantilal C. Pandya et al. (eds.), *Govardhanram Madhavram Tripathi's Scrap Book 1888–94*, Bombay: N.M. Tripathi Private Limited, 1959, pp. 24–5 (hereafter referred to as *Scrap Book*).

Tripathi's gaze fixed beyond the ephemera of events; he defined his task in the privacy of his *Scrap Book* where he recorded his incessant 'internal polylogue'.[8] 'I wish', he wrote:

> to produce, or see produced, not any this or that event but a people who shall be higher and stronger than they are, who shall be better able to look and manage for themselves than is the present *helpless* generation of my educated and uneducated countrymen. What kind of nation that should be and how the spark should be kindled for that organic flame: these were, and are, the problems before my mind.[9]

His 'ultimate' objective was to 'mould' the subject Indians 'into a great people who would be able to take care of themselves'.[10] *Sarasvatichandra* was meant to serve this end. Earlier Tripathi had planned a series of essays. But 'second thoughts' suggested that fiction, creating the illusion of reality, would exercise a more abiding influence. In 1885, he began writing his novel with which, while confronting his people with their depressing reality, he hoped to expand their consciousness and help them dream new dreams.[11] This patriotic idealism progressively dominated the novel, close to 2,000 pages, during the fifteen years of its completion in four volumes.

Labyrinthine in its structure and delighting in excess, especially in the last volume, *Sarasvatichandra* meanders through history, mythology, legends, religion and philosophy fusing them together, as they indeed were fused in people's consciousness. It ranges over

[8] I borrow this felicitous phrase from Jacques Derrida, *Acts of Literature*, London: Routledge, 1992, p. 34.

[9] *Scrap Book 1888–94*, p. 29.

[10] Ibid., p. 51.

[11] See the English preface (April 1887) to the first volume of *Sarasvatichandra*. In a longer Gujarati preface to the same volume, the novelist makes it clear that in his narrative the 'ideal' would dominate the 'actual'. Though the first volume of the novel appeared in 1887 and the fourth in 1901, *Sarasvatichandra* has been regularly reprinted—a measure of its longevity—by N.M. Tripathi Private Limited, Bombay. However, the text that comes out as a testimony to Tripathi's faith in the power of literature to create utopias and reorient people's consciousness is his pioneering essay in the sociology of what he believed to be the classical poetry of Gujarat from the fifteenth to the mid-nineteenth centuries. Delivered as a lecture in 1892, it was published two years later under the title *The Classical Poets of Gujarat and Their Influence on Society and Morals*. This, too, is available in reprint from N.M. Tripathi Private Limited.

just about anything that Tripathi considered relevant for transforming his people, from the 'pigmies' that they were into 'giants' capable of dealing with their masters.[12]

III

On 10 March 1906, having read the massive fourth volume of *Sarasvatichandra*—850-odd pages—in two days, Dayaram wrote to Tripathi.[13] He began with a reference to some criticism that had appeared of the book but remarked: 'I have nothing but praise for your performance.' Dayaram particularly appreciated Tripathi's sensitivity in not ending the novel with the widowed heroine's marriage with Sarasvatichandra. Her marriage, he realized, would have brought suffering to her parents and 'probably' to the couple themselves.

This hardly squares with Dayaram's support to the cause of

[12] Cf. the following entry in the *Scrap Book*: 'The political sagacity and shrewdness, the moral unity and strength, the practical stamina and virtues etc. make the rulers a giant to the ruled pigmy. Yet, in the comparative conscience of British Institutions and people, there is a real and most pregnant hope for the pigmy. It is also a question of turning the pigmies into beings with higher statures.' Illustrative of the paradox that defined the late nineteenth century Indian nationalist response to the colonial connection, the innocence of this observation must be seen in conjunction with what follows three paragraphs later in the same entry: 'I see the European and the Native; and what is great and little in either. The smallest European is a very powerful spark of fire: power for good and for evil, and more for the latter in their present generation in India.' *Scrap Book 1888–94*, pp. 151–2.

[13] This correspondence began on 8 March 1906 with Dayaram thanking Tripathi for the gift of *Sarasvatichandra* and other books. The following day he began reading the monumental fourth volume—apparently he had already read the first three volumes—and a day later he was reacting to it. From the outset the correspondents seem to have realized the value of their exchange. After receiving the first letter from Tripathi, Dayaram wrote to say that he would preserve it and Tripathi could have it anytime he wanted. But Tripathi, who normally preserved only the letters sent to him, was this time keeping copies of his letters to Dayaram. Tripathi died the following year, and in 1909–10 the well-known Gujarati quarterly, *Samalochak*, published this correspondence along with its Gujarati translation. Another interesting detail may be mentioned here. After addressing him as 'Dear Mr. Govardhanram' in the first brief note of thanks, Dayaram dropped the honorific for his old college mate. Tripathi persisted a bit longer in the use of 'Mr.' By the end, indicating the friendly spirit in which this unrelenting correspondence was conducted, the two were addressing each other as 'My dear'. For Dayaram's letters of 8 and 10 March, see *Samalochak*, April–June 1909, p. 70.

women. Given the strength of upper caste Hindu sentiment against widow remarriage—the idea that a woman must remain chaste to her dead husband's memory—he could not have expected such marriages to materialize painlessly. Perhaps the orthodox part of him felt sympathetic towards the affective pulls that held the family together even though they retarded the progress of reform. Be that as it may, the man who had joined issue with Tripathi was no firebrand.

It was this moderate man and admirer of *Sarasvatichandra* who objected to the disregard shown for an intelligent girl's desire to remain unmarried. Would it not have been better, he asked, if both Kusum and her sister, Kumud, the novel's heroine, 'had spent their lives as *Sadhvis*—as sisters of mercy':

> They could have helped Sarasvatichandra that way. They could have started a home or a college for women and shown how unmarried women could be a blessing to the country. This idea must have occurred to you; I wonder why you rejected it and deliberately forced Sarasvatichandra to *commit something like a bigamy in his Sukshma Sharir*. If his heart was given to Kumud [the heroine], how could he honestly give it to Kusum [the sister]! Kumud's rise is his fall. I think you have been very cruel to him.

Dayaram was a friend, collaborator and biographer of Behramji Malabari (1853–1912), author of the celebrated *Notes on Infant Marriage and Enforced Widowhood* (1884) who worked indefatigably for women's emancipation. Going further than the contemporary awareness of the ills of early marriage, Dayaram wanted women saved not only from marriage before a certain age, but also, if they so wished, from matrimony itself. In a society where infant/early marriage was the norm, certainly for its female members, this was a brave and critical extension of the reformist consciousness.[14]

[14] This was a time, we may recall, when even ardent champions of women's cause felt forced to ask only for what appear today pathetic age limits for consummation, not solemnization, of marriage. Thus the Age of Consent Act (1892)—which was passed in the teeth of stormy protests and remained virtually a dead letter—simply raised, from a meaningless ten to a lowly twelve years, the age when a wife could legally consent to the consummation of her marriage (which may well have been performed while she was still in her cradle). When the *Westminster Review* reported that Malabari was proposing an age limit of sixteen, the great reformer wistfully disavowed: 'I have not been able to see my way beyond 12.' Adding: 'And even that I would not see enforced on the people.' *Indian Spectator*, 17 July 1887.

The extension, however, was framed within the context of the emergent nation. Dayaram's advocacy of the right to maidenhood was very much part of his concern for the advance of women.[15] But its justificatory enunciation came in terms of the 'blessing' that unmarried women would be to the country. A different reformist agenda would, similarly, articulate women's 'freedom' in terms of the national need for a new kind of wives and mothers.[16] Indeed, even the opposition to women's emancipation would be rationalized in the name of the nation.

To go back to Dayaram, his stance was not adversarial. He was convinced that, besides serving no purpose, the conclusion of *Sarasvatichandra* vitiated the spirit of its own narrative. His objection, he believed, was an assertion of that spirit. He, therefore, anticipated no major disagreement from the novelist.

Tripathi responded quickly, and at length, on 13 March.[17] To explain the 'final disposal' of his 'hero' and the two sisters, he went back to the primary impulse of his ambitious fictive project. The public whom he wished to educate was 'very backward' when he began the first volume. He had decided, therefore, to make the novel 'rise by grades from the simple to the difficult, so as to induce and enable the general public to accept each succeeding volume with its increasing difficulties as a natural sequel to its predecessor'. His success—thanks to 'Providence'—had surpassed his 'best anticipations' and each volume had so lifted 'ordinary men and women' that they were 'devouring' the novel, including the massive fourth volume. To achieve this, he had purposely sacrificed aesthetic considerations and risked the criticism that his book was 'not quite a novel'.

Tripathi's opening move, linking the novel's end with its extra-literary beginnings, presaged a cultural-normative justification for the impugned denouement. Pregnant with a cultural aggressiveness, the admission of aesthetic solecism was more than a self-effacing

[15] See 'A Symposium of Hindu Domestic Reforms and Anti-Reforms', in Dayaram Gidumal, *The Status of Women in India: Or Hand-Book for Hindu Social Reformers*, Bombay, 1889.

[16] Compare this with the Victorian ideal of 'home' and the Meiji ideal of 'good wives, wise mothers'.

[17] *Samalochak*, April–June 1909, pp. 70–8. Quicker and more regular than now, delivery of letters between Surat and Nadiad then took just one day. Tripathi's reply was sent two days after the receipt of Dayaram's letter.

writer's act to educate his colonized compatriots at the cost of the quality of his work. It was the assertion of a com-munitarian poetics to which the writer in the individual-centred Western culture could possibly have no access. The sense of superiority that followed/inspired this different aesthetic ideal, we shall soon see, also influenced Tripathi's understanding of his characters' choices in critical life situtions.

Far from accepting any discrepancy between the novel's larger design and its denouement, he mapped upon its complicated narrative a teleology that gave the denouement an air of inexorability. In an impressive ex post facto retelling of the tale, he presented the denouement as the inevitable end of the 'psychological development' along which the four volumes had progressed. Beginning with Kusum, on whose behalf Dayaram had protested, Tripathi wrote:

> I have tried to make Kusum entertain an open but unconscious partiality for the hero ever since her first appearance in volume 2, and her mother and aunt think of marrying her to him . . . and she has been as warmly resisting their wishes and aspiring to be happier with a single life—an idea which shocks the elderly ladies as inconsistent with our social conditions.

Tripathi then summarized thus Sarasvatichandra's state of mind:

> The hero, on the other hand, wanted to be an ascetic from the beginning and was diverted from that mood by the attractions of gentle Kumud. He left his paternal roof, forsook Kumud, under the impression that he would not be able to make her happy, but he was prepared to revise the situation [following Kumud's unhappy marriage and subsequent widowhood]. His realisation of the dreadful situation into which his procedure had thrown the girl strikes him with the awful remorse which I have made him exhibit throughout the four volumes.

The ascetically-minded hero, Tripathi emphasized, was not—at any rate no longer—motivated by love. He was prepared to accept domesticity if Kumud so desired. But Kumud desired, or decided, differently. Spending four nights with her lover, talking and dreaming together—separately dreaming the same dreams—she concluded that their marriage was in nobody's interest.

The protagonists' coming together was meant to facilitate a decision. However, the decision was predetermined by the setting chosen for the meeting. The four nights they were by themselves—a bold experiment for an Indian writer in the sexually segregated society of the day—were spent in caves. Conducive to erotic arousal—which, too, the lovers experienced—caves also carried the power to catalyse spiritual ardour. However, the caves' catalytic ambiguity was in *Sarasvatichandra* tilted decisively towards spirituality. They were located within the precincts of an *ashrama*, the religious retreat where the long separated lovers had found refuge and also each other.[18] As Tripathi exulted in his reply to Dayaram, the hero's association with the heroine 'at the caves, where sacred and invisible spirits ministered to the elevation of the inmates of the caves, transforms the two lovers—him and her—into spirits of higher calibre. They enter upon a struggle for elevating reciprocal lot [*sic*] in the higher sense. . . .'

Cleansed of egotistic drives, the exalted heroine is convinced that her sister ought to marry Sarasvatichandra and help him realize his life's mission. The conviction is sealed by the latent love for Sarasvatichandra she discerns in her sister's heart; a love that had remained buried under her resolve to remain single. Thus, in persuading her to marry Sarasvatichandra, the heroine merely enables the sister to follow her heart's inclination.

This is a prosaic precis of Tripathi's ecstatic recall of the denouement in a long paragraph of frenzied prose. Even as it extols the lovers' ascetic self-denial, the paragraph employs erotically charged language. It mentions a twofold fusion that Sarasvatichandra has with the heroine and with her sister. The fusion with the heroine is psychic—*sukshma*—and with her sister psycho-physical. The distinction, however, gets blurred in the linguistic orgasm that follows; it is difficult to convey because critical to its production is the use of culturally pregnant indigenous terms. Tripathi employs the imagery of two sacred rivers—Ganga and

[18] What it meant for the lovers to live among the *sadhus* and *sadhvis* of the *ashrama* is suggested by the following statement made by Sarasvatichandra, significantly enough, in English: '. . . there is nothing in or among these learned saints that is low or vulgar. The very air they breathe is impregnated with the sweet and solemn fragrance of their holy and ennobling souls. Their mode of living is simple and yet refined, to an extent of which none on our Indian plains has any idea or even a dream. Not you but your heart will love and revere them as you are allowed the rare privilege of living among them, and unhappy and unrepentant will be the man that thinks of marring the picture of innocence, sweetness, and sanctity of life which thrives on these hills and is ever kept warm by the high and unheard-of attainments of these modest and simple-looking anchorites.' *Sarasvatichandra*, Bombay: N.M. Tripathi Private Limited, 1968, vol. IV, p. 798.

Yamuna—and their 'merger' with the sea. As a tributary of the Ganga, the Yamuna has its confluence with the sea through the Ganga. The heroine is the Yamuna whom the younger sister, as the Ganga, carries along for fusion with the sea (Sarasvatichandra). The paragraph ends somewhat tranquilly:

> In ch[apter] 50 of the volume, the elder sister touches the chords of the younger one's heart and settles its vibrations which cannot be appreciated without attending to every word from the hearts of both. Sisterly love and appreciation coil into each heart, and the wiser, the more experienced, the more unhappy sister succeeds in making the younger sister accept the judgment of the elder as based upon genuine love, wisdom and highest, truest beneficence of life.

In his reply Tripathi talks about pure love. Even the love the younger sister had unconsciously borne for the hero is pure. 'Her love', Tripathi tells his sceptic correspondent, 'was for his great and selfless soul and not for his body of which not a thought has crossed her brain in the book.' She felt not the charm of his person, but 'the significance of his ascetic frock—the *kantha*—which at times she wore as well'. Tripathi interprets as other than physical even a kiss, apparently her first that the young lady plants on the lips of her ascetic husband a whole year after their marriage. Distressed that a kiss in the India of his day meant only 'a symptom of physical *kama*', he writes: 'But elsewhere and in ancient India, fathers kissed daughters—a kiss in such cases is the effusion of *sukshma* love as well.' He further explains: '. . . her kiss follows as but the consummation of her love for a *soul*, unlike the kiss which in Cupid's world is but the starting point—the thin end of the wedge—serving but to make the drunkard to [*sic*] have a beastly craving for more drink'.[19]

[19] In keeping with his exuberance, Tripathi elaborates the point in the next sentence: 'In Kusum's case the kiss is but the external automatic tread of a fruitional vision that fills her in her heart with a sacred spiritual reality and is not the thievish first step of cupid towards crushing out the spiritual vision from the inner temple to make room for an infernal Satan.' This argument, like much else in Tripathi's exegesis, carries an element of special pleading. He happily forgets the functional variety denoted by the act of kissing—Kusum's was a kiss on the lips of her husband—and the protocol different societies prescribe for the purpose. A more spontaneous reaction to kissing appears in the following from his *Scrap Book*: 'I went to bed—wife was sleeping in her swinging-bed—I paused, stood, and looked at her sleeping face and attitude of restless sleep. . . .

Of this final scene of the novel, Tripathi tells Dayaram in a final flush of fervour, he as the novelist could draw 'but a *poor* picture'. However, to suggest what it symbolized, he had the scene witnessed by Kumud, the heroine, making her its 'happiest [*sic*] and only eye witness and connoisseur'.

Here, as the letter nears its end, Tripathi's rhapsody tapers off. And resignation takes over. Voyeurism—the 'natural propensity of human curiosity to have a peep behind the scene'—would drive 'each class' of readers to interpret the kiss 'according to *their* ideals'. He could do nothing about it. His powers were exhausted with the final volume. 'God,' he concluded the letter, 'allots to each stage of an author's life what it can then alone best achieve . . . and my present stage would not question the sanctity of its predecessor.'

With this self-effacing grace subsided the tide of Tripathi's spiritualism which had brushed aside the young girl's vow of virginity and Dayaram's anxious enquiries on her behalf. So dismissive was Tripathi of her vow that his letter would not even comment on it. What mattered to him was the seed of love for Sarasvatichandra that her heart had unknowingly carried from the moment of her first appearance in the novel. That unconscious attraction, the overriding reality of her being, rendered illusory her vow of celibacy.[20]

The distinction Tripathi postulated in this letter between himself and the author of *Sarasvatichandra* was gestural. So was his admission of the readers' right—*adhikar*—to make what they liked of the text. He seemed convinced of his own superior *adhikar* to expound the text he had authored. Faith in his spiritual-intellectual cultivation strengthened the conviction, facilitating the teleology within which his letter had straitjacketed the novel.

Dayaram was not impressed. As he wrote on 14 March in reply to Tripathi's long letter of the previous day,[21] he had on his own

---

Her facial beauty was worth a kiss. . . . But—but—a kiss would awaken her, and cause a cruel break in her much-wanted sleep—Nay, we are too old for a kiss—a kiss between us is a matter of the past—we are both ascetic friends and body-less lovers, or rather sympathisers.' Tripathi was at the time still a month away from his thirty-ninth birthday, *Scrap Book 1894–1904*, p. 33.

[20] In the historical-cultural context of this exchange, maidenhood implied sexual abstinence.

[21] *Samalochak*, July–September 1909, pp. 132–4.

'noticed much of what you have kindly referred me to'.[22] But he, Dayaram, had read it all very differently. To begin with, if Sarasvatichandra was 'above *raga* and *dvesha* and above *Mayavic* forces' (an ascetic freed from attachments, enmities and other existential illusions) 'remorse' was 'a word hardly applicable to him and ought not to furnish a motive'. More importantly, the love that supposedly bound the hero and the two sisters was not practicable. As Dayaram analysed it, for Sarasvatichandra to live 'a physical and psychical life with Kusum and a psychical life with Kumud is an ideal which can't become "human nature's daily food" perhaps for centuries to come'.

During the four nights in the caves, Dayaram reminded Tripathi, the hero had not been 'above embracing Kumud physically'. The reminder was in order. As against the uninhibited portrayal in the novel of the physical intimacy into which the caves bring the hero and the heroine, Tripathi's letter had censored physicality altogether and waxed eloquent about *sukshma* love. How, Dayaram asked, could this mortal hero, subject to ordinary human emotions, have given his heart to both the sisters 'without disloyalty either to the one or the other'? Real men and women, incapable of transcending the gross, could not belong to the ideal spiritual realm of the *sukshma*. Hinting at the complications such arrangements were liable to in the everyday world,[23] Dayaram clinched the argument in an idiom preferred by Tripathi:

> On the relative plane we have duties to perform, and the *sukshma sharir* [body] is on the relative plane, and reacts on the *sthula* and can't think of two lovely women—both sisters—as wives with impunity. The situation on the relative plane becomes an impossible one—and in the realm of the absolute it can only become possible by becoming indescribable in words.

Dayaram could, however, now see a purpose behind the ending of *Sarasvatichandra*. Perhaps, he admitted to Tripathi, 'the inspi-

[22] Dayaram actually began this letter by saying that he had noted in a previous volume the 'rapturous exclamation' by a friend of the hero regarding the younger sister: 'Oh, she would be the proper wife for Sarasvatichandra'.

[23] This led Dayaram to remark that even if he were to accept the need for the younger sister's marriage, her spouse had to be someone other than Sarasvatichandra. 'If socially,' he told Tripathi, 'there was a difficulty in finding a proper husband for Kusum—you as a novelist could have created a proper one for her.' This, however, did not imply any compromise on the young woman's right to maidenhood.

ration which has led you to this conclusion is after all right'. But his reasoning bore no resemblance to the novelist's explication of *sukshma* and *sthula*. It was the reasoning of a social reformer who, trusting to the cathartic effect of tragedy, felt that, following the separation of the widowed heroine from her lover, the novel 'can't fail to do a vast amount of good'.[24] 'But for that conclusion, the indignation and the compassion aroused in the minds of your readers, the personal interest as it were felt in the characters might not have been so fruitful as they [*sic*] have been.'

Where Tripathi saw the bliss of union, Dayaram saw tragic separation.[25] Nor was he exceptional in diverging radically from the authorial design. Many among the succeeding generations of *Sarasvatichandra's* readers have been moved by it as a tragic text, even though its tragic intensity has withered somewhat over the years.

Dayaram did not know this, but around the same time as *Sarasvatichandra* was completed, Rabindranath Tagore—still some way away from his Nobel Prize—had shown the power of tragedy in his *Chokher Bali* (serialized in the *Bangadarshan* between 1901 and 1903). Perhaps the most delicate delineation in Indian fiction, until then, of the cheerless existence of the Hindu widow, *Chokher Bali* unravelled her irrepressible, socially unrecognized, yearnings. It brought its female protagonist, Binodini, close to marriage with Bihari who was willing to marry her despite her widowhood because of his love for her. But, in the event, the novel denied the lovers the fulfilment of their love in marriage. As a novelist, Tagore would not act mightier than the tyrannous social authority that tabooed

[24] Though he did not see the end of *Sarasvatichandra* as tragic, Tripathi appreciated the cathartic effect of tragedy. Radicalizing, for example, the great Indian epic *Ramayana*, he viewed its popularly deified hero, Rama, not as 'the highest ideal of filial duty'—renouncing a kingdom to accept exile for his father's sake—but as a 'martyr' to an oppressive patriarchy. Rama, he argued, was 'intended to be an object of sympathy, and not an ideal for imitation, the sympathy being excited to create antipathy against the patriarchal rule'. *Scrap Book 1888–94*, pp. 261–2.

[25] In a postscript to this letter, and in a language familiar to the two correspondents—a judge and a lawyer—Dayaram wrote about Tripathi's disposal of the relationship between Sarasvatichandra and Kumud: 'Why should two souls, made for each other so to say and attracted to each other and wedded in spirit, be divorced thus? I am afraid you have been a very arbitrary Divorce Judge.'

widow remarriage. The starkness of the widow's predicament appeared unmitigated in his novel. It soothed the reader neither with a happy resolution nor with the etherialization of vital physical-emotional needs.[26] No wonder, *Chokher Bali* has weathered the passage of time and changing tastes better than *Sarasvatichandra* and most other fictive engagements of that period with the Hindu widow's tragic destiny.

To return to the correspondence, Dayaram's persistent scepticism produced a lull of ten days after the initial rapid exchange of letters. Tripathi, accustomed to dance to his own eloquence, had not expected it to leave Dayaram serenely unmoved. This time Tripathi strained himself to the extreme. The upshot was a far more interesting reply, interesting both for its cultural aggressiveness and its numerous contradictions. Dated 24 March, the reply began: 'Yours of the 14th raises very interesting critical points some of which were not present to my mind when I wrote my last, but so far as I can remember, were not absent from my mind when I wrote the book.'[27]

This was a confident opening—everything critical said by Dayaram had been taken care of in the novel. Tripathi cited, by way of proof, some of the radical passages of the novel that had questioned organized orthodoxy. This, obviously, corroborated Dayaram's lament that the denouement had, without serving any purpose, aborted the radicalism implicit in the girl's resolve to avoid matrimony.

Then followed an argument which conceded that Dayaram's suspicion regarding the self-effacement of the hero and the two sisters might 'appear quite sound from Nature's standpoint'. That admitted, Tripathi went on in the same sentence to claim for Hindu culture a singularity all its own: 'but Hinduism itself is a many-sided rebellion against what the whole world follows as Nature'. The denouement represented typically Hindu, not some abstract 'natural' or 'unnatural', behaviour.

This triumphal statement was, however, informed by the realization of an inexorable loss of selfhood. What could be more self-

[26] Entitled *Binodini*, after the novel's female protagonist, an English translation of *Chokher Bali* by Krishna Kripalani was brought out by Sahitya Akademi, New Delhi, in 1959.

[27] *Samalochak*, July–September 1909, pp. 134–8; October–December 1909, pp. 194–9; January–March 1910, pp. 2–7.

defeating for Tripathi, the Hindu author of *Sarasvatichandra*, than to have to explain to gifted fellow Hindus like Dayaram a behaviour pattern that they should have recognized as culturally their own? Under the hypnotic spell of an alien dispensation, of which English education was the most seductive agent, Hindus—educated Hindus—were tending to be themselves and also something else. Indeed, even Sarasvatichandra and Kumud, both tainted by the new education, had to go through fire, as it were, before they could joyously act as Hindus.

This sense of loss, and of a divided self, had for Tripathi an autobiographical resonance as well. His *Scrap Book* documents, with obsessive regularity and in fine detail, a life of ceaseless oscillation in opposing directions. Happy to be steeped in his own Hindu/ Indian culture, he also resented it vigorously. Feeling it both existentially and intellectually, even if not quite grasping the dialectic between the existential and the intellectual, Tripathi had seen this paradox as the defining mark of the educated Indian subject.[28] He was now near the end of his life; in fact he died ten months later. With the advantage of a whole life's experience of this unresolved paradoxicality behind him, he wrote with a lucidity that rarely comes to one about one's own time. Referring to Hinduism's rebellion against nature, he noted:

> We educated natives swing between that nature and that revolt, and when I evolved my leading characters I was calculating the work of the undulations of the swing, and at times deliberately ventured on inconsistencies which would harmonize with life in India if only one could realise the work of the swing not only in our life but in our ideals and in the resultants, which as time goes are sure to startle our world by the motives of their natures, aspects, strength, and weaknesses.

The undulations of the swing made different levels of life in India a series of inconsistencies. No contemporary or progenitor of Tripathi seems to have had this insight in quite this way. However, as often happens with those who hit upon such illuminating insights, Tripathi was not always equal to his own thought. Having dared a depiction that would harmonize with the inconsistencies of Indian life, he created a narrative closure that flattened all dissonances to produce

[28] Without figuring directly, the issue of subjection resonates unmistakably through much of this correspondence.

a single harmony. When, as in Dayaram's reading of it, the novel refused to be reduced to the authorially intended end, Tripathi tried all his interpretive resources to Procrusteanize the text.[29]

Having invoked the singularity of Hinduism, Tripathi turned to a Western work of fiction to claim for his denouement a universal naturalness. Referring to Kumud's sacrifice of her love so that Sarasvatichandra may marry her younger sister, he wrote:

> Going to Western idea [*sic*] I may draw your attention to a converse case where an elder brother disposes of the lady affianced to him by marrying her to his own younger brother *on the ground that she loved the latter without her being conscious of so loving*! . . . a scene which *perhaps* was a precedent present to my mind when I developed my conclusion—though I have no exact memory on this point. (emphases in the original)

This referred to Emile Zola's *Paris*—the last in his *Les Trois Villes* trilogy—in which Guillaume Froment, a scientist, realizes that his fiancee, Marie, and younger brother, Pierre, are actually in love and arranges to have them married. There is a finely tuned vagueness about Tripathi's recollection of the way *Paris* 'perhaps' resonated in his mind while the conclusion of *Sarasvatichandra* was taking shape. In contrast, he is categorical about the similarity between his conclusion and Zola's in *Paris*. This was made possible by a memory of the reading of the French text which blotted out all the differences that militated against the assumed similarity.

Unlike Sarasvatichandra and Kumud who, as Dayaram put it, were made for each other, the relationship between Guillaume and Marie commences with incompatibilities that seem to portend their eventual separation. Guillaume, who is old enough to be Marie's father, acts as a sort of guardian to her, and the consequent closeness produces a feeling that they believe is love. Pierre's advent on the scene forces a new perspective on Guillaume as he notices an attachment forming between his youthful brother and Marie. Their youth,

[29] This time Tripathi seems to have taken Dayaram more seriously than he did in the first letter. Describing him as a searching critic whose interpretation could 'only assist the author', Tripathi wrote: 'It gives me great relief to find in you one raising these points so ably where others raise the same without hardly knowing where they are. These *others* I usually meet either with a silent smile or with a superficialism enough to meet superficialism without troubling either brain.'

pointing to the potential fecundity of their love, confronts him with the likely sterility of his own marriage with Marie. Also, he is moved by the younger brother's efforts to steal away once he awakens to the existence of a triangle. Guillaume finally decides that he is the one who should be sacrificed. He is human enough, however, to suffer on account of the sacrifice, and feel jealous of his luckier sibling. Contrastingly, Kumud is blissful as she decides that her lover, Sarasvatichandra, should marry her younger sister. Indeed, she is under oath from Sarasvatichandra, the ascetic to whom it does not matter either way, 'to arrive at no conclusion which implied a *swarpan* [self-sacrifice] on her part'. Similarly unsoiled by a sense of sacrifice are the final actions of the lover and the younger sister.

The invocation, through *Paris*, of *the* 'Western idea' of normal behaviour may have been meant to carry greater conviction with the likes of Dayaram. But it seems also to have assuaged Tripathi's own inner need to see 'naturalness' in his novel's end. However exhilarating this fictive resolution may have been for him personally and for his 'somnolent' people, whom he was seeking to awaken, no similar miracle had blessed his own conflicted being, nor theirs.

The swing in which the educated Indians were caught was one that would prompt, and also foredoom, attempts to escape it. In obedience to this dilemma, and impervious to the incongruity of the exercise, Tripathi followed up, as he had preceded, the invocation to *Paris* with further emphasis on Hindu uniqueness. His characters, he said, were governed by 'the duty of Hosts to Guests', whereby an individual must act like 'a host to every one coming in contact with him or her, and to wish or expect nothing in return'. Acting thus, each of the protagonists, Sarasvatichandra and Kumud, was 'anxious' to 'sacrifice everything' in order to make the other happy and prevent her/him 'from incurring any sacrifice'. So overpowering was this anxiety that they were even 'prepared to give up all scruples as to one's own saintliness and to yield to the physical impulses of the other if that course turn out to be the medicine necessary to make the other happy'.

In the event, each saved the other from weakness, and emerged 'relieved of all inner storms and outer fears'. In the process, Tripathi admitted, they 'momentarily seemed to have sought' a few 'so-called "embraces"'. But this was no more than 'a fierce and final struggle between flesh and soul', at the end of which the soul came out 'with flying colours, and crushed all flesh'. Slurring over the cave scenes to suit his teleological exegesis,[30] Tripathi explained:

> The charms of physical or sexual love and amorous exchanges between the hero and Kumud are the baby's stumbles, unsought, unwelcome, attempted to be resisted and finally overcome and replaced by higher conditions. Like foot-prints on sand they are scarcely noticeable to the eye of those whose feet have imprinted them without meaning to waste their energies on the shadowy marks.

Turning to the argument that this was 'Utopian and opposed to human nature', Tripathi saw in it reason to celebrate Hinduism. Just one paragraph after his allusion to *Paris*, he posited a critical difference between the Hindus/Indians and the Europeans. Though Dayaram had written nothing to provoke the outburst,[31] Tripathi held forth in hyperbolic terms:

> We, sons of the ancient Rishis, rightly or wrongly [and I believe rightly], look to our ideals as the goals to be reached by *manushyadeha* [human body] in the next life if not in this; and if the goals are stars in the heavens and not diamonds of earth, I would rather soar up to the stars however inaccessible than handle the toys of earth which adult children call precious stones. The European novelist and scientist deal with the earthly matter and animal life of man. We of India had better look at our spiritual and not animal factors, as really belonging to our human nature. Man is an animal plus more. . . . I had better be this 'more' than this 'animal' for man's animal part is sure to take care of itself whether one wishes it or not. It is this higher part that requires special care, and to it are devoted those parts of my book for which I have worked most anxiously.

He justified his denouement again in terms of his patriotic and pedagogical conception of the writer's social role. The conclusion he had 'worked out' for the hero and the two sisters may not, he agreed, form human nature's daily food. But these children of his imagination were 'high souls' who could 'keep happy and live without eating the earth which the vermin in human nature seeks

[30] Carried away by his teleological impulse, Tripathi provided an interpretation of his novel that matched its final resolution, word for word, with the epigraphs from Goethe's *Faust* and Shelley's *Prometheus Unbound* that he had inserted at the beginning of the first volume.

[31] 'These general remarks,' Tripathi told Dayaram, 'may seem irrelevant to your inquiries to which I shall now specially address myself, and use the above remarks in connection therewith.'

for its daily food'. He had imagined these souls in order that they could 'fire some of my own countrymen and transform them into the active guardian angels of our country's welfare'.[32]

Tripathi was nearing the end of this long letter when he descended from the upper reaches of his fancy to attend to the question that had occasioned this correspondence. To Dayaram's suggestion that Kusum, the younger sister, could as a virgin have become a sister of mercy, Tripathi replied matter-of-factly: 'For sisters of mercy in our country there is no room so long as the present situation lasts.' He cited the case of Pandita Ramabai (1858–1922), the great crusader for the cause of women to corroborate his realism. Emphasizing that 'poor Ramabai' was a widow, not a spinster, he wrote: 'The work that is so out of question for our widows will be still more so for our hypothetical spinsters even if future India will learn to tolerate such a class.' The inference was unmistakable: 'Our ladies starting alone for such work will not only have no assistance in their work, but will only be snubbed or crushed out of society.'

Realism was not the sole reason for rejecting maidenhood as an alternative for women in India. That would have meant a contingent argument which would disappear once India had learnt to accept maidens. Tripathi's resistance went deeper. Even if, he wrote, 'a sister of mercy could work out her way', she could not on her own discharge a mission that would 'equal' the role that awaited Kusum as Sarasvatichandra's spouse and helpmate. No sister of mercy, then, could equal a man.[33]

Tripathi had already dealt with Dayaram's other objections, e.g.

[32] Tripathi, as a patriot, had a long-term conception of the regenerative mediation that his writing would effect within the affairs of his nation. This is best summarized in the following entry in the *Scrap Book*: 'To produce a particular event—be it a rebellion, or be it a political constitutional agitation or a social reform effervescence—this is too little for my mind and aspirations. . . . I wish to produce, or see produced, not this or that event, but a people who shall be higher and stronger than they are, who shall be better able to look and manage for themselves than does the present helpless generation of my educated and uneducated countrymen. What kind of nation that should be and how the spark should be kindled for that organic flame: these were, and are, the problems before my mind.' *Scrap Book 1888–94*, p. 29.

[33] This inference, it may be noted, does not rest on Tripathi's opposition to spinsterhood. It rests, rather, on the reason behind his opposition, as also on the role he assigns to women as their husbands' helpmates. Kusum's mission, Tripathi tells Dayaram, is forged 'out of the hero's dreams and day dreams'.

the irrelevance of remorse in the case of one like Sarasvatichandra who had risen above *raga* and *dvesha*. With his observations on 'sisters of mercy', he believed that their discussion had reached its end. He was satisfied he had settled all the points.

Dayaram was not so persuaded, and replied the following day.[34] 'In Japan', he wrote, 'they tell a story of a lovely girl Kesa who was married to A and was passionately loved by B (to whom she had been first promised) and who by a contrivance had herself murdered by B in order to save her husband and her mother from the wrath of B—to save her chastity also—and to give repentance to her lover. All such stories of renunciation have their uses and Kumud's renunciation has no doubt its uses.' But why should her renunciation have been accepted by Sarasvatichandra?[35]

The correspondence ended, inconclusively, with the kind of rapid exchange with which it had commenced. Three letters changed hands on three successive days. The last was written by Tripathi. Unhappy that Dayaram should have dashed off a reply before he could possibly have absorbed Tripathi's formidable explication of 24 March, he responded in what was, by his standards, a short letter. This, he hoped, 'will suffice to make clear to you my standpoint, though I do not go the length of saying, it also ought to convince you of the soundness of my conclusion'.[36]

All this was to no avail. Dayaram remained convinced of the injustice done to the girl who had wished not to be crippled by matrimony.

IV

What stands out in this correspondence, along with the lack of discussion on the central issue of maidenhood, is the nature of the contradiction into which Tripathi slipped when he did, briefly, grapple with that issue directly. Insofar as the discussion was set off by that issue, the centrality of maidenhood is not offset by the near absence of discussion on it. It is, indeed, the dialectic of lack and profusion that suggests the larger politico-cultural context in which, of necessity, the entire discussion took place. It suggests also the hidden cont-

[34] *Samalochak*, April–June 1910, pp. 67–71.

[35] True to his scepticism, however, Dayaram did say, as he had done in his earlier letter as well, that Tripathi could 'be right after all'.

[36] *Samalochak*, April–June 1910, pp. 70 ff.

straints that held back even sensitive contemporary minds—female as well as male—when it came to making the case for women's freedom.

Of the many contradictions into which the correspondence ensnared Tripathi, one that overarched the others—and reconciled them functionally—was the contradiction between idealism and realism. His eloquence, no matter how inconsistent internally, spurned considerations of the possible/probable to venture into the ideal/imaginary and trivialize the charge of the incredibility of the denouement. Humans, not being vermin, could transgress what was supposed to be natural about them. Hindus, particularly, excelled in that.

Yet, Tripathi lost faith in the human spirit when he denied the possible effectiveness of an Indian sister of mercy. She could overcome neither social nor 'natural' handicaps. Even the example of Pandita Ramabai, whose career had shown (to those willing to see anything) the fragility of those handicaps in the face of an inspired woman, confirmed his belief to the contrary. Indeed, Tripathi was unable to value the Pandita even as a tragic heroic figure. This was a striking failure. For, projecting his own self-image as a silent and unsung martyr, he had cast Sarasvatichandra in precisely such a tragic heroic mould.

It is not that Tripathi expected quick results from these heroic figures, and Ramabai failed the test. Social change, he realized with his suspicion of the 'event', was a slow and painful combat between a self-perpetuating orthodoxy and those unhappy with the existing social state. In this combat, as he pictured it in the *Scrap Book* around the time of the exchange with Dayaram, 'orthodoxy, with nature's gift of instinctive self-preservation, must hold its own as an iron wall, and reformers grow wiser and less sorrowful with their frequent knocking of heads against the wall, until the wall begins to crumble and the heads grow stronger by frequent exercise in knocking and breaking. . . .'[37]

Although Tripathi put it like that, it was not the existing state of Indian society that brought home to him the futility of independent initiatives by women. The causality rather worked the other way around. He seemed to assume the natural dependence of women on men, and the assumption influenced his perception of the empirical

[37] *Scrap Book 1904–6*, p. 67.

reality. Showing how realism can deepen one's perceptual traps, he found even in Ramabai a confirmation of his belief about women: That no woman could on her own achieve what she would as her spouse's helpmate. Induced by the assumption of women's dependence, Tripathi's empirical experience in turn rationalized the selfsame dependence.

This happened despite his concern about the predicament of women and his desire for its betterment. Kumud and Kusum, the two daughters of his imagination who were in advance of the times, were intended to erode people's reactionary attitudes. That, though, did not improve things for his own 'biological' daughters. But that kind of common mismatch between profession and practice is not germane to my argument here. What is germane is the ease with which, in spite of feeling torn, Tripathi could justify his submission to orthodoxy. Take, for example, his acquiescing to the marriage of his eldest daughter in her twelfth year, which was the orthodox limit for a girl's marriage. This is how he justified himself in the privacy of his *Scrap Book*:

> . . . *nolens volens*, I must submit to the custom of seeing her married now. On theory and principles, what justification is there for undertaking to see this? But I cannot ignore consequences. She is born in this society . . . her happiness must be sought by taking this situation into consideration. I must insure her life and happiness in *this* situation, and marriage at this tender age is a condition precedent which the society requires me to perform in order to secure this insurance.[38]

Marriage at a tender age was only part of a larger condition that the society required of parents who cared for their daughters' happiness. The condition, in plain terms, meant bringing up girls in a manner that would make them acceptable—pliant—to their husbands and in-laws. Tripathi seems to have accepted it entirely. In the novel designed to enlarge the mental horizon of his people, he introduced a telling bit of conversation between Kusum's father

[38] This was written in 1891, a few months before the marriage of Lilavati, his eldest and favourite daughter whose early death in 1902 as a martyr to the prevailing socio-domestic order would agonise Tripathi for the rest of his life. *Scrap Book 1888–94*, p. 89. As a safeguard against simplifying Tripathi's position, it may be mentioned that turning to the proposed marriage, he wrote in yet another entry two months later: 'The decision upsets me, plucks me; . . .' Ibid., 90.

and her English mistress. The conversation—carried on in English in this Gujarati novel[39]—begins with the mistress enquiring if she could teach Kusum English accomplishments like piano, singing and painting. 'Well', the father responds politely, 'considering her social surroundings, it is not possible to say that these otherwise good things will also prove her blessings.' 'How?', the clueless mistress wonders, and the father echoes the *Scrap Book*: 'You perhaps know that she is bound to marry and we don't know whether her unknown husband and his people will relish these things.'[40]

Tripathi clearly could not countenance women's freedom to eschew marriage—or even acquire skills that might hamper their smooth acceptance of the domestic reality. As against the ambivalence that he betrayed on most other issues,[41] he had for years retained this clarity on the question of women and marriage. Even his most consistently radical text had, arguably, expressed little revulsion against what it described as 'the national institution of allowing no woman to grow up unmarried'.[42] In his 1892 lecture

[39] Reflecting the way English had begun controlling the thinking of educated Indians, on numerous occasions characters in Tripathi's novel, including animals, break into that language. These occasions are not confined, as one might expect, to the intellectual discussions in which the novel abounds. English is used at times even in emotionally charged situations. Also, three of the novel's four volumes—the second volume carried no preface—have English prefaces. That he maintained his *Scrap Book* in English and occasionally even dreamt in that language shows how profound that control already was. More so, since Tripathi in these respects typifies his times, what makes him unique is the quality and range of his mind.

[40] *Sarasvatichandra*, vol. IV, p. 194. This leads the mistress to protest: 'Why should she [Kusum] be bound to marry? She has a mind to remain as single as I am. You mean *you* will be cruel to her and force her to marry. Such a sweet bird to be forced into marriage? No, no, my good sir, I swear you shan't do anything of that kind!' The conversation ends as the father remarks with gentle—in retrospect, ominous—evasiveness: 'My good lady, you first get your point solved by her and her mother and then we shall see.'

[41] I have discussed this at length in *The Oppressive Present: Literature and Social Consciousness in Colonial India*, New Delhi: Oxford University Press, 1992 (paperback, 1994).

[42] One may remark that, except for the *sanyasi*, this applies effectively to men as well. That may empirically well be the case. But the universality of marriage for women lies precisely in the denial to them of even the choice of *sanyasa*; which for them is a post-marital choice, following upon widowhood, failure of marriage, old age, etc.

on 'The Classical Poets of Gujarat and Their Influence on Society and Morals', he had stated without a trace of disapproval: 'One universal Hindu idea from the oldest times has been that a woman is bound to marry. And a lifelong spinster is a creature of Utopia. The very idea of an adult spinster is foreign to the Hindu mind.'[43]

Utopia was for Tripathi a precious word. It symbolized the will to counter an oppressive present with an alternative future. *The Classical Poets of Gujarat* was itself a utopia that presented a long radical tradition in Gujarati poetry so as to inspire subject Indians with an endogenous model of change. Grander in scale and more cosmopolitan in its inspiration, *Sarasvatichandra*, too, was a utopia. However, when it occurred to Tripathi in the context of maidenhood, 'utopia' lost its resonance, becoming something alien to which the Hindu mind would not warm up.

It was consonant with this consistency, so much the stronger for being atypical, that Tripathi reacted the way he did to Dayaram's defence of maidenhood. Yet, despite the foregoing evidence, Tripathi was, at a level deeper than the consciously intellectual, divided on the question of voluntary maidenhood. *Sarasvatichandra*, we have already noted, is polysemic enough not to be reduced to an authorial exegesis such as the one presented to Dayaram. Similarly, even if we accept for the sake of argument the author's assertion that the novel moves inexorably towards its conclusion, that conclusion cannot exhaust the novel's possibilities. Despite that end, Kusum's expressed resolve to remain unmarried cannot be said to be a mere device to demonstrate its contingent futility, natural impossibility, and cultural undesirability.

This deeper existential/novelistic tension made Tripathi anxious to stall the drift of his text away from what he *knew* was right.

[43] Tripathi states this while discussing Samal, a poet whose 'social heterodoxy' especially attracted him. Being 'wonderfully in advance of his times', Samal had in the seventeenth century considered spinsterhood natural. There is, however, one ambiguous sentence here which may sound like disapprobation of institutionalized prohibition of spinsterhood. But the same sentence also finds 'appalling' a girl's 'vow of celibacy'. I am not sure about the import of this sentence's ambiguity. Referring to a poem by Samal in which a girl mentions her vow of celibacy, the sentence reads: 'The whole idea is original, and the appalling vow of celibacy is a comic reflection against the practice of vows as well as against the national institution of allowing no woman to grow up unmarried.' *The Classical Poets of Gujarat and Their Influence on Society and Morals*, pp. 41–3.

What in this case was right demanded the preservation of an existing social custom—compulsory marriage for women and their subordination to men. The resulting defence of 'existing customs' acquired an overwhelmingly conservative hue. Even idealism, which Tripathi had otherwise used as a liberating force, served the status quo in his exchange with Dayaram.

Tripathi, the exchange testifies, could not have guarded against defeat by his own novel. He had articulated, through Kusum, a subversive female desire and set forth for women a model that threatened a good deal of what he, and many in his society, might wish to preserve.

V

Ironically, the desire to be free from the bondage of marriage entailed the renunciation or absence of another fundamental desire. It implied virginity. Though, normatively, avoidance of marriage meant abstinence for both men and women, the chances of actual denial were much greater for unmarried women than for unmarried men. This was no ordinary sacrifice in the course of searching for a measure of freedom. But the sacrifice was acceptable neither to organized indigenous orthodoxy nor to the colonial dispensation. The two, contrary to received belief, often acted in tandem to maintain the phallocentric status quo.

I may here move from the domain of the *imaginaire* to the hurlyburly of a 'social drama' in 1884–8, roughly coinciding with the first volume of *Sarasvatichandra*, which shook the Hindu/Indian society and reverberated even in England. Having detailed this drama elsewhere,[44] I shall touch upon that part of it which illustrates the melancholy inseparability of deprivation and women's desire for freedom.

The drama was the fallout of a suit filed by a husband for the restitution of his conjugal rights. Married for eleven years, he had never lived with his wife. During the interregnum he had shown himself to be a good-for-nothing consumptive while his wife, Rukhmabai, had grown into an intelligent young woman of twenty-two. Having seen the man go from bad to worse, she had developed for him a 'dislike' strong enough to induce her to resist his claim to cohabitation.

[44] Sudhir Chandra, *Enslaved Daughters: Colonialism, Law and Women's Rights*, New Delhi: Oxford University Press, 1997.

The first of the four judgments in the case, all delivered by English judges of the Bombay High Court, was in Rukhmabai's favour. Inspired by the 'barbarity' of forcing a woman of culture into the arms of an uneducated idler, the judgment rested on the legal ground that a suit for restitution of conjugal rights did not lie in a case of unconsummated marriage such as this.[45] The judgement also emphasized that the provision of a suit for restitution of conjugal rights was unknown to Hindu law. Nor was it right to import into India a 'discredited' English legal practice; discredited in the sense that the English had in their own land defanged the law relating to restitution of conjugal rights by removing its penal provisions.[46]

Though it delighted the reformistically inclined, the judgement appeared to the organized orthodoxy as subversive of the Hindu/Indian socio-domestic order which rested on parentally arranged early marriages. The suit suddenly became a *cause célèbre*. On its resolution seemed to depend not just the fate of two litigants, but the course of rival social forces. Organized Hindu orthodoxy made the husband's case its own, and encouraged him to file an appeal against the judgement. As for Rukhmabai, she had from the beginning had a vague sense of larger principles informing her refusal to go to a man she disliked.[47] This awareness, which soon blossomed into a determination to be a martyr to the women's cause, was shared by those who felt for the cause.

Among the arguments advanced by Rukhmabai one that is

[45] Making a fine distinction between *institution* and *restitution* of conjugal rights, the judge admitted that he could so interpret restitution as to include institution. But, especially in such a case, he was disinclined to enlarge the application of an unfortunate English legal practice which should never have been introduced in India. Ibid., pp. 37–41.

[46] Illustrating the phallocentrism of the English legal system, the harshness of the restitution law was done away with when a woman, in *Weldon* vs. *Weldon*, pressed for the restitution of her conjugal rights. Having been ordered by the court to go to his wife, Mr Weldon made generous provisions for his wife to induce her not to insist on 'cohabitation'. She, however, moved the court to execute the restitution decree or else subject him to penalty for recusancy, which was six months' imprisonment or/and forfeiture of property. These penal provisions were legislated away within months.

[47] Defying the logic of parentally arranged marriages—in which the bride was not a subject but the object of a gift by her father/guardian to the groom (*kanyadan*)—Rukhmabai refused, early in her case, to be bound by this marriage. Married when she was eleven, and incapable of giving intelligent consent, she made it clear that she was no party to the marriage.

germane to this paper is related to comparative hardship. If her husband was put to some hardship by her refusal to live with him, she noted, this was nothing in comparison to the iniquity of her hardship. So revolting was the idea of living with a man like him that she would rather court 'the inconveniences of a solitary life'.[48] The marriage effected in her childhood was for her a 'brutal embrace'.[49] Unlike her husband who, as a Hindu male, was free (whether he won the case or lost it) to marry as many times as he wished, she as a Hindu wife was condemned to this 'embrace' for life.[50]

Rukhmabai's was a revolutionary negation. It was acceptable neither to organized indigenous orthodoxy nor to the colonial masters; assuming axiomatically, as both did, women's subordination to men. This attitudinal similarity, which lay beneath their mutual cultural confrontation, occasionally surfaced during the Rukhmabai case. The husband's claim on Rukhmabai meant the erasure of the woman as a person in her own right. The claim was starkly stated by his lawyer who told the two-judge appellate bench that 'the wife formed a portion of the husband's body and should live with him'. Bayley, one of the judges, was quick to have some fun as he queried: 'How would you apply that rule to the Thakore of Bhownuggur who, according to the Rajput practice, married four wives the same day?' 'Well', replied the husband's lawyer manfully, 'the Thakore's identity was then divided into four fractions.'

The laughter that followed was understandable. Not so Bayley's belief that he as an Englishman/European was above the attitude towards women that he had ridiculed. For, as a contemporary Indian authority on law argued:

> The Hindu law, while it yields to no system in maintaining the unity of man and wife, is more equitable than other systems such as the English, as

[48] Rukhmabai's counsel asked the court to examine her and ascertain: 'She is a most intellectual person, as educated as an English lady, while this man is little better than a coolie. It is no secret that the defendant is a writer of some eminence; and it is altogether revolting to one's sense of decency to think that she should give up her person to such a man as this.' The counsel also emphasized that to force her to go to her husband 'would be the greatest hardship to inflict on a human being'. Ibid., p. 85.

[49] I borrow this poignant expression from Behramji Malabari (1853–1912), a crusader for women's liberation who made Rukhmabai's case his own.

[50] That is what actually happened. Soon after the termination of the case, the man married again while Rukhmabai left for England to train as a medical doctor and came back to lead a life of quiet service.

it leaves to women a much larger share of freedom in the exercise of their rights during coverture . . . the identity of person between man and wife does not extend to civil purposes; . . . the peculiar and often embarrassing consequences of the legal identity of husband and wife in the English law, such as that the husband cannot make a gift to the wife, and that the wife cannot sue or hold property alone, do not exist in our law.[51]

By no means subtle and discerning, Bayley was particularly prone to look down upon the culture of the subject peoples. A more realistic reflection of the pervasiveness of the belief among the rulers of women's inferiority to men is found in some of the remarks made by Chief Justice Sargent who presided over the appellate bench in the Rukhmabai case. At one point, for example, he remarked: 'I should have thought it scarcely worth while citing authorities to show that, according to Hindoo law, a wife's proper place is her husband's house.' Though he made this remark in the context of Hindu law, Sargent believed it to be universally valid. He subscribed to 'the general view of marriage' which prescribed: 'Women *obey* your husbands, and husbands love your wives' (emphasis added).[52]

Not surprisingly, these judges set aside the first judgement, which was in favour of Rukhmabai, and ordered a retrial. The retrial, as ordered by them, was bound to end adversely for Rukhmabai. While her defence rested exclusively on principles, the retrial was to be based on the 'merits' of the case. However, in a moment of inspired defiance, Rukhmabai converted legal defeat into a moral triumph. Instead of offering her defence, she told the court that rather than obey its verdict, which she expected to be against her, she would submit herself to the maximum penalty admissible under the law. To that man she would not go.

The more striking for coming from a woman, and for anticipating passive resistance as political praxis, Rukhmabai's defiance unnerved both Hindu orthodoxy and the colonial dispensation. The Viceroy telegraphed his Law Member: 'I hope you are keeping your eye on the Rukhmabai case. It will never do to allow her to be put into prison.' The Hindu orthodoxy, for its part, advised the husband to leave the woman alone and not press for actual cohabitation. Anxious to make the best of a bad bargain, it argued that the reversal of the first judgement had removed the threat to

[51] See Gooroodass Banerjee, *The Hindu Law of Marriage and Stridhan*, Calcutta: S.K. Lahiri and Co., 1915 (1st published, 1879), pp. 138–45.

[52] *Enslaved Daughters*, pp. 88–9.

the sanctity of Hindu marriage and family. In any case, it was best to leave such a woman and take a new wife.[53]

Once the risk of Rukhmabai's martyrdom was over, the normal state of callousness or resistance to change returned. The advocates of the women's cause, however, continued to press for alterations in the law relating to the restitution of conjugal rights. But they, too, realizing the growing difficulty of persuading the colonial masters, were constrained to lower their demands. For the brief while that the young rebel's incarceration seemed imminent, it seemed possible to propose the very abolition of suits for restitution of conjugal rights but as the controversy waned it became impossible to push through any changes. Finally, the protracted drama ended in 1895. Let down by his own colleagues, the Law Member was forced to drop an innocuous bill that had sought to vest the courts with discretion in the matter of punishing recusancy in a case of restitution of conjugal rights.[54] Their graceless retreat was not reason enough for the colonial masters to feel shame-faced about their professed concern for women. Indians, they claimed, were not yet ready for the proposed change. Even lapses from principles, as the London *Times* had shown in the Rukhmabai case, were for the rulers a matter of principle:[55]

> The government of India by England is, we are often told, autocratic, despotic and irresponsible. Is there any other dependency of any other country where an outrage—against which the feeling of every member of the ruling and many of the better men among the ruled people revolted—would be nevertheless reluctantly connived in, out of respect for the degrading custom of the subject race?[56]

[53] In keeping with what Pierre Saint-Amand describes as the 'perverse logic of image making that degrades the most courageous female models of liberation', Rukhmabai was reviled by the hostile orthodox press as a woman of easy morals. She was said to be the kind who would prefer six months in jail to sacrificing her licentious freedom. See Pierre Saint-Amand, 'Terrorizing Marie Antoinette', *Critical Inquiry*, 20, Spring 1994, p. 400; *Enslaved Daughters*, pp. 124–6.

[54] *Enslaved Daughters*, pp. 165–93.

[55] *Times* quoted in the *Civil and Military Gazette*, 8 April 1887.

[56] The rulers had by this time conveniently forgotten that a discredited legal practice imported from their land into India was responsible for Rukhmabai's legal problems.

The whole thing appeared very different from the women's perspective. It was stated by Ramabai with the passion of a crusader:

It is very easy to bring excuses before the world, but they will be poor instruments of defence when we stand before the judgment throne of heaven. I wonder if such outrageous acts of the English Government will be excused by heaven simply because they have promised to please the males of our country at the cost of women's rights and happiness. . . . I have myself studied the Hindu Law, and do not find anything in it that will warrant such conduct on the part of the Government.[57]

VI

Renunciation, sacrifice, martyrdom reflect a contradictory aspect of women's relationship with the reigning structures of authority. These inter-resonant terms encapsulate the working of varying combinations of conflicting attitudes ranging from acceptance or resignation on the one hand, to a desperate, almost suicidal, urge for justice on the other hand. At one level, this stands out in Dayaram's refusal to accept the authorial explication of *Sarasvatichandra*; and, at another level, in the contrast between Kumud's[58] silent self-sacrifice and Rukhmabai's public invitation to suffering.

The contrast between Kumud and Rukhmabai may seem a function of another contrast: that between a fictive female character idealized through male intervention, and a woman in flesh and blood struggling against what to her was unacceptable. But, as we know, such was the efficacy of socialization that men and women were not divided *as* men and women on the question of women. Moreover, even self-conscious exponents of change were exposed to contradictory pulls.

The final disposal of Kumud's fate squared with a dominant sensibility into which both men and women were being socialized. Tripathi's own daughter had pleaded with him not to bring Kumud—because she was a widow—into marital union with Sarasvatichandra. She who so pleaded was herself a victim of the Hindu woman's

[57] A.B. Shah (ed.), *The Letters and Correspondence of Pandita Ramabai*, Bombay: Maharashtra State Board for Literature and Culture, 1977, p. 177.

[58] A more radical reading of *Sarasvatichandra* must see in the denouement a sacrifice on the part of Kusum as well.

ideal of self-effacement, and would succumb to it before the publication of the final volume of *Sarasvatichandra*.[59]

Of equal significance for understanding the women's question is Tripathi's struggle to overcome the death of his daughter as 'a martyr to the cause of our Hindu Social System'. She, he confided to his *Scrap Book*, had virtually been killed by her husband's unfeeling family. The guilt that he himself had consigned her to that family further aggravated his suffering.[60] When, however, he mourned her death in an elegiac poem, *Lilavatijivankala*, what ensued was an idealization without those disturbing details. This censoring was not entirely due to consideration for the indicted family. A similar idealization marked Tripathi's 'Chuni the Suttee: A Story of Hindu Life' (1902). Inspired by his daughter's death, the story could have given the grieving father the cover of fiction to expose his daughter's 'killers'. The story does describe the travails of Chuni in her husband's family, but there is nothing sinister like the disclosures in the *Scrap Book*. Retroactively even this tempered description loses some of its grimness as the story ends with Chuni's 'ascension':

> It was believed for long that Vishnu himself had visited Chuni in the guise of a *sadhu* . . . that Lakshmi had sent a *Viman* to take her to Vaikunth, and that some people actually heard the bells of the angels and saw the Sati borne away in the celestial vehicle into the region where the clouds gather, the stars twinkle, and spirit meets spirit.

Tripathi's variously expressed grief—in the *Scrap Book*, *Lilavatijivankala* and 'Chuni the Suttee'—is yet another manifestation of the contradictions of which, as we have noted, he could be acutely aware and yet also unconscious. Even the elegy and the story, in fact, possess an ambiguity that seems to both valorize and condemn an order that privileges women as willing agents of self-sacrifice. That explains why Malabari, the great champion of women's cause, serialized 'Chuni the Suttee' in his *East and West*.[61] He must have felt in the pathos and details of Chuni's story a more critical potential and effect than seems to have been intended by Tripathi: or, perhaps,

[59] Being a man and a social reformer did not prevent Dayaram writing to Tripathi: 'I share your beloved deceased daughter's feeling as to Kumud'; *Samalochak*, April–June 1909, p. 70.

[60] See *Scrap Book 1894–1904*, pp. 220–30.

[61] See *East and West*, July–September 1902.

appears to a latter day scholar whose reading of the story is informed by an awareness of Tripathi's work as a whole.

VII

Recent feminist scholarship has indicated the wide prevalence of ambivalence, both among men and women, on the women's question. It has also documented, across cultures, the simultaneously subversive and conservative function of renunciation, sacrifice and martyrdom on the part of women. I shall, in this brief concluding section, refer to Victorian England to confirm the underlying resemblance, already indicated in the context of the Rukhmabai case, between the dominant attitudes towards women among both the rulers and the ruled.

Victorian England idolized the family—home—and idealized the woman as the 'angel in the house'. Dedicating her body and soul to a husband, this angel was pronounced by her very nature to be inclined towards service and sacrifice. Acceptance of nuns notwithstanding, marriage was prescribed as the definitive career for women.[62] The subordination it entailed for them was stated in stirring terms by Charles Kingsley who wrote in his *Yeast, A Problem* (1850) that 'for true woman, the mere fact of a man's being her husband, put it on the lowest ground that you choose, is utterly sacred, divine, all-powerful'.[63] A powerful parallel—which was stated as a contrast—comes in the lament of a Hindu about Rukhmabai: Uncorrupted by Western 'notions of independence and freedom', she would have realized that her husband, no matter how unworthy was '*nevertheless* her husband' (emphasis added).[64]

While the Victorian 'social myth' about women triumphed over 'female reality', it was also seen through and challenged. That ambivalence is thus summarized by Gail Malmgreen: 'A class-bound

[62] See L. Davidoff and C. Hall, *Family Fortunes: Men and Women of the English Middle Class, 1780–1850*, London: Hutchinson, 1987.

[63] Quoted in Susan P. Casteras, 'Virgin Vows: The Early Victorian Artists' Portrayal of Nuns and Novices', in Gail Malmgreen (ed.), *Religion in the Lives of English Women, 1760–1930*, London: Croom Helm, 1986, p. 136. Recall the scene in George Eliot's *The Mill on the Floss* where Stephen tells his fiancee-to-be: 'Now, then—the recitative, for the sake of the moral. You will sing the whole duty of woman—"And from obedience grows my pride and happiness",' p. 323 of the Wordsworth edition, 1995.

[64] *Hindoo Patriot*, 14 March 1887.

Victorian domestic ideology of female service and self-abnegation, confused and confusing in its effects, fuelled the multifarious projects of female philanthropy and social improvement which male commentators like Dickens alternately ridiculed and sentimentalised.'[65]

The same ambivalence characterized even the sharpest Victorian women critics of their society. They were, as Deirdre David has shown, 'both resistant to and complicit with the culture that both encouraged and demeaned them'. As a result, they 'did not feel themselves to be part of a "separatist" female intellectual life'. Focusing on Harriet Martineau, Elizabeth Barrett Browning and George Eliot in her study of the 'burdened and conflictive figure' of the Victorian intellectual woman, David shows how the career of such women 'is constituted by an ensemble of discordant, harmonious, and complex relations between different politics, different texts, and different imperatives, all of which sometimes complement each other and also sometimes contend with each other. . . . The conscious resistance to Victorian patriarchy becomes that much more heroic and interesting in the context of the inescapable cooperation with it.'[66]

Suffering, renunciation and martyrdom—of the silent kind—dominate George Eliot's portrayal of Victorian women. The point is, indeed, made with poignant explicitness in the 'Prelude' to *Middlemarch*. Saint Theresa, 'the little girl walking forth one morning hand-in-hand with her still smaller brother, to go and seek martyrdom in the country of the Moors', figures here as a metaphor for the common destiny of women who 'found for themselves no epic life': 'Their ardour alternated between a vague ideal and the common yearning of womanhood; so that the one was disapproved as extravagance, and the other condemned as a lapse.'[67] This ceaseless oscillation between extremes is Maggie's lot in *The Mill on the Floss*. It terminates only with her death, which is by drowning. The

[65] Gail Malmgreen (ed.), op. cit., p. 9.

[66] Deirdre David, *Intellectual Women and Victorian Patriarchy: Harriet Martineau, Elizabeth Barrett Browning, George Eliot*, London: Macmillan, 1987, pp. x–xi, 5–6.

[67] *Middlemarch*, Wordsworth edition, 1994, pp. 3–4. Virginia Woolf's equally tragic metaphor of Judith Shakespeare comes as a reminder of the continuation, at least at the level of perception by gifted women, of that common destiny into the twentieth century.

novelist, while bringing the novel to an end, keeps the oscillation going.

Sarasvatichandra ends, apparently, with a serene resolution of conflicting human passions. Dayaram, without going very far, was able to discern the 'unnaturalness' of the resolution. He was prepared to assume that the ardour of renunciation felt by Sarasvatichandra and Kumud—not to mention Kusum—was genuine. But he was not prepared to accept that the kind of passion the protagonists had experienced while together in the caves would not recur and overpower them. For him the tale continued beyond Tripathi's formal closure. He could not, realistically, banish a sense of a latent post-denouement storm, ready to erupt any time. Nor was there for him, as a practical social reformer, much comfort in Tripathi's insistence on the exceptional character of the two protagonists.

Inventing Oneself as 'Mu-Luba' in Zaire: State, Citizen, and Ethnic Power in Modernity

T.K. Biaya

MBUJIMAYI, A SPECIFICITY IN THE ZAIRIAN CRISIS

By the end of 1996, Zaire was in the midst of political chaos and a severe economic crisis. The democratic transition, which commenced in 1990, only confirmed a given fact: a dominant social group had confiscated the Zairian state and was using it to maintain itself in power. This group had turned the government into a means of personal enrichment. Unable to put an end to the political contestation and social movements that shook the country since 1976, structural violence became their primary mode of governing everyday politics and its citizens (Biaya, 1997a). During the 1980s, the Zairian state failed to satisfy the imperatives of international economic agreements concluded with the World Bank and the International Monetary Fund (IMF) in order to revitalize its moribund economy. Consequently, all aid to Zaire was cut off in 1993. Thus the structural adjustment program, imposed since 1977, worked together with the institutionalization of multiparty politics in 1990 to aggravate the crisis.

Successive devaluations of the national currency, widespread unemployment, a significant decline in purchasing power, shortages of goods and foodstuffs, and skyrocketing prices all destabilized Zairian society. Inflation rose from 3,000 per cent in 1994 to approximately 10,000 per cent in 1996. This promoted the development

*Since this article mainly refers to a period when the country concerned was called 'Zaire' and since Luba identity was constructed in relation to this name, I prefer to retain it, even though in 1997 the country was re-baptized 'Congo' by the new President Kabila.

of the informal economy, which already in 1985 represented about 60 per cent of national revenues (MacGaffey and Windesperger, 1993). The deteriorating state changed the national currency almost every two years in order to mask rampant inflation. This strategy of 'demonetization' resulted in the substitution of the national money for foreign currency in financial and economic transactions. Lacking liquidity, the banks gave way to street-based money changers. In Lubumbashi and Mbujimayi, Lebanese and Zairian merchants exchanged currencies in their entrepôts.

In this ruined country, only the city of Mbujimayi and its province, East Kasai, exhibited relative economic health. Economic activities in this area were estimated at some US $ 200 million, with transactions reaching a value of US $ 1 billion a year.[1] The city and its province disposed of its own local money, the old zaire, which was no longer in use in the rest of the country. They had recourse to the American dollar for inter-regional commerce. Nonetheless, the Mbujimayi bourgeoisie maintained peaceful relations with members of the state apparatus, with whom they shared or negotiated political and economic spaces. This complex socio-economic and political architecture was the fruit of the province's denizen and artisan: the Luba. This group was able to edify its specificity in the heart of the Zairian nation-state due to the success of their diamond-based bourgeoisie, but also with the help of an ethnic consensus arising out of the historical experience that followed decolonization. This experience allowed certain groups in the Kasai to recreate themselves as both an ethnic group, 'the Luba', *and* as modern citizens of Zaire without raising secession as an issue. This identity construct and its cultural practices also permitted them to negotiate the general autonomy (economic, political, administrative) of their city and its province *vis-à-vis* the state, albeit sometimes at the price of popular revolts ending in bloodshed.

One of the aims of this article is to analyse the ethnic identity of these Luba groups as well as the particular political and economic situation of the city of Mbujimayi during the crisis in Zaire. I also hope to shed light on the intriguing relationship that has developed since 1960 between the state, on the one hand, and Mbujimayi and

[1] These estimations were confirmed by H. Declerq, after his return from a research trip in Mbujimayi and by A.R. Ilunga-Kabongo at CEDAF, Brussels, June 1996.

the Luba of the area, the city and its bourgeoisie, on the other. These complex relationships constitute the crossroads where the double identity—ethnic and civic—of these Luba was forged. This construction was enacted during the very time when the state insisted upon a rigorous nationalism. However, the creation of identity also took place in a context of great mobility of Zairians in general and the Luba in particular. Both movements were confined within the double project of the construction of a supra-ethnic nation-state and the homogenization of national culture. The politics of authenticity, launched in 1971, pursued this juridico-ideological enterprise of so-called national integration (MacGaffey, 1982).[2]

The broader context of the present study is defined by the history of the Luba and that of Zaire from 1960 to 1996; the two are intimately linked to one another. It is against this background that this study focuses on the production of ethnic identity and citizenship among the Luba, specifically among the Luba of the Mbujimayi region. It analyses the construction of an alternative Luba ethnicity centred upon Mbujimayi, the only postcolonial Zairian city formed without state assistance. It ends with the explosion of an overall Luba identity within the confines of the nation-state. A methodological note and a brief presentation of 'the Luba' will serve as an introduction to this analysis.

A NEW APPROACH TO LUBA HISTORY

During the century-long existence of Zaire, first as the old independent state of the Congo, then as the Belgian Congo, and finally as an independent Republic (cf. Jewsiewicki, 1984), the history of the Luba and that of the formation of their double identity as Zairian citizens and as ethnic Luba has thus far been recounted without enough attention to cultural history. One line of thought (Vansina and Boseker, 1963; Young, 1969; Ilunga-Kabongo, 1974) integrated certain presuppositions of colonial ethnography as well as the theory of acculturation. These writings ignored the political culture of the Luba or related it only to the historical Luba empire. However, this empire, founded in the sixteenth century, was located in Nsanga Lubangu (in the present-day Shaba Province) and the Luba groups

[2] Zaire includes more than 350 ethnic groups which speak 250 different languages.

that is of concern here had already emigrated from this area at the beginning of the eighteenth century. This view of 'the' Luba as split-off segments of the central empire was so dogmatic that these researchers ignored the emergence and originality of new political concepts. Ultimately, this resulted in the failure to distinguish between colonization, the exogenous origins of the state, and the cultural dynamism of Zairians in modernity.[3]

The second school of thought (Kalanda, 1959, 1963; Muya, 1985; Kambayi and Mudinga, 1992) also pays scant attention to the knowledge of Luba culture and its diverse cultural practices in modernity even though it offers a serious critique of colonial ideology (Jewsiewicki, 1987; Kalele, 1993). While this writing does concentrate on the construction of the unitary and multi-ethnic nation-state, it ignores the politics of cultural homogenization (especially the endogenous dimension of this process and the specific rationalities guiding citizens' conduct in confrontation with the state). This perspective reproduced certain colonial and postcolonial clichés, not to mention the ideology of the regime in place. Finally, the failure to imagine Zairians as anything but subjects lacking in modernization has resulted in conservative approaches which, for example, identify the Zairian state with that of earlier phases of European history.[4] These studies imply that the experience and the historical trajectory of the Western state constitutes the pre-eminent paradigm of modernity.

The present study is based on the recognition of Luba political culture as a source of ethnic power. It is inscribed in a twin analysis of the dynamic of modern ethnicity and the reinvention of capitalism (cf. Bayart, 1994), both within *and* facing a nation-state constructed out of exogenous attributes and an externally-defined historical legitimacy. This state, inherited from colonization, blocked any integration of endogenous ethnic cultural dynamics in its formation

[3] This line of thought has never been seriously questioned. It is pursued with respect to many themes without its epistemological base ever being interrogated. The very useful studies of B. Verhaegen (1966), J.C. Willame (1972), as well as A.R. Ilunga-Kabongo's dissertation (1974) exemplify this undifferentiated vision which harks back to the Enlightenment and its conceptions of the black race, ethnicity and the state (cf. Gilroy, 1994). This gave rise to a series of other local studies on Zairian ethnicity such as K. Samba (1982) and others.

[4] Cf. for instance, Callaghy's comparison—in itself interesting but susceptible to dangerous exaggerations—of Mobutu with Louis XIV (Callaghy, 1994).

despite its emphasis on national integration and national development (Bokonga, 1975). However, these two elements—modern ethnicity and local capitalism—are at the very heart of Luba culture and the creation of its economic and political space. This was already manifest in the struggles against the colonial and postcolonial states which failed to contain the exodus of Luba citizens from the cities in present-day Shaba, where they had become targets of ethnic wars as early as 1959. These Luba groups chose to migrate to the west, to the Bakwanga area, calling themselves *Nkonga Muluba*: the 'chosen Luba' people returning to their 'promised land'.[5] In this region, a small mining centre, Bakwanga had developed, but the which the state (colonial and postcolonial) protected the area from urbanization in accordance with the interests of the MIBA (la Minière de Bakwanga), the company that exploits the local diamond resources until this day. The vicissitudes of the decolonization process left these people with no other alternative than to reinvent themselves as Ba-Luba and at the same time as the modern citizen in order to survive in their own country.

This instance of identity creation established a model of alternative ethnicity that diverged from that which the (post) colonial state had imposed on its citizens since 1885. This alternative ethnicity was rooted in Luba culture, but it was also an opening on modernity and the world. It gave these people control over their own resources as well as access to regional and international economies which, in turn, acted as a catalyst for the emergence of this specific identity. This politico-economic configuration rested on an ethnic ideology and widely ramified ethnic networks; it defied or subverted state laws through a game of opposition, alliances and complicity between the state, the Luba bourgeoisie, and local political personalities. Moreover, with time, the double Luba-Zairian identity evolved in the context of inter-ethnic relations which were more often marked

[5] The term *Nkonga Luba* by itself reflects the complexity of the emerging Luba ethnicity. It can be translated as 'the one who re-unites the Luba', but it refers also to the mythical founder of the Luba empire. Later, it became the name of a political party. In this context, it referred to the return of the urbanized Luba from Katanga/Shaba—harassed by the 'autochthons' of the area—to the Bakwanga region, where their ancestors had settled a century ago. However, these same Luba groups claim that, in a more distant past (eighteenth or nineteenth century), they had split off from the Luba empire which was situated in present-day Shaba Province.

by tension and exclusion than by friendship and cooperation. This is illustrated by many contemporary sayings: 'There was an accident. Three Zairians and a Luba were killed,' or 'As soon as you are named minister, find a Luba; he will run your cabinet.'[6]

THE AUTONOMY OF SOUTH KASAI WITHIN THE ZAIRIAN NATION-STATE

The birth of the province of South Kasai goes back to 1959, or to what the Luba of Kasai call the 'white treason' (*la trahison du blanc*). The Luba—who since 1885 have served as the pre-eminent collaborators of the colonial trinity (state, Catholic church, capitalist enterprise)—most readily accepted colonial acculturation up to the end of the Second World War. They accepted the school, the missions, and salaried work, and served the administration and industry throughout the country (including Rwanda and Burundi which were annexed to the colonial state in 1924). The Ngala and the Kongo, while equally educated, rarely left the western part of Zaire, their region of origin. Luba peasants in contrast, were able to establish themselves through voluntary migration near the plantations. Moreover, they flocked to the small agricultural centres that blossomed along the Bukama-Kamina-Ilebo railway, constructed during the 1920s, which became a crucial link in the transportation and export of the products of the whole region south-east of the colony.[7] This movement supplemented earlier, compulsory resettlements which occurred when the colonial administration transplanted ethnic groups from the diamond zone to rural areas populated by 'resistant' groups, such as the Kanyok, the Luluwa, and the Kuba. This forced resettle-

[6] Numerous similar proverbs and adages put forth the 'Luba danger' in all its ambivalence. For example: a Kongo, a Ngala, and a Swahili die and arrive in Heaven where God greets them by rising from his chair to shake their hands in keeping with Bantu courtesy. The Luba is the last to arrive. In a forward manner, he salutes God extending his hand. God rises to shake it and the other Zairians whisper: 'Don't get up or he will take your place.' And God sits back down hastily.

[7] Tshijuke 1980. Indeed, the town of Ilebo—the riverhead of this railway, from where products where transported to Leopoldville (Kinshasa), Matadi and on to Antwerp—became a relay station in the spread of the Luba throughout the south-eastern and south-western parts of the colony (Katanga/Shaba, but also Kasai and up to Leopoldville).

ment helped the colonizers put an end to the resistance of local people and to create a belt composed of immigrants around the mining zones, the plantations, and the commercial centres or white citadels. The dispersion of the central Luba people had transformed the colonial Kasai province into the 'breadbasket of the Congo' by 1927. Moreover, this rapid 'acculturation' of the Luba was supported by the colonial policy of 'divide and rule', which portrayed the resistant peoples of the province as lazy, backward, and barbarous.[8]

In 1950, the Luba, who had become very numerous in southern and south-eastern cities like Luluabourg (present-day Kananga) and Elisabethville (now Lubumbashi), constituted also the third largest population in Leopoldville (Kinshasa), following the Kongo and Ngala. The Luba language, which was taught in all of Kasai up to Otetela country, was also the language of the administration. Towards the end of the colonial period, the Luba were so generally established in the large cities of the country that they had a long urban experience. This characteristic is confirmed by life histories (Biaya, 1987; Archives, Department d'histoire, Université de Laval, 1980-91; Jewsiewicki, 1993). Their consciousness as urban migrants was expressed in statements emphasizing their collaboration with the whites and their ethos of hard work, such as: '*Muzungu ni Baba, kazi ni Mama*', the white is my father, work is my mother. It was also marked by a certain radicalism in the social and political demands they articulated between 1940 and 1960, and their adherence to the Mouvement National Congolais, the nationalist party of Lumumba. Contrary to ethnologists' theses about ethnic fragmentation, their urban consciousness was the motor of the radicalism that marked the eventual construction of Mbujimayi. But this radicalism soon antagonized the colonial trinity. After the Second World War, the same colonials who had represented the Luba migration as an example of an 'excellent adaptation to modernity' changed their discourse. They began to support the formation of tribal associations of so-called 'indigenous' groups, even though these had been legally forbidden. This ideology was directed against the

[8] The colonizers, be they Catholic missionaries or agents of the state, 'laziness is the greatest sin of the Lulua'. The Presbyterian mission of Luebo, being under the influence of this ideology, made the baptism of the Lulua and Kuba catechists conditional upon them having prepared sufficient fields for cultivation. They only revised their position on this imposition in 1940 (Anderson, cited by Vernon, 1965).

urbanized Luba who were accused of being dominant foreigners who should return to their region of origin.

A crucial event in this changed attitude was the mutiny of the garrison of Luluabourg (Kananga) in 1944. The rebels were supported by the customary Luba and Lulua chiefs in the rural areas. Their followers, wishing for liberation from colonization, attacked the white farmers and their families (Mukaya, 1972; Biaya, 1987). The urban Luba elite, in contrast, refrained from participating in the mutiny; in stead they protected whites hidden in the town's cathedral, thus showing their fidelity to the colonial authorities (Libata, 1984). They supposed, in all good faith, that the colonials would reward them by recognizing their status as '*évolués*' and by improving their social condition. Their demands were formulated in the 'Luluabourg manifesto'. However, while this manifesto was being debated with some anxiety in administrative offices, a persistent rumour emerged among urban Luba in Katanga/Shaba that the Congo would soon be liberated by black American soldiers. The administration tried to contain the unrest inspired by this rumor by offering Luba leaders the financial means to start a commercial venture in Kasai, thus drawing them away from Shaba (ARSOM, 1983). Nonetheless, all this reinforced the idea of an anti-colonial conspiracy among the Luba and reversed the favourable attitude that the administration and the Catholic church had held with respect to the Luba.

In this country, where a camouflaged apartheid reigned, the demands put forward by the Luba were seen as a challenge to the civilizing mission of colonization. Consequently, in 1953 the colonial administration and the Catholic church encouraged the formation of tribal cultural associations—Lulua frères and Confédération des associations tribales du Katanga—which they explicitly set against the Luba. These associations were used to create the myth of a Luba danger which led to the inter-ethnic and civil wars of Kasai and Katanga/Shaba during the period 1959–63. The Belgians presented the urbanized and educated Luba as overly ambitious, greedy for power and ready to replace them (the Belgians) in order to subjugate the other ethnic groups of Zaire. Fears thus raised were confirmed by the results of the municipal elections, which were followed by a 'Luba hunt.' However, it was only to be expected that the Luba, who were mostly urban and living outside their region of origin, would carry off the municipal elections in the *cités* of Katanga/Shaba in 1958 and later in Kasai, where the indigenous ethnic groups were minorities (Ilunga-Kabongo, 1974; Young, 1969). At the 1960 provincial legislative elections, just preceding independence, the Luba, under the aegis of the Mouvement Solidaire Muluba (MSM) obtained a small majority in Kasai. However, the other ethnic political parties had formed a cartel, thus preventing them from taking control over the provincial government. After that, ethnic wars between the Luba and the Lulua, which had already started in 1959, spread throughout the province of Kasai.

After Independence (1960), a second wave of inter-ethnic, anti-Luba conflict blazed through Kasai and the entire country. These inter-ethnic struggles against the Luba exhibited the same basic pattern. The conclusion of the 'Dequenne Report', which some Luba secretly took from the administrative office in Luluabourg in 1959, was explicit about the cause of the fighting and the recommended solution: the Luba, who were strangers and spoilers, were to leave the Lulua lands (Kalanda, 1959). This assertion pushed the MSM to a more radical position, transforming it into a more explicit political movement. It adopted the name *Nkonga Muluba*, that is the 'reuniter' of the Luba, dispersed by colonization. The choice of an ethnic name reflected a dialectical response to the whites' position and the anti-Luba ethnic associations. Moreover, it underscored the rejection of the Luba colonial identity that had been imposed upon them as much as it implied the emergence of a postcolonial identity.

Therefore, in the face of the failure to form a provincial government of Kasai and the inter-ethnic hatred fomented by the colonizers, all the Luba residing in Kasai (that is, outside the bounds of their native areas) decided to return to Bakwanga. Their experiences made them distrust the agreements of Lake Munkamba and Brussels signed in 1959 and 1960 respectively between the colonial authorities and the customary chiefs and other Luba leaders, which guaranteed individual choice and the liberty to leave or to stay in Luluabourg (Kananga). Now the Luba demanded their own province. A. Kalonji, one of the Luba leaders, radicalized this position by founding the *Nkonga tuyaya kwetu, washala panyima mbwende bwalu* movement (Let us return home; those who refuse will be left to fend for themselves). On 8 August 1960, Kalonji implemented the secessionist threat previously put forth by the urban elite of Luluabourg (Kalanda, 1959). The creation of a 'mining state of Bakwanga' was greeted with general enthusiasm by the Luba of Zaire. This 'state' appeared to be a solution for some two million

Luba who found themselves in uncertain circumstances. It also stimulated their sense of ethnic pride and their desire to possess their own territory, as well as a Luba Parliament and government. Approximately 4,00,000 people responded to this call and returned to Bakwanga. This figure indicates that not only Luba from the former province of Kasai, but also those coming from the industrial cities of Katanga/Shaba joined the movement.

The colonial elites—in the literature often called *les évolués*, that is those Congolese who had acquired some education and thus made career in colonial service—organized the province according to the political culture which had emerged during the precolonial Luba emigration from Katanga/Shaba to Kasai at the beginning of the nineteenth century. Its ideology of city-states (*ditunga*) with elective power rotating among clans inspired the Luba vision of democracy. The notion of *Nkonga Muluba*, which was chosen in opposition to divisive, colonial policy and inter-ethnic fighting, came to express an explicit political choice of identity:

Nkonga ngani?
Nkonga mwana'a Muluba
Mwan'a Muluba nnganyi?
Mwan'a Muluba N'ditunga.

Who is the one who re-assembles (the Luba)?
The re-assembler is the son of the Luba.
Who is the son of the Luba?
It is the son of *Luba N'ditunga* (the Luba city-state).

To understand the last phrase it is important to note that these political and historical metaphors do not refer to the myths and founders of the Luba empire, but to a different strand in Luba history. This distinction is important since it establishes Luba modernity on the basis of a double rejection: first, of the myth of the renaissance of the Luba empire contained in the expression *Nsanga Lubangu* (the tree that was the symbol of the Luba empire); and second, of colonial identity (Vansina, 1966; Biaya, 1985; Petit, 1996). Instead, it indicates a deliberate choice for the modernization of Luba ethnic political culture.

After several months, Kalonji proclaimed himself emperor, contravening the political culture on which the institutions of South Kasai had been founded and in spite of the strong opposition of the

South Kasai assembly and the customary chiefs (Muya, 1985). The subsequent political confusion and conflict among the Luba did not end with the exile of Kalonji to Madrid in 1962. Fighting continued until 1964 and a political arrangement was only reached in 1965, when J. Munkamba was elected governor.[9] After 1962, the town of Bakwanga was renamed Mbujimayi, after the river which runs through the area. The symbolism of this change was that the new name expressed the unity of the Luba clan groups and their willingness to develop a democracy based on ethnic power.[10]

It should be noted that the 1962 law on the administrative partition of Zaire legalized South Kasai as a separate province (which it had been de facto as of 1960). The law of 1966 extended the province to include all central, northern and southern Luba (who formerly had been in conflict), and the Otetela. The province of South Kasai then took the name of East Kasai.

During the first two years (1960–2), the South Kasai leaders were not heading for secession, as Katanga/Shaba did under M. Tshombe. Contrary to the UMHK, the famous Mining Union of Haut Katanga (in present-day Shaba), which suspended tax payments to the Zairian state and supported the Katanga state and its structures, the Minière de Bakwanga (MIBA) continued to pay taxes to the Zairian state even though it invested almost 200 million Congo francs in South Kasai. The Zairian state, being incapable of imposing taxes on the increasingly autonomous provinces, became involved in prolonged national and international negotiations regarding its status. The position of the state oscillated between hegemonic centralization and the confederation or federalism demanded by Kalonji and Tshombe. In such a context of a weak state, the declaration of secession by the state of South Kasai was first and foremost a political threat directed against Lumumba. Later this idea became

[9] The ministerial portfolios and provincial Parliament seats were divided between the two predominant Luba clans just as in the historical city-states. In 1965, the Parliament finally elected J. Munkamba, who came from a politically neutral clan, as governor. His task was to establish 'consensual democracy'. Generally accepted by the Luba people, he continues to play this role up to the present day (cf. infra, Ilunga–Kabonga, 1974).

[10] In this regard, the phrase, 'autonomous state of South Kasai' was harmonized phonetically in Luba: '*mu'ta utwa nyima hanshi*'. This translates as 'live in the state (where it is nice) to rest your bottom' meaning sit and enjoy your local resources.

Kalonji's war-horse, as he tried in vain to remain on both the national and international political scene.

However, Kalonji's ideology of *Nkonga Muluba* was also supported, at least partially, by Luba intellectuals and nationalists who believed in the necessity of a Luba province as a condition *sine qua non* for lasting peace among the ethnic peoples of a united Zaire.[11] It should be noted that these very intellectuals had been pushed out of Mbujimayi in 1961. Many of them were young university students who had joined the 'movement of return', eager to put their knowledge at the service of the young province and hoping to help in the construction of a model administration. However, their leadership was soon decried as a return to colonization. Thus most of these young intellectuals returned to Kinshasa, leaving control of the province in the hands of older local elites who had emerged in collaboration with the colonial administration.

SURVIVAL AND CONFLICT OVER RESOURCES, 1962–1982

The exploitation of diamonds in the Bakwanga area was started in 1917 by FORMINIERE, the company which had been exploiting the mineral wealth and forests of the Belgian Congo since 1905. Later the same company expanded its activities to the Tshikapa area in Western Kasai which, however, did not prove to be very profitable. So, in 1957, the company abandoned industrial exploitation in the western parts of Kasai, turning its full capacities to the diamond zone of Bakwanga. In 1960, it took the name Minière de Bakwanga (MIBA). Today, it is a state-run enterprise whose stock is less than 50 per cent foreign-owned. The law of 1928 divided all concessions containing precious minerals into two zones, A and B. A is the zone of direct mineral exploitation while B, the adjacent zone, is debarred from all urban development since it might give rise to diamond fraud. This law was respected up until 1960; but after the arrival of numerous newcomers in Bakwanga (the 'return' of the Luba, mentioned earlier), it was increasingly and consistently violated.

The city of Mbujimayi, constructed in zone B, for all practical purposes limited the MIBA concession to zone A, called 'the fence'.

[11] This preoccupation and its implementation was for the most part in keeping with the legalist position of Lumumba (Verhaegen, 1961; Gérard-Libois and Verhaegen, 1961).

Those who arrived with the 1960 exodus looked for a place to settle near Bakwanga, then a small town (about 16,000 inhabitants) of MIBA labourers. This forced the company into negotiations with the local administration. MIBA did indeed take steps to accommodate the newcomers: it set up the 'New City,' a chic neighbourhood for functionaries and magistrates; financed schools; and conducted other charity works. In exchange for this contribution, it obtained the provincial government's promise to prevent the expansion of diamond fraud. But this proved to be unsuccessful since the majority of city-dwellers refused to return to 'the bush' and diamonds were the only means of survival for them. Only 18 per cent agreed to return to their native villages and go back to agriculture. Meanwhile, the rural youth, who disdained agricultural labour as well as schooling, came *en masse* to Mbujimayi, drawn by the sparkle of the diamond and urban life despite police controls and a ban on new constructions. Diamond fraud reached its pinnacle during the period 1964–7 ('Rapport annuel de MIBA', 1965, 1967; Biaya, 1985).

MIBA's complaints to the provincial and national governments about the increase in fraud were in vain due to the laxity of the first Republic (1960–5). During the first two years of South Kasai's existence, Kalonji's official discourse castigated fraud. However, he was extremely ambivalent on this point, supporting the opposite position as well. At first, this seemed to escape the interpretive skills of MIBA. But, as it became ever clearer that, in practice, Kalonji even encouraged fraud, open conflict erupted between the provincial government and MIBA. At the same time, it stimulated the creation of a local diamond-based bourgeoisie which was antithetical to the well-being and productivity of MIBA. After Kalonji's fall from power in 1962, the provincial and national governments gave stronger support to MIBA. They set out to combat diamond fraud through legal measures and police activity, both of which were reinforced over the years. The hunt for traffickers went on until 1982, when diamond exploitation in the eastern Kasai was liberalized. This struggle against fraud was often bloody but despite the great efforts made by the state and MIBA, it was not very successful.[12] The emergence of a Mbujimayian bourgeoisie went through three stages,

[12] Another aspect of these developments was that the Bakwanga, who were natives of the region, were increasingly marginalized. Many had already been deported as agricultural labourers by the colonial administration to Lulua land around Luluabourg/Kananga and to Kuba and Lele in the west and north-west (Tshikapa, Mweka, Ilebo—see the map).

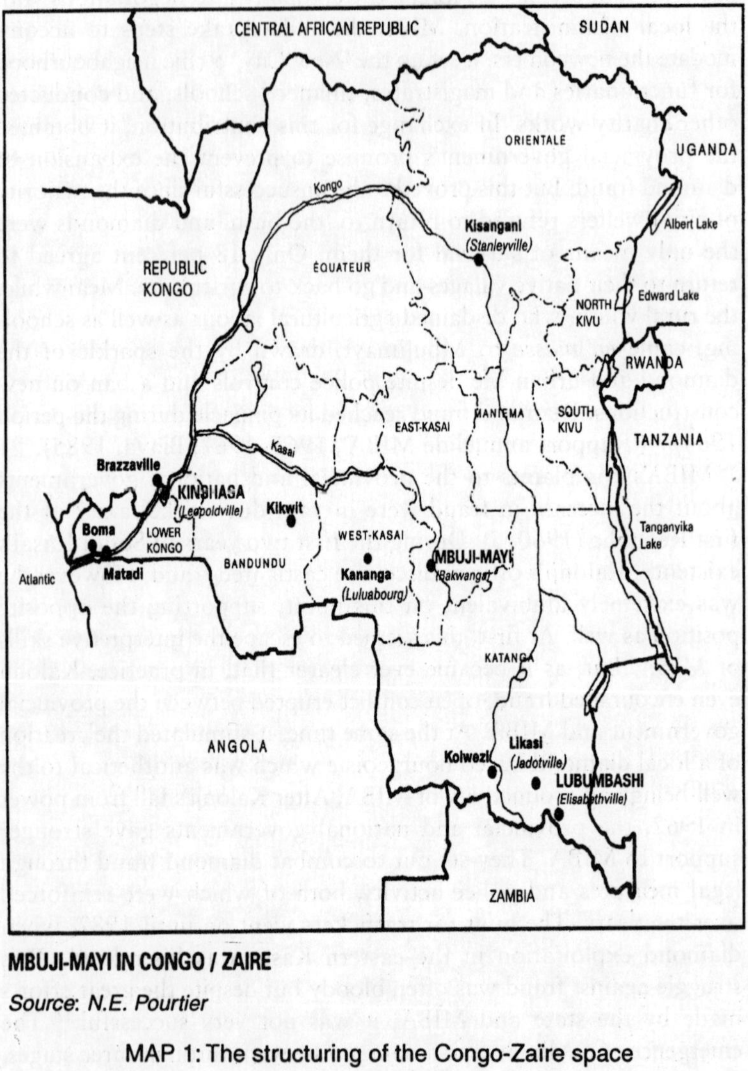

MBUJI-MAYI IN CONGO / ZAIRE

Source: *N.E. Pourtier*

MAP 1: The structuring of the Congo-Zaïre space

all marked by tense, conflictual, and sometimes ambiguous relations between this local bourgeoisie, MIBA, and the state. Between 1960 and 1967, diamond fraud constituted an important activity of the youth and the local politicians, to which they devoted themselves without reserve. Such groups sold the diamonds to West Africans who then exported them. Its members were known as *les riches*, or more poignantly as upstarts, *bena citanci*. In an earlier publication, I have characterized this group as *les cuistres* in view of their reputation of being rude, ill-mannered and highly adventurous (Biaya, 1985). They were looked upon with some disdain by the educated Luba intellectuals. Yet, these *cuistres* were the ones who would reconstruct the local economy and manage, in their own way, to merge it with the global economy.

These *cuistres* spent their money in an ostentatious manner: on drink, prostitution, polygamy, clientelism, etc. The fraudulent exportation of diamonds increased and allowed Congo-Brazzaville and Burundi to enter the ranks of exporting countries by opening purchasing agencies ('Rapport annuel de MIBA', 1965, 1966). As of 1967, the *grands trafiquants*, the big Luba 'traffickers', wrested the market from the West Africans, who were soon forbidden by the state to reside in either zone A or B. As an alternative, they turned to pro-visioning the town with foodstuffs and essential manufactures. This served to intensify the diamond fraud, as well as MIBA's anxieties. The latter demanded that the state reinforce its anti-fraud measures. And this, in turn, pushed the bourgeoisie to fine tune its economic practices and adjust its ideology. This social class blossomed only after 1970, when it finally succeeded in nullifying the efficacy of the new anti-fraud measures.

This Luba bourgeoisie was made up of two factions. The first, *les grands trafiquants*, were the kingpin of this class; they specialized in diamond exports, which they bought from 'diggers' who worked rather like artisans. Building up their own network of friends, they no longer needed the buying agencies of Brazzaville and Bujumbura, once used by the West Africans. Instead, they remobilized colonial circuits leading to East Africa (Tanzania, Uganda, Kenya) via the Goma-Butembo axis as well as the South African circuit via the Lubumbashi-Lusaka axis. By 1976, this fraction of the bourgeoisie succeeded in integrating itself ino the global circuit which links the eastern international diamond networks (Cairo and Bombay) and the western ones (Antwerp and London) even today. They laundered their money by selling the foreign currency they earned to merchants who imported goods. Through this, a second fraction of the bourgeoisie—the importers—was able to build up a local commercial structure (plantations, commercial houses, hotels, small industry, etc.). And they diversified their commercial activities through innovative strategies, increasing the worth of their holdings by investing in other regions of the country.

This diversification allowed this bourgeoisie to escape the draconian laws of the state. It also permitted the Luba bourgeoisie to establish and control an inter-regional commercial network alongside that which existed for international import, with Mbuji-mayi as its centre. The commercial fraction invested in industry and plantations outside of eastern Kasai. Well-organized and of considerable economic sophistication, this bourgeoisie provisioned the city and its region in local and imported products such as beer (*Simba, Temba*) and cornmeal from Shaba, manioc and beer (*Skol*) from Kananga, rice from Kindu and Thailand, etc. By 1981, the Luba bourgeoisie no longer used the official banking system for its financial transactions, not only because it was infiltrated by the mining police, but also because the demonetization of Christmas 1979, which hid runaway inflation, weakened their habitual propensity for savings. They established a system for transferring money by air freight—called *tindage*—so as to escape state controls and to minimize the impact of future demonetization by 'keeping money in merchandise'. Although monetary transfer by air was more costly, it was rapid, efficient, and secure both for exchanges and purchases.

During the same time, the high cost of living in Mbujimayi (indeed, the highest in the country) was compensated for by the fact that there were no shortages and prices were stable. Socially speaking, the rise in the cost of living precipitated the downfall of middle class bureaucrats and teachers. Over the long term, their collapse engendered a fall in status of intellectuals and of education in social life and urban culture. Increasingly, money as such came to be perceived as the key to social success.

Moreover, the draconian anti-fraud laws and the ban on new constructions in Mbujimayi in 1967[13] marked the start of open hosti-

[13] These measures included prison sentences of up to 20 years with confiscation of real estate and furnishings; the creation of the mining police and their special court; an armed industrial guard trained by retired Belgian officers, the shooting of illegal miners by the army; the destruction of unlicensed neighbourhoods, etc. (cf. Biaya, 1985).

lities between, on the one hand, the state represented by Kinshasa and the provincial administration, and, on the other, the Luba who, already having elaborated their own sense of 'citizenship', became more and more convinced that the state, by supporting MIBA, was working against the Luba and their own attempts to develop their own city and region. Thereafter, the Luba consolidated their local political base by both reviving the 'return home' *Nkonga* ideology and participating more actively in the regional chamber of commerce. In their view, the white treason (*la trahison du blanc*) had been followed by a similar betrayal of the Luba by the postcolonial and tribalist state, as identified with Kinshasa. Their *Nkonga* ideology valorized the economic success and political resistance of the Luba ethnic group, without which the bourgeoisie would have been incapable of directly confronting the state as happened in 1991 (Biaya, 1997b).

THE DIAMOND BOURGEOISIE AND THE LUBA INTELLECTUALS: A TORTUOUS RELATION

The 'democratic' elections of 1977 (under a dictatorial regime) and the blunders of the Mobutu regime brought together two Luba social groups: the mostly illiterate local bourgeoisie and the intellectuals of Mbujimayi and Kinshasa (whether associated with the state or not). Their rupture dated back at least 15 years. The constitution of South Kasai as an autonomous region between 1960 and 1962 raised a number of issues concerning the access to and management of its mineral resources, and more specifically the political leadership of the *Nkonga Muluba* movement. These issues opposed the local bourgeoisie which had emerged during the colonial period and the younger university intellectuals, who mostly had either just finished their studies or were still at the university. The older leaders formed political parties and succeeded in gaining control of the *Nkonga* movement of the Luba 'return' to Bakwanga, and subsequently of the provincial administration in collaboration with the customary chiefs. Their participation in diamond fraud led to the integration of semi-literate local traffickers into their ranks giving rise to the diamond bourgeoisie mentioned earlier. When the younger university elite returned to the area in 1960, with the hope of contributing to the development of their province, they were denounced as 'colonial' for their classical manner of administration. They were deemed as reactionaries and anti-Luba since they fought the diamond fraud and openly supported the claims of MIBA.[14] Under threat of death, these university men then withdrew to Kinshasa where they established themselves through their knowledge and competence, gaining positions as high level officials and members of the state bourgeoisie. However, they used their new positions of power to intervene on behalf of the South Kasai bourgeoisie in an effort to avoid open conflict between the centralized, hegemonic state and the provincial leaders who lived, to a large extent, off the diamond fraud.

These relations, which were fraught with mistrust and ambiguity (Mbujimayi *versus* Kinshasa, the Luba *versus* the central state), ruptured in 1967, when the 'revolutionary constitution' affirming the hegemony of the state and its centralized administration over the provinces came into effect.[15] The new state confronted the diamondbased bourgeoisie, which had succeeded in spreading its tentacles in spite of the hostile environment created by MIBA and the draconian anti-fraud laws. The bourgeoisie's hatred for the Luba intellectual was proportionate to its success and determination to

[14] Between 1960 and 1977, two political discourses coexisted among the Luba with highy polyvalent connotations, expressing the conflicts of interests of the various Luba sub-groups which date back to the time of the 'independent state of South Kasai'. On the one hand, the intellecuals struggled against fraud and sought to establish a local administration in accordance with the laws of the national state. This vision and its concomitant practices countered the wishes of the general population who felt they had built South Kasai and who felt that their survival depended on this fraud—a position supported by their leader, Kalonji. The emergent semi-literate political and commercial bourgeoisie upheld this popular vision and gave the university intellectuals over to popular anger, accusing them of working for the destruction of the independence of 'the sons of Muluba': that is, they claimed that these intellectuals supported the 'white treason' and partook of the Lumumbist ideology which called for the extermination of the Luba. M. Kalanda recounts this story in terms of a political science which is, alas, profoundly influenced by a colonial perspective (Kalanda, 1963).

[15] The 1967 constitution marked the triumph of the hegemonic vision of the nationalists, among whom were the Luba intellectuals. It imposed further centralization, abolishing the provincial governments and assemblies. The governor became a nominated functionary. Being foreign to the region he governed, he was ultimately dependent upon the Ministry of Territorial Administration. In the Kasai, this reinforced Luba micro-nationalism and the sentiment of being oppressed by 'strangers'.

develop the region without the backing of the state. They accused the state of taking their resources without investing in the province or attending to the well-being of the Luba, the real owners of diamonds. The Luba intellectual who participated in this pillage was seen as a traitor to the Luba cause and an ally of their enemies.

The first step towards reconciliation between these two social groups came in 1977. It occurred at the time of the democratization of the regime, which restored the post of Prime Minister (eliminated in 1966) and established open elections for a new Parliament with accrued powers of control over the government, and even free elections for the political bureau, the main decision-making organ of the one-party-state (Lumanu, 1989, pp. 39–58). The results of the elections were such that the Luba intellectuals felt deceived by their exclusion from the affairs of the state which they themselves had helped to create. They returned to Mbujimayi in search of legitimacy for new political activities, opting for a strategic withdrawal in order to build an oppositional core in the heart of the one-party-state. In this endeavour, they obtained the support of the Luba leaders and the 'customary chiefs'. They also came to an agreement with the local bourgeoisie. Thus reconciled with rival political actors and, in a more general sense, with regional history, the intellectuals set out to negotiate their return into national politics, this time supported by the local bourgeoisie which was also keen to penetrate at the national level. In order to assure themselves of the support of local leaders, the intellectuals promised to further defend and promote Luba interests in Kinshasa. According to the agreement concluded between them, the intellectuals would run for Parliament while the local bourgeoisie would aim for the political bureau, the superior of the two national political bodies.

The massacre of almost 300 Luba diamond workers from Katekelavi and Luamwela by the army in 1979 created an advantageous situation for those Luba intellectuals who had indeed succeeded in getting into Parliament and who made themselves popular in the Luba region and throughout the country by their critical interventions against the regime. This group profited from the violence by supporting the protests of its electorate stronghold and by their condemnation of the state for its disdain for human rights. The Luba opposition against the one-party-state and its chief evolved rapidly into a call for democratization and federalism, giving rise to a clandestine political party, the Union pour la démocratie et le progrès social (UDPS), in 1982. The return of the Luba intellectuals to their political base in their province and their alliance with the local bourgeoisie both reinforced popular support for the UDPS in eastern Kasai. Their political courage also inspired admiration among many Zairians for their ethnic group. Mobutu's regime attempted to reduce the clandestine party to a caricature by referring to it as simply 'a Luba affair' and as an instance of tribalism against the supra-ethnic nation-state (even though its leadership included members of various ethnic groups).

It is clear, however, that the return of the Luba intellectuals to national politics was also inspired by their rivalry with the local Luba bourgeoisie which tried to enter the national arena on its own terms. This bourgeoisie's close rapport with the national elite resulted from its expansion outside its home province, East Kasai, and the overtures made by the regime and the state bourgeoisie following the failure of Zairianization (1973–7). The latter involved the nationalization of small and middle-sized foreign companies in an effort to create a Zairian commercial class. This rather ill-defined plan of action created an inter-ethnic space for *affairisme* and 'elbowing' which allowed the Luba bourgeoisie to affirm itself as a group of dynamic, 'postcolonial' entrepreneurs in their relation to non-Luba Zairians. But it also made this same group conscious of its national, Zairian identity and the concomitant opportunities offered by this identity. Encouraged by this experience, the local Luba bourgeoisie made its own move towards Kinshasa where, by 1983, they had forged alliances with the state bourgeoisie and the national commercial class. This strategy, based on mutually advantageous alliances, helped the Mbujimayian bourgeoisie to avoid the traps of the predatory state bourgeoisie, who were intolerant of competition and the idea of sharing national economic activities. The Mbujimayians thus implicated themselves in the state 'kleptocracy' by affirming that '*ku Tshinsansa ku mpwila mambu*': Kinshasa is where final decisions are made. This political deal-making and economic realism reflected the local bourgeoisie's views on their relations with both the state and the state bourgeoisie and their economic intrigues.[16] In the long run, the Luba intellectuals could not remain politically indifferent.

[16] In 1983, the Groupe Fontshi—Fonds de Tshilenge—opened the first Luba-owned diamond purchasing agency in the towns of Mbujimayi, Kananga,

In this political and socio-economic arena—which had been polarized by political opposition, shifting political alliances, violent popular repression, and the controlled liberalization of diamond production—all parties (the local Luba bourgeoisie, the state elite, and the regime) tried to play their cards without, however, throwing the precarious equilibrium of these variable forces off balance. In this context, Munkamba played a determining role for all groups involved, including the Luba people. Since 1965, this intellectual emerged as the Luba political personality par excellence, being both a modern nationalist and an undisputed representative of the Luba *Nkonga* ideology. Elected governor by the South Kasai assembly, defiant *vis-à-vis* the intellectuals and their anti-*Nkonga* positions, he achieved the peaceful transition from the juridico-political laxity of the first Republic, which tolerated diamond fraud, to the centralized and hegemonic power of the second Republic, which severely repressed it from 1967 to 1982. Contrary to other intellectuals associated with the same regime, Munkamba did not lose credibility among the Luba. In 1983, the growing opposition of the UDPS was followed by rumours that he would be designated head of the province or of MIBA which, until then, had been under the direction of non-Luba who applied an employment policy which disfavoured the Luba in their own region. When he finally did become director of MIBA in 1987, even his immense popularity did not protect him from violent attacks and pressures from the Luba, who began to consider him as the 'eye of the regime' amongst them.[17]

Tshikapa, and Kinshasa. The group was the first to create its own airline company (Fontshi Air Service). The Hôtel Tanko in Mbujimayi, which belonged to Tatu Nkolongo, succeeded in getting the monopoly over housing for state functionaries travelling through the city; Bimansha started construction of the first Luba-owned building in Kinshasa but he died and it remained unfinished.

[17]Munkamba had so much difficulty dominating the spirited Luba that he often had to risk his life. The regime used him to undertake negotiations with the traffickers who lost their miners in the 1979 massacre and who, especially around Christmas of the same year, were hit hard by the demonetization. In 1983, he offered them the possibility of investing in national purchasing agencies of 'open' diamonds. In 1985, with the assistance of the Catholic church, Munkamba participated in the unsuccessful reconciliation of Mobutu and the UDPS. During the popular revolt of May 1991, the partisans of the UDPS ransacked his house and he escaped death only by fleeing together with the

Paradoxically, it was the same Munkamba who established the Council for the Development of East Kasai (CODEKOR), a sort of Luba civil association that further contributed to the Luba self-development programme. The predecessor of this organization was the so-called *Mutuelle des Baluba* or *Nsanga Lubangu*, an informal association of the Luba intellectuals of East Kasai living in Kinshasa. They had organized themselves in 1978 in order to give medical aid to the rural populations of Lukelenge, where a sleeping sickness epidemic had broken out. In 1985, this ethnic association was transformed into CODEKOR, but it lacked significant finances and a centre for coordination. In 1987, Munkamba revitalized it by financing it with funds derived from MIBA's social investments. Although this act was in response to popular pressure on Munkamba to use his position in the national state—as a member of a regime that oppressed and exploited the Luba in order to defend Luba interests, it was not without ambivalence. Mukamba's intention may have been to use CODEKOR in order to divide the UDPS party, which was led by other Luba intellectuals who were also well established in the province.

In less than three years, and with the assistance of both MIBA and Luba people living in Zaire and elsewhere, Mukamba had this Kinshasa-based non-government organization (NGO) transferred to Mbujimayi and arranged for a firm juridical basis. His personality, his abilities, and his political weight served to reassure the regime as much as other members of the state-based bourgeoisie and the undecided Luba. In the province itself, he received the support of the local bourgeoisie *and* the intellectuals. He called a first general assembly in 1989. In 1991, CODEKOR began to devise and manage economic, social, and cultural initiatives for the Luba in an effort to compensate for the state's failure to respond to the needs of the Luba people and of the province. A plan for autonomous development was put up—including the revival of the construction of the

---

provincial governor to Kananga. This popular revolt led to an armed confrontation between the Luba and the national armed forces. This lasted seven days, during which time the administration's offices and archives were destroyed and burned. The Luba also burned companies, houses, and stores that were thought to belong to the allies of Mobutu (Luba and non-Luba). The UDPS counted 47 deaths and numerous disappeared persons (Biaya, 1991a and b, cf. Documents UDPS, 1991).

hydro-electric dam abandoned by the state, the creation of the university of Mbujimayi, a beer plant, and other projects—to be financed by Luba entrepreneurs and their international partners. However, the NGO was careful not to invade the economic domain of the local bourgeoisie. Since 1970, the latter had taken over diverse tasks of the state—*res publica*—such as medical care, the pumping and distribution of water, schooling and so forth. CODEKOR incarnated Luba civil society insofar as it also tried to channel the tensions between the local bourgeoisie and the state. Moreover, the support of influential members of the state bourgeoisie gave CODEKOR room to manoeuver in the face of the state and the ruling class, for whom it managed certain political and financial interests in 'the hot' Luba region.

THE IDENTITY CLASH BETWEEN FORMER LUBA 'BROTHERS', 1993–1996

During the *Nkonga Muluba* movement between 1960 and 1962, many Kasaians—Luba workers who had migrated to industrial Katanga/Shaba since 1928—joined the return to 'their' area as has already been seen. The Luba workers who had remained behind endured a second wave of anti-Luba tribalism 30 years later. This was 'the Shaba incident'. Mobutu's complicity with this movement was in keeping with his instigation of ethnic hatred among provincial authorities (Braekman, 1993). In 1974, seven years after the nationalization of the *Union Minière*, which became GECAMINES, Mobutu set about 'ethnicizing' this company, which was the most important in the country and the main source of the economic and social development of Shaba. He appointed people from the region to the directorship, replacing Luba staff. These new authorities then implemented a pro-Shaba, anti-Luba employment policy. They let it be known that Kasaians, those 'foreign migrants', were to return home and find employment with MIBA. The latter were said to occupy the places of the 'natives', who were to replace them. However, the Kasaians had been settled in the towns of the region for at least two or three generations. Inter-ethnic tension, already manifest during the 1980s, turned into armed conflict in 1990, with the formation of political parties. In 1991, the youth of the pro-Shaba parties blockaded and attacked meetings held by the UDPS, which they considered a Kasaian party even though it was led by people from Shaba. In August 1992, the election of Tshisekedi, a Luba, as prime minister in Kinshasa infuriated the militia of the Union des fédéralistes et républicains indépendants (UFERI/Shaba) who engaged in violence against Kasaians in the centre and south of the province with the help of the national police and gendarmes. They killed Luba who dared defend themselves, burning their homes and belongings. UFERI and the provincial governor rallied with Mobutu in this political transition, justifying this premeditated and unpunished massacre as a rectification of past misdeeds (Kalumba and Ngoy, 1995, p. 141). This reinterpretation of regional history by Shaba intellectuals rekindled frustrations accumulated from the colonial period up to the second Republic and identified those responsible for all evil: 'It's the other, the foreigner, and especially the Kasaian' (Dibwe, 1996, pp. 10–11).

From 1992 to 1994, Kasaians in the urban centres of Shaba (excepting Lubumbashi) were driven out. Many fled to the Likasi train station where the Red Cross and Doctors without Borders had erected a refugee camp. There, they awaited their 'repatriation' to eastern Kasai (for the Kabamba Luba) and western Kasai (for the Lulua and Luntu). Some 1,50,000 persons returned to eastern Kasai. Those coming to Mbujimayi were 'welcomed' and installed in refugee camps at Muene Ditu, a small town 120 km away from Mbujimayi. In general, the cold reception they received from their 'brothers' in Mbujimayi was a deep disappointment. Most of them—especially workers and unemployed youth with their families—never made it to the city. They soon concluded that 'ethnic solidarity did not work' and returned to their abandoned homes and belongings in Shaba. They swore that they never wanted to return to Mbujimayi and that the 'the Luba there were no longer their brothers'. On the other hand, the intellectuals and the entrepreneurs among the refugees did go to the city, where they found employment in the diamond industry or in private teaching. Others established small enterprises or obtained some kind of employment. The rapid integration of the intellectuals contrasted sharply with the lot of the less fortunate and less educated, who were labelled refugees and, for those who remained in the Kasai, were relegated to agricultural labour to survive.

In the face of this calamity, the Mbujimayan bourgeoisie, which had investments in Shaba but was revolted by the massacre and the exodus of their Kasaian 'brothers', suspended all economic dealings with that region. They terminated their investments in industries (breweries, tobacco companies, mining, maize plantations, etc.) and transferred their capital to Kinshasa and elsewhere. They declared a boycott of all products from Shaba (beer, fish, flour, etc.), which they replaced by imports from South Africa. But they did not offer any humanitarian aid to the refugees in the camps at Muene Ditu. This partial engagement was indicative of the nature of modern ethnic solidarity. It is a clear sign of the dynamics of Nkonga ideology which served to legitimize this historical rupture. An important implication of this ideology seems to have been that it underscored the emerging distinction between Luba 'brothers', thus re-writing the history of ethnic identity construction. The fact that *les Kasayiens*—the Luba who fled during the second exodus from Shaba in the 1990s—were not integrated into East Kasai is indicative of the importance of ethnic political culture. When such a common culture is lacking, ethnic solidarity becomes a matter of ethnological thought or folklore. This experience illustrates how distant and distinct those Luba 'brothers' had become, whose different identities as *Koréens* (or *Kasayiens orientaux*: those who had come with the first *Nkonga* exodus of the 1960s to East Kasai) and as *Kasayiens* (the Luba refugees of the second exodus from Shaba) were constructed out of a common colonial genealogy that had followed different historical trajectories. Indeed, the history of *Nkonga Muluba* is in no way that of the *Kasayiens* who chose to remain in Katanga/Shaba in the 1960s. They had not accepted the idea of the 'white treason' and so they never cut themselves off from the colonial culture that lingered into the postcolonial period.

ETHNICITY AND MODERNITY: THE PLURALITY AND FRAGMENTATION OF LUBA IDENTITY

The history of Luba modernity is, above all, a history that intertwines the cultural and the political. It reflects the specific Luba conception of ethnicity and their experience of citizenship in the postcolonial state of Zaire. It is founded on the incessant struggles that the Luba waged against the state (colonial and postcolonial) and its consistent anti-Luba policies which have been manifest ever since 1944. Since the exodus of 1959–63, most Luba have interpreted, wrongly or rightly, any intervention by the state as persecution and an attempt to push them towards suicide by imposing a specific identity upon them: that of an 'acculturated' people. The Luba rejected this treacherous label in a forceful effort to create their own identity, an identity based on the quest for their own territory, the *Nkonga* political culture, and a particular vision of history. This complex arrangement upset Lumumba's nationalist project and his attempts to reduce the province of South Kasai to a state of civil war that would bring about the extermination of the Luba people. Against this, the political culture of *Nkonga* evoked the ideas of a 'promised land' (following the model of the city-state) and the Luba as the 'chosen people'.

Appealing to the ethnic prestige of the Luba in precolonial times, the urban Luba tried to combine their wish for democracy (born from their urban political experience) with the reinvention of capitalism which would endow them with a modern economic and political structure. This was complicated by their ambivalent and antagonistic relations with the state and MIBA, the one oppressive, the other only interested in diamonds. Despite this, the urban Luba elite succeded in recreating a modern city-state. Thus Mbujimayi was to rearticulate varying identities and to rework the secessionist and pro-nationalist aspirations of the urban masses, who had lived 'the white treason'. By refusing to relate their history to the originating myths of the Luba empire, they chose to build a future on a different political culture which was also available in their history: the culture of the city state and the idea that democracy presupposes the refusal of tyranny, whether of precolonial kings or of postcolonial dictators. All efforts of the Zairian state to control this city-state—or, in a larger sense, South Kasai—were perceived as a threat to democracy as well as to the territorial integrity of the Luba. Basically, it was a conflict over access to resources, but the Luba were prepared to defend these more general principles even with their lives. This struggle became the leitmotif for the Luba people, and for their survival in the heart of the unitary and anti-Luba nation-state.

It is important, however, to distinguish between this view of Luba history and that of Luba myth which was constructed by outsiders out of the Luba success as individuals and as members of an ethnic group. This tribalist discourse is still enshrined in Zairian collective memory, but it only takes into account the aspects of the construction of Luba identity that are compatible with the ambivalent ethnic discourse of colonial and postcolonial power, inspiring both hatred and admiration. It underscores the ambiguity of the sentiments among other ethnic groups and citizens toward the Luba. On the one hand, they admire them for opposing the kleptocratic and dictatorial state, and for having constructed Mbujimayi as an economically stable oasis in spite of state hostility. On the other hand, the Luba myth marks the group as a mortal danger for other groups. This myth is based on a selective historical memory, erasing the history of peaceful interaction between the Luba and other ethnic groups (Lulua, Konyok, Otetela, Shaba) in various national and regional contexts. Furthermore, this construct indicates the extent to which these national ethnic groups have taken up the colonial ideology based on the notion of 'Civilization', as well as the postcolonial ideology of 'Fathers of the nation' (Memêl-Fote, 1991), both of which assert that ethnicity and modernity, or tribe and citizen, are contradictory terms.

An alternative view of Luba history is inscribed in the dynamic of a modern political ethnicity. As an alternative ethnicity, it rests on an ensemble of political practices informed by local political culture, as well as by a vision of a modern society and a nationalist state. Thus local political culture is articulated with modernity through a reinvention of capitalism. This process of cultural fixing is antithetical to the functioning of the 'State of the Other' (Buakasa, 1996)—the 'external and kleptocratic state'—which is multi-ethnic, oppressive, and authoritarian-nationalistic, hiding its neglect of the citizen behind its strongly centralized administration. Luba ethnicity provides an alternative insofar as it helped to create a civil society that showed the hegemonic state its limits through a combination of negotiations and open conflicts or even wars. It is an alternative ethnicity to the extent that it developed outside the confines set by the *savoir colonial* of ethnologists and administrators which shaped the trajectory of ethnic identity in so many parts of Africa.[18] In contrast, *Nkonga* power gave rise to a consciously elaborated double Luba-Zairian identity which led to the self-nomination of the Luba as '*Koréen*' in the face of other Zairians, especially the Kasaians, their former brothers in the colonial labour migrations to urban Shaba. Luba political culture illustrates the affirmation of Luba

[18] See Hobsbawm and Ranger (1983); see also Gilroy (1994), on the direct link between Enlightenment ideas and the ethnic conceptions informing colonial policies.

micro-nationalism as well as their determination to remain Zairian in the context of a federal state that has allowed them to develop their province by exploiting its resources. Far from being tribalist, the Luba are both nationalist and ethnic in their quest for a democratic Zaire, sensitive to ethnic difference and rejecting narrowly defined cultural homogenization or imposed ethnicity. In this way, ethnic differences will constitute an important cultural fact in the constitution of citizen identity and national development. The example of the Nsanga Balende soccer team illustrates this effort to be both 'Luba' and 'citoyen'.

Mbujimayi has three soccer teams whose composition reflects the dividing lines of colonial history. *Musangana wa Mbongo* ('the native owns the diamonds'), financed by MIBA, has the worker's children. *Nsanga Balende* brings together the 'well born' (*bien nés*), recruiting players who originally came from the Swahili speaking towns in the eastern part of the country (Shaba, Kivu, and Haut-Zaire). *A.S. Bantou* is constituted of people from Kananga, Lusambo, Kabinda, Mweka and Tshikapa—that is, from the former colonial province of Kasai. The expression of these different identities in soccer teams was seen by both the advisers of the Mobutu regime and researchers working on ethnicity as a disturbing factor that engendered ethnic fragmentation. However, subsequent developments have shown that soccer could also become a site of a modern Luba identity, based on their experience of *Nkonga*.

In 1982, while Mobutu tried to denounce parliamentary opposition as mere 'Luba subversion' against the one-party-state, *Nsanga Balende* won the national soccer championship in Kinshasa against a local team. This victory, and the ways in which it was consecrated, obliged the nationalist elite to recognize the integrating force of the memory of the Luba exodus as a crucial element in the new Luba identity and its role at the national level. Contrary to the expectations of some, this victory did not lead to inter-ethnic violence. On the contrary, it exposed the notion of 'the Luba danger' as a myth. The players and their fans from Mbujimayi performed their magic *ndoci* war dance on the field before receiving the trophy. Subsequently, the youth of Kinshasa appropriated and popularized this dance, which became the 'top' dance of 1982 throughout the country. This sporting victory made the Luba and their presence in all parts of Zaire more visible; and this was boosted by their participation in the African Cup championships.

This story of the Luba seems to end in victory. The relative economic, monetary, and political autonomy of the Luba of Mbujimayi did not lead to secession since this would have countered the effort to be both Luba and *citoyen*. Indeed, the spectacular success of Mbujimayi in some ways reproduced the history of South Kasai between 1960 and 1967; the latter was also characterized by economic autonomy and juridico-political submission to Kinshasa. But in the recent history of Mbujimayi, this configuration reproduced itself on a larger scale: the rejection of the national currency and recourse to the old zaire and the American dollar symbolized the Luba adherence to the nation-wide struggle for democracy as well as their wish to protect their ethnic identity. This was a 'nationalist' project insofar as it aimed to break down the dictatorial, and essentially colonial, political order.

The Luba experience of modernity and its relation to the construction of the Zairian nation-state indicate that analyses of the state, ethnicity, and popular movements for democracy which emphasize the fragmentation of the Luba into different groups and sub-clans tend to neglect the varying dynamics of local political culture. Without this it becomes difficult indeed to attain a deeper understanding of ethnicity and to foresee the future dynamics of groups organized around ethnicity. The shock of the abrupt reunion of the 'old Luba brothers', the *Koréen* and the *Kasayiens*, illustrates this. It informs us not only about the historical character of urban identities—as the outcome of a complex and dynamic arrangement of political culture, history, and economy—but also of the inadequacy of political science in predicting the failure of a crumbling colonial ideology of ethnicity.

The trajectory of the construction of the nation-state in Africa, based as it was on an outright rejection of endogenous ethnicity, stimulated Luba micro-nationalism and an anti-centralist reaction through its continuation of colonial policies and its ideology of integration. It thus led to the emergence of a combined Luba and Zairian identity as a sort of double but non-antagonistic consciousness, which did not deny the idea of the nation-state as such. On the contrary, it served to reconcile the Luba with other groups who equally wanted the nation-state to be federalist and democratic. A crucial feature of Luba ethnicity is that it succeeded in surpassing colonial constructions of ethnicity which tended to block the dynamics of local culture. The danger of such standardized, 'colonial' versions of ethnicity are still exemplified by tribalist ideologies, as in the continuous vindication of the need to redress 'historical injustices' in Shaba, in the hunt for Bakuyakuya 'strangers' in Kisangani, or in the incessant references to the 'Luba danger' by certain national leaders in Kinshasa. The resurgence of Mbujimayi seems to highlight the force of alternative forms of ethnicity that appear to be able to stimulate autonomous regional development and relate it to the national configuration and, beyond this, even to international economic circuits.

REFERENCES

Africa Confidential, 1996, 'Zaïre: Décollage du Kasaï. Diamants et solidarité ethnique expliquent la prospérité de la province du chef de l'opposition', 22 January, pp. 6–7.

Africa Watch, 1993, 'Zaïre: Inciting Hatred: Violence Against Kasayiens in Shaba', vol. 5, 10.

ARSOM (ed.), 1983, L'effort de guerre au Congo Belge, 1939–45, Brussels: ARSOM.

Bayart, J.-F., 1981, 'La fronde parlementaire au Zaïre, 1979–80', *Politique africaine*, 3, pp. 90–3.

——— 1994, *La réinvention du capitalisme*, Paris: Karthala.

Biaya, T.K., 1985,'La "cuistrerie" de Mbujimayi. Structure, fonctionnement et idéologie de la bourgeoisie africaine de Mbujimayi, Zaïre', *Genève-Afrique*, vol. XVI, 1, pp. 65–84.

——— 1986, 'L'Église catholique, la foi et les peuples du Kasaï colonial, 1887–1960', *Éducation et Libération*, 13, pp. 14–27.

——— 1987, *Récits de vie de Deux Dignitaires de l'Ordre National du Léopard*, Kananga: La case d'Édition P.U.

——— 1991a, 'Le Massacre de Mbujimayi: Ce que la Commission parlementaire n'a pas dit', *L'Appel africain*, 4, 1, pp. 5–8.

——— 1991b, 'Les Baluba sont maltraités même chez eux', Interview du Colonel Kankolongo, *L'Appel africain*, 4, 1, p. 13.

——— 1992, 'L'ethnicité au coeur de l'idéologie nationaliste', in M. Kankwenda (ed.), *Zaïre: vers quelles destinées?*, Dakar: CODESRIA, pp. 2–17.

——— 1996, 'La culture urbaine dans les arts populairs d'Afrique, L'analyse de l' "ambiance" zaïrose', *Canadian Review for African Studies*, vol. 30, 3.

——— 1997a, (forthcoming), 'State and Ethnicity in Zaire', in O. Nnoli (ed.), *Ethnic Conflicts in Africa*, Dakar: CODESRIA.

——— 1997b, 'Jeunes, culture de la rue et violence urbaine à Kinshasa, Zaïre', *Rapport d'enquête*, Ibadan Institut français de recherche en Afrique.

Bokongo, B., 1975, *La politique culturelle au Zaïre*, Paris: UNESCO.

Braekman, C., 1993, 'Le Zaïre à feu et à sang en de vastes régions', *Le monde diplomatique*, November.

Buakasa, G., 1996, *Réinventer l'Afrique*, Paris: L'Harmattan.

Callaghy, T., 1994, *The Struggle State—Civil Society in Zaire*, New York: Colombia University Press.

Dibwe, M., 1996, 'L'épuration ethnique au Katanga et éthique du redressement des torts du passé'. Paper for Annual Conference of the Canadian Association of African Studies, McGill University, Montréal.

Dunant, G., 1961, *La politique Hammarskjold au Congo, Le tragique paradoxe*, Brussels: Remarques congolaises.

Gérard-Libois, J. and B. Verhagen, 1961, *Congo 1960*, 2t., Brussels: CRISP.

Gilroy, P., 1994, *Black Atlantic. Modernity and Double Consciousness*, Cambridge: Harvard University Press.

Gould, D.J., 1978, 'From Development to Underdevelopment of an Administration, The Zairian Case', *Les Cahiers du CEDAF*, 6.

Hobsbwam, E and T. Ranger (eds.), 1983, *The Invention of Tradition*, Cambridge: Cambridge University Press.

Ilunga-Kabongo, A., 1974, 'Luba Ethnicity'. Ph.D. Dissertation in Political Science, Berkeley: University of California.

Jewsiewicki, B. (ed.), 1984, *Etat indépendant du Congo, Congo belge, République démocratique du Congo*, Zaïre, Sainte-Foy: SAFI.

——— 1987, 'The Construction of Luba Ethnicity in Belgian Congo, 1920–60', in L. Vail (ed.), *The Construction of Tribalism in Africa*.

——— 1993, *Naître et mourir au Zaïre, Un demi-siècle d'histoire au quotidien*, Paris: Karthala.

Kalanda, A., 1959, *Baluba et Lulua, une ethnie à la recherche d'un nouvel équilibre*, Brussels: Remarques congolaises.

——— 1963, *Tabalayi Bana Betu*, Léopoldville: Imprimerie Concordia.

Kalele, K.B., 1993, 'Regionalist ideologies', in M. Kankwenda, (ed.), *Zaire: What Destiny*?, Dakar: CODESRIA, pp. 18–46.

Kalumba, A and L. Ngoy, 1995, *Le Katanga et la transition zaïroise: L'Église nous parle*, Lubumbashi: Saint Paul.

Kambayi, B. and Mudinga, 1992, *Le Citancisme, Histoire d'une mentalité*, Kinshasa: Éditions Saint Paul.

Libata, M., 1984, 'Les mutineries de Luluabourg de 1895 et 1994', *Les Annales de l'ISP-Kananga*, vol. III, 4.

Lumanu-Mulenda, B.S., 1989, 'Les révisions constitutionnelles au Zaïre: Etude d'une dynamique de construction-destruction d'un ordre politique', *Genève-Afrique*, vol. XXII, 2, pp. 39–58.

MacGaffey, J. and G. Windsperger, 1993, 'The Endogenous Economy', *The Long Term Perspective Study of Sub-Saharan Africa*, vol. 3, Institutional and Sociopolitical Issues, Washington, DC: World Bank, pp. 81–90.

MacGaffey, W., 1982, 'The Policy of National Integration in Zaïre', *Journal of Modern African Studies*, vol. XX, 2, pp. 49–70.

Memel-Foté, H., 1991, 'Des ancêtres fondateurs aux Pères de la nation, introduction à une anthropologie de la démocratie', *Cahiers d'études africaines*, XXXI, 3, pp. 263–85.

Mpoyi, L., 1964, *Histoire wa Baluba*, Mbujimayi: Centre Pastoral.

Mukaya, N., 1972, 'La révolte de Mukalamushi de 1944', Pré-mémoire en histoire, Ecole normal moyenne de Luluabourg.

Muya, B.L.L., 1985, *Les Baluba dans la crise congolaise, 1960–6*, Lubumbashi: Saint Paul.

Mwamba, W.M., 1996, 'Le développement du Kasaï oriental au temps de Jonas Munkamba Kadiata Nzemba', *Le Potential*, 824, pp. 4–5.

Petit, P., 1996, '"Les charmes du roi sont les esprits des morts": les fondements religieux de la royauté sacrée chez les Luba', *Africa*, vol. 66, 3, pp. 349–66.

Samba, K., 1982, *Phénomène d'etnicité et conflits ethno-politiques en Afrique postcoloniale*, Kinshasa: Presses Universitaires du Zaïre.

Tshijuke, K., 1980, 'L'évolution sociales et économiques le long du rail, 1928–60', Thèse de doctorat en histoire, University of Lubumbashi.

Vansina, J., 1966, *Les anciens royaumes de la savane*, Léopoldville: Éditions Universitaires du Congo.

Vansina, J. and Boseker, B., 1963, 'Luba and Ibo Receiptivity to Change', *Political Science Journal*.

Verhaegen, B., 1961, *Congo*, 1960, 2 vols., Brussels: CRISP.

——— 1962, *Congo*, 1961, Brussels: CRISP.

——— 1966, *Rébellions au Congo*, Brussels: CRISP.

Vernon, A., 1965, *Still Leading in Triumph*, North Carolina: Presbyterian Church of United States.

Willame, J.C., 1972, *Patrimonialism and Political Change in The Congo*, Stanford: Stanford University Press.

Young, C., 1969, *Introduction à la politique congolaise*, Kinshasa: Éditions Unversitaires du Congo.

DOCUMENTS

'Congo, 1959–Congo, 1967', Documents du CRISP, Brussels.

'Dépositions sur les événements Malheureux de Mbujimayi, du 13 au 17 avril 1991', UDPS-Fédération du Kasaï.

'Lettre au Commissaire de district du Kasaï', Manifeste Lulua, Luluabourg, 1953.

'Manifeste des évolués de Luluabourg', Luluabourg, 1944.

'Les massacres de Katekelayi et Luamuela (Kasaï oriental)', Mbujumayi, 1980.

'Lettre ouverte au Citoyen Mobutu Sese Seko, Président-Fondateur du Mouvement Populaire de la Révolution et Président de la République Mobutu', Kinshasa, 1980.

'Rapport annuel de MIBA', 1960–6, Mbujimayi.

Bogumil Koss Jewsiewicki collected life histories of Zairian men and women (author's archives) of which copies have been placed at the archives of the Department of History, University of Laval, Québec.

From Conquest to Consent as the Basis of State Formation: Reflections on Rwanda

Mahmood Mamdani

In the year 1994 the African intelligentsia lost its innocence.[1] Literally, in the same week that South Africa began a historic journey to reconciliation in Rwanda the genocide became an epic tragedy. If one had been told a few years earlier by some clairvoyant that there would soon be a genocide in one country and a reconciliation in the other, I wonder how many would have been able to guess their identities right.

I had been to South Africa, but not to Rwanda. Being a Ugandan, I had closely followed the march of the RPF to Kigali, and had wondered about the role my country played in the unfolding tragedy, and about the responsibility of Ugandan intellectuals. Eventually, in July 1995, I did go to Kigali, and then to Gitarama, to the university in Butare, to Ntarama, and finally to Nyamata. It was a short visit, but it would be followed by several others. During which, I slept little and thought much. What follows are my reflections after that first visit. I am aware that the time I spent in Rwanda was short, the cross-section of people I met narrow, and my preparation for the visit inadequate. Even so, I have chosen to stay on the side of boldness. If the distance and detachment of the

[1] This is a revised version of a paper presented to the conference on 'Crisis in the Great Lakes Region', organized by the Council for the Development of Social Research in Africa (CODESRIA) in Arusha, Tanzania, 4–7 September 1995, and subsequently to the SEPHIS Conference on 'The Forging of Nationhood and the Contest over Citizenship, Ethnicity and History' at Delhi, India, 1996. The author would like to acknowledge research funding from the program on Peace and International Security of the MacArthur Foundation.

outsider can often be a source of ignorance, I can only hope that these may sometimes also prove to be a source of insight.

A STARTING POINT

I began with my own research into the colonial state in equatorial Africa, a context from which to underline the distinctive aspect of Rwandan history.[2] I had understood the colonial state as a bifurcated apparatus under which crystallized two distinct forms of authority: the first a civil power speaking the language of rights, the second a 'customary' power speaking the language of tradition. While civil power claimed to protect rights by enforcing civil law in civil society, the claim of customary power was to enforce custom. The bifurcated state was described by a duality in legal theory which separated the civil law governing relations of non-'natives', both among themselves and with 'natives', while 'customary' law kept 'natives' in their place. This bifurcated power reproduced a dual identity. Civil power was racialized; both the non-'native' beneficiaries of civil rights and the urbanized 'natives' denied rights were imprinted with a racial identity. Customary power, by contrast, was ethnicized or tribalized. The Native Authority defined and enforced an official version of custom as customary law. The stranger under the Native Authority was not a racial but an ethnic stranger: customary power reproduced an ethnic identity.

In the African colonial experience, custom was broadly defined to include not only personal law but land. To the extent that land and labour were defined as customary, they remained beyond the scope of the market: force was the only way to drive them out of the customary realm. Briefly, the regime of custom tapped into authoritarian possibilities in culture. Custom became the language of domination, masking a regime of force. When the use of direct force was outlawed in British colonies after the First World War, and in French colonies after the Second, this applied only to civil power. Native Authorities continued to exercise their right to use force, so long as that force was customary—and force used by Native Authorities was, of course, considered customary. The tautology was complete. Colonial rule consolidated, not the force of tradition, but the tradition of force.

[2] Mahmood Mamdani, *Citizen and Subject: Contemporary Africa and the Legacy of Late Colonialism*, Princeton, London and Cape Town: Princeton University Press, 1996.

Rwanda, however, was distinctive. While most colonies were organized as polyglot formations—with a central civil authority and a constellation of district-based customary authorities, each with a distinct ethnic identity—in Rwanda district authorities did not correspond to ethnic powers. Instead, the Batutsi were like a layer of cream spread over the entire society, administering a subject peasantry, the Bahutu. To understand the difference, one needs to grasp the distinctive nature of the process of state formation in Rwanda.

My grasp of post-genocide Rwanda has been shaped by a consideration which has three main aspects: first, Bahutu and Batutsi (the prefixes are 'mu' for singular, 'ba' for plural) are bipolar identities reproduced by a form of the state that institutionalized them as such: there cannot be one without the other. In this relationship, first shaped by the pre-colonial Rwandan state but fully crystallized by the colonial state, Batutsi came to be identified with power and Bahutu with subjecthood. Second, despite its limitations, the 'social' revolution of 1959, which turned this relation upside down, was a subaltern revolt, akin to Mau Mau in Kenya and the Zanzibar Revolution of 1963. So 'Hutu Power', the official ideology of that revolt, crystallized a consciousness that was both popular (from below) and limited to the relations of power (chief and peasant) that animated the working of the local state. In this sense it was a subaltern but truncated consciousness, shaped and limited by the institutional context of the indirect-rule state. Without understanding this, it is difficult to grasp the link between proponents of 'Hutu Power' and the subaltern Bahutu masses in the genocide—for while this power was extreme, it was not marginal. The foot-soldiers it mobilized understood the genocide as a defence of the social gains of 1959. They referred to the killing as 'work', and indeed communal work, a 'customary' obligation, organized and directed by 'customary' authorities in the state. Finally, while I have no 'solution' to the problem of Rwanda, I do claim that the search for one must incorporate three insights: that failure to ensure that those responsible for the genocide are brought to justice will only multiply instances of revenge; that a broad-based regime in a tense post-civil-war situation must include all political tendencies willing to renounce violence, even 'Hutu Power'; that the construction of a broad base from the level of the elite can only be a stop-gap measure unless it is reinforced by institutional reform of the conquest state from below.

THE BAHUTU-BATUTSI QUESTION

Who are the Bahutu and the Batutsi? This is a question that came up in every discussion I had. While the Bahutu opposition had been a target of the massacre, this was a political matter; the Batutsi faced true genocide—the attempt to eliminate them as a people. Given this single fact, which illuminates the tragedy of Rwanda for the world at large, I was nonplussed to be told over and again by leading people in the RPF: 'We speak the same language, have the same culture, and live on the same hills; we are the same people.' But in casual conversations and out on the streets, some of the same individuals would readily identify Muhutu and Mututsi. Sometimes by physical appearance, but in a place like Ntarama in the southern lowlands, where Batutsi made up as much as a third of the population, and where there had been many intermarriages—I was told a third of the Batutsi daughters were married to Bahutu—this was hardly a reliable method. During the killings, people were asked to produce their identity cards.

Not surprisingly, one of the issues hotly debated in the Rwandese Alliance for National Unity (RANU), formed by refugees in Uganda in 1979, was whether the difference between Bahutu and Batutsi was one of class or ethnicity. I remembered what I had heard from a Nigerian colleague at a conference organized by the Dakar-based Council for Development of Social Research in Africa (CODESRIA) early in 1995, that if he went to a discussion on Rwanda and Burundi, he could close his eyes and tell the identity of a speaker from these countries by the twist of their arguments. If a person claimed that there were no differences between Bahutu and Batutsi, or that the difference was one of class, the speaker was most likely a Mututsi. A Muhutu intellectual was most likely to argue otherwise, that the difference was one between distinct ethnic—or even racial—groups. It is difficult to believe that the Bahutu-Batutsi difference is based on class for both groups are internally differentiated. One finds Bahutu and Batutsi in the same class: the Batutsi pastoralists I saw in the southern lowlands were as poor and wretched as the Bahutu peasants I met along the way. If the view that there is 'no difference', or only a class difference, tends to focus on socio-economic processes, the preoccupation of the 'ethnic difference' perspective is with the biological and the historico-cultural. If the 'no difference' view tends to suffer from historical amnesia—specifically of how power was organized in the pre-colonial Rwandan state, that of 'ethnic difference' tends to freeze the history of the Rwandan state at its colonial stage, turning a historical outcome into a primordial difference. If loss of historical memory leads to a tragic political innocence, historical fixation leads to a no less tragic pathology. One side overlooks the limits of politics, the other fails to appreciate the possibility of political action. Neither is able to come to grips with the political potential in a given situation.

THE PRE-COLONIAL RWANDAN STATE

When I returned from Kigali, I immersed myself in whatever literature I could find on Rwandese history. I realized that the further back one went, the mistier the historical background became. Shrouded in a rich mythology is the question of the origin of the Batutsi. Caught up by the notion that differences and conflicts in human society are the result of racial differences, early European explorers and administrators came up with the 'Hamitic hypothesis': that the Batutsi were a superior non-Bantu race who had come from the direction of Ethiopia and conquered indigenous agriculturalists (Bahutu) and forest-dwellers (Batwa). This racist theory was discredited in the heyday of anti-imperial nationalism, but there is still no consensus amongst historians and anthropologists on the origin of the Batutsi. At least three accounts can be found in the literature. The first explanation of difference is based on nutrition and is most identified with Walter Rodney. In his influential work *How Europe Underdeveloped Africa*, which, strangely enough, was standard reading for the RPF cadres in the late 1980s and early 1990s,[3] Rodney argued that the Batwa remained 'pygmies' because 'they wandered around in small bands, hunting and digging roots, thereby failing to assure themselves of plentiful or rich food'. The Bahutu 'were more socially advanced than the Batwa' because 'they did not live entirely on the whims of nature'. But, in comparison to the Batutsi, the Bahutu remained 'short and stocky' because 'the quality of their food fell short of protein-rich Batutsi diet'. And so the Batutsi pastoralists, 'subsisting on a constantly accessible and rich diet on milk and meat' turned out to be 'one of the tallest human groups in the world'.

[3] Walter Rodney, *How Europe Underdeveloped Africa*, Nairobi: East African Educational Publishers, p. 138.

The second explanation accepts the migration theory, that the pastoralists came from outside Rwanda, but argues that their relations with the agriculturalists were peaceful and symbiotic: they exchanged dairy products for garden vegetables. Forcefully expounded by the late Samwiri Karugire, the noted Ugandan historian, it has since been embraced by various political protagonists, including the President of Uganda and many in the leadership of the RPF.

Neither the dietary hypothesis nor the theory of peaceful coexistence gets to the question that I think is the key to understanding the pre-colonial period: the nature of the political power organized as the Rwandan state. Rodney accepts that 'the system of social relations which emerged in Rwanda was more completely hierarchical . . . than in most parts of Africa'.[4] Similarly, Edward Steinhart, taking inspiration from the late Samwiri Karugire, concludes with reference to Ankore that 'the system of pastoral domination, which had evolved from meagre beginnings in the fifteenth century, had by the early nineteenth century become one of the most rigid and authoritarian systems of political and social exploitation in the intralacustrine region'.[5] All scholars are agreed that if there was a system more hierarchical than that in Ankore, it was in Rwanda.

A third explanation has recently been put forth by Archie Mafeje in a book called *The Theory and Ethnography of African Social Formations*.[6] While Mafeje dismisses the Hamitic hypothesis, his work is based on a critical summary of colonial anthropology. Mafeje's starting point is Bunyoro where, 'somewhere in the fifteenth century', there occurred the 'first known processes of political centralization' in the intralacustrine region. In Bunyoro, 'the introduction of pastoralism as an elite pursuit must be attributed to . . . invaders who, probably, migrated from south eastern Ethiopia and southern Somalia with their long-horned cattle'. But the Bachwezi dynasty did not last long in Bunyoro. In 'a few generations', the Bachwezi 'were chased out by Babito invaders' from the north, moving in 'a south-westerly direction where ecological conditions are ideal for cattle-keeping', and 'reappeared as conquering Bahima herders in

[4] Ibid., p. 139.

[5] Edward Steinhart, *Conflict and Collaboration: The Kingdoms of Western Uganda, 1890–1907*, Princeton: Princeton University Press, 1977, p. 10.

[6] Archie Mafeje, *The Theory and Ethnography of African Social Formations: The Case of the Intralacustrine Kingdoms*, Dakar: CODESRIA, 1991.

Ankore, Rwanda and Burundi'.[7] It would seem that the Bachwezi 'disappeared' on the way from Bunyoro to Ankore, and 'reappeared' as the Bahima in Ankore, and the Bahima 'disappeared' on the way to Rwanda where they 'reappeared' as the Batutsi.

Mafeje is at pains to point out that at the outset Batutsi migration was largely peaceful: 'land was plentiful in the areas of migration of the Bahima'. Later, though, this seems to have led to forcible conquest and the creation of the Rwandan state: 'as the population increased and more Tutsi kept on entering the country and more land had to be tilled to feed them and as cattle were increasing', the Hutu had to move from the most fertile soil.[8] But the very fact that our author has to speak of 'disappearance' and 'reappearance' suggests that what is involved here is a stringing together of facts which are otherwise separated by many a historical gap. The result then is likely to be as much fiction as fact.

That much of what passed as historical fact in academic circles has to be considered as tentative—if not outright fictional—is becoming clear as post-genocidal sobriety compels a growing number of historians to take seriously the political uses to which their writings have been put, and their readers to question the certainty with which many a claim has been advanced. In the process, several claims that had come to be regarded as sacred cows no longer appear so self-evident: for example, David Newbury questions the long-held assumption that the Bahutu were always agriculturalists and the Batutsi pastoralists. He argues that 'the people who came to be known as "Hutu" had cattle here long before those known as Tutsi appeared on the scene'.[9] Certainly, if Bahutu had in fact had a natural aversion to cattle-rearing and had always been cultivators, it would have made little sense in the pre-colonial period to put restrictions on Bahutu owning cattle. We must acknowledge that these identifications are less mere facts unrelated to power than historical artefacts created alongside the institutionalized power of the pre-colonial Rwandan state.[10]

[7] Ibid., pp. 19–21, 26.

[8] Ibid., p. 23.

[9] David Newbury, 'The Invention of Rwanda: The Alchemy of Ethnicity', mimeo, University of North Carolina, Chapel Hill, November 1995, p. 7.

[10] This could certainly make greater sense of Mafeje's observation that, 'as in Ankore', there was in Rwanda too 'a conscious effort to deny non-Batutsi access to cattle in general'. See Mafeje, op. cit., p. 60.

CONSTRUCTING A STATE

This history is important, not because of where the Batutsi and the Bahutu originally came from, but because in their coming together they created certain political institutions which outlived that history and shaped a tragic future. The key political institution forged through their contact was the pre-colonial Rwandan state. It established a double domination, of a pastoralist aristocracy over a subject peasantry, and of Batutsi over Bahutu and Batwa. While the question of the historical origin of the Batutsi is shrouded in mystery, that of the nature of the state they built is not.

The parameters of the cultural complex called Kinyarwanda are much larger than the domain of the state called Rwanda.[11] The disparity between their size was even greater in the pre-colonial period than it is today. Outside of Kiswahili, Kinyarwanda is said to have the largest group of speakers of any African language, roughly ten million.[12] Long before the consolidation of the Nyiginya dynasty as the state of Rwanda in what is known as the central court complex, people speaking variants of Kinyarwanda were widely settled in the region. Outside central Rwanda where the pre-colonial Rwandan state was based, there were at least two zones that were culturally, but not politically, Kinyarwanda. The first of these is today divided between northern Rwanda and western Uganda, settled by a people known as the Bakiga—'the people of the mountains'—who shared the same language but not the same social and political culture as those within the ambit of the Rwandan state. Not only did they have different settlement patterns, clan categories and marriage forms, but their political life was highly decentralized and community-based, in sharp contrast to the centralized hierarchy of the state of Rwanda. Here there were no Batutsi and no Bahutu, at least not until German colonialism integrated part of this area into the Rwandan polity. The cultural difference between what then became northern Rwanda and the rest of the country would later reappear, under the two Hutu Republics, as the difference between northern and southern Bahutu. The second

[11] For a detailed discussion, see Newbury, 'The Invention of Rwanda', pp. 14–17.

[12] The numbers are approximately ten million. If, however, one includes Kirundi in the Kinyarwanda language family, as do most linguists, the numbers would go up to fifteen million. See Newbury, 'The Invention of Rwanda', p. 14.

major cultural zone that lay outside the pre-colonial state of Rwanda is today divided between western Rwanda and eastern Zaire. These speakers of Kinyarwanda live south and west of Lake Rweru (Edward), and north and south of Lake Kivu in Zaire. Unlike the Bakiga of the north, the Banyabwisha of the west had long accepted delegates from the central court: their social institutions closely resembled those in the central region. All Banyarwanda spoke Kinyarwanda, the Banru language originally spoken by the peasant population of Rwanda. Thus we come to the point that the people called Batutsi, and those who came to be called Bahutu, spoke the same language, lived on the same hills, and had more or less the same culture, depending on the cultural zones in which they lived. But they had yet to become one people.

I will make my point by contrasting two states that were organized in the intralacustrine region—Rwanda and Buganda. Like Buganda, Rwanda was a highly centralized kingdom, with a standing army and an official bureaucracy. But unlike Buganda, the state in Rwanda defined rulers and subjects as belonging to two distinct social groups, pastoralist and agriculturalist, one noble, the other commoner. The kings, considered divine, were all Batutsi as were all army commanders. While the entire population was affiliated to the army, there is, once again, no agreement amongst historians as to whether the warriors were exclusively Batutsi or whether this held true only for an earlier period. Nonetheless, most seem to agree that participation within the army was structured hierarchically. In this context, as Antoine Lema puts it, 'the corpse of a Mututsi had more value than that of a Muhutu or a Mutwa . . . the Bahutu were deprived [of] the right to [a] glorious, honorable, heroic death, since the Batutsi had also social monopoly on that'.[13] In the civil bureaucracy, the Mwami appointed and dismissed all chiefs, of which there were three types: *the chief of men* who was in charge of recruiting soldiers, the *chief of pastures* who ruled over grazing lands, and the *chief of landholding* in charge of agricultural land and production. The chief of landholding was more likely to be a Muhutu, for agriculture was said to be a Muhutu calling. In the lower ranks of the administrative hierarchy, non-Batutsi functionaries were more common.

[13] Antoine Lema, 'Africa Divided: The Creation of Ethnic Groups', Ph.D. thesis, University of Lund, Sweden, 1993, p. 53.

There was one institution in pre-colonial Rwanda that prevented the Batutsi-Bahutu distinction from hardening into a caste-like difference, just as it prevented the formation of a Bahutu counter-elite that would in time challenge Batutsi domination. This was *Kwihutura*: the rare Mahutu who was able to accumulate cattle and rise through the socio-economic hierarchy, could *kwihutura*, shed Hutuness—and achieve the political status of a Mututsi. It is clear that one is talking of a political distinction, one that divided the subject from the non-subject population, and not a socio-economic distinction, between exploiters and exploited or rich and poor.

This is why the ruling aristocracy in pre-colonial Rwanda needs to be understood as both pastoral and Batutsi. The Bahutu made up the *subject* population, while the Batutsi—even when not part of the ruling group—had more of an identification with power and a more privileged relationship to the state. While socio-economic processes led to class differentiation, particularly amongst the Batutsi, the political differences created by how the state was organized reflected more than just class differences. It seems to me that the Batutsi developed a political identity—they 'formed a distinct social category, marked by marriage and ethnic taboos', as Mafeje says;[14] a self-consciousness of being distinguished from the subject population. Thus, the mere fact of some physical difference—often the nose, less often the height—could become symbolic of a great political difference. The colonial state built on this political difference, making it the central political artefact around which was constructed the state's local apparatus. As a result, these otherwise incidental physical differences came to bear the weight of an entire history of state formation.

THE COLONIAL STATE

While the Rwandan state clearly lost its independence with colonization, what was not so apparent was that its apparatus actually expanded during the colonial period. The territory it administered reached its widest span under German colonialism since it was only with German military support—particularly 'the subjugation in 1912 of the northern districts'—that Mwami Musinga was able to enlarge the state's boundaries.[15] The Germans had but 5 civil

[14] Majefe, p. 29.

[15] Lema, 'Africa Divided', op. cit., p. 56.

and 24 military officers, commissioned and non-commissioned, on Rwandan soil in 1914. They could rule only through the institutional reach of the Batutsi-created state apparatus. The irony is that imperialism played a critical role both in the final consolidation and in the ultimate collapse of this state apparatus. For if German colonialism provided the force behind the final expansion of this apparatus, one can see that the power behind its destruction was Belgian.

The Germans understood Africa through the optic of late-nineteenth-century imperial Europe, which saw humanity as a conglomeration of races which required identification and hierarchical classification. Such was the inspiration behind the new discipline of physical anthropology, whose foot soldiers now began to classify the Batutsi and the Bahutu as separate races, one 'Hamitic' and superior, the other 'Bantu' and inferior. But it was the Belgians who, from 1929 to 1933, turned this theory into the very basis of organizing the administrative apparatus of the colonial state. They classified the population into the Batutsi and the Bahutu (and the Batwa) and issued passes identifying all. Even the relative flexibility of the pre-colonial period—*kwihutura*—was removed, and the distinction was frozen into a rigid caste-like structure. Indirect rule became the norm through cooperative elements in the Batutsi oligarchy—those who managed the lowest rungs of the colonial administration which were also the highest rungs of the subordinate but semi-autonomous district-level state apparatus.

The reorganization of the pre-colonial state was highly important. The key shift was in the redefinition of the powers of the state agents called chiefs. The previous trinity of chiefs was abolished and powers which had hitherto been separate and differentiated were fused in a single agent. To quote from Rene Lemarchand's study of colonial Rwanda, 'the old balance of forces between cattle chiefs, land chiefs and army chiefs, which in previous times had served to protect the [Ba]Hutu peasantry against undue exactions' was abolished. This 'concentration of powers in the hands of a single chief, exercising unfettered control over his people, was bound to lead to abuses': not only did it deprive the Hutu of opportunities to play one chief off against another, but it also eliminated the channels of appeal offered by the previous arrangement.[16] At the

[16] Rene Lemarchand, *Rwanda and Burundi*, New York: Praeger, 1970, pp. 119–20.

same time, most Bahutu chiefs on the lower rungs of the colonial administration were dismissed and replaced by those classified as Batutsi. Such institutional change not only augmented state power but made it more despotic in character.

Belgian rule was harsh by any standards. Force was integral to the process of exploitation—particularly forced labour. And the indigenous mask of this brutal foreign domination was the hierarchy of Batutsi chiefs. So severe was Belgian rule, and with such impunity was it translated into practice by the Batutsi chiefs, that hundreds of thousands of Bahutu peasants fled into Uganda in the decade after 1928 to take up jobs as migrant labourers in the coffee farms of Buganda. At first, the colonial power found it convenient simply to pass on every demand—say, the upkeep of roads—to 'customary' chiefs so that they used their 'customary' prerogative to get the job done, without payment and with a minimum disruption of order. The chiefs also found it convenient to add their own demands to this list of 'customary' exactions. So the list grew. The land tax—*butake*—traditionally said to be one day in every five, was increased by chiefs to two or even three days in every six. Soon, this was supplemented by other forms of *corvee* which had never before existed, such as an obligation to construct chiefs' houses from durable materials. The smaller the chief, the more arbitrary could be the imposition. As one Church observer noted, a *petit* Mututsi chief and his wife 'could take almost anything they please—bananas, yams, etc.—and the [Mu]Hutu must comply lest he be expelled from his fields'.[17]

Every so often, the Belgian authorities would try to rationalize the system, mainly to reduce the scope for levying extra-legal exactions. The main method was to replace corvee with an annual tax to be paid in cash. But, as often as old forms of corvee were converted to a cash levy, new exactions in kind would be levied, justified as 'anti-famine' or 'development' measures. Throughout this oscillation between the monetization of old exactions and the introduction of new impositions in kind, there was one form of corvee which the colonial power refused to convert into a monetary payment. This was *ubureetwa* which was 'imposed specifically on Hutu' and left unreformed because officials thought that to do away

[17] Mgr. Classe in 1916, quoted in Lemarchand, *Rwanda and Burundi*, p. 122. For further examples, see pp. 121–4.

with it would be to 'undermine the chiefs'authority over the population'.[18]

By the 1920s, the threefold institutional framework underpinning the colonial state was fully in place. The first was fused power; the new chief was no mere administrative officer, he combined legislative, executive and judicial powers. Second, these powers were justified as 'customary', and 'custom' was proclaimed by the very authority sanctioned by the colonial power as 'customary'. This tautology was crystallized in the legal institutions of colonial rule which cordoned off the system of civil laws administered in civil courts for 'non-natives' from an administratively driven system of 'customary' laws designed to govern relations between 'natives'. Third, this 'customary' legal authority was the force behind a range of extra-economic measures also said to be 'customary'. It is this organized power propelled by the institutional triad of fused power, administratively driven justice, and extra-economic coercion, that I define as the conquest state.[19] My argument has little to do with foreign power and indigenous subjects. The conquest state crystallized in the colonial period proper, as a decentralized despotism, a subordinate but autonomous district-level Batutsi apparatus operating under an overall Belgian colonial authority.

MONEY AND SCHOOLING

But not everything under this political system was hard. There were two broad processes under way—the expansion of a money economy and school-based Western education—that would erode Batutsi economic supremacy while, for a time, leaving intact their political supremacy. The money economy opened up opportunities for enrichment other than through the ownership of cattle, weakening the bonds of pastoral servitude that had been the colonial *ubuhake* contract between patron and client.[20] In this context, the expanding

[18] Catherine Newbury, *The Cohesion of Oppression: Clientship and Ethnicity in Rwanda, 1860–1960*, New York: Columbia University Press, 1988, p. 112.

[19] This argument is fully elaborated in my *Citizen and Subject.*

[20] Writers on Rwanda, and generally on the region of the Great Lakes, used to assume that clientship was a universal and determining feature of social inequality, generalizing backwards from the high ground of the colonial era. In shaping this perspective, Jacques Maquet (*The Premise of Inequality in Ruanda,* London: Oxford University Press, 1961) was very much the pace-setter. Even

school system of the 1940s and 1950s provided the structural basis for the emergence of a Bahutu counter elite. School education for children of Bahutu families was a Church initiative. Admission records of the *Group Scolaire* in Astrida (now Butare), a Church institution which admitted students from the three Belgian colonies of Rwanda, Burundi and the Congo, show that Bahutu students were virtually excluded until after the Second World War,[21] but the attitude of the European clergy underwent a major shift in the mid-1950s. Post-war newcomers, according to Lemarchand, were likely to come from '*le petit clerge*' of 'relatively humble social origins', and with a 'previous experience of social and political conditions in the French-speaking provinces of Wallonia', they were 'more generally disposed to identify with the plight of the [Ba]Hutu masses'.[22]

When the Bahutu graduates of the *Group Scolaire* at Astrida entered the job market in the mid-1950s, they found there were few vacancies for an educated Muhutu. Literally shut out of jobs in the civil service and the private sector, they turned to the Church for opportunities, not just to make a living but also to articulate their major social grievance: the institutionalized exclusion of Bahutu from what they saw as a Belgian supported Batutsi monopoly over all avenues of advancement. With the support of a sympathetic clergy, they took control over Church publications—the most

---

though more empirical and locally based studies, conducted during the 1970s and 1980s, challenged the universalist assumptions of this school of thought, it still has its adherents. Probably the strongest critique of Maquet came from the pen of Catherine Newbury (*The Cohesion of Oppression*, especially Chaps. 5, 6 and 7) who showed not only that there were different forms of clientship—some leading to solidarity within a class, others to servitude between classes—but that each had its own historical trajectory and none was universal or primordial. The pre-colonial cattle contract (*umuheto*) was more like a bond of solidarity that tied lineages in the periphery of the kingdom to patrons in the central court; while unequal, it was reciprocal. By contrast, the colonial cattle contract (*ubuhake*) took more the form of servitude: the clients were now individuals, not lineages. But the *ubuhake* clients, constituting no more than a fifth of the total population, were still predominantly Batutsi, not Bahutu. *Ubuhake* clientship thus expressed both a growing social differentiation amongst the Batutsi and a social grid pre-empting the emergence of a more prosperous Bahutu stratum in the cattle economy. They had a higher status than the *ubureetwa* clients: these were exclusively Bahuru, at the bottom of the social scale.

[21] Lemarchand, op. cit., pp. 134–8.

[22] Ibid., pp. 106–7.

important being the Kinyarwanda-language magazine *Kinyamateke*—and began to address whoever would listen sympathetically, mainly the Bahutu masses below and visiting UN Commissions above.

Though administered by Belgium, Rwanda was a UN trust territory. Under UN tutelage, the process of decolonization unfolded as a series of electoral reforms. Elections set the context in which the Bahutu counter-elite forged their consciousness against the Batutsi elite. Such a consciousness emerged from the throes of a political contest. Batutsi identity, forged with the creation of the Rwandan state, long preceded Bahutu identity. Batutsi consciousness was a consciousness of power while Bahutu consciousness would come to be one of lack of power, in fact of a struggle for power.

The development of a Muhutu consciousness was a protracted affair, stretching over the entire span of the colonial period. As late as Independence in 1962, the 'Bahutu' of the north-western region insisted on being considered as Bakiga, like their neighbours in south-western Uganda, not Bahutu. The Muhutu-consciousness developed in phases: before the Second World War, it was a consciousness of subjecthood that transcended all locally-anchored identities; in the 1950s it became the consciousness of a people seeking power. This shift took place only with the emergence of a Bahutu counter-elite which, propelled centre stage by a series of electoral contests, promoted 'Hutu power' as a programme for overcoming their identity as a subject people. Branded with a subject identity—'Bahutu'—the counter-elite emerging from the ranks of the socially oppressed would hold it up as a badge of pride: Hutu Power! In turning a chain into a weapon, Spartacus-style, in trying to forge an identity for liberation from an emblem of servitude, it was neither the first nor would it be the last. One only need think of a related example: Black Power!

STRUGGLE THROUGH ELECTIONS

The backdrop to these electoral contests was a series of UN decolonization missions that were regularly despatched to its trust territory after the Second World War. Elections were held in 1953 to create advisory councils to state organs; then in 1956 the first general election, another in 1959, and two more in 1960 and 1961. This series of elections, and the anticipation of a transfer of power, triggered a chain of events leading, first, to a loosening of the hold of the Batutsi elite on the lower reaches of the state apparatus, and then, to extreme political polarization between the Batutsi and the Bahutu—a prelude to an anti-Batutsi pogrom. The shift from indirect to direct elections showed that there was considerable likelihood of a Bahutu victory at the polls. There was a clear victory in the 1956 elections of Bahutu candidates at the sub-chief level, where the vote was direct, but not at higher levels where the vote was indirect. This was accompanied by an ideological polarization between Batutsi and Bahutu, dramatized by two rival documents issued in anticipation of the 1957 UN trusteeship mission. First was *Mise au Point*, a proclamation for an all-Rwandan emancipation issued by the Mwami's High Council, calling for a transfer of power to ease racial tensions between black and white. Within a month followed the *Bahutu Manifesto*, written by Kayibanda and eight other Bahutu leaders, all Church-affiliated, and a Belgian priest. The difference between the two documents could not have been sharper. Independence first was the view of the Batutsi elite, it was also the claim of the pre-colonial rulers for a restoration of their prerogatives. Democracy before Independence, the view of the Bahutu counter-elite, spelt out its demand for power. One highlighted the racial contradiction in the colony—between white and black—while the other underlined the social contradiction amongst the colonized.

On 19 October 1959, in anticipation of the next round of elections, and with the blessing of Church authorities, a Bahutu political party, the Parti du Mouvement de l'Empancipation Hutu (PARMEHUTU), was created out of the old cultural association, Mouvement Social Muhutu. Almost immediately, there followed confrontations between PARMEHUTU militants and those of the pro-monarchy Batutsi party, the Union Nationale Rwandaise (UNAR), and Batutsi chiefs in charge of the local state apparatus. These came to a head in and around Gitarama the next month. When news spread that a group of young UNAR militants had attacked the PARMEHUTU leader Dominique Mbonyumutwa, pogroms started all over the country. The visiting UN mission of 1960 estimated the killings at two hundred but added that 'the number may be even higher since the people preferred to bury their dead silently'.[23] Some Batutsi chiefs were killed, others were forced to resign. A state of emergency

[23] Lema, *Africa Divided*, p. 38.

was declared and the country put under the command of Colonel Bem Guy Logiest. It was in this context that Belgium carried out nothing less than a coup d'etat. Arguing that the presence of Batutsi as sub-chiefs and chiefs 'disturbed the public order', Bem Logiest began the replacement of Batutsi chiefs with Bahutu, thus shepherding a 'revolution' against what had hitherto been the colonial power's own authorities. Half the chiefs and sub-chiefs on the eve of the 1960 and 1961 general elections were Bahutu—and the chiefs had control of the ballot boxes. Without this reconstitution of the local state hierarchy, it is difficult to explain the dramatically different outcome of subsequent elections. Two tendencies gelled around PARMEHUTU and UNAR. In the 1961 election, PARMEHUTU secured 77.4 per cent of the popular vote, UNAR 16.8 per cent.[24] Independence followed on 1 July 1962; the new government was based on a power-sharing arrangement between PARMEHUTU and UNAR.

THE 'COCKROACH' INVASION

Unstable as it was, this power-sharing came to an end with the attempt by the Batutsi refugees, who had fled in 1959 to Burundi, to return to power through an invasion called *Inyenzi*—cockroaches.[25] On the second attempt, they managed to cross the border with two or three hundred men, overran the Rwanda military camp under construction at Gabo where they stocked up on arms and ammunition and a few jeeps. They were welcomed as heroes at the camp in Nyamata by Batutsi refugees who later rallied behind them, only to be decimated 12 miles from Kigali, at the Kanzenze bridge on river Nyabarongo, by units of the Gendarme National Rwandaise, then under Belgian officers. The response was an organized countrywide killing of prominent Batutsi personalities, who had been previously arrested, and sections of the Batutsi population. Each of the country's ten *prefecteurs* was made an emergency zone under the command of a minister who organized 'self defence' groups among the Bahutu population. It is difficult to know how many were killed. The UN guessed 1,000 to 3,000; the World Council of Churches estimated 10,000 to 14,000. Writing in *Le Monde* on

[24] Ibid., pp. 70–l.

[25] The following account sums up ibid., pp. 71–3.

6 February 1964, Bertrand Russell termed it the most horrible systematic extermination of a people since the Nazi extermination of Jews. No African state except Burundi even raised a voice. The smashing of the counter-revolution, for that is how this pogrom was hailed, eroded any middle ground. The Batutsi who were killed were precisely those who had cut themselves from the court and from the monarchists, and had hoped for a republican regime in which they could serve.

In the context of this long historical account, one can draw the following conclusions:

- The distinction between Batutsi and Bahutu is a socio-political distinction. It is not just a colonial creation. Created in the pre-colonial period, the distinction was polarized by the colonial state, and would be inflamed and institutionalized by the postcolonial state.

- The Batutsi identity crystallized at the time of the formation of the pre-colonial Rwandan state. It was a self-consciousness of being in or near power, or simply identifying with power. By contrast, the Bahutu identity which gelled later was a self-consciousness of those subject to power. The Bahutu identity—and its springboard, the 1959 revolution—cannot be dismissed as simply a sign of backwardness. This identity was limited to the framework of the colonial state, particularly the Batutsi hierarchy of chiefs. It is from this Bahutu point of view that 1959 looks like a revolution, and 1994 must look like a counter-revolution.

- Those who insist that the Bahutu and the Batutsi are separate ethnic or cultural groups should ponder one fact: the identity Bahutu-Batutsi is bipolar. Neither can exist in isolation. Rwanda's First Republic understood that so long as there is a socio-political identity called Batutsi, there will be another called Bahutu. So it tried to entrench and keep alive both identities by re-enacting the 'revolution' as Hutu power through periodic pogroms, expulsions and the redistribution of property to its militants in 1959, 1963 and so on. In time, the re-enactments borrowed imagery from the French Revolution. 'Committees of Public Safety' posted lists of 'counter-revolutionaries'; in 1972, these were Batutsi who were found in prominent positions in the educational system or the civil service. The pogrom of 1972 gathered in intensity as Bahutu refugees were pushed into Rwanda, seeking shelter from a rampaging Batutsi-dominated army in neighbouring Burundi. In this context, the Minister of Defence, Jouvenal Habyarimana, staged a *coup d'etat*, proclaiming that the 'cultural revolution' of 1972 would complete the 'social revolution' of 1959.

• The Second Republic tried to bring the 'permanent revolution' that, in reality, was a permanent terror, to an end by embedding the Bahutu and Batutsi identities in institutions. This institutionalization went hand in hand with a double shift. The first was a regional shift of political focus, from the Bahutu to the northern Bahutu as the true custodians of the 'revolution'—perhaps because the north was the last part of contemporary Rwanda to be brought under Batutsi domination. The second was an institutional shift in the locus of power, from civilian to military rule; the army, after all, was the child of the 'revolution', forged in the heat of the battle against the *Inyenzi*. Habyarimana institutionalized a hierarchical pluralism that he justified as a form of reverse discrimination (affirmative action) that would restore balance to Rwandan society through a system of quotas designed to redress the grievances of a hitherto oppressed majority. The Batutsi would be allowed a subordinate status in civil society. In this context, Habyarimana made every attempt to ensure a symbolic Batutsi presence in the state apparatus; in late 1990, there was one Mututsi in a 19-member cabinet, one ambassador, 2 deputies in a 70-seat National Assembly, and 2 members in the 16-person central committee of the ruling party, the MRND.[26] Did not the 1959 revolution turn the world that the Bahutu knew upside down, but without changing it in other ways? If the corpse of a Mututsi had more value than that of a Muhutu in an earlier era, did not the revolution arrive at a point where the corpse of a Mututsi had less dignity than a human corpse? If the upwardly mobile Muhutu could shed his Hutuness (*kwihutura*) and enter the ranks of power, was not Habyarimana's nominal integration of Batutsi in the state hierarchy, right up to the cabinet, a sort of a *kwitutsira*?

The allocation of resources and positions within the state was said to reflect the actual numerical weight of the majority and the minority in society so the demographic question became a hot political issue. The Second Republic maintained that the Batutsi

[26] Catharine Watson, *Exile from Rwanda: Background to an Invasion*, Washington: U.S. Committee for Refugees, 1991.

constituted no more that 9 per cent of the total population of Rwanda—this had the status of a state-sanctioned truth and the figure remained unchanged over decades. Officialdom had little to say about intermarriages between Bahutu and Batutsi and the official identity of children of these marriages. The demographic question would become important when the genocide became the central political issue. Many would wonder, if the population of Rwanda was 7.5 million in 1994 and 9 per cent were Batutsi, and if one million were killed in the genocide, and even if a half million returned, how many Batutsi could there possibly be alive today inside Rwanda?

- To break out of this notion of the state as a representation of a permanently defined majority is the challenge. For any society to continue to exist, democratic competition—whether party-driven or not—presumes the existence of an order based on the consent, not of a majority, but of all. If political competition is not destructive of life, all those who participate in it—whether they win or lose—must accept the rules of the game. The creation of a consensus based political community must precede the adoption of any majority driven political competition. Failure to learn this lesson will place Rwanda once again in a state of permanent tension. How to move from an order based on conquest to one based on consent is the challenge for Rwanda today.

GENOCIDE, JUSTICE AND RECONCILIATION

On 22 July, I went to Nrarama, about an hour and a half from Kigali by car, on a dirt road going south towards Burundi. I arrived at a village church, made of brick, with a roof of iron sheets. Outside there was a wood and bamboo rack bearing skulls. On the ground were sacks of assorted bones, stuffed together, but sticking out of the torn cloth. The guard explained that the bones had been gathered from the neighbourhood. A veteran of sites in the Luwero Triangle in Uganda, I felt a sense of *deja vu*, even if the numbers of skulls and sacks were greater in quantity than I had ever seen at any one site.

The church is about 20 by 60 feet. Inside, wooden planks placed on top of stones are meant to be used as benches. I peered inside and saw piles of belongings—shoulder-sacks, tattered clothing, a towel, a wooden box, a *suferia*, plastic mugs and plates, straw mats and hats—the worldly goods of the poor. Then, amidst it all, I saw bones and skeletons, each frozen in the posture in which the person had died. Even a year after the genocide, I thought the air smelled of blood, mixed with that of bones, clothing, earth. A human mildew.

I scanned the walls with their gaping holes. The guide explained that these were made by the *Intrahamwe*—the youth brigade of the ruling party, the MNRD—so that they could throw grenades into the building. He said that those in the church were lucky. They died almost instantly. Those outside had a protracted, brutal death, in some cases drawn out over as long as a week, with one part of the body cut off daily. On the walls of the church there were still some old posters. One read: '*Journee Internationale de Femme*'. And below it in bold letters: '*EGALITE—PAIX DEVELOPEMENT*'.

I was introduced to a man called Callixte, a survivor of the massacre in Ntarama. 'On the 7th of April [1994], in the morning', he explained,

> they started burning houses over there and moving towards here. Only a few were killed. The burning pushed us to this place. We thought this was God's house, no one would attack us here. On the 7th, 8th, up to the 10th, we were fighting them. We were using stones, they had pangas, spears, hammers, grenades. On the 10th, their numbers increased. On the 14th, we were being pushed inside the church. The church was attacked on the 14th and the 15th. The actual killing was on the 15th.
>
> On the 15th, they brought Presidential Guards. They were supporting Intrahamwe, brought in from neighbouring communes. I was not in the group here. Here, there were women, children and old men. The men had formed defence units outside. I was outside. Most men died fighting. When our defence was broken through, they came and killed everyone here. After that, they started hunting for those hiding in the hills. I and others ran to the swamp.

I asked about his sector, who lived in it, how many Batutsi, how many Bahutu, who participated in the killing. 'In my *secteur*, Bahutu were two thirds, Batutsi one-third. There were about 5,000 in our *secteur*. Of the 3,500 Bahutu all the men participated. It was like an order, except there were prominent leaders who would command. The rest followed.'

I asked whether there were no intermarriages in the *secteur*.

> Too many. About one-third of Batutsi daughters would be married to

Bahutu. But Bahutu daughters married to Batutsi men were only 1 per cent: Bahutu didn't want to marry their daughters to Batutsi who were poor and it was risky. Because the Batutsi were discriminated against, they didn't want to give their daughters where there was no education, no jobs . . . risky. Prospects were better for Batutsi daughters marrying Bahutu men. They would get better opportunities.

Batutsi women married to Bahutu were killed. I know only one who survived. The administration forced Bahutu men to kill their Batutsi wives before they go to kill anyone else—to prove they were true *Intrahamwe*. One man tried to refuse. He was told that he must chose between the wife and himself. He then chose to save his own life. Another Muhutu man rebuked him for having killed his Mututsi wife. He was also killed. Kallisa—the man who was forced to kill his wife—is in jail. After killing his wife, he became a convert. He began to distribute grenades all around.

The killing was planned, because some were given guns. During the war with the RPF, many young men were taken in the reserves and trained and given guns. Those coming from training would disassociate themselves from Batutsi. Some of my friends received training. When they returned, they were busy mobilizing others. They never came to see me. I am fifty-seven. Even people in their sixties joined in the killing, though they were not trained. The trained were Senior 6 or Technical School leavers.

I asked how such young killers could have been his friends. 'I was a friend to their fathers. It was a father-son relationship. I think the fathers must have known.'

HOW MANY MURDERERS?

Gradually, I began to make sense of the magnitude of the genocide. The number of people killed, I was told, was around a million. Unlike the Holocaust, this genocide was not carried out over years, but months—only three. 'It wasn't just a small group that killed and moved,' explained a political commissar in the police. 'Because genocide was so extensive, there were killers in every locality—from ministers to peasants—for it to happen in so short a time and on such a large scale.' Unlike in Germany, where the Holocaust was mainly the work of state functionaries, in Rwanda there was an attempt to involve the entire Bahutu population. Though planned from above, it was executed by sections of the civilian population. It was as if every attempt was made to involve everyone, so there would be no one left to point a finger. A political commissar in the army puzzled over it, 'When we captured Kigali we thought we would face criminals in the state; instead, we faced a criminal population.' And then, he reflected upon the other side of the dilemma: 'Kigali was half empty when we arrived. It was as if the RPF was an army of occupation.'

Who was involved in the genocide? I posed this question everywhere I went. Callixte had this to say: 'In our *secteur*, there were six leaders. The six should be killed. The others should get appropriate punishment. There were even some intellectuals involved who were being led—but knew—they should be given more punishment. On average 15 to 20 years in jail. It is not possible to kill them all.' A member of the Army Political Group put it as follows: 'The genocide had a broad base extending from those who planned it to the intermediate level that organized the logistics and did the briefings, to those who carried out the activity.'

I came to Kigali prepared to argue against those who saw the question of justice in a purely legalistic way: that those who can be shown to have killed must be punished. My view was that the legal perspective must be subordinated to an overall political imperative. When I put this argument to the Army Political Group, I found that I was preaching to the converted. In the course of various conversations, I could sense a consensus growing at different levels of the state that justice must pave the way to reconciliation. But to extend that consensus to society seems a dilemma. To return to the Army Political Group,

> Are we looking at it from the point of view of genocide or of the people who lost relatives? . . What do you tell people who say, where shall we stop, shall we not kill everyone? Is the point to punish an individual, or to highlight a crime against humanity? Will the answer maintain the broad base [the coalition government], or dismantle it? Those not directly affected by the genocide don't share the pain, feelings and point of view of those directly affected.

The head of the Army Political Group told me, 'If you can bring to trial those who planned the genocide, then the question of the peasant who caught people on the hills is political. We can overlook that.' A similarly placed official said, 'The numbers of those held responsible doesn't matter.' Another said, 'Exposure is more important in the trials than punishment. Morally, those who survived on the politics of ethnicity will have been undermined.'

RECONCILIATION WITH JUSTICE

The growing consensus in the state involves two propositions. First, the number legally responsible for genocide and the number that one can politically afford to hold responsible are not the same. A political answer to the question, 'Who planned the genocide?', cannot begin with an identification of individuals. The brief response must be 'the state power'. Only then will the responsibility for genocide be political, not ethnic. Second, if the point of the genocide was to divide the population entirely into two—killers and victims—then justice must seek to identify and isolate those who sought to do this; to bring to public attention those who refused to participate or even dared to shelter Batutsi people; and to declare a general amnesty for the rest, and thereby establish the political basis for reuniting the population. But this consensus is neither crystallized nor unanimous. There is also a view, a minority view, which reflects a growing opinion outside Rwanda, particularly in political circles in the West, that the demands of justice may contradict those of reconciliation, and that the latter should have priority. It is a view that the UN Secretary General is said to have put, that the broad base of government should include the previous regime. Before I went to Rwanda, I had also found this view persuasive. But, as I found out through my discussions in Rwanda, it is not politically tenable.

In Butare I went to the Universite National du Rwanda, where 400 Batutsi students had been massacred, betrayed by fellow students and faculty. I met a Muhutu professor, and listened to her story.

> One of the [Batutsi] lecturers had a Muhutu wife. They had a boy of sixteen. We hid the child of the couple, and then took him along to the [French-created] *Zone Turquoise* when we ran there for safety. The wife survived. . . the husband, a Mututsi, had tried to hide, survived for two months, was found in June and was killed. . . . She heard about us, and came to the *Zone Turquoise* to get the son, but never told us we were being talked about as killers. So when we returned, we were arrested a week later. We put our lives at risk for hiding the boy for three months.

She was released after three months, but her husband—also a professor—is still in jail, charged with participating in the killing. She described the conditions in jail, 'There were 3,500 in jail with me, now increased to 6,000. Prison capacity is 1,500. Of the 6,000, more than 50 per cent are innocent. Among these there are 10 lecturers who I know are innocent. If they were brave enough to come back, they must be innocent.'

I asked her whether the demands of justice are a hindrance to reconciliation. The answer was quick and clear:

> Those responsible must be tried. They must be given punishment which should be broadcast so the culture of not punishing is brought to an end. I don't believe in forgiving. This was something which was planned at the level of political parties. It was not accidental. . . . There is no tension between justice and reconciliation. Once those victimized see perpetrators punished, they will feel better and will be able to live with the rest.

'The culture of not punishing', the culture that those in power need never answer for anything, is so deep-rooted in Rwanda that it has a name: Impunity. This culture seems to have begun in the colonial period. This prerogative—generally of rulers against the ruled, known in the colonial period as 'white privilege' in towns, and 'customary' privilege of chiefs in the countryside—was turned into a state culture after colonization ended. As such, it has been common to state authorities in Rwanda and Burundi, whether Bahuru or Batutsi. I asked a church official in Kigali to explain the significance of impunity. 'In 1972, Batutsi in Burundi went to secondary schools and eliminated over 200,000 Bahutu students. That's what the Burundi Bahuru call "impunity". Nobody bothers, nobody does anything.' But impunity, claims a Political Commissar in the Rwanda police, goes deeper than state culture. It permeates every institution: 'Children were taught in school to distinguish between Batutsi and Bahutu, that the former were oppressors and the latter oppressed. It created complexes. The teachers intimidated Batutsi children from the beginning, and taught Bahutu children that they had the right to oppress Batutsi. . . . What's wrong with killing an enemy? Kill the snake!' Callixte explained what it was like to live under those conditions:

> People here got used to killings. Even though there were no killings in our *secteur* before the genocide [in the Second Republic], there were often killings in surrounding *secteurs* like Nyamata. . . . But the killings would create refugees, who would come to our village and tell us of those from our village who were part of the *Intrahamwe*, who had participated in killings of other *secteurs*. Then the killings stopped, life just continued as usual.

Even if one did not witness killings, one got used to living next to known killers.

One has to bear in mind a specific factor in the genocide. Because broad sections of the population—willingly or under threat—participated in it, it has divided every neighbourhood and every institution. Every commune, every hospital, every school, every church, bears the scars of the genocide. If justice is not forthcoming from the state authorities, a rough-and-ready justice will be meted out by survivors to those they consider perpetrators. The alternative to justice is not reconciliation, it is revenge. This is why without justice, there can be no reconciliation: 'If the genocide is not handled properly, it is a time bomb that will explode.'

JUSTICE DELAYED IS JUSTICE DENIED

One is struck by an overriding fact in Rwanda today: the only institution that functions is the army. Over a year after the end of the genocide and the assumption of power by the RPF-organized government, there has been not a single trial of a person accused of responsibility for the genocide. There is not even a judiciary in place. The problem, I was told in discussions with the Army Political Group, is twofold: lack of means, and the lack of a definition of who counts as a perpetrator. It is difficult to accept that lack of means can be an adequate reason for this delay. If arms, and perhaps even specialized military personnel, can be brought in from the outside, why not the legal personnel to set justice in motion? If the problem is financial, why is there no effort to call for legal volunteers from the region? Most of all, why the failure to understand that justice and reconciliation—and not defence narrowly understood—are the first priority for Rwanda today?

The business of defining who is guilty, by contrast, is a real issue. While there is a growing consensus that neither government nor society can afford to try all those responsible, I found many in ruling circles who believed or assumed that most of the Bahutu population of Rwanda must accept responsibility for the killing. A highly placed person said: 'Categorize according to responsibility. Let those with responsibility be shot in the national stadium. Then go ahead and say that for all those who participated, the three to four million, let them say we did the wrong thing.' If this number is to be believed, the proceedings must be the domain of a South African-style 'truth with justice commission'—and must indeed explain the political paralysis of those in charge of justice.

I have little doubt that the problem is political. The state language in Rwanda, the language one hears from every official, and also from many who are not, divides the population of Rwanda into four categories: returnees, victims, survivors and perpetrators. The returnees are the mainly Batutsi (and some Bahutu) exiles and refugees who returned with the RPF. The victims are said to be both Batutsi and Bahutu—the latter victims of massacres of the internal political opposition. But survivors is a term applied only to the Batutsi. This is because the genocide was aimed at only the Batutsi, I was told. The implication, never spelled out openly, is that the perpetrators are the Bahutu who are still alive and, to put it plainly to be Muhutu is to be presumed a killer.

HOW DID THE SURVIVORS SURVIVE?

I think of the professor at Butare who, with her husband, hid the son of a colleague. In Ntarama, I met a 45 year old Muhutu who was the guard of the church—he had been a soldier in Habyarimana's army, was pensioned off and became a policeman. He had hidden eleven Batutsi, some in his house, others elsewhere. In Ntarama, and the southern lowlands of which it is a part, I was told it was possible for Batutsi to hide in the surrounding swamps and survive; but not so in most of the country. You could not hide in the hills. So hopeless was the quest to survive that there were many who eventually resigned themselves to being killed and presented themselves at roadblocks. There were even those made to queue before rivers to have their heads chopped off as they reached the front of the line, so that the corpse may roll into the river with but a nudge, saving the killers any extra effort. And yet, there were survivors. How? Conversations with people, official and non-official, gave me a clue. For most who survived outside the lowlands, there must have been at least one Muhutu family who protected them. For this group, however, there is no term; it is politically and publicly invisible.

The political cost of delayed justice may be extremely high. When I asked Callixte at the end of our discussion whether he wished to say anything else, he replied; 'I would wish to see justice being done. If we are needed to testify, we will do it. We are uncomfortable with the situation when nothing has been done.' Callixte was echoing a growing concern amongst Batutsi survivors: that the returnees from exile may not share their sensibilities about justice since they did not share their experience of genocide. The political consequence of this fact was uneasily but honestly underlined by one RPF official:

> We have a difficult situation. The people [Batutsi] here say we have been here for a year and nothing has happened. No one has been brought to justice. They say we were opportunistic, just wanting to come to power, for which they paid the price. Before the RPF came, they were oppressed, but not massacred. Now, they have suffered a genocide but have no justice. Survivors want punishment for the perpetrators. What do we do?

The more justice is delayed, the more people will take matters into their own hands—the more revenge will be the order of the day. Rwandese society will once again turn in on itself. This is already happening. According to the professor from Butare, 'The main problem for reconciliation is arbitrary arrest and those who have not participated being harassed. There are even cases of Bahutu who hid Batutsi being arrested now. It is demoralizing. Those who killed left, didn't remain behind. Now, even those who were hidden by Bahutu are not coming out to say so, to protect those who hid them if falsely arrested.' Why? 'One reason is that the victim is often the only survivor. She feels bad, feels others should be in her position. There is sometimes the desire for revenge. Up to now, those hidden by Bahutu don't visit them, speak for them or visit when in prison.' So the demand for prompt justice is not a demand confined to those Batutsi who survived the genocide. It is also a demand of important sections of the Bahutu. Delayed justice is already eroding political support for reconciliation, and with that, whatever moral and political basis the present government has.

The RPF seems not to have understood that justice and reconciliation have to be their first priority, for everything—defence, development, democracy—will fail without them. It is difficult otherwise to understand the decision of the RPF to make justice the responsibility of a single ministry. In any country with an emergency, it is not handled by a single ministry. It is recognized as the responsibility of the entire government. Genocide is more than an emergency; it puts in balance the survival of a whole people.

REGIONAL RESPONSIBILITIES

The RPF invasion of October 1990 occurred at a time of internal reform, not repression, in Rwanda. Supporters of the RPF have simply remained silent on this point, while opponents claim this single fact underlines the diabolical and power-hungry nature of the RPF. In my view, the invasion only makes sense if understood as a response to developments within the region, rather than Rwanda alone. More than any other country in the region, the fate of Rwanda would seem to be tied to that of Uganda. The RPF invasion that finally led to the downfall of the Second Republic in Rwanda came from Uganda. If the long-term historical trend that created a growing pool of refugees in the region—through a combination of periodic pogroms and expulsions of the Batutsi—can only be explained by internal developments in Rwanda, the organization of the refugees as an armed force and the timing of their armed return in October 1990 is explained mainly by internal developments in Uganda. For what has come to be known as the RPF invasion of Rwanda also needs to be understood as an expulsion of Rwandese refugees from Uganda.

The Rwandese who moved into Uganda over this century—excluding the Kinyarwanda-speaking population of Bufumbira county in Uganda—can be divided into two groups. The first were mainly Bahutu peasants who began flowing across the border from the mid-1920s in response to the tightening regime of forced labour and forced cultivation in Rwanda. The second were mainly Batutsi pastoralists and middle class people who fled the cycle of terror unleashed by the 1959 revolution. The former are termed migrants, the latter refugees. The social destiny of the two groups has turned out to be markedly different. Migrants came into Uganda to take up jobs in farms. From that starting point, they became a part of the local society more than refugees ever could, gradually assimilating, taking on local names, clan affiliations, spouses and even an overall identity. Refugees, by contrast, were destined for camps in which they lived under a commandant, in circumstances that clearly divided them from the host society. By 1990, migrants numbered between 500,000 and 750,000. Refugees were roughly 200,000.[27]

The division between the Bahutu and the Batutsi in Rwanda was

[27] Ibid., p. 5.

reproduced outside Rwanda as a difference between migrants and refugees. The RPF was a force socially anchored in the refugees more than in the migrants. The lot of the Rwandese refugees in Uganda was arguably the worst in the region. In Tanzania they could take up citizenship relatively easily, and the government actually demarcated a separate district for them; in Zaire, they were at times offered citizenship, though at other times the offer was withdrawn. Successive Ugandan governments, by contrast, considered even the children of refugees to be refugees. Even though some of the children left the camps, went to schools and even universities, and came to form an elite educated stratum whose members could be found in the professions, business, and the civil service, they had to hide their identity to do so, pretend to be what they were not: Banyankole, Baganda, or Banyoro. Even then, many had to bribe their way into institutions. The closest parallel I can think of to their situation was that of Palestinian refugees in the Middle East. The butt of popular prejudice and official discrimination, the readily available explanation for any situation difficult to explain—from poverty to sabotage—it was amongst the Rwandese refugees in Uganda that a refugee self-consciousness came to form first and foremost in response to anti-refugee prejudice promoted by the state and shared by many in the society at large. This is also why the mainly Batutsi refugees in Uganda came to think of themselves as Banyarwanda (Rwandese), and not as Batutsi.

It was the refugee intelligentsia in Uganda that set up the first organization of Rwandese refugees in the region, the Rwandese Alliance for National Unity (RANU) in Kampala in April 1979. RANU was primarily an organization of intellectuals, given largely to debate, discussion and representation. It was not quite equal to the fast developing situation in Uganda in which every discernible minority was becoming the target of state hostility and popular suspicion. The trend surfaced dramatically with the expulsion of Kenyan Jaluo workers in 1970, and the expulsion of Asians two years later. It would soon be the turn of the Rwandese. The Rwandese expulsion did come, but in 1982–3, under Obote II. On 1 October 1982, a combination of local chiefs, the youth wing of the UPC and a unit of the paramilitary Special Forces began an operation in south-west Uganda whose target were the 'Banyarwanda', but which included Bakiga and Bahima. The refugees' houses were destroyed, and there were 'killings, rapes, and maimings'. Over 40,000 fled into Rwanda before the Kigali government closed its side of the border. The rest divided into two. While adults fled to camps, many a youth headed for the growing army of NRA guerrillas in the bush. In December 1983, local chiefs and UPC youth wingers evicted over 19,000 Banyarwanda from Rakai and Masaka districts. With the Rwanda border closed, half fled into Tanzania, the other half divided once again, between the security of camps and the promise of guerrilla ranks. About the same time, 'a similar but less calculated attack on the Banyarwanda was taking place' in Teso in the east and Lango in the north, grazing areas where Banyarwanda pastoralists had moved, either in search of grass for cattle, if they owned any, or in search of employment more suited to their skills.[28]

The counterpoint to these expulsions was the spreading guerrilla war in the Luwero Triangle, an area whose population included large numbers of migrants. The largest group amongst the migrants were Banyarwanda, estimated at roughly 15 per cent of the district's population. In response to this inter-ethnic mix, the NRA developed a notion of popular organization and rights that would highlight the unity of the population, not its internal divisions. In deciding who could belong to popular village assemblies called Resistance Councils, vote in them, and be elected to village Resistance Committees, they pushed aside criteria of birth and descent as divisive and adopted those of residence and labour.

RWANDESE IN THE NRA

From the very outset, the presence of Rwandese in the guerrilla war was important. Two of the 27 who are said to have begun the guerrilla war with the ambush at Kabamba in 1981 were Banyarwanda—Fred Rwigyema and Paul Kagame. Rwigyema was to become Deputy Commander of the NRA after it came to power and Deputy Minister of Defence in Kampala. Paul Kagame would be Acting Chief of Military Intelligence of the NRA. The senior officers who under the command of Major General Rwigyema formed the leadership of RPF when it crossed into Rwanda, included six other senior NRA officers: Lt. Col. Wasswa, and Majors Kagame, Baingana, Kaka, Bunyenyezi, and Nduqutse.[29] These senior officers,

[28] Ibid., p. 10, US Committee for Refugees, 1983.
[29] Catharine Watson, personal communication, September 1995.

like Bunyenyezi who was a mobile Brigade Commander, were just the tip of the iceberg. Had they joined the guerrilla struggle in Luwero, as some argue, to gather skills and weapons and build an organization so they could move to Kigali at the first available opportunity? Or was the move to Kigali a result of developments that took place after the NRA assumed power in Kampala, developments that would bring home to the refugees a bitter truth: that in Africa today, once a refugee, always a refugee. As a senior RPA commander put it to me in Kigali in 1995, 'You stake your life and at the end of the day you recognize no amount of contribution can make you what you are not. You can't buy it, not even with blood.' No doubt their ranks included some who were convinced from the outset that there was no alternative but to return. Just as surely, these ranks could not have grown without others who thought naturalization the more viable alternative. After all, it was as late as 1988 that a conference of Rwandese exiles on naturalization could take place. What happened to leave such a bitter after-taste?

Once guerrillas returned to society from the bush, they returned to a world of citizens and refugees, a world they thought they had left behind forever. With hardly any delay, the round of expulsions began once again and Rwandese cattle-keepers were forcefully evicted from Teso in 1986. The NRA tradition of giving preference to curcumstance of labour and residence became distant history. When it came to promotions, especially where a Munyarwanda was involved, what began to count, more than anything else, was descent. Ironically but understandably, to Rwandese officers and men in NRA, the period after 1986 must have begun to seem like a betrayal by none other than their former comrades-in-arms.

One of the founders of RANU recalled the mood of the moment,

> The NRA experience was a catalyst in mobilizing the Banyarwanda in NRA. As far back as 1983, our position was that people should join the struggle in Uganda voluntarily. It was worthwhile. It was not a deliberate effort to organize an army inside an army. The discrimination and harassment puzzled them, made them look for alternatives. They turned to senior RANU members, like Baingana. The discrimination did mobilize quite a few for us.

Out of this predicament was born the RPF in 1987, crystallizing two points of consensus: that the leadership of the refugee struggle would come from Rwandese in the NRA, and that the return home could only be military. Unlike RANU which had represented a left-leaning ideological tendency, RPF was to be a broad front; and unlike RANU which was mainly an elite intellectual formation with a deliberative impulse, RPF would be socially anchored in the refugee population and would be driven by an activist impulse. But there was still no agreement on the future of the refugees, whether to return or naturalization.

Then came the 1990 parliamentary debate on the land bill. The Rwandese refugees had always been charged with responsibility for land shortage where grazing pastures overlapped with arable land. Equally, pastoralists had always sought a way out of the squatter situation into which they had been locked by their refugee status. The land bill aimed to repossess large ranches—originally distributed to influential bureaucrats in the 1960s—subdividing them into smaller plots and redistributing them to squatters.[30] It was a bill that was introduced in the midst of an escalating conflict between ranchers and squatters, the former having over time turned into landlords who rented out grazing land to squatters. The ranchers portrayed the bill as an instrument of refugee Banyarwanda interests, backed up by governmental, and particularly military, power. As the debate progressed, both sides armed themselves. The issue provoked one of the most heated debates in Uganda since 1986, ultimately pitting the President against his own Minister of State for Defence.

The decision that Parliament finally made forbade non-citizens from owning land; Banyarwanda refugees, and their children, were expressly mentioned as non-citizens. Major General Fred Rwigyema was removed from his position as Deputy Minister of Defence by the Chairman of the High Command and 'was no longer on active duty with the NRA at the time of the invasion in October 1990'. 'It is believed', argued Katenta-Apuli, Uganda's ambassador to the US in a letter to Human Rights Watch (26 August 1993), 'that the combination of these two fundamental decisions convinced Rwandese refugees that they did not have a bright future in Uganda and precipitated the mass desertion from the NRA and the decision to invade Rwanda to regain their rights in their country of origin.' To drive the point home, on the day of the invasion, the Ugandan government declared all Rwandese who had left the NRA to attack Rwanda as deserters under the Operational Code of Conduct. 'That means',

[30] *New Vision*, Kampala, 25 July 1990.

the ambassador clarified, 'on conviction by a court martial, they would be punishable by death. This is no incentive for them to cross back into Uganda.'

To most Ugandans, the ambassador's claim may appear laughable. After all, many in the RPF, particularly its leadership, did cross into Uganda at several points during the war, and the RPF enjoyed active support from Uganda. After all, the Banyarwanda in the RPF were not strangers to Ugandan society or the Ugandan state. Some observers even thought of the RPF as functioning like a state within the state. But in spite of all this, one thing is clear: the precondition for this support was that there be no return. The bottom line was that the RPF continue to push into Rwanda. The refugee soldiers who formed the core of the RPF, who were nearly 3,000 of the roughly 14,000 NRA who took Kampala in 1986, and were estimated at around 4,000 in 1990, found themselves between the Rwandan devil and the Ugandan deep blue sea. The refugee crisis that led to the October 1990 invasion was a question that was both Rwandan and Ugandan. It was, in a nutshell, an African crisis.

INTERNATIONAL RESPONSIBILITIES

The October 1990 invasion made for an explosive situation inside Rwanda. Both France and Belgium sent troops in support of the government. While Belgium quickly developed cold feet—citing a legal obligation to remain neutral in situations of war it withdrew its troops—France proved to be the regime's most reliable backer. French assistance ranged from providing funds, training, and arms to giving financial guarantees for arms purchases from intermediary countries such as Egypt and South Africa.[31] So public was France's role in the training of the armed militias that soon would be the stormtroopers of the genocide—particularly the *Intrahamwe*—that in Kigali it was common to hear the French President called *Mitterahamwe*.

An equally visible and enthusiastic supporter, but of the Kigali regime, was President Mobutu of Zaire. In contrast to France and Belgium, Mobutu despatched a special Presidential unit, and it immediately went into direct action against the RPF. For Mobutu,

[31] For details, see Africa Watch, *Arming Rwanda: The Arms Trade and Human Rights Abuses in the Rwandan War*, New York, 1994.

the war was a heaven-sent opportunity to prove to France—who had begun to cold shoulder him recently—and to anyone else who would care to take note, that he could always be relied upon for support during critical times. According to African Rights, Zaire's involvement continues to be that of an intermediary between the Bahutu extremists and their main benefactor, France.[32]

The quantifiable side of the international involvement has been its more obvious side, and it has been well documented by two human rights NGOs, first by Africa Watch, and more recently and more comprehensively by African Rights. Less obvious, however, has been the non-quantifiable side of this involvement, its sum and substance being diplomatic and financial pressure in favour of a policy shift. The vulnerability of the country's political and social structure was greatly increased by a collapse in coffee prices and the imposition by the World Bank of a severe structural adjustment programme. The pressure for a policy shift came from powers that included the US and Canada; their demand was for political reform and an opening of negotiations with the RPF. Reform, they said textbook fashion, meant the introduction of a multi-party political system. Western democracies, that instinctively respond to internal insurgency by restricting political freedoms, compelled the government in Kigali to open up the political system in the face of a civil war, or else face diplomatic isolation and a cessation of aid. A leader of an opposition party in the early 1990s, who is now a minister in Kigali, recalled the consequences, 'The multi-party system—and the related organization of youth—put this country in a situation of permanent tension.'

One would have thought that expanded discussion and negotiation would have been the most adequate antidote to rising tension. But political representation at the Arusha negotiations in 1992 provided little room for expression and representation to the extremist wing of the ruling coalition in Kigali. In fact, it turned out to be more of a consultation exercise between the RPF and the opposition parties which had joined the government in Kigali and bagged several portfolios, including Foreign Affairs, in the ongoing political reform. The eventual Arusha Accord of August 1993 provided for the RPF to furnish 40 per cent of the troops and half of

[32] African Rights, *Rwanda Death, Despair, and Defiance*, revd. edn., London: African Rights, 1995, pp. 1101–9.

the high command of the remodelled armed forces. The 'Hutu power' tendency, with no say at Arusha, regarded such provisions as anathema; extreme though it was, the 'Hutu power' tendency was hardly a marginal force. The more it felt excluded from the negotiations, and the more they moved to a resolution that it saw as a disgraceful capitulation, the more Bahutu extremism looked for a 'final solution' to the Batutsi question. The assassination of President Habyarimana in April 1994 furnished the genocidal wing of 'Hutu power' and its apparatus—notably, the *Intrahamwe*, the *Impuzamugambi* and the *Milles Collines* radio station—with the pretext and opportunity to unleash the mass killing.

The terror was directed against the two forces they held responsible for an outright betrayal of the 1959 revolution. Encompassing first the massacre of the Bahutu opposition, and then the genocide of the Batutsi minority, this terror cannot simply be explained as the response of an elite in danger of losing power though it was that too. We have seen that the genocide was a highly decentralized affair in which villagers killed their neighbours, just as those in school and hospitals exterminated their colleagues, notwithstanding the fact that there were others who risked their lives to save those being hunted. One is confronted with the 'popular' nature of the genocide and compelled to look for clues that may explain the motivation of the subaltern masses.

The 'Hutu Power' claim that the RPF stood for nothing less than a Batutsi resurgence which would reverse the social gains of the 1959 revolution, restoring a rule reminiscent of the Batutsi chiefs under colonialism, made sense to significant sections of the Bahutu population, including peasants and the urban poor, many hard hit by economic crisis and austerity. Mobilized by the Bahutu power structure born of the revolution, they participated in the mass killings which, as has already been seen, they called communal work. This popular response highlights the limits of a subaltern consciousness: defined by the memory of the colonial period, it was limited to the experience of oppression by the agents of indirect rule. From this point of view, 1994 was only a continuation of 1959, an orgy of revolutionary violence meant to nip counter-revolutionary violence in the bud, whose subaltern motivation was no less than to defend their own threatened humanity. Hegel remarked at one point that human beings are differentiated from other forms of life by their capacity to give life for a cause they consider higher than life. He should have added, and to take it.

When they finally glimpsed the magnitude of the oncoming crisis, the leaders of the international community responded by shirking their share of responsibility. Instead of building up the UNAMIR force already inside Kigali to protect Batutsi civilians, as its commander recommended time and again, they withdrew it! What is the Rwanda problem today from the point of view of this international leadership? They fear that the assumption of power by the RPF will simply trigger another cycle of ethnic revenge. Their tendency is thus to detach the question of justice from that of reconciliation, and to push for reconciliation without justice. The trouble with this position, as I have already suggested, is that it will encourage incidents of rough-and-ready justice and turn them into waves of revenge inside neighbourhoods and institutions, dividing each and all. The international leadership also believes that at the heart of the problem—in Rwanda as in Burundi—lies an ethnic conflict, amenable only to an ethnic solution. So any solution must involve ethnic power-sharing between the Bahutu and the Batutsi, reflecting the numerical majority of the former. This is what a multi-party democracy would mean: one or many minority Batutsi parties facing one or many majority Bahutu parties. And the problem with this position, I will suggest, is that power-sharing will not be durable without a reform of the structure, so that majority and minority are not permanent artefacts institutionalized in the structures of the state and confirmed by the political process set in motion by that state. In other words, while the recognition of the Bahutu and Batutsi identities needs to be the starting point for a process of reconciliation, the point of the process must be not to reproduce these dualities but to transcend them.

I will argue against the notion that multi-party democracy can lead to democratic outcomes regardless of context, for this can only be when all participants accept the rules of the game. Logically and historically, the creation of a political community must precede multi-party competition. It bears repeating that the creation of a political community requires a minimum consensus of all within that community. The definition of a people is not ethnic, nor racial, nor cultural; it is mainly political. This is why one can think of forging a people in a multi-ethnic, multi-racial and multi-cultural situation like South Africa through a political process. To create a political community based on consent is to create a Rwandese people.

BROAD-BASED GOVERNMENT

Common to those countries which have gone through the trauma of civil war is an emphasis on a broad-based government. Uganda and South Africa are two examples. Rwanda is another. The experiences of constructing a broad base are various and even conflicting. I would like to highlight several issues. First, where civil war has fractured the political elite into antagonistic factions, the starting point of the broad base has been an agreement about power-sharing at the top. Uganda and Rwanda show two different instances of how power-sharing may be conceptualized. In Uganda, the broad base incorporates individuals in power led and organized by the victorious group in the civil war, the NRA. In Rwanda, the background to the broad base is the Arusha Accord of 1993. The broad base of 1994 includes three types of representatives: the RPF, political parties that did not participate in the genocide, and individuals outside the RPF invited by it to join Uganda-style. The Ugandan way might seem opportunistic. It does not recognize the right of political organizations to choose who shall represent them and thus their right to hold individuals accountable. But the contrast between Rwanda and Uganda has several aspects. One of these is that the broad base in Rwanda seems more nominal than that in Uganda. Even if the majority of the cabinet in Rwanda is from outside the RPF, its identity more Bahutu than Batutsi, one suspects this majority is in government at the behest of the RPF. I often heard the comment that the parties in government have no base, that somehow a base would have to be created. The proposition would seem to be true for one reason only—that the genocide has greatly eroded that base.

Second, the key question confronting the RPF in its construction of a broad-based government is who should be included and who excluded? The issue assumed vital significance after 1995 with the dismissal from the cabinet of two key Bahutu leaders, Faustin Twagiramungu, the Prime Minister, and Seth Sendosonga, the Minister of the Interior. Both were excluded hecause they were proponents of 'Hutu power'. This rationale contradicts the lesson learned from the broad base in Uganda and South Africa—in an explosive post-civil war situation, every effort must be made to include each political tendency. There should be only one pre-condition to participation: the renunciation of violence as a method of attaining objectives. In Uganda the broad base included members from all the previous dictatorships, from Amin and Obote II to Lutwa, along with ethnic, chauvinist and monarchist supporters. In South Africa, it includes supporters of Black Power and White Power. The RPF includes within its ranks proponents of 'Tutsi power'. Why then should the broad base in Rwanda not include their counterparts, those champions of 'Hutu power' who are willing to renounce violence as a means for an objective, keeping out those who favour Hutu dominance—rule by the sociological majority? To exclude Bahutu is to exclude those whose views have support in the majority of the population. It is to erode the middle ground and narrow the broad base.

While justice is a necessary condition for reconciliation, it is not a sufficient condition. Reconciliation will also require the construction of a shared history, and in this there will be no more difficult task than arriving at a shared interpretation of 1959. I met Bahutu figures, including some in the present cabinet, who uphold 1959 as a 'social revolution' which emancipated the majority. Today history is no longer being taught in schools in Rwanda, mainly because there is no account of 1959 that is acceptable to both Bahutu and Batutsi, even to those inside the government. Is not to exclude the non-violent proponents of 'Hutu power' from the broad base tantamount to undercutting the process of reconciliation by declaring their account of 1959 illegitimate? Reconciliation in Rwanda is likely to be a task more difficult than in Uganda or even South Africa. Even if the RPF is to pursue justice and construct a broad enough base for governance, reconciliation is likely to remain a distant goal.

As one political commissar put it to me, 'The genocide created more suspicion amongst the people than the broad base can contain.' The point is that one has to go beyond power-sharing at the top, to building consensus from the bottom up. Power-sharing can at best be curative; preventive measures require the building of a minimum consensus. That, in my view, is not possible without institutional reforms that will dismantle the conquest state in a step-by-step fashion.

BUILDING A DURABLE CONSENSUS

We have seen that while the *institutional* infrastructure of Belgian colonialism was no different from that of other colonies on the continent, its *social* representation was. While ethnic groups in other African countries lived in spatially distinct locations, each more or less confined to its own locale, this was not the case with the Bahutu and the Batutsi in Rwanda—who lived in the same hills. So that while the district-level apparatus of indirect rule in other African colonies tended to crystallize a local hierarchy that was ethnically no different from the local peasantry, giving rise to the social experience of colonialism as rule by one's own, this was not so in Rwanda. The district-level antagonism in other African colonies erupted as local civil wars inside each ethnic group but local antagonism in Rwanda took on the character of a conflict between Bahutu and Batutsi which transcended local boundaries.

While 1959 changed the state personnel from Batutsi to Bahutu, it did not change the institutional character of the state apparatus. Power remained as fused and authoritarian as before. This authority continued to be enabled through 'customary' law, which rationalized extra-economic coercion. I do not mean to say that nothing changed with the 1959 'revolution', for control over the allocation of land passed to the majority. The year 1959 signified free access to land and freedom of labour for the Bahutu peasantry. It was a historical gain that was real, and remained so, until the end of the late 1980s. To the extent that the Bahutu masses partook directly in the genocide of 1994, they did so to protect the gains of 1959.

Indirect rule was an ideological term for a decentralized despotism. To reform it is to dismantle the institutional legacy of the colonial state, a task for which there is no blueprint, and nor should there be any. The answer, or more likely answers, will have to be found in practice, through a creative process of trial and error. The only starting point can be an analytical summing up of our experience to date. I believe the Ugandan example to be of relevance here. To be durable, a broad base—to use the language of contemporary Ugandan politics—needs to be constructed from both above and below; the power-sharing from above to defuse the immediately explosive tension, and institutional reform from below to begin to build a durable consensus. Without the latter, the former will be no more than a stop-gap measure. The Ugandan example is known as the RCC (Resistance Council and Committee) system. Its strength and appeal has been in the countryside, where it dismantled the trinity of chiefly authorities which had ruled since colonial times, and replaced them with popular committees elected by village assemblies. At the same time, a separation of powers was achieved, separating legislative from executive and judicial powers. Village councils (Resistance Councils) operated on the basis of discussion and consensus. The executive committees (Resistance Committees) they elected worked on the basis of consensus when possible, majority when not. The introduction of participatory forms of government created plural majorities, not one countrywide majority confronting one minority, but as many majorities and minorities as there were recognized communities.

TOWARDS A COMMON POLITICAL COMMUNITY

I have argued that the identities Batutsi and Bahutu were created in the process of the formation of the Rwandese state and could not have been reproduced without a form of state power that institutionalized these identities. While the identities are socio-political, those who proclaim 'Hutuness' and 'Tutsiness' have writ these identities even larger, with a resonance that is also socio-cultural. There is no point in arguing whether the Bahutu and the Batutsi are the same, or culturally or even physiologically similar. Our starting point should be what Bahutu and Batutsi people think of themselves today. From that perspective, the irony is that the current government does not tire of shouting from the rooftops that 'we are all one people, we are all Rwandese'. I believe that there has been no time in the history of Rwanda when the Bahutu and Batutsi were so polarized. Their long and tragic history has brought us to a point where we must today consider Rwanda as being like most other African countries—multicultural.

From this point of view, Rwanda shows that where majority and minority turn into permanent artefacts, neither minority nor majority rule necessarily leads to viable regimes. Both experiences ended in disaster—the former in a cycle of pogroms, and the latter in a genocide. The construction of permanent divisions between the majority and the minority in a multi-cultural context is the outcome of a nation-state paradigm, of the state as an expression of the right to self-determination. This paradigm can be seen as the source of three problems.

First, one learnt from Europe that a nation is a cultural community living on a common territory, and that its self-determination requires that it create its own state. One forgot that, in the making of nation states, Europe went through an entire history of ethnic cleansing. Where it did not, it branded cultural minorities as permanent 'national minorities' alongside the cultural majority as the 'nation'. One's reality is of multi- and not uni-cultural communities. If one's past has anything to teach, it is how diverse cultural communities can begin to constitute a single political community. But if one is to adopt the paradigm of a nation creating a state, is he prepared to follow Europe into a future of ethnic cleansing, or one of ethnic apartheid? Second, the language of self-determination immediately created a contest around notions of majority and minority. In multicultural contexts, it created an inter-cultural tension, and at times an explosion. But in uni-cultural contexts where a political community did not exist, it turned the slight differences that had survived a long history of cultural diffusion—the nose, height, diet, endogamy—into strategic political artefacts around which state power created a central and legitimizing political difference.

The existence of permanent minorities and permanent majorities is not compatible with the democratic process, no matter what safeguards are introduced into the process, as anyone familiar with the history of Native Americans and African-Americans will testify. For a political process to be democratic, minorities and majorities must be constructed in the course of that process, rather than being a foregone conclusion. My argument is that before one can find in the notion of self-determination the touchstone to the process of state formation, one has to answer the question of identity. In one historical period, Europe answered that question more or less unanimously: the nation, a common cultural community. In the African context, the answer has to be different if we are not to end by cutting one another's collective cultural throats. The 'we' cannot be a common cultural community; it has to be a common political community. To realize a political community in a multi-cultural context, one needs to move away from the ideal whereby politics must be an affirmation, even a mirror-image, of culture, and begin to think of the autonomy of politics from culture.

Third, where politics is seen as an affirmation of culture, politics will permeate and shape that culture. The nation-state is a construct in which politics is only primary, not omnipotent. This much is evident not only from the course of 'Hutu power' in Rwanda, but also from an examination of the colonial state in Africa as a whole. The point of indirect rule, of a central power working through 'customary' local authorities, was precisely to tap into and develop authoritarian possibilities in culture and to sanctify them as 'customary' while simultaneously undercutting the autonomy of culture. The difference is that while the customary was always a contradictory construct in colonial Africa—it was the language of both power and protest—it seemed to have achieved a claustrophobic triumph as the language of power in Rwanda after 1959.

CONCLUSION

What is likely to be the future of Rwanda? Short of being hurled into another destructive cycle, I can think of three possibilities. In the discussion with the Political Group of the army, a political commissar dismissed with contempt one such possibility: 'Set up a Tutsiland to save an engendered species?' Nonetheless, this possibility could become reality should Rwanda return to the cycle of revenge and reprisal, massacre and genocide.

The closest parallel this region has to offer to the 1959 revolution in Rwanda is the 1963 revolution in Zanzibar. The history of state formation in Zanzibar is less disputed than that in Rwanda. There is no debate I know of about when and where the Arabs came from. Over a period of, there was an integration of Arab and African cultures: the Arab and the African populations spoke the same language, practiced the same religion, and lived on the same island. They created the core of a cultural community, but not of a political community. In time, the identities Arab and African became more socio-political and historical, less socio-cultural. The colonial state in Zanzibar institutionalized these identities. Britain ruled through an Arab administrative apparatus symbolically headed by a Sultan. The revolution in Zanzibar led to the collapse of the minority state and the formation of a majority state in the midst of pogroms reminiscent of Rwanda of 1959. It was a trajectory that could easily have led to a cycle of revenge and attrition, an institutionalized terror in the name of a permanent revolution, except for one factor—the union with the mainland and incorporation into Tanzania. This regional solution, incorporation into a neighbouring political entity, is the second alternative that Rwanda may face if its political leadership is unable to find a way out of the cycle of revenge and mutual self-destruction.

The third alternative is one that has neither a historical parallel nor a model. Precisely for that reason, it is likely to be the more creative and the more promising. My sketch of some of the steps along such a path—justice, a broad-based regime and a reform of the state to forge a common political community based on consent—should be taken more as an attempt to illuminate signposts on the tortuous road ahead than as the formulation of a definitive alternative. It is difficult for me to exude optimism and propose a solution, let alone one formulated outside the parameters of daily practice. No one asked Jews and Germans to live together in post-Holocaust Germany. But imagine if they had been asked to do that—under a Jewish-dominated government and with roughly a third of Germans living outside the country. Allow further for one salient difference: that the genocide in Rwanda was a far more decentralized and 'popular' affair than the Holocaust. Such is the context in which reconciliation must proceed in contemporary Rwanda.

The Story of Three Songs: Illuminations on the Cultural Politics of Thai Citizenship

Kasian Tejapira

WO BU SHI ZHONG GUO REN (*I am a Chinaman*)

One night, in the middle of January 1993, an annual banquet of the Machine Tools & Ironware Business Association of Thailand was held in a grand Chinese restaurant in downtown Bangkok. I was invited by my elder sister, who happened to be an executive member of the Association, to join in the feast. I arrived to find that most if not all of the more than one thousand guests at the banquet were ethnic Teochiu Chinese.

Typical of this type of gathering, as anyone who is used to it can readily testify, there is always an accompanying musical show on the stage to which hardly anyone pays attention. When I entered the banquet hall, a song was being sung by a nicely-dressed male singer, scarcely audible amidst the din of chit-chat and chaotic clattering of spoons and chopsticks. Having studied Chinese mandarin in my youth, admittedly by no means a happy experience since I was forced to do so by my father, I happened to recognize, and was struck by, the words of the song whose title I found out later to be '*wo bu shi zhong guo ren*' (I am a Chinaman). It reads:

Reticence is not cowardice.
Patience is not apathy.
Confucius' traditional teachings guide our steps.
Arduous, eight-year war of resistance
Has proven my tenacious people.
Not until the final critical moment
shall we lightly take up arms.
When provoked beyond endurance,

I shall step forward bravely.
When my fellow countrymen suffer
and my land awaits salvage,
I shall firmly remember.
No matter where I was born,
I am a Chinaman.
No matter where I die,
I swear I'll be a Chinese ghost.[1]

No one else there seemed to hear it, let alone be moved by such a heartfelt patriotic call from their homeland. I had to ask why?

Perhaps, first of all, because most if not all of them, being literate in Thai and the Teochiu dialect but not in Chinese mandarin, simply did not understand what '*wo shi zhong guo ren*' meant. And second, because, for better or worse, no matter what their life experiences, the spatio-temporal formation they inhabited, and the particular cultural-political governance to which they were subject, they were not 'Chinamen', but Jeks or Lookjins.[2] What precisely does it mean?

THAILAND UNITES THE THAI BLOOD AND RACE

To understand this, we need to listen to another song, the Thai National Anthem, whose words begin: 'Thailand, unites the Thai blood and race. A people's state, all parts belong to Thais. . . .'[3]

[1] The song was composed by Liu Jia-chang and sung by Zhang Minmian in 1988, see Casette tape jacket information, '*wo shi zhong guo ren*' (I am a Chinaman), Zhang Mingmian (Dragon Casette, 1988, D-398). The translation is mine.

[2] 'Jek' is a common and informal term used by ethnic Thais to call the Chinese immigrants and their descendants and considered derogatory by the latter whereas 'Lookjin' literally denotes people of Chinese ancestry who were born in Siam and has no negative connotation.

[3] My own translation. An alternative, semi-official version is that of Mr Phairoj Kesmankiu, which reads in full as follows:

'Thailand, cradle of Thais wherever they may be;
The homeland of our people, the whole land is the land of the Thais.
United and in the spirit of brotherhood we are ever able to defend our land.
Thais love peace but never fear the battle.
Never shall we let our independence be surrendered.
We shall shed every drop of our blood to defend our beloved country.
May glory and victory reign over our beloved Kingdom. Hurrah.'

It encapsulates the crux of Thai official nationalism,[4] as conceived by King Rama VI or Vajiravudh (1910–25), the chief ideologue of Thai royalist absolutism, which was later consolidated, expanded and intensified by Prime Minister Field Marshal Plaek Phibunsongkhram (1938–44 and 1948–57), who can be seen as the Führer and pioneer of Thai militaristic statism. The opening lines of the Thai national anthem, obligatorily broadcast, are played and sung throughout the country twice a day, to accompany the raising and lowering of the Thai national flag since 1938. It is undoubtedly the most frequently heard song in the country; the song proceeds to define the Chinese immigrants in Siam as 'the Other' or even 'the enemy within'. Chinese immigrants, in these lines, are automatically excluded from the rightful membership of the Thai polity and are derogatorily dubbed 'Jek' and 'the Jews of the Orient'. It was the state-incited fear and hatred of the Chinese spectre that originally gave rise to Thai official nationalist consciousness, which is based solely on the Thai race and politically centred on, as well as arbitrarily defined by, the state. Upon the ruins of the historically multi-cultural, multi-ethnic Siamese Kingdom was laid the ideological foundation of the supposedly mono-cultural, mono-ethnic national imagination of the Thai state. We shall look at some basic canons of its doctrine.[5]

Quoted in Montri Tramot, 'Prawat phleng sansern phrabarami lae phleng chat' (The History of the Royal Anthem of Thailand and the Thai National Anthem), *Sinlapakorn*, XVI, 2 (July 1972), 93.

[4] My use of 'official nationalism' here follows that of Benedict Anderson in Chapter VI of his *Imagined Communities*, which refers to 'an anticipatory strategy adopted by dominant groups which are threatened with marginalisation or exclusion from an emerging nationally-imagined community', 'a means for combining naturalisation with retention of dynastic power', and 'a willed merger of nation and dynastic empire'. See Benedict Andersen, *Imagined Communities: Reflections on the Origin and Spread of Nationalism*, London: Verso, 1991, pp. 86, 101.

[5] The following analysis of Thai official nationalism draws on my own article, 'Pigtail: A Pre-History of Chineseness in Siam', *Sojourn*, VII, 1 (February 1992), pp. 95–122; and Chai-anan Samudavanija, 'State-Identity Creation, State building and Civil Society', *National Identity and its Defenders, Thailand, 1939–89*. Craig J. Reynolds (ed.), Clayton, Victoria: Centre of Southeast Asian Studies, Monash University, 1991, pp. 59–85; as well as Dr Somkiat Wantana, 'Song satawas khong rat lae prawattisatniphon thai' (Two Centuries of the Thai State and Historiography), *Thammasat University Journal*, XII, 3 (September 1984), pp. 152–71.

During the initial phase of its formation under King Vajiravudh, which may be called 'the negative politicization of Thai ethnicity', the majority Thai ethnic group was politically interpellated as the dominant mainstay of the multi-ethnic Siamese nation.[6] This is evident in the King's oft-quoted poem entitled '*Sayamanusati*' (Maxim for Siam), which conceptually maintains the distinction between '*la patrie siamoise*' and '*le peuple thai*' as follows:

If only Siam still stands,
then all of us can survive.
But if Siamese land is lost, alas,
it's as if Thai lives and race were gone.

However, King Vajiravudh's willful politicization of the Thais was achieved negatively by singling out the Chinese as their archenemy.[7] The King branded the Chinese in Siam with such epithets and perceptions as 'Yellow Peril' (pp. 72, 83); '(Siamese) are no more like the Chinese than any of the European races are like the Jews' (pp. 72, 113); 'persistency and pride of race' (pp. 72, 73, 75); 'neither knows nor understands nationality or patriotism' (p. 73); 'loyal to the power that owns his fickle allegiance only so long as his own interests happen to coincide with those of his masters' (p. 73); 'somewhat undesirable' (p. 73); 'regarding their residence as temporary and . . . refuse to be assimilated' (pp. 73, 83, 113); 'locusts' (p. 73); 'with the avowed purpose of extracting as much wealth as they could and then go away, without any thought of obligation at all' (pp. 73, 96); 'never becomes a real citizen' (p. 75); 'share the benefits of citizenship . . . but . . . evade . . . duties' (p. 75); 'undisguised contempt for his neighbour' (p. 75); 'never dreams of dealing honestly or fairly with any of us . . . thinks that we others

[6] This idea is derived from Louis Althusser's concept of ideological interpellation. See his 'Ideology and Ideological State Apparatus', in *Lenin and Philosophy and Other Essays*, London: New Left Books, 1971, pp. 121–73.

[7] It is at this point that Chai-anan Samudavanija's incisive indictment of Thai official nationalism reaches its critical ceiling and loses its bite. Whereas he has no qualms in tearing to shreds Field Marshal Plaek's later mono-ethnic and statist version of Thai nationalism, he remains conspicuously silent about the openly negative, strongly anti-Chinese and hence primarily racist nature of its forerunner, i.e. King Vajiravudh's royalist nationalism. This consistent blind spot in Chai-anan's writings about the Chakri monarchs separactes his liberal conservative politics from that of, say radical social critic Sulak Sivaraksa.

exist for the special purpose of being cheated and outdone by him' (pp. 75–6, 85); 'every bit as unscrupulous and as unconscionable as the Jews' (pp. 76, 80); 'his courtesy is merely assumed and his fair-speech mostly lying flattery' (p. 76); 'insolent' (p. 76); 'acute . . . money-making instinct' (p. 79); 'money (as) the Be-all and End-all . . . will do anything for the sake of money . . . willing to sell their lives . . . suffer starvation and every form of hardship . . . for money' (pp. 79, 120); 'utterly without morals, without conscience, without mercy, without pity . . . where money is concerned . . . will cheat with a smile at their own cleverness and rob and murder with utter callousness for the sake of getting a few dollars . . . fiendishly clever at devising schemes, be it of fraud, robbery, or piracy' (pp. 80, 82); 'no more Buddhists than are the Jews Christians' (p. 80); 'worship . . . one God only . . . the Money God' (p. 82); 'Honour and Good Name, Honesty and Truth, Love and Mercy, the Milk of Human Kindness, all are offered on the altar of the Money God' (p. 82); 'a completely individual system of morality' (p. 82); 'soulless' (p. 83); 'aliens, by birth, by nature, by sympathy, by language and finally by choice' (pp. 83, 93, 98, 99, 101, 102, 105, 113); 'vampires who steadily suck dry an unfortunate victims,' life-blood' (p. 84); 'bound one day to come into bloody conflict with the inhabitants' (p. 84); 'no love lost between my compatriots and Chinamen as it is' (pp. 84–5); 'born intriguers and conspirators' (p. 86); 'exclusive and unneighbourly' (p. 95); 'quite unreasonable . . . will not believe anything that we Siamese say' (p. 96); 'are Siamese by words of mouth only' (p. 97); 'Chameleon' (p. 97); 'very troublesome' (p. 103); 'extremely thrifty' (p. 120), etc.[8]

The King posits, in independent Siam, a colonial 'plural-society-like situation' (à la J.S. Furnivall)[9] where people of different ethnicities 'mix but do not combine' and 'live side by side but separately', and simply denies any possible co-identity, union, combination and even mediation or middle ground between the two races and communities. Hence,

[8] Asvabahu (King Vajiravudh), *Phuak yew haeng booraphathis lae meuang thai jong teun thoed phrom duai lai phra ratchahat khamplae phasa angklis* (The Jews of the Orient and Wake up Siam with English translation in the King's Handwriting), Bangkok: King Cajiravudh Memorial Foundation, 1985. Translation is mine.

[9] See J.S. Furnivall, *Colonial Policy and Practice*, London: Cambridge University Press, 1948.

> One is either a Chinaman or a Siamese; no one could be both at the same time, and people who pretend that they are so are apt to be found to be neither. Such people, like the Chameleon, change their colour to suit their surrounding; when they come among us they are Siamese, but when they go among the Chinese they become Chinese, while many of them also owe their allegiance to some European Power. These latter are usually the 'politicians' among the Chino-Siamese community, the self-constituted leaders of 'Modern Thought', the demagogues and journalists of Bangkok. . . .
>
> . . . we can only count as Siamese those who have *definitely* decided to adopt the Siamese nationality, cutting themselves quite completely from all Chinese association. They must throw their lots in with us *absolutely* before we accept them as one of us. We cannot accept those who call themselves 'Chino-Siamese as Genuine Siamese'. (emphasis in the original)[10]

What this amounts to is the imagination of an 'uncommunity' between the Thais and the Chinese in Siam or, in short, an 'imagined uncommunity'[11] where a Chino-Siamese or Sino-Thai ethnocultural identity is discursively impossible.[12] However, whereas Furnivall inferred from his 'plural society' assumption that colonial Burma was incapable of nationhood, King Vajiravudh concludes that the only way to hold the Siamese 'uncommunity' together was to let it be dominated culturally and politically by the Thai race.

The conclusive phase of the formation of Thai official nationalism took place under Prime Minister Field Marshal Plaek Phibunsongkhram, who, having overthrown the Chakri absolute monarchy in 1932 as a junior military member of the People's Party, proceeded to take over, transform and develop the legacy of Thai imagined

[10] Asvabahu, *Phuak yew*, pp. 97, 113.

[11] Obviously, this is a pun on Benedict Anderson's pivotal concept in his influential *Imagined Community*.

[12] I use the word 'imagination' here advisedly because the objective existence of such an uncommunity has never been conclusively proven and it also runs completely counter to my childhood experience. On a narrow lane linking Yaowaraj and Jaroenkrung roads in the middle of Bangkok Chinatown, there used to be a movie house outlandishly called 'Texas', where my mother and I were frequent visitors. Totally unrelated to its namesake in the United States it showed exclusively Indian movies that were all dubbed in Thai. Its regular audience consisted mostly of Chinese and to a lesser degree Indians and Thais who enjoyed themselves and applauded, laughed and cried together peacefully and harmoniously for many, many years.

uncommunity. On the one hand, he de-emphasized the monarchy.[13] On the other, he deepened and expanded its residual racist, statist tendency, to the cultural-political exclusion of not only the Chinese but also all other non-Thai ethnic groups, resulting in the wholesale ethnicization of the Siamese polity as, this time, exclusively and monolithically Thai. Thus, beginning in 1939, a whole series of Ratthaniyom (i.e. Cultural Mandates) were issued by the Phibun-songkhram Government which decreed, among other things, the change of the country's name from Siam to Thailand, and adopt the new words of the *post-ancien regime* official National Anthem.

Members of non-Thai ethnic groups, to maintain their achieved socio-economic status and gain acceptance and membership of the Thai polity, were expected to 'assimilate' themselves culturally to the 'Thai' identity. Formally, this involved the adoption of a Thai name, literacy in the officially-standardized Bangkok-Thai language obtained through the state-centralized system of national education, perhaps a career in state bureaucracy, and last but not least, the search for a Thai political patron. Substantially, it entailed the adoption of a number of essentially 'Thai' traits, values, attitudes and precepts. Some examples are:

— '*Allegiance to the King of Siam*' (King Vajiravudh)[14]
— '*Love of National Independence, Toleration, and Power of Assimilation*' (Prince Damrong, one of the King's uncles)[15]

[13] This is evident in what the Prime Minister once said to his cabinet colleagues in 1942: 'The Japanese have their Emperor to adhere to but we have nothing of the sort. What we have are Nation, Religion, King and Constitution. And yet Nation is impalpable. Religion can't win people's faith securely. The King is still a boy and seen only in pictures. Consititution is just a document. Without anything to adhere in times of national emergency. I therefore decide to let the people follow the Prime Minister' (my own translation). Quoted in Charnvit Kasetsiri, *Prawat kanmeuang thai yuk pajjuban* (History of Contemporary Thai Politics), Bangkok: Faculty of Liberal Arts, Thammasat University, 1990, p. 121.

[14] Asvabahu (King Vajiravudh), 'Khwampenchat doi thaejing' (Real Nationhood), *Pakinnakakhadi* (Miscellanies), Bangkok: Khlangwitthaya Press, 1975, pp. 241–7, in which he 'decreed': 'In order to determine the real nationality of whoever, one must consider to who he pays his allegiance? If he pays allegiance to the King of Siam, then he is a real Thai.'

[15] Prince Damrongrachanuphap, *Laksana kanpokkhrong prathes siam tae boran* (The Character of the Administration of Ancient Siam), Creation Volume of Mr. Dao Buphawes, Rasbamrung Temple, Chon Buri, 1 December 1968, pp. 5–8.

— *'Thailand is a conformist and obedient nation'*; *'Thais are excellent fighters'*; *'The country is the home, the military its fence . . .'* (Phibunsongkhram); etc.[16]

Needless to say, the foregoing 'Thai' identity or ethno-ideology of Thainess is a very selective reading of Thai traditional culture and history. It leaves out plenty of traits, values, attitudes and precepts associated with highly independent, critical, dissenting, even rebellious, liberal or radical personalities and groups in modern Thai history such as Thianwan, Narin Phasit, Thawat Riddhidej, Siao Huadseng Sibunreuang, Kulap Saipradit, Pridi Banomyong, the Kekmeng Party, the Workers' Party, the Chino-Siamese Communists, or even the left wing of the People's Party itself.

Based as it was on the elites' subjective and selective wishful reading of traditional traits, values, attitudes and precepts of the Thai peasantry and bureaucrats, the ethno-ideology of Thainess represented their attempt to coercively 'assimilate', above all, the Chinese immigrant urban middle and working classes. These constituted the most dynamic economic forces, with the greatest potential for political autonomy in contemporary Thai civil society and for opposition to the conservative, authoritarian, militaristic and clientelistic political culture of the state and rural sectors.[17] They were to be prevented from any attempt to transform their economic power into political and thence state power.[18]

[16] Thaemsuk Numnon, 'Meuangthai yuk cheua phoonam' (Thailand in the Believe-the-Leader age), *Thammasat University Journal*, VI, 1 (June–September 1976), pp. 144–5.

[17] The Thai state's subjection of the urban Chinese middle and working classes to statist and clientelistic political culture comes out clearly in the childhood experiences of many a Lookjin who grew up under the Governments of Field Marshal Plaek Phibunsongkhram and Sarit Thanarat (*c.* 1948–63). See for example Yutthaphong Phoorisamban Personal interview on his life, poetry and political activities by Kasian Tejapira, Bangkok, 30 January 1989.

The late Yutthaphong (1948–89), alias Rawi Domephrajan, a famous fiery radical poet of the 14 October 1973, uprising, was a Haianese Lookjin who spent his childhood in the northern province of Phitsanulok under Plaek and Sarit regimes. In the only lenghty interview he ever gave to a Thai researcher (i.e. myself) shortly before his untimely death of cancer, he told very revealingly of his early ardent Thai nationalist and anti-Chinese feelings, his unfulfilled wish to join the army, his love of peasant culture, and his aversion to mercantile character and habits.

[18] This point is succinctly formulated by Chai-anan Samudvanija in his 'State-Identity' article, pp. 67–8.

This is evident in the anti-Chinese writings of King Vajiravudh and the King's comment at one point that, despite their many resemblances, there was nonetheless one major difference between the Jews and the Chinese, i.e. the former had no country of their own while the latter still had one. Consequently, the political activities, interests and ambitions of the Chinese immigrants were oriented towards their homeland in China, rather than their land of temporary residence in Siam. Luckily so, the King said, otherwise 'they might prove very troublesome'.[19] On another occasion, he composed a short political satire entitled '*Rai-ngan kanprachum paliment siam*' (Proceedings of the Meeting of the Siamese Parliament) to caricature the call of Thianwan, a self-educated Thai commoner-reformer, for the establishment of a parliamentary system of government. Interestingly enough, in the noisy and chaotic Parliament of his nightmarish imagination, not a few MPs were Chinese who, during the meeting, behaved in a very disorderly manner, shouted 'Damn the Government!' repeatedly, and ended up being dragged out of the chamber by the police.[20] Without the literary pretensions and dramatic flourish of his immediate predecessor, King Prajadhipok (1925–35) was blunter on this point. He wrote in 1927 a memorandum entitled 'Democracy in Siam' to Prince Damrong, his uncle and trusted aide:

> Now I am also inclined to think that a real democracy is very unlikely to succeed in Siam. It may even be harmful to the real interests of the people. One could readily imagine what a parliamentary form of government would be like in Siam, and there is no need to go into details. I shall just mention one fact, that is the parliament would be entirely dominated by the Chinese Party. One could exclude all Chinese from every political right; yet they will dominate the situation all the same, since they hold the hard cash.
>
> Any party that does not depend on Chinese funds cannot succeed, so that politics in Siam will be dominated and dictated by the Chinese merchants. This is indeed a very probable eventuality.[21]

[19] Asvabahu, *Phuak yew*, p. 86.

[20] King Cajiravudh, 'Rai-ngan kanprachum paliment siam' (Proceedings of the Siamese Parliament's meeting), in Chai-anan Samudavanija and Khattiya Kannasut (eds.), *Ekkasan kanmeuang kanpokkhrong thai* (*Ph. S. 2417–77*) (Documents of Thai Politics and Government, BE 2417–77), Bangkok: Siamese Studies Institute, Social Science Association of Thailand, pp. 150–5.

[21] Quoted in Benjamin A. Batson, *The End of Absolute Monarchy in Siam*, Singapore: Oxford University Press, 1986, pp. 303–4. The late Dr Batson, who managed to unearth this revelaing document from the Damrong papers.

In that regard, the issue of 'Thai-Chinese relationship' was actually a state-capital relationship shrouded in racist discourse; and the widely-acclaimed so called 'cultural assimilation policy' of the Thai state towards the Chinese was actually a political emasculation policy against capital and labour.[22]

But it was also an economic emasculation policy against the peasantry: for while the Thai bureaucratic state has always resisted the political power of the capitalist class, it has never deviated from the path of unequal capitalist economic development which extracts cheap labour and natural resources from the countryside to further the growth of both the urban economy and the state apparatus. Thus it has helped to create a patron-client relationship between the Thai state bureaucratic elite and the Chinese business class (regardless of their different races!), on the one hand, and a yawning gap, a genuine—as against imagined—socio-economic structural uncommunity, between the city and the countryside in Thailand, on the other. This has been the case, especially since the launching of the first National Economic Development Plan under the Sarit dictatorship in 1961. By 1972, Suguru Suyama, a Japanese economist, made the following incisive comment on the economic plight of the Thais in his *The Economic History of the Overseas Chinese* (in Japanese): 'There is no merchant class among the Thais. The accumulation of national capital is almost impossible. These *economically emasculated* Thais have no choice but to end up being a peasant, or, if lucky, a well-to-do idler, or, if somewhat educated, a professional or government official.'[23]

[22] Owing to the deliberate and consistent policy of succesive Siamese monarchies of the Chakri dynasty since the early nineteenth century to encourage immigration of Chinese coolies *en masse* into the kingdom to satisfy the growing demand for wage (as against corvee) labour on the part of the Siamese absolutist state and its burgeoning market economy, there developed a pattern of ethnic division of labour in Siam in which the Chinese were primarily merchants, artisan-craftsmen and labourers, whereas the Thais worked mainly in government and agriculture.

See G. William Skinner, *Chinese Society in Thailand: An Analytical History*, Ithaca, New York: Cornell University Press, 1957, pp. 91–8, 117–18, 300–6.

[23] Quoted in Suwinai Paranawalai, *Borisat yipun kab kanpennik khong prathesthai* (Japanese Corporations and Thailand's Nicdom), Bangkok: Faculty of Economics, Thammasat University, 1989, pp. 27, 29 (emphasis added translation mine). Critical analyses of the growing class and sectoral disparities resulting from the unbalanced socio-economic development are voluminous, the

Thus, despite his virulent anti-Chinese discourse, King Vajiravudh had no qualms about taking the support of the Chinese when it came to the hard facts of economy. Not only did the King have Chinese entrepreneurs as business partners and even as his favourite attendant, ennoble them and help them out financially time and again,[24] he also preferred, as a matter of economic policy,[25] Chinese

---

more political ones among which are Saneh Chamarik, 'Problems of Development in Thai Political setting', *Democracy and Development: A Cultural Perspective*, Bangkok: Local Development Institute, 1993, pp. 219–67; and Chermsak Pinthong, 'Prathesthai: kanphatthana thi khad khwamsomdul lae pentham' (Policy Impact on Rural Incomes and Poverty in Thailand: The case of Inequitable Growth), *Saranrom*, 47 (10 February 1990), pp. 65–91.

As to recent figures of the unequal distribution of income in the country, Central Bank of Thailand Governor Vijit Supinit reported that the average revenue per head of workers in Bangkok and its environs was 7.7 times that in the north-east, 5 times that in the north, 3.7 times that in the south and 2.6 times that in the central area ('Central Bank Urges Economic Restructure', *Bangkok Post*, 7 September 1993, p. 21).

[24] For example, several ennobled and commoner Chinese were among the major shareholders (3 out of 9) and executive board members (2 out of 7) of the Siam Commercial Bank, in which the Privy Purse held a 10 per cent interest. The Bank survived two financial crises caused by a business slump, panic among depositors and huge embezzlement during the reign of King Vajiravudh owing to generous support from the Privy Purse. Furthermore the King had, among his retinue, a Chinese merchant by the name of Bunrod. Being very close to the King, Bunrod accompanied him to many *Kongseuapa* (the King's pet militia) manoeuvres until he was ennobled as Luang Phiromphakdi. Bunrod would later found the first beer brewery in Siam to produce the famous Thai Singha beer in 1931 under the personal patronage and promotion of King Prajadhipok. See Sungsidh Piriyarangsan, *Thunniyom khunnang thai* (*Ph. S. 2475–2503*) (Thai Bureaucratic Capitalism [BE 2475–2503], Bangkok: Chulalongkorn University, Social Research Institute, 1983, pp. 55–61.

[25] I say 'economic policy' advisedly. This is evident in the following excerpt from a letter of Chaophraya Yomaraj, the then Minister of the Capital (Nakhornban), to King Vajiravudh dated 1 March 1916, in which he commented on the economic value of the Chinese immigrant population in Siam as follows:

> The Kingdom of Siam is large, but her population is small, not to mention how lazy the people are. Without importing foreigners into the country, the population will not grow quickly enough, and consequently neither will the revenue. To develop the country, both in its military and civilian aspects, requires a great deal of public funds. If the revenue development does not progress at the same pace, development of the country will slow down accordingly, and fail to catch

investors to Thai ones since the former usually had more capital, business experience and hence a better chance of success.[26] Much the same can also be said of Field Marshal Plaek's subsequent economic nationalism. Later researches have revealed that while most if not all of the allegedly 'nationalist' state enterprises set up under his authoritarian rule turned into lucrative sources of his henchmen's free-wheeling corruption and embezzlement of personal wealth, almost each and every one of these people sat cordially besides Chinese businessmen in the executive boards of many Chinese-owned/operated companies and banks under their political patronage.[27]

---

up with the times. . . . To take a nearby example, the Privy Purse is now earning over 4,000 [*sic*] a month from its bazaar at Nakhom Pathom, and the money is from the Chinese vegetable growers. Without them, the bazaar would be left in ruins, not to mention the loss of the rent. As a matter of fact, if there were fewer Chinese in Bangkok, the rent income from the row houses would also decrease.

Quoted in Seksaan Prasertkul, 'The Transformation of the Thai State and Economic Change (1855–1945)', unpublished Ph.D. thesis, Department of Government, Cornell University, 1989, pp. 133, 281–2.

As it turned out, a great deal more than vegetables and row houses rent were at stake with regard to the Chinese 'golden-egg-laying geese'. According to dates relating to the Siamese government revenue from 1894–1902, the cumulative percentage of state revenues from the Chinese population-based taxes on opium, gambling, liquor and the lottery, amounted to 46.43 per cent of total state revenue throughout the period. See Benedict Anderson, 'Studies of the Thai State: The State of Thai Studies', in Elizer B. Ayal (ed.), *The State of Thai Studies: Analysis of Knowledge, Approaches and Prospects in Anthropology, Art History, Economics, History and Political Science*, Athens, Ohio: Ohio University, Center for International Studies, Southeast Asia Program, 1979, pp. 212, 221–3.

[26] For instance, in 1923, two Thai investors, in response to King Vajiravudh's clarion call for greater participation by the Thai in 'alien'-monopolized business activities in his 'Wake up Siam' essay, asked for a teak forest concession in Tak province from the King. However, much to the two woken-up Thai patriots' dismay, the King decided to grant the concession to a Chinese firm instead. On top of that, it turned out that the Chinese owners of that firm were not even Thai citizens at that time, but French subjects! See Seksan Prasertkul, 'The Transformation of the Thai State and Economic Change', p. 282, f. 134.

[27] Sungsidh's meticulously researched *Thunniyom* is a pioneering work and still the best on this issue. See especially Chaps. 3 and 4.

Miraculously, this racist opportunism or sinophobic-by-words but sinophiliac-by-deeds attitude of the Thai nationalist elite seems to extend even into the nether world. For in his will, made on 10 November 1920, that is 5 years and 16 days before his eventual departure, King Vajiravudh, being of clear and sound mind, dictated that:

> During the seven days of alms-giving when my body lies in state and also in my cremation ceremony, a gongtek[28] rite should be held. If no one has faith in holding it for me, my heir should find priests of the Annamite or Chinese Sects to hold it for me.[29]

Alas, one can never be sure under which godly authority one would land in the other world!

TWO DRAGONS IN HIDING

The Laws of Dialectics have it that every ideological subjection entails qualification; and every social structure is both a constraint on, and an opportunity for, action.[30] Thus, under the cultural-political regime of Thai official nationalism, the study of Chinese in formal educational institutions was severely restricted and discouraged, and Lookjins of Chinese alien parentage were barred from the rank of officers in the Armed Forces and had their voting and candidacy rights curtailed.[31] However, the Lookjins learned to adapt them-

[28] Chinese religious rite for the dead in which paper miniatures of personal belongings, luxuries, money, mansions, livestock, vehicles, even maids and servants are burnt so that they may follow the dead and be of service in the hereafter.

[29] The entire will of the King was published in Prayut Sitthiphan, *Pramahathirarajjao* (King Vajiravudh), Bangkok: Siam Press, 1972, pp. 411–14.

[30] These notions are borrowed from Goran Therborn, *What Does the Ruling Class Do When It Rules?* London: Verso, 1980, pp. 176–9; and Anthony Giddens' theory of structuration in his *Central Problems in Social Theory: Action, Structure and Contradiction in Social Analysis*, Berkeley: University of California Press, 1979.

[31] See details in Richard J. Coughlin, *Double Identity: The Chinese in Modern Thailand*, Hong Kong: Hong Kong University Press, 1960, Chaps. 7, 8. As of now, whereas the state restrictions on Chinese education have been abolished recently by the liberal and forward-looking Anand Panyarachun government and there is a better change for Thaified Lookjins to get into the Armed Forces' officers corps, the restrictions on candidacy right of a Lookjin of alien parentage,

selves opportunistically, adopt (or, if one prefers, feign) the official nationalist '*Thai identity*', and play '*Thai*' according to the requisite political cultural code. During the decade following the Second World War, we have two interesting and contrasting examples of *Lookjins* who adopted a Thai name, learned the standard Thai language, and took a 'Thai' job for political purposes—Khow Tongmong and Chou Shoulim.[32]

KHOW TONGMONG[33]

Born to Khow Huad (alias Chai Kanjanawat or Meun Suwansiriphong), a wealthy Chinese rice-miller and ennobled village headman, and his Thai wife named Somjin in the Bang Khanak Village, Bang Namprieo District, Chachoengsao Province, on 20 June 1915, 'Ti Noi Tongmong' ('Little Brother Tongmong' as he was then called) was sent by his father to attend the Kuomintang-founded, Teochiu-speaking, Chinese Xinmin School in Bangkok, reputedly the best of its kind in the country at the time.[34] After graduation around 1933, he was recruited as a teacher by his Alma Mater on account of his good knowledge of Chinese and English. Quickly, he earned his Thai secondary education degree, and rose to become the principal of another leading Chinese school called Huang-hun, later renamed in Thai as Sahakhun Seuksa. Under the sponsorship of the Kuomintang government, Khow Tongmong, along with ten other Chinese teachers from Thailand, was selected and sent to

---

in effect since 1933, still stand. To be qualified to run in a parliamentary election, he/she must have completed a secondary or university education. This regulation automatically excludes, among others, four of my own younger brothers from ever becoming an MP or a PM for that matter under the current Consitution. See Article 105 of the Consititution of the Kingdom of Thailand, BE 2534 (AD 1991) and its BE 2535 Amendment as well as Article 19 of the Election of Members of the house of Representative Act, BE 2522 and its BE 2535 Amendment.

[32] The following account of Khow Tongmong and Chou Shoulim is based on Kasian Tejapira, 'Commodity Marxism: The Formation of Modern Thai Radical Culture, 1927–58', unpublished Ph.D. thesis, Cornell University, 1992.

[33] The following biographical profile of Khow Tongmong is based on 'Prasit kanjanawat', *Phoonam Thurakij*, III, 26 (February 1989), pp. 15–64.

[34] Skinner, *Chinese Society*, pp. 159, 169. The name of the school was transliterated as 'Hsin-min' by Skinner.

receive further pedagogical training at the Jinan University in Shanghai for a year, and then on a study tour through north-eastern China for another three months.

Khow Xiansheng, or Teacher Khow's promising teaching career was cut short, however, upon the wholesale closure of Chinese schools in Thailand by the nationalist-playing Phibunsongkhram Government in 1939–40.[35] Adapting himself adeptly to the changing times, Khow Tongmong enrolled in Thammasat University, got a new job as a translating clerk at the Department of Commercial Registration, Ministry of Commerce, and changed his unfashionable un-Thai name to the officially-favoured Thai Prasit Kanjanawat. Having graduated from Thammasat, Prasit resigned from his government job and set up a private law office called Manukij with a number of his Thammasat friends.

While Prasit's law practice and joint financial ventures with some of his friends prospered, his objective was something else. Partly to indulge his dilettantish literary and journalistic interests, but mainly to create a handy publicity instrument for his personal political ambition, he started to invest money and engage his close business colleagues in various publishing and printing enterprises. From about the end of the Second World War, he founded and edited a weekly newspaper, *Karnmuang*, bought the controlling interest of the *Thai Mai* daily newspaper, had a fine printing block-making shop also called Thai Mai, and was closely involved in establishing the Rungnakhorn Printing House.[36] Capitalizing on the regular public exposure he commanded as a newspaper owner, and deploying his editorial staff in his election campaigns, Prasit ran three times for Parliament. He was elected as a pro-government MP in his home province for the first time in February 1952. By no means a serious journalist in any professional sense of the term, 'Hia Sit' or 'Elder Brother Sit', as he was affectionately called by his newspaper employees, was rather a crafty politician who used his papers as a stepping stone on his path to greater political power and higher governmental positions. Thus he was MP from Chachoengsao (February–December 1957), Deputy Minister of Cooperatives

[35] Ibid., pp. 267, 269.

[36] Royal Thai Government, Department of Commerical Registration, Ministry of Commerce, 'Rungnakhorn Company Limited', Registration Profile File no. 2349, (n.d.).

(August-October 1958), a member of the Bangkok Bank's Board of Directors (May 1968), Senator (July 1968), Deputy Director of the Economic, Fiscal and Industrial Division of the ruling military Revolutionary Group under Field Marshal Thanom Kittikachorn (November 1971), Deputy Minister of Economy (November 1971), Deputy Minister of Commerce (December 1972), MP from Chachoengsao (January 1975–April 1976), President of the House of Representatives and the National Assembly (February 1975), Vice-President of the Bangkok Bank (January 1976), Deputy Minister of Justice (April 1976), Deputy Prime Minister (5 October 1976), Senator (April 1979), and President of the Bangkok Bank (since August 1984).

CHOU SHOULIM

Born to a Chinese father and a Thai-Khamu half-breed mother in the northern province of Phichit, Chou Shoulim[37] was sent to study in China from his childhood and went on to Datong University in Shanghai.[38] He was probably recruited into the Chinese communist movement while in China. He later returned to Siam, married a Thai woman, and continued his underground political activities. Unfortunately, under the pseudonym of 'Piatoe', he was arrested

[37] Biographical data of Chou Shoulim are drawn from various interviews and memoirs of some of his former comrades and friends as well as a few secondary sources which made use of government documents on communist activities of the period, especially Suwadee Charoenphong, 'Bot thi 5: Patikiriya khong ratthabal prhabatsomdej phrapokklaojaoyoohua to kankhleuanwai thang khwamkhid sangkhomniyom khommunit (Ph. S. 2468–75)' (Chapter 5: The Reaction of King Prajadhipok's Government to the Communist-Socialist Ideological Movement, AD 1925–32), in Chai-anan Samudavanija and Suwadee Charoenphong (eds.), in *Kanmeuang-kanpokkhrong thai samai mai: Ruamnganwijai thang prawattisat lae ratthasat* (Modern Thai Politics and Government: A Collection of Researches in history and Political Science), Bangkok: Chulalongkorn University 1979, and Thongchai Phuengkanthai, 'latthi khommunit lae nayobai totan khong ratthabal thai Ph. S. 2468–2500' (Communism in Thailand and Government Policy against Communism AD 1925–57), unpublished M.A. thesis, Department of History, Graduate School, Chulalongkorn University, 1978.

[38] According to Mr. Phin Bua-on, who worked closely with Chou Shoulim in the Thai communist movement during the late 1950 (Phin Bua-on, personal interview on his life and the history of Thai communist movement by Somsak Jiamthirasakul, Bangkok, 31 July 1985).

along with his comrades while holding a meeting in a Chinese school called Jintek in Phichit.[39] As the official investigators found him politically knowledgeable, he was told to write a testimony on communism and Siam which he did in Chinese. The translation of his testimony, was sent to Prince Boriphat, the then Minister of Interior. Having read the testimony, the Prince concluded that Piatoe was a full-fledged communist, that given a chance he would certainly incite the Thais against foreigners, and hence should be banished. But to declare him *persona non grata* was more easily said than done, since, even though this 'full-fledged communist' had been brought up and educated in China and could only write his testimony in Chinese, legally speaking, a Thai national having been born in Siam and being married to a Thai woman could not be deported. Unable to bring himself to believe that a Thai could also be a communist, the Prince submitted to King Prajadhipok Piatoe's testimony along with his own report. 'People who believe in communism like Mr. Piatoe', he commented, 'are likely to cause a lot of troubles. It should not be taken simply for granted that he is a Thai by birth since his disposition is by no means Thai . . . [He] should not be allowed to depend on His Majesty's merciful protection any further.'[40]

The King wrote back that he agreed with the report and the Prince's suggestion that Piatoe be exiled. However, when the case came before the criminal court, the judge thought otherwise. Having successfully claimed his Thai nationality and thus prevented deportation, Piatoe or Chou Shoulim went to Bangkhwang Penitentiary after being sentenced to 15 years imprisonment and a fine of 5,000 baht.[41]

In Area 6 of Bangkhwang Penitentiary, reserved exclusively for political prisoners, Chou Shoulim was far from lonely having more than 100 Chinese and Vietnamese comrades as fellow inmates.[42]

[39] Suwadee, 'Patikiriya', pp. 315, 318, 332, 349; Thongchai, 'Latthi Khommunit', pp. 115–19, 121.

[40] *Nangseu krab banghomthul khong kromphra nakhornsawanworaphinit* (Report to his Majesty from Prince Boriphat) (439/125116, 6 January 1930), quoted in Suwadee, 'Patikiriya', p. 318.

[41] Thongchai, 'Latthi Khommunit', p. 118.

[42] The ensuing account of Chou Shoulim's life in prison is drawn from Leuan Saraphaiwanich (Captain Phraya Saraphaiphiphat), *Fan rai khong khaphajao*

Shortly afterwards, 250 new arrivals joined them. Far from being communists these so-called Bowaradej rebels had been involved in an armed attempt in 1933 to overthrow the People's Party government and restore power to the monarchy under the leadership of Prince Bowaradej, a former Minister of War under the *ancien regime*. The coup was bloodily crushed.[43]

For six years or so the communists and Bowaradej 'politicos' were together in jail. These 350 prison inmates were indeed strange bedfellows, in both the figurative and literal senses. Ethnically, the communists were Chinese and Vietnamese while the politicos were mostly Thai. Sociologically, the former were teachers, merchants and coolies while the latter were mostly senior or junior civil servants and military or police officers, respectively deemed of low and high status according to traditional Thai social standards. And perhaps most important of all, ideologically, the two groups were poles apart, i.e. communist revolutionaries versus conservative or liberal, royalist counter-revolutionaries.[44]

Nevertheless, they now shared several things in common. They were suffering the same ordeal, living in the same jail, being bound in similar chains, doing the same menial work, eating the same unsavoury food, wearing the same blue uniforms, in the custody of

---

(My Nightmare), Bangkok: Bannakhan Press, 1959; Phimphawal Sethaputra, *Chiwaprawat kanthamphotjananukrom angklis-thai thai-angklis khong so sethaputra* (So Sethaputra and the Making of his English-Thai, Thai-English Dictionary: A Biography), Bangkok: Phimphawal Sethaputra, 1971; M.R. Nimimongkhol Nawarat, 'Chiwit haeng kankabot song khrang' (The Victim of the Two Political Purges), *Meuangnimit lae chiwit haeng kankabot song khrang* (The Sight of the Future Siam and the Victim of the Two Purges), Bangkok: Aksornsamphan Press, 1970; and Phayap Rojjanawiphat, *Yuk thamil* (Evil Age), Bangkok: Anthai Press, 1989.

As to the general official history of Bankhwang Penitentiary, see Somphop Jantharaprapha, et al., *Prawat kanrajthan 200 pi* (200 Year History of the Penitentiary), Bangkok: Department of Penintentiary, Ministry of Interior, 1982, pp. 372–82.

[43] For a general account of the Bowaradej rebellion, see Chaiwat Yonpiam, *Fan rai khong meuang thai* (Thailand's Nightmare), Bangkok: Chaophraya Press, 1985.

[44] Leuan, *Fan rai*, pp. 34–6, 125–7, 155–6; Phayap, *Yuk thamil*, p. 63; Phimphawal, *Chiwaprawat so*, p. 170; Nimitmongkhol, 'Chiwit', pp. 330–3, 336–7, 441.

the same hostile government and jailors. Leading a kind of life that was perforce largely collectivized and maddeningly leisured, they were gradually drawn to one another, especially the better-educated and more experienced among them. After all, different as their backgrounds had been, they were politicized intellectuals whom the government saw it necessary to imprison in the same way.[45] Therefore, it was not suprising that they found it convenient to share the same cell during those nights when they pursued their diverse intellectual activities together.[46]

Initially, they began their relationship by teaching foreign (i.e. non-Thai) languages to one another. The communists taught Chinese, Cantonese and French to the politicos, whereas the latter taught English and Japanese to the former.[47] The teaching went on for several years, and, judging from the circumstances, the linguistic medium of teaching must have been none other than Thai. Then, they moved on to politics, discussing, in both Thai and Chinese, among other things the communist ideology and doctrine, the strategy and programme of the communist revolution in Siam, the 'politically correct' conception and evaluation of labour, especially menial labour, the communists' personal feelings about imprisonment, ideological commitment, past experience and future plans. The argument and exchange of ideas between the two groups of prisoners was pleasant, instructive, and fruitful when the communist interlocutors were senior people of 'leader or teacher rank' (*chan huana* or *nchan ajan* in Thai), with their mature, educated, polite, and refined manner.[48]

One such communist inmate was Piatoe, whom Leuan Saraphaiwanich calias Captain Phraya Saraphaiphiphat, a former high-ranking aristocrat and Bowaradej inmate, remembered as 'a good friend', 'of teacher-rank', 'polite and well-mannered'. Piatoe, or Chou Shoulim, whose other Chinese names included Mongji, simply Toe or the derogatory Jek Tow, had not only acquired sufficient knowledge and skills of the Thai language in prison, but also found it politic to have Leuan coin his first Thai name for him as Toe

[45] Leuan, *Fan rai*, pp. 100–2, 149–58, 180, 185, 302; Phiphawal, *Chiwaprawat so*, p. 180.

[46] Leuan, *Fan rai*, pp. 153–4; Phiphawal, *Chiwaprawat so*, pp. 168–9.

[47] Leuan, *Fan rai*, pp. 153–4, 180–1, 301.

[48] Ibid., pp. 154–8, 180–2, 195–6.

Jutharak (meaning Big Protector of the Crown or Head, which cleverly reflects both the sound and meaning of his Chinese names, i.e. 'Piatoe' and 'Chou Shoulim' as 'Shoulim' or 'Shouling' in Mandarin denotes head, leader or chieftain).[49]

Later on, he would also invent for himself such fanciful Thai *noms de plume* and *noms de guerre* as Phayap Angkhasing (meaning 'Northwest Leonine', which indicates his regional homeland in Siam), Phichit na Sukhothai (meaning 'Conquest at Sukhothai', which refers to his mother's home province of Sukhothai), Pho.No. Sukhothai (an abbreviated version of the former), and Prapanta Virasakdi (meaning 'Writing with Honour of Courage', which was the one he used in public as the Spokesman of the Thai Communist Party).

Why so much ado about naming? One needs only to read another essay of King Vajiravudh entitled '*Priab namsakul kab cheusae*' (A Contrast of Family Names with Clan Names, 1913) to gauge the immense political significance of these nominal changes by Chou Shoulim, and Khow Tongmong for that matter. In that essay, the King aggressively called for the replacement of Chinese clan names ('Sae' in Teochiu or 'Xing' in Mandarin), still widely in use among Jeks and Lookjins in Siam, with Thai family names. He associated the latter with blood ties, love, modernity, civilization, social hierarchy, national unity and political obedience, while linking the former with belligerent gangster solidarity, archaism, barbarism, group inclusion, national division, and political insubordination.[50] It thus followed from this fantastic Vajiravudhian cultural logic that a Lookjin communist with a Thai family name could not but be a living discursive impossibility or, in other terms, a political contradiction in terms.

And yet, there he was, Toe Jutharak, alias Phayap Angkhasing, or Phichit na Sukhothai, or Prapanta Virasakdi, a Lookjin communist armed with not only one but many Thai family names, stepping

[49] *Pho. Meuangchomphoo (Udom Sisuwan), Soo samoraphoom phoophan (phrom phak phanuaki) pai meuang hang* (To the Phoophan Battlefront with an Appendix: To the Hang Town), Bangkok: Matichon Press, 1987, p. 210. Udom, another leader of the Thai Communist Party and a close colleague of Chou Shoulim, was in charge of the party's publication department during the 1950s.

[50] King Vajiravudh, *Pakinnakakhadi*, pp. 79–94.

out of Bangkhwang and then going on to Yunan to help with the Chinese Revolution, bringing Mao Tsetung's thought back to Siam, publishing a couple of books on communism and the Thai revolution in Thai, and becoming the first spokesman of the Thai Communist Party![51]

Actually, he could have been elected the Secretary at the Second Congress of the Party in February 1952 in place of the former acting-secretary but for one seemingly trivial but politically damaging blemish of his 'Thainess' to which the majority of party delegates objected—he spoke Thai with a thick Chinese accent.[52] *Aiya, ik wok nok easie-ak all to become a Thai khommunik*![53]

[51] Leuan, *Fan rai*, p. 156; Phin, Interview, 31 July 1985; Pho. Meuang-chomphoo, *Soo samoraphoom*, pp. 21, 46–9, 51–2, 132–3, 135, 141; and Udom Sisuwan, personal interview on communism and literature in Thailand by Craig J. Reynolds, Bangkok, 19 January 1984.

[52] One cannot stress strongly enough the political significance of unaccented Thai speech for the recruitment of Thai elite, 'reactionary' and 'revolutionary' alike. Thus, even today one can still (over)hear complaints, in both private and public, that, say, the Rector of Thammasat University, the Chairman of the Board of Directors of Bangkok Bank, or the President of the National Assembly '*phood thai mai chad*' (literally meaning 'speak Thai unclearly' but actually denotes 'speak Thai with a thick un-Thai acent'). Amazing is the ludicrous extent to which some Lookjin elite are willing to go to confirm their Thainess. For example, a leading Chinese business tycoon was alleged to have his Chinese-sounding name, Wan Sanseu, changed expediently to a Thai-sounding 'Van Chanseu' once he was elected the President of the senate and hence ex-officio President of the National Assembly. Be it true or not, the allegation obviously upset him so much so that, whenever opportunity rose, he kept on reiterating his correct 'Thai' name as well as explaining its meaning to the Thai public in the following manner: Van = kind, Chan = steep, Seu = honest, therefore, Van Chanseu = the kind of people with a high degree of honesty, *OED*! See Bunchai Jaiyen, *Ruai baeb jaosua 1* (Rich-Tycoon style, vol. 1), Bangkok: Bunchai Press, 1990, p. 78.

[53] For a Chinese of the Teochiu dialect group (which has been predominant among the Chinese in Thailand), his inability to speak Thai clearly and articulately ('*phood thai mai chad*' in Thai) has a peculiar characteristic typical of all Teochius, i.e. the inherent absence of certain consonants (e.g. d and r) and vowels (e.g. euan, -n) from their original Teochiu speech and hence their replacement by other consonants (e.g. l for d and r) and vowels (e.g. -ian for -euan; -ng for -n) in Thai speech.

DRAGON'S HEIRS BEGIN TO SPREAD THEIR WINGS

As to the majority of Lookjins who did not deliberately play 'Thai' politics, the state-supervised and centralized national education system, and the rapid state-promoted capitalist economic development launched by the military government of Prime Minister Field Marshal Sarit Thanarat in 1961, together transformed them and their offspring into a significant plurality of the new multi-ethnic national urban middle class[54] which

— are of Chinese blood but basically illiterate in the Chinese language (especially written Chinese);
— speak, read and write in Thai and therefore, paradoxically, are relearning Chinese culture, reviving their ethnic consciousness and re-imagining their own Chino-Siamese identity through the medium of the Thai language;
— work in the most vibrant, dynamic, advanced, open, cosmopolitan, modern sector of the economy and culture, but remain under one of the most inefficient, corrupt, rigid, authoritarian, clientelistic, outdated bureaucratic states in South-East Asia;
— are generally civic-minded and patriotic but normally apolitical, favour an open and accessible pluralistic parliamentary government to military dictatorship, hold the state bureaucracy in very low regard, but have confidence in the private business sector;

[54] Roughly speaking, the middle class in Thailand, broadly defined to include professionals, technicians, administrators, managers, businessmen, merchants, shopkeepers, clerks and skilled salaried workeers in both private and public sectors, numbered around 900,000 in 1950, 1.8 million in 1970, and nearly 5 million out of a total population of over 54.5 million in 1991 (Kasian Tejapira, *Lae lod lai mangkorn: Ruam khokhian waduai khwampenjin nai siam* (Looking through the Dragon Design: Selected Writers on Chineseness in Siam), Bangkok: Kobfai's Publishing Work, 1994, pp. 69-70; Ben Anderson, 'Withdrawal Symptoms: Social and Cultural Aspects of the 6 October, Coup', *Bulletin of Concerned Asian Scholars*, IX, 3 (July–September 1977), p. 16. As to the Chinese in Thailand, one recent source estimates that they account for 10.5 per cent of the total population (Charles F. Keyes, *Thailand: Buddhist Kingdom as Modern Nation-State*, Bangkok: Editions Duang Kamol, 1989, p. 16). While no precise figure is available, it is plain as a pikestaff that the Chinese constitute a far greater percentage of the middle class population than the overall average.

— are gaining greater power as the largest group of entrepreneurs and consumers in the increasingly cohesive and unified, nation-wide economic and cultural market but lack any genuine, adequate and elective representation in formal political institutions;
— and, therefore, cannot really control the state, even though the survival and prosperity of their business enterprises and consumerist lifestyles are becoming more and more vulnerable to state policy and action.

Increasingly regarding the over-centralized but under-unified power structure of the fragmented pyramid-like Thai bureaucratic state as the main impediment to their further economic prosperity and political freedom, the more politicized among them have gone out onto the streets and into the jungle waging battles, peaceful and armed, against the state since the early 1970s, culminating in 14 October 1973 uprising, 6 October 1976 massacre and *coup d'etat*, the communist-led armed struggle in the countryside, and, last but not least, the May 1992 uprising. However, contrary to the middle class' somewhat naive expectations, the intransigent bureaucratic elite have steadfastly resisted and undermined any attempt at the decentralization of power. They continued to cling to the old state structure, despite the middle class' many efforts and sacrifices in the May Democratic Movement of 1992. On top of that, their political frustrations are further aggravated by the dismal performance of the elected politicians, the lacklustre under-achievement of the elected governments, and the crisis prone dysfunctioning of the existing parliamentary system. These frustrations are now given full vent in the nation's booming print and electronic media through the very vocal and strident voice of a new generation of middle-class intellectuals.

Broadly representing the middle-class interests and concerns, globalized in their outlook and liberal democratic in their political views (subject, of course, to their varying emphases and interpretations), well-educated (in the country or abroad), and multi-lingual (in foreign and local languages) their reach is wide. They consist of the state economic and technical technocrats; the executives, consultants, researchers, developers, creative designers of the private business sector; intellectuals working in various kinds of media, cultural, educational and academic institutions, both public and private; and intellectuals in non-government organizations (NGOs) in both the urban and rural areas. Armed with such IT communication paraphernalia as personal computers, cellular phones, fax machines, satellite dishes, cable TVs, CD or digital cassette tape players, VDO or laser disc players, pack-links, E-mail services, etc, which were used very creatively and effectively in waging a communication guerrilla warfare against the state's misinformation encirclement campaign during the May 1992 crisis, they have since then, been re-imagining a new Thai national community. The main features which emerge in their published articles, radio and TV news commentaries, talk shows and advertisements, indicate[55]

— it is a multi-ethnic, multi-cultural community with the King as the centre of the people's allegiance;
— it is peaceful and calm because traditional social relations and cultures whose continued existence has been threatened by socio-economic changes are securely restored;
— it upholds Buddhism as the national religion, but generously allows believers of other faiths to live peacefully together therein;
— it has bright prospects since its children are getting a good up-bringing;
— it is a member of the community of affluent nations;
— it accepts economic inequality and yet the poor are happy because they get kindly help from the rich;
— it is ruled by a modern, benevolent, compassionate, efficient, wise, visionary and accessible national government that employs lenient methods to achieve national security, independence, sovereignty and material prosperity; and
— the rule of law, constitutional-guaranteed rights and freedom, militaristic belligerence and values, and rural farming are either

[55] This outline of the new middle class imagined community draws upon recent writings of Nidhi Aeusrivongse, the most perceptive observer and commentator of Thai nationalism and middle class political culture. See his *Chatniyom nai khabuankan prachathipatai* (Nationalism in the Democratic Movement), 'Sinlapawatthanatham khong khong chan klang thai' (The Culture of the Thai Middle Class), *Thammasat University Journal*, XIX, 1 (1993), pp. 31–41; 'Khwampenthai nai khosana tivi' (Thainess in TV ads), *Phoojadkan Daily*, 14 June 1993, p. 33; 'Latthiphithi sadej pho ro 5' (The Cult of Rama V), *Sinlapawatthanatham Monthly Magazine*, XIV, 10 (August 1993), pp. 76–98. Also see the debate on the current renaisaance of Chinese culture in Thailand in Kasian Tejapira, Seksan Praserthkul and Suphalak Kanjanakhundi, *Wiwatha: lod lai mangkorn* (Debate on 'Through the Dragon Design'), *Journal of Political Science*, XVIII, 2 (October 1992), pp. 101–27.

left out altogether or de-emphasized in the new imagined community.

And yet, the Lookjin middle class, for all their wealth and cultural power, are numerically in the minority. And here lies the key to their unsuccessful attempt to control and reform the Thai state so far, since the state relies on, and manipulates, the genuine socio-economic and cultural political division between the urban civil society and the rural communities—the real national uncommunity, as I have called it—to maintain its power. Until that gap is bridged, until the Lookjin middle class finds ways to unite with the Thai and other ethnic groups who constitute the majority in the countryside in a common front against the state, a free and genuinely multi-ethnic, multi-cultural national community will be possible only in their imagination.

At this point, I shall return to my account of the banquet. At the end of the two hour-long eating marathon, the same male singer reappeared on the stage and announced to the well-fed audience that he was going to sing another song especially for this auspicious occasion, this time in Thai. This time, when the music and the singing began, there was a sudden palpable hush among the audience who listened attentively as though something of crucial importance to them was being sung.

That song turned out to be the title song of an extremely popular TV drama series entitled *Lod lai mangkorn* (Through the Dragon Design), which was shown in late 1995. Adapted from a Thai novel of the same name written by Praphassorn Sewikul, a successful popular novelist of ethnic Thai origin, it was reputedly based on the real life stories of two late Chinese immigrant multi-millionaire tycoons—Chin Sophonpanich of the Bangkok Bank and Thaim Chokwatthana of the Sahaphathanaphiboon consumer products-manufacturing conglomerate. It narrates the path from rags to riches of Ah-Liang Seuphanich, a Chinese immigrant who arrived in Thailand penniless on the eve of the Second World War and then painstakingly, parsimoniously and ingeniously built up a family business empire through war, bankruptcy, coups, military dictatorship, political exile, family conflicts and tragedies.

Drawing on, as well as realizing in imagery and images, the widely-held belief about inherent Chinese immigrant entrepreneurial virtues (diligence, patience, enterprise, self-reliance, self-help, discipline, determination, parsimony, self-denial, business acumen, friendship, family ties, honesty, sincerity, shrewdness, modesty, etc.), '*Lod lai mangkorn's* tragic, heroic, triumphant plot has an unusually strong and profound appeal for the Chinese immigrant and Lookjin community in Thailand. It defies the conventional representation of the Chinese in Thai literary circles and the entertainment industry in which Chinese characters are almost always caricatured as crooked mafia-boss villains, stingy bloodsucking shopkeepers, or uncultured buffoons all of whom, needless to say, are '*phood thai mai chad*'. Here the protagonist is a '*phood-thai-mai-chad*' Chinese immigrant merchant instead of the usual Thai foreign-educated nobleman or police/army/navy/air force captain. Moreover, the unschooled Chinese merchant manages to win the heart of the story's beautiful heroine (a half-bred Sino-Thai girl) despite fierce and persistent competition with her ethnic Thai university-educated boyfriend![56]

I give the lyrics of the 'Lod lai mangkorn' song in my own English rendering:

From the Chinese land overseas
on a small boat drifting afar
penniless like a beggar
[he] arrives in the Gulf and land of Siam.
Like a dragon in hiding
flees away from the flame of war
to a shelter one feels grateful for
he is ever more determined to make good on this life.
Builds a legendary business and romance
to win public acceptance and reputation
Gives birth to a new generation
the new wave of great energy.
Fights the battle of the business world
with flexible wisdom and nerve.
But, alas, as to the battle of love,
harsh wounds are inflicted on the heart.
Through the days and nights of toil

[56] Praphassorn Sewikul, *Lod lai mangkorn* (Through the Dragon Design), Bangkok: Doyka Press, 1992. As of February 1993 the novel has gone through its eleventh printing. The successful adaptation of the novel for TV drama owed much to the creative effort of the script-writer, 'Wilasini' (alias Wichian Thangsuk).

Contemplates the coin of past struggle.
Dragon begins to spread its wings
paying back things it owes to this land.[57]

It struck me there and then that this was the long missing anthem of their own imagined community.

POSTSCRIPT

It has been suggested to me by the organizers of the SEPHIS workshop in Delhi, where I first presented this paper, that some further contextualizing would help to bring out the political weight and emotional depth of the issues it deals with. Perhaps a simple, if rather idiosyncratic, way to do this is to recount in plain terms how I myself have come to hear, sing and make sense of these three songs in the context of my own cultural political life as a Thai citizen. I was born a Jek, a descendant of Chinese immigrants in Thailand, and it is an important factor in my life.

For one thing, it defined me from the start as an ethnic un-Thai or 'the Other Within' in Thailand. I still remember vividly how, in my school days, my teachers always urged me and other Jek students to have our Chinese clan names changed into Thai family names so as to smooth our future path to a government service career, and how disturbed and uneasy I became after having learned from the official Thai history textbooks that it was none other than my Chinese great-great grandfathers who had driven the great-great grandfathers of my Thai classmates and teachers out of northern China all the way down south to Siam about a thousand years ago. No matter how unfounded and untenable that myth of the anti-Chinese ethnogenesis of the Thai race was, as I later came to learn, it splendidly served the overall anti-communist and domestic anti-bourgeois political causes of the Thai state during the Cold War of the 1960s (as both happened to be Chinese), and made me generously tolerant of my Thai school friends' bullying.

It was only with my political baptism of fire in the aftermath of

[57] The 'Lod lai mangkorn' title song was composed by Suwinai Sornkhamkaew, arranged by Nukul Kiatklang, and sung by Prawit Preuang-aksorn in 1992, see Cassette tape jacket information, *Teng neung chud lod lai mangkorn* (The Favourite: Through the Dragon Design), Prawit Preuang-aksorn et al. (opna Stereo, 1993).

the student-led popular uprising against the military dictatorship in October 1973 that I overcame my cultural and political alienation from Thailand, and came to regard it as *ma patrie* and love it. As an activist in the radical student movement of that brief, three-year democratic interval in a long history of conservative authoritarian rule, I wholeheartedly identified myself with and ideologically adopted the alternative and unofficial radical democratic, populist and egalitarian nationalism developed and propagated by the Thai leftist intellectuals. Widespread popular protests, political polarization and state-backed right-wing hooliganism were the order of the day in that particular period. They lead inexorably to a series of right-wing terrorist attacks, scores of political assassinations of popular protest leaders, and eventually a massacre of student activists in Thammasat University by police and right wing hooligans on 6 October 1976, in which at least 40 students, including a few of my close friends, were brutally murdered. The official Thai nation tried to kill us but I survived, so to speak.

Therefore, immediately after the 6 October massacre and the military coup, I was among the 3,000 students and intellectuals who went into the jungle to join the rural armed struggle led by the Maoist Communist Party of Thailand. I spent a couple of years in a CPT base in Democratic Kampuchea under the Khmer Rouge, and another two and a half years in the north-eastern jungle of Thailand as a cadre of the People's Liberation Army of Thailand. Life then was hard. We went through protracted government military blockades and countless anti-insurgency campaigns, chronic malaria and typhoid epidemics, and starvation, during which my comrades and I resorted to eating all kinds of wild plants and animal meat including elephants, bears, lizards, boars, snakes, horses, monkeys, and birds. However, it was not physical hardship, but ideological and political differences between the more liberal and nationalistic urban students and intellectuals and the totalitarian and pro-China CPT that finally split the movement. In the early 1980s, with the Thai government's timely declaration of a general amnesty for the students and intellectuals, we broke with the CPT and left the jungle *en masse*, and the communist-led insurgency collapsed on its own. We were by and large peacefully and smoothly reintegrated into Thai society and were referred to as 'co-developers of the Thai nation', if only partly and temporarily. I resumed my undergraduate study and continued my interest in Marxist theory of the Western and New Left variants, and afterwards went to Cornell to pursue a doctorate in government.

Two important things happened to me in Cornell: first, I gave up Marxist ideology, though not Marxism as a heuristic theoretical tool and cultural discourse. Second, I discovered my own Chineseness. Much of this was due to Professor Benedict Anderson, my adviser at Cornell, who provided me with a new way of thinking and looking at the problems of ethnicity, identity and nation. He made me realize how crucial these issues had been in the cultural-political making of the official Thai nation and how inadequate Marxism-Maoism was as a discourse to tackle them. Nationality and ethnicity had never been openly and fully dealt with in the Thai communist movement which, ethnically speaking, was heavily un-Thai from the outset. The communists could not raise it, because it was impossible for them to do so within Maoist-Marxist discourse. Nationality and ethnicity were for them a non-problem that would automatically disappear once class exploitation was abolished and the vanguard of the proletariat was installed in power. Neither was it easy for the Thai intellectuals in general to discuss these issues because of the long running hegemony of official Thai nationalism. That was the point of departure for my rethinking of the cultural politics of Thainess, un-Thainess, Chineseness and communism in Thailand, which resulted in my doctoral dissertation entitled 'Commodifying Marxism: The Formation of Modern Thai Radical Culture'.

I came back to Thailand in January 1992 just in time for another popular uprising against the military-led government in May of that year. Now, as a university lecturer and a newspaper columnist, I regard my own role as that of a cultural politician whose job is to demolish, or deconstruct if you will, the deadly and murderous cultural political infrastructure of official nationalism in Thailand. The battle has become increasingly complex in recent years, for it is not simply a matter of championing or arguing the case of alternative unofficial nationalism of the 1970s against age-old official nationalism, but also that of finding an appropriate and adequate strategy to cope with the new 'non-nationalism' or even 'anti-nationalism' of globalization, bypassing both state and nation. For, in my opinion, we are being confronted with a potent cultural force that, on the one hand, helps liberate the Thai public in general and the Thai middle classes in particular from the straitjacket of official nationalist culture, but on the other hand threatens to obliterate any concern with the Thai nation and the victims of development in Thailand, who are likely to miss out all over again on globalization due to their lack of access to cultural and economic resources.

So, new songs have yet to be sung. The real national anthem of a multi-ethnic and multi-cultural Thailand in the age of globalization has not been written yet.

Contributors

ROSSANA BARRAGÁN is a historian at the University of San Andrés (UMSA-La Paz). She is the director of the journal *T'inkazos. Revista Boliviana en Ciencias Sociales* of the Program of Strategic Research in Bolivian Social Sciences (PIEB–La Paz). She has studied Bolivian history in the nineteenth century focusing on the constitution of the state in postcolonial society and the dynamics of class, race and gender during this period. Presently she is enagaged in a research project on the social history in Bolivia in the twentieth century.

Recent publications are *Espacio Urbano y Dinámica Etnica. La Paz en el siglo XIX* (La Paz, 1990), and, with Silvia Rivera, *Debates Post Coloniales: Una introducción a los Estudios de la Subalternidad*. La Paz: Historias, Sephis, Aruwiyiri, Coordinadora de Historia, South–South Exchange Programme for Research on the History of Development y THOA.

T.K. BIAYA is a researcher affiliated to CODESRIA (Council for the Development of Economic and Social Research in Africa), Dakar and LASK (Laboratoire d'Analyses sociales de Kinshasa), Kinshasa. He lives and works in Addis Ababa, Ethiopia. His published works include *Acteurs dans la prévention et la médiation des conflits en Afrique de l'Ouest* (1999), *Les jeunes, la violence et la rue à Kinshasa* (2000), and jointly with G. Bibeau, was editor of *L'Afrique revisitée 'Anthropologie et Sociétés'* (1998). He has also published many articles in specialized journals and contributed to many books on popular culture, sexuality and gender identity, ethnicity and religion.

SUDHIR CHANDRA is author of *The Oppressive Present: Literature and Social Consciousness in Colonial India* (OUP, 1992, paperback 1994, 1999); *Enslaved Daughters: Colonialism, Law and Women's Rights* (OUP, 1998, paperback 1999); and *Continuing Dilemmas: Understanding Consciousness* (Tulika, forthcoming).

PETER GESCHIERE taught History and Anthropology at the Free University (Amsterdam), the Erasmus University (Rotterdam) and the

EHESS (Paris/Marseille). At present he is Professor of African anthropology at Leiden University and the University of Amsterdam. His recent publications are *The Modernity of Witchcraft: Politics and the Occult in Postcolonial Africa* (University of Virginia Press, 1997); and (with Birgit Meyer) *Globalization and Identity: Dialectics of Flow and Closure* (Blackwell, 1999). He is member of the steering committee of SEPHIS.

ANDRES GUERRERO is Professor at the Universidad de Cordoba (Argentina), chargé de cours at the Université de Vincennes (France) and Professor at Facultado Latinoamericana de Ciencias Sociales (FLACSO-Ecuador). He recieved scholarships from the Social Sciences Research Council, J.S. Guggenheim Foundationa and Rockefeller Foundations—IEP. He has written several texts: 'La semántica de la dominación: el concertaje de *indios*' (Libris Mundis, 1991), 'La loi de la coutûme et la loi de l'Etat: Domination éthnique et constitution de l'état national en Equateur' (EHESS, 1992), 'A Ventriloquist Image: Liberal Discourse and the "Miserable Indian Race" in the Late 19th Century Ecuador' (*Journal of Latin American Studies*, 1997).

MAHMOOD MAMDANI is Herbert Lehman Professor of Government in the Departments of Anthropology and Political Science, and Director of the Institute of African Studies, at Columbia University in New York. He is the author of *When Victims Become Killers: Colonialism, Nativism and Genocide* (Princeton, 2001); *Citizen and Subject: Contemporary Africa and the Legacy of Late Colonialism* (Princeton, 1996), and several other books. Mahmood Mamdani was elected President of the Council for the Dakar-based Development of Social Research in Africa (CODESRIA) in 1998.

GYANENDRA PANDEY was Professor of History at the University of Delhi from 1986 to 1998, before moving to his present position as Professor of History and Anthropology at the Johns Hopkins University, Baltimore, USA. He is the author of *The Ascendancy of the Congress in Uttar Pradesh*; *The Construction of Communalism in Colonial North India*; and *Remembering Partition: Violence, Nationalism and History in India*; and a founding member of the Subaltern Studies project. He served as a member of the steering committee of SEPHIS (South-South Exchange Programme in the History of Development) from 1995 to 2000.

KASIAN TEJAPIRA is is an Assistant Professor of Political Science at Thammasat University in Bangkok. The author of *Commodifying Marxism: The Formation of Modern Thai Radical Culture, 1927–1958* (Kyoto University Press and Trans Pacific Press, 2001), he is also a noted columnist and was formerly a radical activist and guerrilla fighter in the jungle of north-eastern Thailand.

NIRA WICKRAMASINGHE is presently Senior Lecturer in the Department of History and International Relations at the University of Colombo and Senior Fellow at the International Centre for Ethnic Studies, Colombo. A historian by training, she obtained her D.Phil. from St. Antony's College, University of Oxford. Her published works include *Ethnic Politics in Colonial Sri Lanka, 1927–1947; Introduction to Social Theory* (co-edited); *History Writing: New Trends and Methodologies; Civil Society in Sri Lanka: New Circles of Power* (in press) and; *Dressing the Colonised Body* (forthcoming).

HAIYANG ZHANG is Professor at the Department of Ethnology, Central University of Nationalities and lectures on physical anthropology, political anthropology, comparative study of Chinese and the Western cultures. Research on China's cultural diversity and Chinese identity; the relationship between the protection of eco-environment, ethnic minorities rights and ethnic cultures.